ST. MARKS IS DEAD

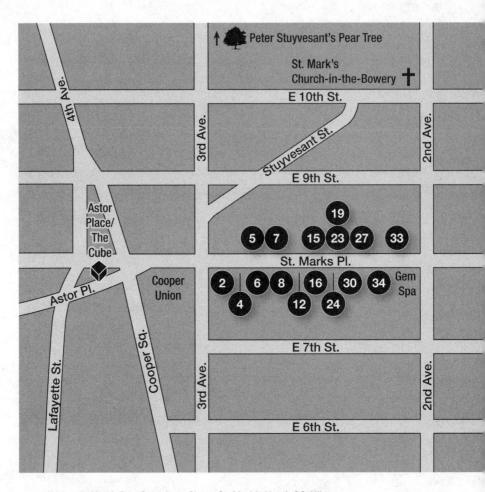

2 Valencia Hotel, Five Spot, Late Show, St. Mark's Hotel, GG Allin

4 Alexander Hamilton, Jr., Bridge Theater, The Fugs's "Night of Napalm," Trash and Vaudeville

5 Khadejha Designs, Gringo mural

6 James Fenimore Cooper, The Modern School, St. Mark's Baths, Mondo Kim's

7 Blind Tom, Carl Solomon, Kristina Gorby

8 Madame Van Buskirk, Juliet Corson's New York Cooking School, La Trinacria

12 German Shooting Society, @ Café, St. Mark's Bookshop

15 Paul McGregor's salon, BoyBar, Coney Island High

16 Royal Unisex Hair Style

19–23 Arlington Hall, Polish National Home, The Dom, The Electric Circus, All-Craft

24 Limbo, Dojo

27 House of the Thrill

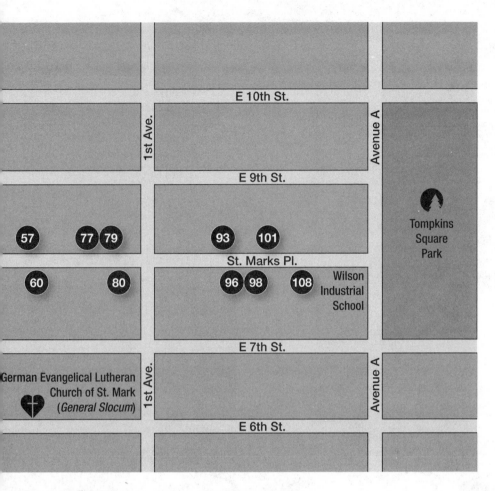

ST. MARKS IS DEAD

THE MANY LIVES OF AMERICA'S HIPPEST STREET

ADA CALHOUN

W. W. NORTON & COMPANY

Independent Publishers Since 1923   New York | London

Clockwise, first title page: "Little Missionary" Sara Curry, ca. 1890, courtesy Eileen Johnson; General Slocum passengers, collection of the author; Valencia Hotel, 1930, courtesy Library of Congress; view from author's window, 1991; Al and Jessica Forsyth, 1976, photo by Libby Forsyth; Lewis Warsh on his wedding day, 1967, photo by Peter Schjeldahl; Amanda R. Cecil and Melanie Walker on the fire escape of no. 102, 1994, photo by Michele Quinn; Gringo mural, photo by Alysia Abbott.

Clockwise, second title page: Mr. Zero at The Tub on Thanksgiving 1929, collection of the author; Jimmy McMillan's car, photo by the author; BoyBar Beauty Miss Peau de Soie, ca. 1986, photo by Matthew Kasten; the "Death Star" under construction, photo by the author; contact sheet of St. Marks between First and Second Avenues, photos by Annie Lionni.

For information about permission to reproduce selections from this book, write to Permissions, W. W. Norton & Company, Inc., 500 Fifth Avenue, New York, NY 10110

For information about special discounts for bulk purchases, please contact W. W. Norton Special Sales at specialsales@wwnorton.com or 800-233-4830

Manufacturing by RRD Westford
Book design by Chris Welch
Production manager: Louise Mattarelliano

ISBN 978-0-393-24038-2

W. W. Norton & Company, Inc.
500 Fifth Avenue, New York, N.Y. 10110
www.wwnorton.com

W. W. Norton & Company Ltd.
Castle House, 75/76 Wells Street, London W1T 3QT

1 2 3 4 5 6 7 8 9 0

Dedicated to my parents,

who looked at the apocalyptic 1970s East Village

and thought, *What a great place to raise a kid.*

The author and her mother, Brooke Alderson. St. Marks Place
and First Avenue, 1976. Photo by her father, Peter Schjeldahl.

Visit New York for the first time;
Walk in any direction
Until you're thirsty.
Drop anchor at any bar and grill;
Talk to the bartender;
Tell him you're a stranger,
Never saw the city before.

What will he say?

"You should have seen it in the old days."

—*Percy Seitlin*, That New York, *1960*

CONTENTS

INTRODUCTION

I grew up in Manhattan's East Village. My parents have lived in their three-bedroom, top-floor walk-up on St. Marks Place since 1973. I was born in 1976, an only child. As a little girl in the eighties, I navigated sidewalks cluttered with crack vials, used condoms, and junkies on the nod, and witnessed the Tompkins Square Park Riots from my window. As a teenager in the nineties, I bought egg creams at the old-time newspaper shop Gem Spa and hair dye from the punk shop Manic Panic, rented movies at Kim's Video, and worked the register at St. Mark's Comics.

"You grew up on *St. Marks Place*?" people sometimes ask, as if they didn't know children could. Or: "*You* grew up on St. Marks Place?" implying that I seem too normal to hail from a place with so many Mohawks and tattoo parlors. Then, invariably, these strangers will pity me for having missed the street's golden era, which they identify variously as the 1950s, 1960s, or 1970s.

They're right. I missed a lot. I did not love-in or be-in or do anything *in*. I never sat on a trash can outside the Five Spot jazz club listening to Thelonious Monk. I did not see Andy Warhol introduce the Velvet Underground at the Mod-Dom. I did not hang out with the Ramones or the New York Dolls. Nor did I see W. H. Auden promenade to church wearing his slippers, much less Peter Stuyvesant stumping down the same lane on his silver-and-wooden peg leg.

I am, however, as familiar as a deacon's daughter with the religion of St. Marks Place. The street has provided generation after generation with a mystical flash of belonging. Having interviewed more than two hundred current and former residents, I marvel at how many of them describe experiences of mortal peril, dissipation, and misadventure, and then conclude by saying that their era on St. Marks—in 1964 or 1977 or 2012—was the best time of their lives.

St. Marks Place evangelists insist the street is not just special for them, but that it has affected everyone—whether they know it or not—by pioneering everything from preschool, at no. 93 St. Marks Place, to prewashed jeans (no. 24). More than forty songs—by musicians as diverse as Lou Reed, the Replacements, and Tom Waits—name-check the street. Nearly all of these songs are about getting drunk or high; many also describe loss, posturing, and sunsets. (The Dictators' "Avenue A" manages to work in all of the above.)

While the revolutionary Leon Trotsky, the painter Joan Mitchell, and the lunatic GG Allin lived elsewhere before or after their time on St. Marks Place, by residing at no. 77, no. 60, and no. 2, respectively, they all joined, whether they meant to or not, a cult stretching backward and forward in time. St. Marks Place devotees often call the street "hallowed ground."

But the history of St. Marks Place is more complex than even many of its cheerleaders realize. The street has undergone constant, and surprising, evolution. In the 1600s, this land was Dutch director general Peter Stuyvesant's farm. In the 1830s, prominent statesmen lived here. In 1904, it was devastated by New York's deadliest tragedy before the terrorist attacks of 2001. In the early twentieth century, gangsters and bootleggers thrived. In the 1940s, it was a working-class immigrant neighborhood; a man who grew up on the street around the time of World War II told me that, as a kid, he chose his route home from school based on whether he preferred to be beaten up by Polish or Italian toughs that day.

The street has been rich and poor and rich again. The cycle of wealth and poverty has spun like a wheel for four hundred years. The street is prosperous now, featuring comically high rents and shimmering new glass buildings. But it is insanity to think, as a friend of mine recently suggested over lunch at one of the many busy new restaurants on St. Marks Place, that rents will "keep going up forever"—that a place where change has come so often will never change again.

Even so, some things about St. Marks have remained constant: This part of the city has always welcomed runaways. In the seventeenth century, Stuyvesant took refuge here from the noise and commerce at the tip of the island. In the late 1800s, Peter Cooper, Juliet Corson, and Sara Curry founded peaceful schools on St. Marks to help the poor escape their overcrowded tenements. And since the middle of the twentieth century, kids from all over the country, and the world, who wanted to be writers or artists or do drugs have come to St. Marks Place to find one another and themselves.

Disillusioned St. Marks Place bohemians—those who were Beats in the fifties, hippies in the sixties, punks in the seventies, or anarchists in the eighties—often say the street is dead now, with only the time of death a matter for debate. Typically they say the street ceased to be itself in the late 1980s: 1988, say, when the Gap opened, heralding the arrival of corporate national franchises, or 1989, when Billy Joel desecrated the street by using it as a backdrop for his chipper "A Matter of Trust" video.

They're not wrong; the St. Marks Places of the Beats, hippies, and punks are dead. But this book will show that every cohort's arrival, the flowering of its utopia, killed someone else's. Older Slavic and Puerto Rican residents thought everything went to hell when unwashed artists started commandeering their front stoops to promulgate the virtues of free love and Communism. Native Americans could cite the 1640s, when the Stuyvesant family turned their glorious hunting grounds, bountiful for millennia, into a sprawling Dutch farm.

"There goes the neighborhood" has been heard on the street in many tongues ever since. Someone is probably saying it right now. A college student told me that St. Marks Place died just a couple of years ago with the closing of the Cooper Union Starbucks—a business that was initially hailed as the final nail in the street's coffin. As students, James Estrada and his friends lounged there all day free of hassle. "I came back from break," says Estrada, "and it was gone. We used to hang out there and get cups and fill them with strawberry champagne and feel glamorous. There's no room for life to be lived there now." The gentrified are gentrifiers who stuck around.

At the gateway to St. Marks Place, near the venerable college Cooper Union, stands a sculpture: Tony Rosenthal's *Alamo* (1967), a fifteen-foot steel cube painted black, set on one of its corners, and spinnable. Texas has only one Alamo to remember; St. Marks Place has one roughly once a decade. Every time a new group comes in, residents fight. Then they adjust to the change. They tally losses like notches on a bedpost, winning by losing—a never-ending game of low-hand poker.

Of late, the Santa Annas of St. Marks have been land-grabbing New York University and rent-hiking, character-free chains like Chase Bank, Chipotle, and 7-Eleven, which some locals see as antithetical to the street's aggressive weirdness. Bohemians here tend to revile the new and revere the old. "Bohemia is always yesterday," writes Malcolm Cowley. And how ironic that a street famed for experimentalism should be home to such prickly nostalgia.

In the Gospel of Mark, Jesus protects the secret of his divinity. Elsewhere in the New Testament, witnesses are encouraged to spread the news of his dual nature, but in Mark, the disciples are told, "Unto you it is given to know the mystery of the kingdom of God." So, too, a countercultural brotherhood maintains the gospel of St. Marks Place, a half mile that is sanctified and forever besieged by colonizers who cannot—and even must not—understand its true meaning.

Father Michael Allen, the "hippie priest" of St. Mark's Church-in-the-Bowery, fostered the 1960s East Village art explosion. In the chapel, he let experimental filmmakers show work that veered to the pornographic, gave poets like Allen Ginsberg a home at the Poetry Project, and supported the avant-garde Theatre Genesis, which launched the career of playwright Sam Shepard. When several black and Latino parishioners stood up during a Sunday service in 1969, handed the priest a list of demands, and marched out in protest, Allen followed them out the door and gave them everything they asked for, including $30,000 in cash.

Shortly before he died in 2013, Allen told me that the Gospel of Mark is not the best place to look for the theology of St. Marks Place. He pointed instead to Old Testament prophets like Elijah and Elisha, who saw the future when even their leaders couldn't, and whose presence Allen felt on the street in the 1960s. "The artists and the poets were the ones doing theology," he said. "They were the ones telling the truth." He added that his years at St. Mark's were the most exciting of his life.

PART I

"A VERY EDEN"

10,000 BC–AD 1904

Manhattan, 1609.

Markley Boyer/The Mannahatta Project/The Wildlife Conservation Society.

1

PETER STUYVESANT'S FARM

Four hundred years ago, on a long, thin island flanked by two rivers, the Lenape camped in the forest that would become St. Marks Place. Several trails converged at what they called Kintecoying, "Crossroads of Three Nations"—today, Astor Place, where you can catch the 6 train uptown to Grand Central or downtown to the Brooklyn Bridge. Bordered on one side by a salt marsh thronged with bullfrogs and on the other by a trail worn free of grass by centuries of bare feet, this was where Lenape men hunted deer and wild turkey, women gathered blackberries, and children cuddled cornhusk dolls.

Those were the days.

Today, the marsh is Tompkins Square Park, and the path is the Bowery. The area's development began early in the seventeenth century. In 1609, Lenape at the southern tip of the island saw on the horizon what they imagined to be a "monster of the sea": the sails of Henry Hudson's ship *Halve Maen* (*Half Moon*) cutting through waters then still inhabited by whales, seals, and porpoises. The first of many alien encounters to take place in Manhattan was cordial; the men agreed to share the land's wealth of wild game, lumber, and oysters.

Soon the Dutch West India Company had established a small settlement. Their company town at the tip of Manhattan, New Amsterdam, traded mostly in pelts—especially beaver, the height of European fashion. This tiny, barely defended colony wasn't as valuable to the motherland as those colonies that supported the spice, sugar, and slave trades. Still, the Dutch settlers saw promise in this new territory. In the words of Dutch poet-about-town Jacob Steendam, New Netherland was the "noblest spot on earth."

It is the land where milk and honey flow;
Where plants distilling perfume grow;
Where Aaron's rod with budding blossoms blow;
A very Eden.

The Dutch mocked the natives for not having taken better advantage of the island in their thousands of years of stewardship. In 1626, Dutch trader Peter Minuit famously "purchased" Manhattan in exchange for twenty-four dollars' worth of goods from the Lenape, who lacked a distinct concept of ownership and likely thought they were only granting permission for hunting.

The misunderstanding proved fateful. Dutch traders began to see the lingering Native Americans as former tenants ignoring an eviction notice. Intending to solve the problem, Dutch director general William Kieft ordered colonists to slaughter Lenape men, women, and children during what became known as Kieft's War (1643–1645).

Soon under attack from Lenape seeking revenge, New Netherland's colonists resented the Indian-killer Kieft. They petitioned for a gentler new director general—and got one nearly as ruthless: company man Peter Stuyvesant, who had lost his right leg to a Spanish cannonball in 1644 during a sea battle in the Caribbean.

A strict Calvinist, Stuyvesant was appalled by the sordid behavior he found in New Amsterdam, which lacked New England's puritanism. Stuyvesant built a country refuge two miles north, where he could raise his family away from the town's pirates and prostitutes.

In 1651, Stuyvesant bought from his employers, the Dutch West India Company, the huge tract of land known as Bowery (originally "Bouwerie," Dutch for a self-sufficient farm) No. 1, as well as part of the lot Bowery No. 2 and the meadowland to the north, a total of more than three hundred acres. The purchase included Bowery Village, inhabited by seventy-five freed slaves. Stuyvesant encouraged the import of hundreds more slaves from Angola. By the mid-1660s, seven hundred slaves lived in New Netherland. Stuyvesant himself owned about forty.

Stuyvesant rode north to his vast farm from the town at the island's southern tip along the Bowery Road, a path lined with blackberry bushes, past the mile marker for the Eastern Post Road that led to Boston. Not much is known about specific land use during the seventeenth century, but one theory is that the area that would become St. Marks Place, at the heart of the Stuyvesant land, was an orchard. Stuyvesant loved fruit trees, especially pears.

The Stuyvesant family built a skating pond and a windmill, and in 1660, on what is now Tenth Street and Second Avenue, a Dutch Reformed chapel that would let the family avoid the long Sunday journey to church at the tip of the island. Stuyvesant dedicated his country chapel to the patron saint of sailors, merchants, and repentant thieves: St. Nicholas, more widely known as Santa Claus.

Stuyvesant enlisted Dominie Henricus Selyns, pastor of the Dutch Reformed congregation in Breukelen (now Brooklyn), to travel every Sunday, weather permitting, to conduct services at the little church. Soldiers met Selyns on the banks of the East River to escort him through the forested salt marsh. The preacher and his guards walked a rough path cut through the ninety-acre swamp stretching from today's Houston Street to Twelfth Street and from Avenue A to the East River, encompassing the area now known as Alphabet City. The men armed themselves with weapons against the wolves and the Lenape. But soon a more powerful enemy appeared.

In 1664, British ships surrounded the colony. Stuyvesant grudgingly surrendered at his Bowery farm. Despite colonists' pleas over the years for more troops, weapons, and settlers, the Dutch West India Company had never properly invested in the place, and so it fell without a fight.

The British Articles of Capitulation were hardly onerous. As long as the Dutch settlers took an oath to the British king, they could retain their property and go on as before. Stuyvesant nevertheless hated the English from then on. When he returned to New York after a trip back to Amsterdam to face criticism for the fall of the colony, he retired to his farm. Foreswearing city life, he wrote poetry and attended to his collection of exotic birds. Meanwhile, his little church increasingly attracted wealthy families establishing farms nearby.

Washington Irving, who later attended St. Mark's Church with friends, wrote about the retired peg-legged governor in his satirical *Diedrich Knickerbocker's History of New-York*. ("Knickerbocker," the fanciful Dutch surname Irving chose for his narrator, became slang for those who'd been in New York City since colonial times, and eventually the name of the city's orange-and-blue-clad professional basketball team.)

In his *History*, Irving imagines Stuyvesant's retirement: "No persuasions could ever induce him to revisit the city—on the contrary, he would always have his great arm-chair placed with its back to the windows which looked in that direction; until a thick grove of trees planted by his own hand grew up and formed a screen that effectually excluded it from the prospect." According to Irving, Stuyvesant forbade anyone from speaking English in his home, and in a fit of nationalist forestry, chopped down an avenue of English cherry trees on his property.

Stuyvesant died in February 1672. His body was moved the

short distance from his house (located roughly where First Avenue and Sixteenth Street intersect now) into his chapel vault, an underground cave with marble shelves facing the coffins of his servants. In life, the family and their slaves had spent Sundays in separate parts of the church—slaves were relegated to the balcony—but now they shared the same space beneath it, as they still do.

After the director general's death, children dug for imagined buried treasure on his land. Irving wrote that the locals considered it a "great exploit" to "rob 'Stuyvesant's orchard' on a holiday afternoon." Stuyvesant's descendants, meanwhile, expanded his estate. Peter and Judith's son Balthazar died in the Caribbean in 1675, but their other son, Nicholas William, continued to purchase land. Watching yellow fever epidemics tear through the city, the family anticipated a northward shift. By the eighteenth century, the family's lands ran from what is now Stanton Street to East Thirtieth Street.

By the middle of the 1700s, most of New York's inhabitants had grown attached to their British rulers. Even the Stuyvesant family, now Anglican, must have looked on warily as George Washington gathered his troops for military operations in the vicinity of what would become St. Marks Place. The city's prosperous citizens were mostly unenthusiastic about the revolutionary upstarts.

When the British finally withdrew on November 25, 1783, other colonies rejoiced, but New York despaired. Where once twenty thousand people inhabited the island, now only about half as many dwelled there. Bowery Village—the humble cluster of shops, inns, bars, and homes in the vicinity of the Bowery Road—carried on. But the Revolutionary War was a disaster for the local economy, as were the fires of 1776 and 1778. In 1777, another accidental fire incinerated the old Stuyvesant mansion.

Each generation of the Stuyvesants typically produced only one male heir who survived to adulthood. That was true of Nicholas William, who saw the survival only of his son Gerardus—and also true of Gerardus, whose lone-surviving son, Petrus, born in 1727, brought to the Stuyvesants' vast land holdings ambitious architecture and luxury housing.

Petrus, possessed by a vision of what the city should be, hired a surveyor named Evert Bancker, Jr., to outline a street plan for the family's property. Bancker arrayed the streets along the cardinal directions. Those streets running north to south Petrus named for his four daughters: Judith, Elizabeth, Margaret, and Cornelia. The east-to-west ones he named for male family members: Tenbroeck, Winthrop, Gerard, Governor, Peter, Stuyvesant, Nicholas William, and Verplanck. The last fell roughly where St. Marks Place is today.

Petrus worried that the family's Dutch chapel was decaying above his ancestors' crypt. To protect the remains and to provide a new religious home for his wealthy peers, he hoped to found a new, more exclusive, Episcopal church. There was just one problem: Trinity Church held the lone Episcopal charter in the City of New York. If the Stuyvesants' little country chapel were to be reconceived as an Episcopal one worthy of the finest Anglo-Dutch aristocrats in New York—those with names like Fish, Tompkins, and Beekman—it would have to enter the books as a rural extension of Trinity rather than its own parish.

Petrus donated the land, and plans for a Trinity-maintained chapel began to take shape. But as 1800 approached, the Trinity board decided that it preferred not to shoulder the financial responsibility, and so recommended that St. Mark's be incorporated as an independent entity. Petrus asked Alexander Hamilton, attorney for Trinity Parish (and America's first secretary of the treasury), to circumvent the charter problem. Hamilton wrote a legal opinion permitting St. Mark's

The residence of N. W. Stuyvesant, located at what is now St. Marks Place between First and Second Avenues. Manual of the Corporation of the City of New York. 1857. Picture Collection, The New York Public Library, Astor, Lenox and Tilden Foundations.

Church-in-the-Bowery to be the first Episcopal church in America independent of Trinity. Upon its consecration on May 9, 1799, St. Mark's, a fieldstone church modeled after St. Martin-in-the-Fields in London, began its idiosyncratic relationship to the Anglican mainstream.

Unlike many of his relatives, Petrus saw two of his sons survive to adulthood: Peter Gerard and (another) Nicholas William. When Petrus died in 1805, he left the land north of Stuyvesant Street to Peter Gerard (who would go on to found the New-York Historical Society) and the land south of it to Nicholas William. Peter's mansion was called Petersfield. Nicholas William lived in a white, two-story, two-chimney building called the Bowery House, on what today is St. Marks Place between First and Second Avenues. The house sat on a little hill, surrounded on the sides by woods and facing a spacious lawn and hedge-flanked path. For generations, the

Stuyvesants had been careful stewards of their rural paradise. Watching rabbits hopping through the green grass outside his window, Nicholas couldn't have known that within a decade the city would destroy his father's vision and tear up nearly every square inch of his family's beautiful land.

In 1811, New York State's Commissioners of Streets and Roads implemented a city grid that followed Manhattan's orientation rather than the compass. The Stuyvesants' master plan was literally overruled, with the exception of Stuyvesant Street in front of St. Mark's Church-in-the-Bowery. Today Stuyvesant Street is an anomaly in the city: a street that runs west to east, at an angle to the grid. The street was allowed to maintain its

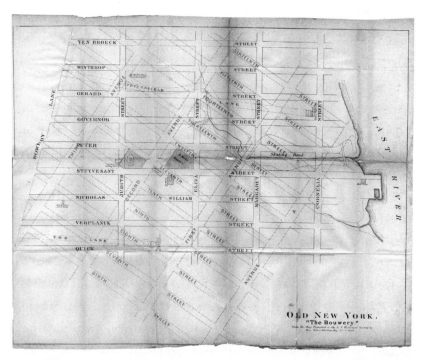

This 1862 map shows the Stuyvesant plan, in which the streets are named after family members, overlaid with the Commissioners' plan that was implemented instead. The Stuyvesants did get to keep one street: Stuyvesant, which runs west–east in front of St. Mark's Church-in-the-Bowery.

orientation after the church and local residents petitioned the state legislature. (It probably didn't hurt that the mayor was on the vestry.)

The Stuyvesants weren't the only ones who opposed the city's grid plan, which many New Yorkers saw as the mad pursuit of industry at the expense of nature. "The magnificent opportunity which was given to the Commissioners to create a beautiful city simply was wasted and thrown away," wrote one critic. "These worthy men decided that the forests should be cut away, the hills leveled, the hollows filled in, the streams buried; and upon the flat surface thus created they clapped on a ruler."

Morbidly, the city left standing a single pear tree planted by Peter Stuyvesant. Where once it flourished as part of the formidable Dutch leader's lush farm, it now stood anachronistically on the corner of the newly and blandly named Thirteenth Street and Third Avenue.

The part of East Eighth Street that would come to be called St. Marks Place began its evolution into a respectable address in 1831, twenty years after the grid's introduction, when prominent real estate developer Thomas E. Davis built a series of elegant townhouses there. Three of these buildings still stand: no. 25, the Hamilton-Holly House at no. 4, and the Daniel LeRoy House at no. 20 (where in 2014 a Ron Paul sign could be seen in an upper window).

Among the first inhabitants of no. 4 were Elizabeth Schuyler and Alexander Hamilton, Jr., the widow and son of the Hamilton who had helped found St. Mark's Church. In 1804, United States Vice President Aaron Burr had killed Hamilton, Sr., in a duel. In a small way, Hamilton, Jr., a lawyer, avenged himself on his father's killer: in 1836, he represented fifty-eight-year-old Eliza Jumel when she divorced the seventy-seven-year-old Burr after just a few months of marriage. Burr died the day the divorce was finalized.

Last of the Mohicans author James Fenimore Cooper lived at no. 6 for a season or two in 1834. In a footnote to his New York historical novel *Satanstoe*, Cooper complains about reserved pews like the Stuyvesants' at St. Mark's Church. He argues that "Distinctions in the House of God are opposed to the very spirit of the Christian religion, and it were far more fitting that pews should be altogether done away with, the true mode of assembling under the sacred roof, than that men should be classed even at the foot of the altar." (In 1969, St. Mark's parishioners would fulfill Cooper's dream by ripping out those same pews.)

Strolling the street in the 1800s, one might encounter the Keteltas family emerging from their red-brick mansion with white doors and marble trimming, which stood into the twentieth century on the northwest corner of St. Marks Place and Second Avenue. The Folsom Mansion with its vast garden (now the Stuyvesant Clinic on Second Avenue) stood nearby. Horse-drawn carriages carried well-dressed residents along city streets, the hooves clattering on concrete. These smooth, new roads were beginning to replace cobblestones, which earlier had replaced dirt and oyster shells.

The name St. Marks Place appears on maps beginning in the 1850s, though it had been the street's unofficial name for years. It was common at that time to glamorize a street's image with "Place," like Astor Place or Beekman Place. The "St. Marks" came, of course, from nearby St. Mark's Church-in-the-Bowery. Having evolved from a Dutch summer chapel on a farm to a parish church in the suburbs, St. Mark's was swiftly becoming a very rich institution in a wealthy neighborhood, of which St. Marks Place was the grandest promenade.

Then, little by little, new families trickled in from outside the social register to subdivide the old one-family homes into more practical apartments, and St. Marks became less fashionable.

Just a few blocks away, on Broadway, a new Episcopal house of worship, Grace Church, rose in 1846. With its façade of sparkling white marble so much more elegant than St. Mark's rustic rubble stone, Grace now drew the well-to-do on Sunday mornings.

Astor Place clung more tightly to its aristocracy. Sewing machine inventor Isaac M. Singer and *New York Evening Post* editor William Cullen Bryant lived there. The millionaire A. T. Stewart maintained his department store on Broadway between Ninth and Tenth Streets. The especially glamorous lived at Lafayette Street's La Grange Terrace, a stretch of Greek revival buildings erected on John Jacob Astor's land in the 1830s, later known as Colonnade Row (a few of these are still standing).

In 1833, Nicholas William Stuyvesant died, and in 1847, the family's reigning patriarch, Peter Gerard Stuyvesant, drowned at Niagara Falls. He left his estate to his nephews, Hamilton Fish and Gerard Stuyvesant. He also named as heir his five-year-old great-grandnephew, on the condition that the boy's name change from Stuyvesant Rutherford to Rutherford Stuyvesant. The child's family moved into Peter Gerard's almost brand-new mansion on Eleventh Street, where his father, an astronomer, built an observatory and took photographs of the moon. Meanwhile, outside this elegant home, immigrants from Ireland and Germany were bringing crowds and violence to the neighborhood. Or so nativists warned.

On May 10, 1849, a battle broke out in front of the Astor Place Opera House between supporters of the English actor William C. Macready and of the American actor Edwin Forrest, who were appearing in rival productions of *Macbeth*. Working-class, fiercely nationalistic Americans found a target for their ingrained anti-British rage: the audacity of a British actor to challenge a hometown favorite on his own turf.

During the riots, the state militia shot into the crowd. Twenty-two people died.

This was only the beginning of the disorder. With more residents and commerce, foot and horse traffic increased precipitously. In 1867, two carriages crashed in front of the Pear Tree Pharmacy at Third Avenue and Thirteenth Street. One slammed into an iron railing on the corner with enough force to destroy the railing and the tree it was built to protect. When the wrecks were removed, witnesses noted that the collision had shattered the stump of the Dutch pear tree that Peter Stuyvesant had planted there two hundred years earlier, the last relic of his farm except for the church and graveyard. Amidst the chaos of the expanding city, few mourned its loss.

2

PETER COOPER'S UTOPIA

The grid had been mapped north only as far as Union Square when a young man named Peter Cooper began his apprenticeship to a coach maker in lower Manhattan. Trash filled the streets, ignored by all but scavenging goats and pigs. There were only a few smoky oil lamps to light the poorly paved streets at night.

As a sensitive child growing up in New York, young Cooper had been horrified by the city's capacity for cruelty. In Washington Square Park, Cooper saw a man hanged for theft and left in the tree for hours while crowds jeered. On the Fifth Avenue side of the same park, he witnessed two black men forced to flog each other. In City Hall Park, he encountered men being beaten at a whipping post, their backs raw. Cooper vowed to devote his life to making New York City more humane, and he believed the best way to do that was through education.

Cooper married, had six children (of whom two survived to adulthood), and made a fortune with inventions and business ventures, including a grocery store near St. Mark's Church and a glue factory. By the middle of the nineteenth century, he was one of the richest men in America.

In 1859, after six years of construction, his visionary school Cooper Union opened its doors. Into its hollow cornerstone, Cooper and Mayor Daniel F. Tiemann—incidentally, Cooper's nephew-in-law—together placed copies of the Constitution, Washington's Farewell Address, and various translations of the Bible, likely provided by Cooper Union's neighboring publisher, the prolific Bible House, which recently had relocated to Astor Place.

Cooper Union's idealistic mission was to offer a free education in the arts and sciences to both men and women. Cooper envisioned it as a beacon to those striving for better lives. On the Bowery, lowlifes lived brutally—this was the *Gangs of New York* era. Cooper Union's position at the top of that road made it the symbolic entrance to a promised land where one could escape the depravity of the Lower East Side.

A Unitarian and an advocate for women's rights, Cooper established programs geared to the working class's needs, including night classes and free public readings on Wednesdays. Among the resources he provided were the Women's School of Design, a debating society, and a public reading room.

Men and women of all classes gathered at Cooper Union for

1905 postcard looking north, showing Cooper Union and the Third Avenue El train. Collection of the author.

"free lectures for the working man." These diverse offerings took the form of concerts, political meetings, entertainments, union rallies, and presentations on social and scientific subjects. No topic was off limits; Bishop Matthew Simpson, for instance, took the stage to warn the audience that the city now had as many prostitutes as Methodists.

Some longtime residents scorned Cooper Union as the death of the neighborhood. They complained about the mixing of the classes that the school promoted and the market sheds that lined the east and west sides of the building, which they cited as evidence that the school was actually a commercial building. Cooper, they said, was trying to avoid paying taxes by passing it off as a place of learning.

Opponents also worried that the building was acting as a magnet for the undesirable immigrants who had overcrowded tenements to the south. St. Marks Place, an unusually broad and bright street, offered one-family homes split up into apartments; the accommodations were luxurious compared to those around Orchard Street.

Indeed, Italians, Jews, and Poles gradually took over St. Marks Place, along with some of the two million Irish people who migrated to America between 1846 and 1860. The Irish and others worked in the shipping industry along the East River. On some evenings, these workers made their way west along St. Marks Place to attend lectures at Cooper Union and discuss the issues of the day, which included the threat of civil war.

Peter Cooper opposed slavery and Southern secession. He inscribed the word "Union," as one biographer noted, "on the most conspicuous front of this building looking to the south," and he encouraged the public to debate these issues in his school's Great Hall. In February 1860, a presidential candidate named Abraham Lincoln arrived at Cooper Union to give a speech before 1,500 people on the tension between North

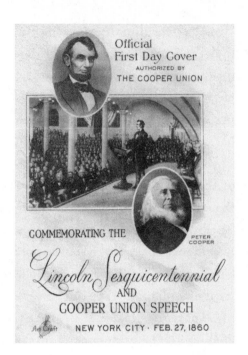

Souvenir of Abraham Lincoln's
1860 Cooper Union speech.
Collection of the author.

and South. Lincoln's own views on slavery were evolving. Privately, he opposed it, but he was running on the Republican platform, which rejected only the spread of slavery into new territories.

Walking onto the stage, the backwoods lawyer initially appeared uncomfortable. "The first impression of the man from the West did nothing to contradict the expectation of something weird, rough and uncultured," wrote one observer, George Haven Putnam, who also noted Lincoln's "large feet," "ungainly figure," and "clumsy hands, of which the speaker seems to be unduly conscious."

After a nervous start, Lincoln began to speak more clearly. "Let us have faith that right makes might," he said, "and in that faith, let us, to the end, dare to do our duty as we understand it." The speech was long, twenty-eight times longer than the Gettysburg Address he would give a few years later. "In the Lincoln canon," writes Harold Holzer in his book devoted to the Cooper Union speech, "it represents an altogether unique rhetorical watershed, the transforming moment separating the prairie stump speaker and the presidential orator."

When he finished, the crowd walked out into the night confident that they had just seen their next president. That speech likely helped Lincoln secure the nomination—as did his shrewd use of visual promotion. On the way to Astor Place that evening, he'd stopped off at Mathew Brady's Bleecker Street photography studio and posed for the commanding portrait that would grace his campaign posters.

The abolition movement was gaining ground and slavery had been outlawed in New York in 1827, but still the practice continued in secret. St. Marks Place served as a headquarters. In 1861, a Spaniard named J. A. Machado, whom the *New York Times* called "the king of the slave-traders in this City" was arrested at his home at no. 33 St. Marks and taken to the city jail called then, as now, the Tombs. He was charged with running slave ships from Africa to Cuba. When he was arrested, it was discovered that he was living in sin with a woman, who could "share his woes, and participate in the profits of his trade."

New York City, including the neighborhood around St. Marks, often found itself on the wrong side of American history, whether in its loyalty to the British in the eighteenth century or its xenophobia in the nineteenth. Lincoln's speech had impressed the Cooper Union crowds, but St. Marks Place, along with the rest of New York, remained largely Democratic and skeptical of abolitionism even after he was elected President. On July 13, 1863, a morning demonstration against the draft became "a sweeping assault against the local institutions and personnel of Abraham Lincoln's Republican Party, as well as a grotesque and bloody race riot." The march started in Central Park and moved downtown, then spread through the whole city in a reign of terror that involved looting, lynching, and arson.

Black men were the primary targets, but Republican strong-holds were also torched, and anyone spotted in a military uniform was killed. The mostly Irish rioters—the same struggling immigrants whom Peter Cooper had been seeking to civilize—burned down the Colored Orphan Asylum, as well as a home for aged prostitutes. Fifth Avenue homes were pillaged. The chaos lasted five days and cost at least 105 lives, ending only when five regiments of Union army troops were called back from Gettysburg to put down the revolt.

Soon after the Draft Riots, black performer Thomas Greene Wiggins, better known as "Blind Tom," arrived on St. Marks Place and found a thriving music scene. While racial tension persisted in the city, this part of the Lower East Side, with its pleasure gardens and bars, as well as Cooper Union's reputation for nurturing respect for the arts, was evolving into a welcoming environment for musicians, an identity that would mark it for many decades to come.

Born in 1849 to Georgia plantation slaves, Wiggins was sold with his family to a Colonel James Neil Bethune. Likely autistic, Wiggins was treated more as household pet than human being, but Bethune's daughter Mary noticed that he had an uncanny ability to imitate sounds. She encouraged him to play the house piano. He applauded himself after every number, laughed often, and said that the wind taught him how to play music. By age eight, he could reproduce any composition to the note.

He made thousands of dollars for his owners while touring. At age ten, he performed for President James Buchanan at the White House, the first black performer to appear there. John Steinbeck wrote about him in the short story "Johnny Bear," and Willa Cather alluded to him in *My Ántonia*.

When General Robert E. Lee surrendered at Appomattox in 1865, Wiggins became free, but the Bethunes decided he wasn't

Blind Tom, 1880. Photo by Golder & Robinson, N.Y. Copyrighted by John G. Bethune. Library of Congress.

capable of living independently. Mary's brother John became Wiggins's guardian. On the train during a concert tour, Mark Twain encountered him in the smoking compartment and made the following observation of the violently rocking man, who was imitating every sound the train made: "What a wild state he was in! Clattering, hissing, whistling, blowing off gauge cocks, ringing his bell, thundering over bridges with a row and a racket like everything going to pieces, whooping through tunnels, running over cows—*Heavens!* I thought, *will this devil never run his viewless express off the track and give us a rest?*"

When Twain later saw Wiggins give a formal performance, he was left with an altogether different impression: "If ever there was an inspired idiot this is the individual. He lorded it over the emotions of his audience like an autocrat. He swept them like a storm, with his battle-pieces; he lulled them to rest again with melodies as tender as those we hear in dreams . . . now and then he threw in queer imitations of the tuning of discordant harps and fiddles, and the groaning and wheezing of bag-pipes, that sent the rapt silence into tempests of laughter."

In 1870, Wiggins and his guardian, the colonel's son John, moved to a boardinghouse at no. 7 St. Marks Place. Wiggins studied with a prominent music teacher, and John married the boardinghouse's owner, Eliza Stutzbach. The marriage didn't last. Stutzbach sued for divorce and soon after, in 1884, John fell under a train and died. He'd already written his ex-wife out of his will, calling her "a heartless adventuress." (This is a little like blaming the sun for shining, heartless adventuring being what people traditionally go to St. Marks Place *for*.) Wiggins's custody reverted to John's father, the Colonel. But Stutzbach sued for guardianship, enlisting the help of Wiggins's mother, Charity, and in 1887 she won. Under her supervision, Wiggins returned to performing. The *New York Times* reported on Wiggins in his later years: "If he felt the wind blowing against him he would exclaim: 'Tom's in a draught. He may catch cold and die. Wouldn't that be terrible!'"

By 1891, some newspapers were saying Blind Tom had consumption and that he had little if anything left of the estimated $750,000 he'd earned in his lifetime. But Wiggins was alive and apparently comfortable. Eliza remarried, and she and Wiggins moved to Hoboken, New Jersey, with her new husband. Wiggins died there in 1908, at the age of fifty-nine. He was buried in Evergreens Cemetery in Brooklyn beneath a gravestone with a portrait; a list of his most popular compositions, including "The Sewing Song: Imitation of a Sewing Machine"; and this quote: "Music inspires, comforts, and is the balm throughout our lifetime."

In the decades after the Civil War, St. Marks Place drew agitators of all classes. In the idealistic tradition of Cooper Union, a fleet of new schools and services for the poor opened there, bringing the indigent and wealthy into daily contact. Women working, the poor studying, unions organizing—by the 1870s, little was left of the Stuyvesants' elegant St. Marks Place.

At Juliet Corson's New York Cooking School (no. 8) in 1875, a new wife could learn how to feed a family of six for fifteen cents. "Before the cook stove all women are equals," proclaimed a Corson profile.

In the mornings, young women from prominent families would take classes, and in the afternoons, some of those society ladies would stay to teach cooking to lower-class women. One poor student who had grown up in the tenements finished the course and then cooked a meal at the Corson school for her fiancé. Her teacher served them. For many young women, schools like this were a route to both marketable skills and dignity.

Around this time, Miss Emily Huntington arrived as headmistress of the Wilson Industrial School for Girls, which had been founded some twenty years earlier. Huntington was an ideal candidate. She had a fervent belief in cleanliness and good habits, and was fond of this George Herbert verse:

A servant with this clause
Makes drudgery divine
Who sweeps a room, as to thy laws
Makes that, and the action fine.

She visited the filthy tenements of the Lower East Side and agreed with the Wilson board that something had to be done about all the children who didn't know how to light a proper fire, clean silver, or fold clothes. She taught by call and response, as documented in her book *Little Lessons for Little Housekeepers*. For example: "How do you make hot suds?" Correct response: "Put a piece of soap on a fork, and stir it briskly in the water."

Situated at the corner of Avenue A and St. Marks, the

Wilson Industrial School was a beacon of efficiency, purpose, and Christian values. So Huntington was not pleased when she learned that she was employing Theosophists—mystics who believed in a common theme among all religions and hosted séances in which they communed with ghostly spirits.

This was a golden age of pseudoscientific exploration. The faraway-eyed Helena Petrovna Blavatsky, along with Henry Steel Olcott and William Quan Judge, had formed the Theosophical Society, a mystical initiate group that stressed a connection between eastern and western religions. Blavatsky wrote books with titles like *The Secret Doctrine* and *Isis Unveiled*, occult mélanges that propose the existence of a universal oversoul. Theosophy was the Scientology of its day: it had powerful members, operated in secrecy, and roused great anxiety in outside observers.

One spring day in 1893, the Wilson School's administrators cracked down.

Miss Rapello and Mrs. Jennings inquired if Wilson teacher Miss Elizabeth Chapin might be a Theosophist. She said that she was a Christian, and that she attended a Congregational church in Brooklyn (near where she lived on Classon Avenue). Then a Mrs. Stone directly asked if Chapin were *also* a Theosophist, and she said yes. She was told she had to resign from either the school or Theosophy. Chapin insisted she would do neither.

When a *Tribune* reporter came calling at Chapin's house, she said she'd been fired and that she found it "unfair and uncharitable," adding that the Theosophical Society had been donating ten dollars a month to support the school. She said it was hypocritical that the board found Theosophists good enough to take money from but not to employ.

A month later, it was revealed that Miss L. J. Kirkwood, a sewing teacher who had been at Wilson for fourteen years and developed a curriculum used in public schools throughout the city, was also a Theosophist, as was the matron, Mrs. E. L. Armstrong. Both were dismissed at the insistence of the Reverend Daniel Redman, the missionary at the school's chapel. Now almost completely bereft of teachers, the school closed. "This staid old non-sectarian Protestant institution has not been closed before, it is said," the *Times* reported, "summer or winter, for forty years."

A close cousin of religious purism was temperance, which also thrived during this time on St. Marks Place. The Temperance Fountain, which still stands in Tompkins Square Park, was erected to tempt the drunks of the area with cold water instead of alcohol.

All up and down St. Marks, religious philanthropists were driven to help the poor. St. Mark's Hospital opened at no. 60 in 1890. Charles Loring Brace's Children's Aid Society opened a "Girls' Temporary House" at no. 27, where homeless girls could learn to cook and do office work. And in the middle of the century, a lawyer's wife from Gramercy Park named Mary Delafield DuBois teamed up with a doctor's wife named Anna R. Emmet to open the Nursery for the Children of Poor Women in a little St. Marks Place house. Until then, poor women had little recourse if they found themselves unable to take care of their babies. Hospitals like Bellevue farmed these newborns out to poor families. Under strangers' sometimes less than ideal care, hundreds of neglected babies died every year.

Nevertheless, DuBois and Emmet drew the line at accepting the children of women of poor character. If the woman was unwed, she had to show that the pregnancy wasn't her fault: "The mother must produce evidence of having borne a good character until the dark shadow of him who ruined her fell across her path."

Forty years later, a tiny, pale woman named Sara Curry opened Little Missionary, a daycare for 150 children, at no.

93. She didn't make the mothers of her charges pass a morality test, and she was clear-eyed about their bleak circumstances. Curry, one of seven children of an Irish immigrant couple, had been orphaned at the age of ten. Though frail, she'd gone to work at a cap mill in Utica, New York, to take care of her two small brothers.

Deeply religious, Curry moved to New York City in 1896 to work as a tenement missionary through the Methodist Episcopal Church. While there, she saw a child run out into the street and get hit by a truck. She carried the child inside, and he died in her arms. On her way out of the neighborhood that day, Curry stopped to talk to some of the mothers about the tragedy. "Have these children no one to look after them—to see that they do not get into danger?" she asked. The women told her: "We must work. They must eat. We can't tie them up like dogs. They must move about. Who's to look after them? You, for instance?"

Curry heard her calling: to provide a safe place for the children of women who needed to work. As part of her campaign to better the lives of tenement children—one that earned her sainthood on the Lower East Side and a fur coat as thanks from Mrs. John D. Rockefeller—"Mama Curry" also marched into countless homes to show poor women how to keep house. Curry got on her hands and knees to demonstrate the right way to scrub the floors, and showed the women how to decorate with fresh flowers or properly cook a steak.

"We'll fix up this place so that your husband will be glad to stay here, and we'll cook him a supper that'll do him good," she told the women she visited, assuring them that a well-kept home was the best way to keep their husbands away from bars.

One of Curry's neighbors also took an interest in the children of the neighborhood. Horatio Alger was born in 1832 in Revere, Massachusetts. He attended Harvard and then tried his hand at journalism in Boston. When he failed at that, he

German shopkeeper Abraham Mayer (on right) with two Polish boarders.
Collection of Mayer's granddaughter, Susan Mayer Wheeler.

became a Unitarian minister in Brewster. After two years, he was run out of town for engaging in "unnatural crimes" with boys. Alger fled south to New York and took up residence in a hotel on St. Marks Place. There, he surrounded himself with the neighborhood's street urchins, about whom he began to write books.

In 1867, installments of Alger's book *Ragged Dick: or, Street Life in New York*, about an ambitious boy named Dick who works hard to become respectable, appeared in a Boston magazine. Alger became a popular novelist, giving voice to the poor boys of St. Marks Place and to a social philosophy in which the downtrodden could pull themselves up by their bootstraps and attain the comforts of middle-class life. While giving a tour of the city to a rich boy, Ragged Dick makes a point of showing off the newly built Cooper Union. Alger offered a philosophy quite different from that of the street's alternately moralizing and indulgent charities: The poor didn't need handouts, he insisted; they needed opportunities to prove their worth. In the wake of the Civil War, the German immigrants colonizing St. Marks Place tended toward Alger's way of thinking. They worked hard until they had eradicated the street's former identity and converted it into what all of New York was soon calling Little Germany. At the end of a period of class uplift, St. Marks Place roared to life in a cacophony of German shopkeepers calling out to their customers, beer steins clinking in the new outdoor bars, and classical music pouring out of windows. The Germans appeared to be happily entrenched, destined to rule over the neighborhood for many years to come. And yet, within just two generations they would be gone.

3

KLEIN DEUTSCHLAND

As a young boy living at no. 93 in the 1870s, William J. Urchs, whose father was a singer, lived among large German families, usually of between five and twelve children. Many of their parents played two instruments, often for the Philharmonic and Symphony Orchestras. "They practiced four to six hours daily, and you can imagine the pandemonium," Urchs recalled in his nostalgic essay "St. Marks Place Manhattan." "The tuning of an orchestra before a concert sounds like an infant's wail in comparison." From his window, Urchs enjoyed watching the police and fire departments, and the National Guard, march from their Tompkins Square Park parade grounds to Astor Place. He and his friends knew the names of every colonel, bandmaster, and police captain.

Between Second and Third Avenue was the Tivoli Garden, a family hangout with an orchestra bandstand and small tables. The proprietors of the Tivoli hosted a variety show with acts like Grimaldi the Clown, who in the course of his act pointed a fake rocket into the crowd and lit the fuse, causing a minor panic. Another source of entertainment for Urchs and his friends was playing in the gravel piles underneath the new elevated train on First Avenue. The Second Avenue El, which operated on First Avenue up to Twenty-Third Street, was one of several elevated lines being built around the city (the others were on Third, Sixth, and Ninth Avenues), casting neighborhoods into shadow and showering them with dirt and noise.

The mounted police drive what the press calls "riotous Communist workingmen" out of Tompkins Square Park on January 13, 1874. Engraving by Matt Morgan in *Frank Leslie's Illustrated Newspaper*, January 31, 1874. Library of Congress.

In the summer of 1876, Urchs watched five thousand people gather in Tompkins Square Park for a protest against government corruption at Tammany Hall. Residents were frustrated by graft and the dilapidated state of the city. In the densely packed neighborhood, Tompkins Square provided a rare opportunity for recreation and fresh air. Its having become a "chaotic wilderness," in the words of one speaker, even after funds had been earmarked for its repair, made it a symbol of the crowd's cause. On a platform lit by Chinese lanterns, speakers wound up the crowd with speeches in both German and English. It was 8 p.m. and they were just getting started.

Along St. Marks Place, Urchs and his neighbors sat on their stoops gazing east toward the park. At first large but orderly, the crowd now threatened to turn into a chaotic mob. The police, a vulnerable symbol of the Tammany system, grew tense with the memory of the recent Draft Riots no doubt fresh in their minds.

Finally, at 10 p.m., as the crowds reached a crescendo of rage, the police decided to act. A mounted policeman raced along St. Marks Place. The residents took that as their cue to get inside. Urchs writes: "The street was cleared like magic, doors were slammed and shutters were closed with a bang."

From his window on the second floor, Urchs watched as the chanting mob squared off against policemen waving batons. Five minutes later, the outmatched rioters fled east, back toward the park. More policemen ambushed the protesters from a hiding spot on First Avenue and swiftly scattered the remaining activists. Tammany would continue to thrive for decades to come.

By now the area's Irish shipping industry had more or less dried up. The East River's old, rotting wooden piers were being rendered obsolete by modern facilities in New Jersey. German immigrants like the Urchs family had taken over the rooming houses and converted single-family buildings of St. Marks Place, working middle-class jobs like dressmaking, baking, brewing, and piano tuning. Where once lived some of the richest families in New York now dwelled residents like S. C. Lynes, Jr., a bookkeeper (no. 47), and Charles Edward Anthon, a history professor (no. 37). In 1871, the painter and caricaturist Lyonel Feininger was born at no. 85.

As elsewhere in the city, the Germans fostered a tradition of beer halls and rollicking parties. The German Shooting Society's headquarters was at no. 12 (on the façade is still written "Einigkeit Macht Stark," or "Unity Makes Strength"). In

1874, German music society the Arion Club threw a party at no. 19–21. Members wore hats shaped like dolphins for the festivities.

William Schwind ran a costume shop at no. 23 until George Ehert bought it in 1887 and combined nos. 19, 21, and 23 into Arlington Hall, a ballroom and community hall space. Tammany nemesis and anti-corruption reformer Theodore Roosevelt would speak there in 1895, when he was the New York City Police Commissioners board president. Around the corner, in the spirit of Peter Cooper, arose the first free public lending library in New York: the Ottendorfer, built in 1884, is still in operation.

Despite its cultural assets, the street's economy struggled through the Long Depression (1873–1879), caused in part by bankers' reckless railroad speculation. The neighborhood began to see an influx of Jews, some of the 1.5 million who would arrive in New York between 1881 and 1910, mostly from Russia. St. Marks Place retained its German flavor but ethnic tensions began to rise, especially in the wake of the near-collapse of America's financial system. Wages fell, manufacturing jobs disappeared, and unemployment in New York City hit 25 percent.

With nowhere to play, boys ran wild through the city in packs. In 1872, Edward Crapsey wrote a book called *The Nether Side of New York*. He describes the operation of an abortionist named Madame Van Buskirk (real name Gifford), whom he calls "one of the boldest and worst of her tribe, and whose den in [no. 8] St. Mark's Place has long been known as one of the most infamous places in the metropolis."

Crapsey also condemned "The Ring," a political conspiracy that allowed "venal rascality" among politicians, who "constantly exhibited themselves to the public gaze loaded with diamonds and guzzling costly wines, like the vulgar knaves they were." Crapsey noted that as vast numbers of poor immigrants came in, Europeans who had been in the United States long enough to amass money, status, and skills moved to bedroom communities in Brooklyn Heights or far uptown, only coming into lower Manhattan to work. "New York was a camping ground rather than a city," wrote Crapsey. New York's Lower East Side, he said, was left with humanity's "dregs."*

Every ethnicity contributed its share of violence. On October 14, 1888, a man named Antonio Flaccomio had dinner with two fellow Mafia members, the Quarteraros—Carlo, a fruit dealer, and his brother Vincenzo—at an Italian restaurant called La Trinacria (another name for Sicily), which had recently replaced Juliet Corson's school at no. 8. They quarreled over a drinking game they were playing called Tocco. A feather-duster manufacturer named Frank Aita told Flaccomio to step outside. Flaccomio did, taking a large knife with him. The arguing men walked to Cooper Union. Vincenzo Quarteraro and Flaccomio flashed their knives at each other. Meanwhile, Vincenzo's brother, Carlo, a stocky thirty-year-old with a heavy black mustache, snuck up and stabbed Flaccomio in the chest with a bread knife he'd grabbed from the restaurant's kitchen. "I've fixed him," he said to his brother in Italian. The men returned to the restaurant and promised to protect each other, but the police later got someone in the group to talk. An inquest determined that the Tocco argument was merely a pretext for a premeditated hit on Flaccomio for ratting out a fellow member of their Sicilian secret society. The press, fascinated by this relatively new crime genre, called it "the 'Mafia' murder."

Flaccomio died in the shadow of the new Third Avenue El train. The huge metal structure seemed to nurture brutality. In the train's shadow were always nestled "thin pale men in old clothes" according to one observer. For the seventy or so years

* This is word for word what would be said about New York in the 1970s.

St. Mark's Church-in-the-Bowery postcard. Collection of the author.

that the El stood on that corner, men drank, fought, and died on the dark sidewalk beneath its girders.

At St. Mark's Church-in-the-Bowery, more troubling disturbances were taking place. In 1876, grave robbers opened the crypt of retail merchant Alexander T. Stewart, whose store stood on Broadway between Ninth and Tenth, and removed his corpse, then wrote to his family demanding a ransom for its return.

The body was ultimately recovered, but the family realized that St. Mark's Church and its surroundings were no longer safe for rich people—even dead ones. The Stewarts moved their patriarch's body to a safer mausoleum on Long Island, and plenty of wealthy St. Marks Place dwellers followed.

The body snatching wasn't the only scandal facing St. Mark's

Church. On May 25, 1889, the rector, J. H. Rylance, sailed for England with plans to return in August. While he was away, a member of the vestry spread word of "a scandal in the Parish." Some vestrymen, including Rutherford Stuyvesant, William Remsen, and N. W. Stuyvesant Catlin, gathered on July 17 to discuss the rumors. By the end of the meeting, they'd decided to suggest the rector resign.

William V. King opened his letter to Rylance, "Dear Sir, Since your departure for Europe certain grave charges have been made against you—affecting your moral character and standing both in the Church and community." King said that if he refused to resign, the case would be presented to the bishop and "scandal and publicity" would follow.

The ensuing flurry of letters never exactly identified the "rumors of indiscretion and improper conduct for a clergymen," but church lore has it that Rylance had been seen with prostitutes. When confronted, he insisted he had only been ministering to them. In the end, King became convinced that Rylance had been wrongly accused and was simply the victim of gossip. He apologized to the rector and said he wanted to distance himself from "this repulsive business."

While Rylance remained abroad, the formidable rector of Grace Church, Rev. Dr. Huntington, took time away from his magnificent temple and its carillon of bells to give an address to the humble St. Mark's on the occasion of its centennial.

"The Lion of St. Mark is not dead," he opened, rather patronizingly, "no, nor even dormant. He is an old Lion, a century old; but to-day he rouses himself, asserts his right to be, and presently he will be heard from."

The once-dominant Germans trickled out of the neighborhood, primarily uptown to nicer apartments, while newer immigrants, mostly Slavs, took over their shops and tenements. But some Germans held on and tried to maintain their cultural traditions, one of which was an annual boat trip and picnic. In 1904, the St. Mark's Lutheran Church's annual Long Island field trip was set for June 15. That day 1,342 parishioners set out aboard a Knickerbocker Steamship Company ship called the *General Slocum*. (The Civil War Union officer and congressman Henry Ward Slocum was known for his controversially slow march into the Battle of Gettysburg—earning him the nickname "Slow Come"—and for helping Major General William T. Sherman take Atlanta.)

The ladies, in their best dresses, cheered as food and drink were loaded on the boat at Third Street. As the craft steamed up the East River, a band played hymns like "Ein Fest Burg is Unser Gott" ("A Mighty Fortress Is Our God"). Flags fluttered from the masts beneath a cloudless blue sky.

The merrymaking on deck was interrupted by the cry of a fourteen-year-old boy, Frank Perditski. As the boat passed Eighty-Third Street, the young passenger noticed smoke in the storeroom, where packing crates filled with straw had been set near oil lamps. The captain ignored him.

A quarter-mile later, a dredge captain on a nearby ship saw smoke coming from the *Slocum*'s lower deck. Other boats signaled, too, but the captain of the *General Slocum* kept going, fanning the flames by heading into the wind. Another boy grabbed a deckhand from the barroom, but the addled man panicked and threw charcoal on the fire, then went to find the mate. Mate Flanagan showed no haste in alerting the captain. The captain made a slow investigation.

When the alarm was finally sounded, the ship had reached 110th Street. The captain yelled contradictory orders: "Go slow! Full speed!" and for another mile, the boat zigzagged up the river. In a later inquiry, the captain would say that he hadn't stopped because he'd been afraid of setting fire to riverside buildings.

The uninspected water hoses split apart when crewmembers

tried to use them. The lifeboats and rafts were wired so tightly to the ship that the passengers couldn't free them. The rotten life preservers sank.

Mary Hartman held onto her two daughters, aged fifteen and twelve, and tried to stay calm waiting for a rescue boat, but the family was torn apart by "two destructive forces moving at roughly the same speed—a huge mob of panic-stricken passengers followed by a wall of orange fire."

What was left of the boat came to rest, aflame, at North Brother Island between the Bronx and Rikers Island. By then most of those onboard, a total of 1,020, mostly women and children, had either drowned or burned to death. The hundreds of dead bodies were laid along the banks of the river. Families were grouped together. The Rheinfrank family lost eleven; the Weis family, ten. Almost every member of the church's kindergarten died.

One survivor, a child, described his surreal journey from the Bronx back to St. Marks Place. When he reached the El train to take him downtown, word had already spread. From his clothes and his face, the subway worker realized that he'd been on the ship and asked him if he were coming from the *Slocum*. When the boy said yes, the worker ushered him through the turnstile and put him on the train downtown.

Back home, the child joined the rest of his community, who had gathered to wait for news with Pastor Haas at the Sixth Street church. In the coming days, nearly every hearse in the city would be pressed into service for the *Slocum* funerals.

In the weeks that followed, the steamship company faced national condemnation and became a symbol of how Tammany's bribery system could cost lives. In court, it came out that a routine inspection forty days earlier had been a sham. President Roosevelt appointed a federal commission, which personally inspected the other 268 vessels in New York Harbor. More than half failed. The captain was convicted on several

Funeral of unidentified victims of the *General Slocum* disaster, June 15, 1904.
Corner of Avenue A and Sixth Street. Gustav Scholer Papers, Manuscripts and Archives
Division, The New York Public Library, Astor, Lenox and Tilden Foundations.

charges, including criminal negligence, and sentenced to ten
years in prison. Roosevelt refused to pardon him.

In James Joyce's *Ulysses*, which takes place entirely on June
16, 1904, a character ordering gin says, "Terrible affair that
General Slocum explosion. Terrible, terrible! A thousand casualties. And heartrending scenes. Men trampling down women
and children. Most brutal thing." Until September 11, 2001,
the *General Slocum* fire would rank as the worst disaster in New
York City's history.

The German population of St. Marks Place was already on the decline at the turn of the century, but after the tragedy of the *General Slocum*, hundreds of men who had woken up husbands and fathers and gone to bed childless widowers saw little reason to stay. Many moved four miles north to Yorkville, a neighborhood on the Upper East Side, and started new lives.

By the start of the twentieth century, William Urchs's glorious German St. Marks Place—with its lively bars and clamor of instruments—was dead.

As the German incarnation of St. Marks Place passed away, New Yorkers began feeling nostalgic even as the city boomed around them. A few years after the horrors of the *General Slocum* disaster, a Broadway show, the *Ziegfeld Follies of 1913*, debuted a song entitled, "New York, What's the Matter with You?" The song suggests that the lights don't burn as brightly as they once did.

As the world approached a cataclysm on a whole new scale— the Great War—St. Marks Place had already ceased to be so many things: a place of natural beauty, a hotbed for philanthropy and free education, and a rollicking German enclave. Many people assumed it would never be anything interesting again.

PART II

"THREE BLOCKS OF UNUSUAL"

1905–1950

Garment workers in front of Arlington Hall, ca. 1915–1920.
Library of Congress.

4

"HAIL MARX" PLACE

Born to a Jewish family in Czarist Russia in 1869, Emma Goldman moved at the age of thirteen to a Jewish ghetto in St. Petersburg, where she lived under the stacked authorities of an abusive father and an autocratic political regime. Emma followed the ghetto's revolutionaries, who dreamed of overthrowing the czar and building a new political system of collective rule.

While working in a corset shop at the age of fifteen to help support her family, Goldman faced pressure from her father to marry. In 1885, she fled to America and settled with two of her sisters in Rochester, New York, where she worked in a factory making overcoats ten hours a day for $2.50 a week. There, Goldman married a fellow immigrant, but the marriage didn't last. "Marriage and love have nothing in common," she later wrote. "They are as far apart as the poles; are, in fact, antagonistic to each other."

Goldman then had what she described as a conversion experience: in the newspapers, she read about the trial of eight Chicago anarchists accused of throwing a bomb during a rally in Haymarket Square. Four were hanged. Goldman decided America was no better than Russia. That night, she wrote, "I had a distinct sensation that something new and wonderful had been born in my soul." She was eighteen.

A teenage divorcée, she headed to New York City with five dollars and a sewing machine. She found herself in the

Emma Goldman on a streetcar,
ca. 1900. Library of Congress.

center of anarchist society and was soon living in a *ménage a trois*
with anarchist Alexander Berkman and his male cousin, an
artist and illustrator named Modest "Fedya" Aronstam (later
changed to Stein). She organized rallies and marches and
went on speaking tours, but she believed the revolution would
require a galvanizing event.

In 1892, several striking steelworkers were killed during
a protest in Homestead, Pennsylvania, that turned violent.
The industrialist Henry Clay Frick, who had joined forces
with Andrew Carnegie to control the steel trade, was taking a
hard line in wage negotiations in an effort to break the union.
Goldman and Berkman decided to assassinate Frick. The plan
was for Berkman to hang for the murder and then for Goldman to turn Berkman into a martyr for the revolution. She
tried prostituting herself on Fourteenth Street to raise money
for a gun but ended up having to borrow the money instead.

Berkman entered Frick's office shaking. He shot the magnate twice before Frick—injured, but not fatally—tackled his opponent. In the struggle, Berkman stabbed Frick multiple times but was pulled off him by another man. As a last-ditch effort, Berkman tried to detonate a powerful dynamite capsule in his mouth, but it failed to go off.

In the end, Frick survived, famously sitting back down and finishing up some paperwork before being taken to the ambulance. "I do not think I shall die," the stoic Frick told the press, "but whether I do or not, the [Carnegie Steel] Company will pursue the same policy and it will win." Berkman, looking to the world more deranged than heroic, was sentenced to fourteen years in jail. Even worse from the revolutionaries' perspective, he cost the strikers the public's sympathy.

Goldman continued to spread the word on her own. She was thrown in jail repeatedly for handing out birth-control information and protesting the draft, as well as for inciting a riot by suggesting to a crowd of thousands in Union Square that the unemployed should take what they needed by force. After serving time for the riot charge, she founded the anarchist magazine *Mother Earth*, which was pro–birth control and antiwar and had a roll of some eight thousand subscribers. On New Year's Day, 1911, she opened the Modern School at no. 6 St. Marks Place. The school offered an alternative to public education for children and continuing-education classes for adults. When it opened, the school had just nine full-time students, including Margaret Sanger's son Stuart as well as Man Ray. Also called the Ferrer Center after the Spanish anarchist Francisco Ferrer, the Modern School taught students to disregard any government restrictions that they didn't support and to plan for a world without laws. Jack London and Upton Sinclair lectured there. In 1912, the historian and philosopher Will Durant became principal, then fell in love with a fifteen-year-old pupil and married her. Together, the Durants would go on to write an eleven-volume set of history books, *The Story of Civilization*.

The anarchist movement of 1914 opposed American involvement in World War I, and its members used dynamite to gain attention for their cause. Several Modern School continuing-education students tried to bomb John D. Rockefeller's mansion. When the bomb failed to detonate, they took the device to *Mother Earth* editor Louise Berger's Lexington Avenue apartment, where it exploded and killed four people.

"In the Ferrer or Modern School, run by anarchists," wrote investigators for the New York State Legislature's Joint Legislative Committee to Investigate Seditious Activities, "children at the most impressionable age were taught an utter disregard for our laws, and imbued with the idea that a state of anarchy was the true blissful state, and that this should be the aim and purpose of the little children who, in all their innocence, believe what their elders tell them. That such an institution should have been allowed to exist for almost ten years is not a very high compliment to the city of New York." The Modern School, which had since moved to East Twelfth Street, was shuttered, and Goldman found herself the marquee name in a nationwide sweep of radicals.

At about 4 a.m. on December 21, 1919, Goldman and 248 other dissidents were herded onto a ship nicknamed the "Soviet Ark." Goldman felt betrayed. "On the deck above us I could hear the men tramping up and down in the wintry blast," she wrote. "I felt dizzy, visioning a transport of politicals doomed to Siberia. . . . Through the port-hole I could see the great city receding into the distance, its sky-line of buildings traceable by their rearing heads. It was my beloved city, the metropolis of the New World. It was America, indeed America repeating the terrible scenes of tsarist Russia! I glanced up—the Statue of Liberty!"

German Odd Fellows Hall, no. 69, 1893.
Collection of the author.

Despite Goldman's departure, St. Marks—now nicknamed "Hail Marx"—Place remained a headquarters for radicals and union organizers. If you wanted to find out if the garment workers were going on strike or what demands the waiters' union was preparing to make, St. Marks was where you went. A 1903 almanac lists several union headquarters at no. 69, including the American Association of Masters and Pilots of Steam Vessels (Manhattan Harbor No. 1); American Federation of Musicians, Local No. 41; and the International Brotherhood of Boilermakers, Iron Ship Builders, Blacksmiths, Forgers and Helpers.

This had been a wildly successful time for the labor movement. In 1909, Yiddish-speaking Ukrainian teenager Clara Lemlich had whipped a strikers' meeting at Cooper Union into a frenzy by saying that as a "working girl" she was sick of listening to mere speeches. She wanted action and she got it, leading the Uprising of the 20,000, the largest strike by women in the history of America. During the protests, which lasted from November 1909 to February 1910, she was arrested seventeen times and six of her ribs were broken, reportedly by heavies enlisted to scare her away from union involvement. The strike transformed the garment industry forever, though not quickly enough to save the 145 of Lemlich's peers locked inside the Triangle Shirtwaist Factory who died in a historic March 1911 fire.

Just a few years after the Triangle Shirtwaist tragedy, a charismatic young radical, the son of rich Jewish farmers in Ukraine, arrived by boat in the middle of the night. It was January 13, 1917, and a cold rain fell on the docks. Leon Trotsky stepped off the ship with his wife and two sons. In broken English, he asked a driver to take them to their new lodgings in what had been described to him as "a workers' district" in the Bronx. For eighteen dollars a month, the family would enjoy modern conveniences, including a gas stove and electric lights. The Trotsky boys were particularly enchanted by the prospect of their very own telephone. The next day, Leon started his job at a revolutionary newspaper office on St. Marks Place.

Trotsky had been a union organizer in Russia. After being arrested for radicalism in 1898, in prison he fully converted to Marxism, admiring its combination of intellectualism and action. In 1900, he and his wife were sentenced to four years in Siberia, where they would have two daughters before he escaped on a hay wagon, remarried, and went into exile.

After stays in Vienna and Paris, Trotsky arrived in New York for a position on the editorial board of *Novy Mir* (*New World*), a Russian newspaper coedited by Nikolai Bukharin and printed in the basement of no. 77. "I left a Europe wallowing in blood," Trotsky wrote of his arrival in New York City, "but

I left with a profound faith in a coming revolution. And it was with no democratic 'illusions' that I stepped on the soil of this old-enough New World." Trotsky found Bukharin fickle and untrustworthy. "You must always keep your eyes on him," he writes, "or else he will succumb quite imperceptibly to the influence of some one directly opposed to you, as other people fall under an automobile." But he was glad for the job.

Novy Mir was "the headquarters for internationalist revolutionary propaganda"—fresher, Trotsky believed, than the "stale odor of sentimentally philistine socialism" emanating from the offices of the Yiddish-language daily paper the *Forward*, then considered the Jewish immigrants' leading social-justice publication.

On March 2 of that year, Trotsky was staring out the *Novy Mir* office window, daydreaming, when he witnessed a disturbing sight. He watched "an old man with suppurating eyes and a straggling gray beard step before a garbage-can and fish out a crust of bread. He tried the crust with his hands, then he touched the petrified thing with his teeth, and finally he struck it several times against the can. But the bread did not yield. Finally he looked about him as if he were afraid or embarrassed, thrust his find under his faded coat, and shambled along down St. Marks Place."

"Revolution is brewing in the trenches," Trotsky said soon after in a speech at Cooper Union. In March 1917, he returned to Russia. That October, the Russian Revolution began.

5

UNDERGROUND TUNNELS

At the turn of the century, a Lower East Side mob boss named Dopey Benny Fein (so called because of his sleepy eyes) ruled St. Marks Place. Dopey Benny formed a bridge between the virtuous labor leaders and the vice-laden underworld because, despite his mile-long rap sheet—as a kid, he had picked pockets in order to buy homing pigeons—he had principles: he was rigorously pro-union. During this period, New York's garment workers became a national power. Clean, organized factories were replacing the chaotic sweatshops, and Fein supported these developments in his own, violent way.

Where other gangsters might beat up scabs one day and union organizers the next, depending on which group was paying them, Fein only took union money, and only according to a reasonable fee schedule: for example, Fein's gang received two hundred dollars to knock out a scab or injure a foreman, and fifty dollars for throwing an informer down the stairs. Fein was also a women's rights pioneer. He routinely employed women; they infiltrated factories to ensure that strike orders were carried out and attacked scabs with hatpins and umbrellas.

Mobsters operated along the Bowery, now known for "nickel museums featuring mermaids, snakes, sword swallowers, lions, dwarfs, and women in various states of undress," not to mention a nightly flophouse population of twenty-five thousand. St. Marks was becoming similarly notorious as a locus

Jewish gangster Dopey Benny Fein, ca. 1914.

for crime, thanks in part to the Astor Place stop on the Third Avenue elevated train, which showered the sidewalks with oil and coal and provided cover for muggers.

Fein commandeered Arlington Hall at nos. 19–23, the former German hotspot, for parties, and bookie joints flourished up and down the street. A raid of no. 9 in March 1900 found more than three hundred men and boys playing pool and gambling. When the police opened the door, revolvers drawn, some gamblers still had money clutched in their hands. Two of those in charge were arrested, but the telegraph operator threw his machine down the dumbwaiter shaft to the saloon below and jumped after it with various gambling paraphernalia under his coat. The officers nevertheless found evidence that the owner of the gambling den was a high-ranking Tammany Hall politician. During a later raid at no. 6, crooks flung furniture at detectives trying to enter and shot at them through an ice-chest door as the cops chopped at it with axes.

An entrepreneur, Fein sought to revolutionize the underworld by drawing up a treaty for the mutual support of his cohort and its non-Jewish fellows: the Hudson Dusters of Greenwich Village and the uptown Car Barn and Gas House gangs. The groups shared resources and followed rules of extradition, delivering to one another enemies who in years past may have hidden out in other parts of the city. There were, however, some major exceptions to this axis of powers: most notably, the Five Pointers, led by Jack Sirocco (who, incidentally, often sided against the unions in labor conflicts), refused to join. That breach led to a showdown on St. Marks Place.

In January 1914, the Harry Lenny and Tommy Dyke Association, some brash Italian gangsters outside Fein's syndicate, rented Arlington Hall for a gala. The Lenny–Dyke party infuriated Fein, who considered Arlington Hall his turf. What's more, members of Sirocco's gang, which had refused to join Fein's syndicate, would be attending. Fein ordered the assassination of his enemies as they left the party. A gun battle erupted between the two groups in front of the building, with some of the shooters using cars across the street as a cover.

Amazingly, not one of the gangsters died. In fact, after the shooting, members of the Dopey Benny crew went around the corner to the Stuyvesant Casino (in the building formerly home to the German YMCA) and partied late into the night. But a court clerk named Frederick Straus, a popular neighborhood figure, was caught in the crossfire and killed. While walking to a Cooper Union lecture with his son, Samuel Lipsig of no. 58 had seen Straus's shooter run up to Edward "Fat Bull" Morris, the bouncer at Arlington Hall, crying, "Fat Bull, hide me!"

When the police questioned Morris, he confessed that the likely killer, the one who'd "taken refuge behind his bulky form," as the *New York Times* put it, was one of Fein's top soldiers, Waxey Gordon ("waxey" for the slickness with which he'd lifted wallets out of pockets as a child). Another gangster put the finger on other members of Fein's group, including Isidore "Jew Murphy" Cohen, Morris "the Mock" Kaplan, and David "Battleship Dave" Sanders.

Though the gangsters were acquitted at trial, Fein was convinced that garment union organizers had conspired to give him up. In 1915, he went to the police and cut a deal, ratting out former friends who were part of a butchers union extortion plot. At the age of twenty-six, having alienated his client base, Dopey Benny Fein claimed retirement from the underworld, moved to Brooklyn, and became a successful garment manufacturer and father of three. He would reappear in the papers again, though, some thirty years later. At the age of fifty-five, he was convicted of being a fence for gunmen who stole $2.5 million in merchandise from garment center warehouses and given a ten- to twenty-year sentence.

Organized crime declined throughout World War I. The gangsters yielded Arlington Hall to a group of Polish immigrants, who renovated it into a complex of Polish businesses and a popular Polish restaurant. They renamed it The Dom, which means "home" in Polish.

But just as the Lower East Side underworld was fading, a new national law revived it: Prohibition. When the Eighteenth Amendment passed in 1920, banning the sale of alcohol, gangsters quickly emerged as key brokers in booze. Speakeasies opened along St. Marks Place, and with them flowered an elaborate system of payoffs, blackmail, and extortion.

The Italian Mafia ran a particularly terrifying racket known as the Black Hand. It worked like this: A letter appeared in your mailbox signed with "The Black Hand." If a certain amount of money was not paid in a certain amount of time— say, three hundred dollars in two weeks—then you could be stabbed or your home bombed. In 1926, Black Hand panic reached its hysterical peak when Mafia members distributed hand-shaped, black candy lollipops at Lower East Side schoolyards as a warning to the children's parents.

Other ethnicities got into the act, too. After a March 1927

blackmail bombing in Brooklyn, police acting on a tip searched an apartment at no. 63. They found a stockpile of dynamite. The man staying in the apartment was forty-year-old Polish worker George Falley, also known as "Fay" or "Sluklitztsy." He was working as a blaster's helper in the subway being excavated at Eighth Avenue and Fifty-Third Street. He said he took the dynamite home from work to build a bomb for a fishing expedition. A newspaper headline about Falley's alibi said it best: "Not Convincing." He went to jail.

At the height of the Prohibition era, the German-Ukrainian Walter Scheib and Bavarian bootlegger and gangster Frank Hoffman ran one of the largest speakeasies in the neighborhood: Scheib's Place at no. 80. To gain admission to Scheib's, customers went into a nearby butcher shop and asked for a shot. They would then be admitted into an alleyway, at which point they would knock on the door. A little window would open. If they knew the password, they were allowed into the club, which had a dance floor and an Art Deco–style, horseshoe-shaped bar.

Hoffman had a secret escape route ready in case the place was raided. He had built tunnels radiating out from the basement into various side streets. He planned to grab bags of money from his basement safes and run down one of his tunnels, then head for the East River. In this way, he could be on a boat heading away from Manhattan before anyone realized what had happened.

But not before destroying the evidence. "Here you can see a single strand of copper wire that links all these together to a zip cord that goes to the magnetic switch for the bomb detonator," says the current owner of the building, Lorcan Otway, pointing to a still-intact wall of the basement rigged by Hoffman. "If you close the second circuit, the building explodes."

The Italian Otway family, Howard and Florence (who had

studied art at Cooper Union in the thirties) moved to the block between First and Second Avenues in 1964 with their young son Lorcan. Soon after moving in, Howard Otway found two safes in the basement and called Scheib, saying, according to his son, "I found two safes. I'm too curious to leave them closed, but too cautious to open them without you."

Scheib came down, and a locksmith spent hours working the lock. The first safe was empty. "It was a real Geraldo Rivera moment," Lorcan recalls.

Then they moved on to the second safe. Inside, they found enormous stacks of bills amounting to nearly two million dollars. To his son's horror, Otway let Scheib keep the money. Lorcan believes the cash was only one of gambler Frank Hoffman's secret troves and that the two million was barely a fraction of Hoffman's hoard. On November 7, 1945, Lorcan thinks Hoffman returned to St. Marks Place after his time as a soldier in World War II and snuck out ten million dollars he'd hidden in the building, then skipped town with his young girlfriend, a Miss Ortega, and another friend.

Hoffman was never heard from again. "My speculation was that the third man that was with them murdered them," says Otway. "There must have come a point in the evening when he realized, *How often do you find yourself alone in a car with $10 million, a twenty-something-year-old Brazilian and a Bavarian-American just back from the war who's easily missed?* Friendship is only so strong."

6

A RUNAWAY GIRL AND
A RUNAWAY CHURCH

Prohibition-era gangsters drove respectable families from the neighborhood, and people fleeing respectability moved in. The savagery of World War I had provoked a "revolution in taste." Experimental novelists, expressionist poets, and abstract painters were drawn to St. Marks Place, where they could feel freer than in comparatively respectable Greenwich Village. An aspiring young painter named Ray Euffa moved to St. Marks Place from her conservative Russian immigrant parents' home on Honeywell Avenue in the Bronx. Her father, a cantor, and her mother, a housewife, didn't understand Ray's fascination with writers like T. S. Eliot and Wallace Stevens.

The Euffas had come over from Kiev in 1915, two years before Trotsky's arrival. Ray's father had originally planned on an opera career in Europe, but his wife was afraid he would have affairs if he went on the road and so persuaded him to become a cantor in America.

Not only had their daughter, Ray, decided to become a painter, but she was also determined to shack up with a Norwegian artist named Mike, who rumor had it was an alcoholic as well as a Gentile. Ray's mother wanted to disown her, but her father prevailed. "I will not lose a daughter, no matter who she lives with," he said.

And so every Friday, Ray was allowed to return to her parents' home for dinner—and to take a bath. Typical of apartments on St. Marks Place at the time, her love nest had no hot running water. The St. Mark's Baths, founded in 1906 at no. 6, offered an option for those lacking parents in the Bronx.

Ray and Mike were close to Ray's brother Henry, a violinist two years older than she was, and Henry's wife. The two couples lived together in the St. Marks Place apartment with their pet cats. They were left-leaning and decried bourgeois society, yet the apartment held a billiards table—an entertainment of the rich—and their rhetoric sometimes outstripped their tolerance. Henry arrived home early from rehearsal one afternoon to find his wife in bed with Mike. He left the apartment and

Ray Euffa ca. 1935, teaching art at the Works Progress Administration (WPA)'s Educational Alliance. Reprinted with permission of the Archives of the YIVO Institute for Jewish Research, New York, and the Educational Alliance.

went straight to the hospital, where his and Ray's sister had just given birth to a baby boy. Henry sobbed at her bedside.

People like Ray who moved to St. Marks Place in the 1920s, and for decades after, were generally from good families. Rejecting their (often immigrant) parents' sense of the good life, they left the middle class for a kind of distinguished poverty. They embraced bohemianism and radicalism, if not as fully as Emma Goldman and Leon Trotsky. They believed that their own personal and sexual satisfaction were important and that tradition wasn't. A common refrain among their disappointed parents was: *We spent our whole lives clawing our way out of the Lower East Side, and now you're choosing to move back.* But it didn't feel like going backward to those young people. It felt brand-new.

Two blocks up from Euffa and Mike's cold-water flat, Father William Norman Guthrie was tormenting the Episcopal Church authorities with his own commitment to rebellion. Guthrie had taken over as rector of St. Mark's Church in 1911, when there were only "some eighteen old ladies who came in Sunday mornings, out of sentiment," and he had wasted no time in shocking them all. He called the Book of Common Prayer a "beautiful museum piece." He wrote original services based on Hindu, Baha'i, and Buddhist traditions, and on the lives of George Washington and Joan of Arc. He eccentrically redecorated the church and churchyard, adding sculptures like *The Little Lady of the Dew*, the installation of which was hailed in the press with the headline "Nude Statue in Church."

Father Guthrie injected qualities of artistic experimentation and ecstatic ambition into St. Marks Place's radicalism. He invited artists and poets to participate in the church's services, saying that these liturgical experiments "will never permit the clergy to become stale, or the congregation to be too sure it knows what is going to happen." He connected the organ to colored electric lights. "Almighty God!" he would intone, pushing a note that flooded the congregation in blue, "to whom all mysteries . . ."—red lights.

He even had the audacity to tinker with the poetic and efficient statement of faith known as the Nicene Creed. After the line with which for centuries Christians have expressed their belief that Jesus was "begotten, not made," Guthrie tacked on, "Be thou unto us this World of the senses—grown, ever, alas, more crass and sordid—made now utterly new—for jaded sight and hearing, taste and smell and touch—by the unearned miracle: even as of a vouchsafed return to bodily vigor and health when our souls had emptied already with the flood of Jordan into the salt Dead Sea, and mounted thence to heaven in the quivering heat of a fiery noon!"

"We inherited a Colonial edifice," Guthrie wrote of St. Mark's Church in the 1927 book *Offices of Mystical Religion*, "chocolate-painted because of the whilom [archaic for 'erstwhile'] brownstone mania, squatting like a dusty, melting caramel, glutted inside with golden oak and brass; outside, a deserted yard, piebald with sour patches of wire-grass, and melancholy with sickly condemned trees." Believing in the idea of art as a medium for worship, Father Guthrie established housing for poets and painters in what he called St. Mark's Garth Apartments.

All of this was much to the chagrin of the new bishop of New York State, former Trinity rector William Manning. They made a comical pair: the bishop, an old school friend of Guthrie's, was short and muscular; Guthrie was long and lean. Manning sent Guthrie letters urging him to remember that he was running a church and not an artists' colony. Guthrie responded by painting the hallowed old church pink.

In 1924, Guthrie went too far. With the rector's blessing, several women performed a dance in the chapel inspired by the 1465 Della Robbia plaque "The Annunciation," a white-

Father Guthrie welcomed dance performances in the chapel, as here in 1923. Collection of St. Mark's Church.

and-blue ceramic relief copy of which hung behind them. It was written up in the press as a "bare-leg, bare-hip affair" (the women were actually just barefoot, but don't appear to be wearing corsets). The dance caused Bishop Manning's "restrained frowning to transform into thundering wrath and public denunciations." For ten years, Manning refused even to visit St. Mark's Church.

Father Guthrie's rebellious congregation constantly hosted events. The groundbreaking modern choreographer Martha Graham danced at the church in 1930. Guthrie invited Edna St. Vincent Millay for a visit. There was a popular reading of "The Prophet" by inspirational poet Kahlil Gibran, who was on the St. Mark's Arts Committee. A Happiness Clinic failed, but the Body and Soul Clinic, run by the neurologist Edward Spencer Cowles, drew hundreds of people several times a week for medical care and mental-health services.

Father Guthrie invited antihero Harry Kemp, a proto-Beatnik known as the "Tramp Poet," to entertain the congregation. According to a Works Progress Administration–supported oral history, Kemp hosted poetry readings for the women in the parish, who were apparently enchanted by this handsome free spirit. In exchange for entertaining these ladies, Guthrie allowed Kemp to move his Poetry Theatre from the West Village to the basement of St. Mark's Church.

Kemp decided he wanted to use Native American tribal rituals in his show, so he took out an ad in *The World* that read, "Real Indians Wanted!" Actors in paint and feathers showed up ready to go but didn't know any authentic rituals, while members of the Five Nations who came from upstate refused to share their sacred customs with bohemians in a dimly lit church basement. In the end, Bronx college students played the Native American parts.

Theatrical heavyweights like Heywood Brown, Alexander Woollcott, David Belasco, and William Brady were among those who sat in the rented chairs. The show was a hit even though the father of one of the stars, nineteen-year-old Clifford Odets, wasn't impressed. Lou Odets said, "The play stank and so did Clifford," but helped his son out by "telling the crowd I'd bust their heads in if they didn't clap."

Kemp, distracted by an affair he was having in his Minetta Lane garret with a married society woman, allowed the Poetry Theatre to fall apart. Guthrie, who had an entrepreneurial streak, wasn't deterred. He was savvy with real estate and helped make St. Mark's Church into a powerful Lower East Side landholder. Together he and his friend Frank Lloyd Wright—with whom he had been in intimate correspondence for many years, at one point advising the architect to leave his mistress and return to his family—planned a trio of residential eighteen-story glass skyscrapers called the St. Mark's Towers.

Sketched out between 1927 and 1931, these buildings were designed to encircle the church. They would have been New York City's first glass towers and the neighborhood's tallest structures by more than ten stories. They were exactly the sort of big, shiny architectural project that would incite howls from later generations. In the mid-1980s, just a block or so away, New York University faced major protests when it built an eighteen-story dorm building on Third Avenue and Ninth Street.

Then the Depression gutted the collection plate and Guthrie's church went broke. He had to crawl to Bishop Manning for a bailout. Manning exacted promises of good behavior from Guthrie in exchange for necessary funds. The ambitious Frank Lloyd Wright towers plan was scrapped.[*] A 1932 *New York City Sun* article proclaimed, "St. Mark's Back within the Fold." For Peter Stuyvesant's 267th birthday, his descendant Augustus Stuyvesant and others gathered to watch a skit about the church's history. Actor Walter Huston, playing Stuyvesant in peg leg and swashbuckling attire, chided those present for letting the church sink, yet again, into disrepair.

[*] More than twenty years later, Wright's St. Mark's Towers were finally built—in Bartlesville, Oklahoma.

7

THE COSMIC THRILL

Just before the stock market crashed in 1929, a Southerner named Don Terry came to town. He was a reporter for Charleston, South Carolina's *News and Courier* sent to report on a street so radical that its "Hail Marx Place" nickname had spread across the country. Much like St. Marks Place tourists today, Terry visited the street specifically in search of wildness.

"The street is three blocks long, but it packs a diversity of life and color," Terry wrote in his long, almost reverent story, "Three Blocks of Unusual." "A place of paradox, its sides are lined with shabby tenements, banquet halls with canopied entrances, political clubs, homes of subdued dignity and the usual sprinkling of modern refreshment parlors."

During Terry's visit, he saw partiers flocking to St. Marks Place clubs, which threw almost daily dances from the teens through the thirties. An invitation to one such dance at no. 53, tendered by Keyspear Social Club on a Saturday in February 1936, advertised "Gus La Rocco and His W H N Orchestra . . . Ladies 25 Cents."

But Terry was more taken with the characters on the street than the meeting halls, bars, theaters, and dance clubs. He chatted with a sixty-nine-year-old woman selling coal, ice, and wood at no. 24. She told him she'd been lugging bags as big as she was up from the basement for twenty years.

Her neighbor on the ground floor of no. 26, "Hobo King" Dan O'Brien, was famous for two things: running for mayor and paying the lowest rent in New York: three dollars a month. Downstairs in the coal bin, the featherbed of a man named Livingston Pratt, "physicist, cobbler, professional walker and secretary of the local chapter of the Hoboes Union," was surrounded by math textbooks.

Across the street from the Hobo King, Terry found a makeshift church at no. 27: the House of the Thrill. W. Lathrop Meaker, with his flowing red hair and fringe-like beard, along with his assistant Abraham Mischon, held services at an altar on which a candle was always burning and over which a pendulum swung in constant motion.

The "Cosmic Thrill" they chanted went like this: "Awake! Awake! Put on thy strength and loose thy bands; / Arise and shine! Thy banners all unfurled; / Go forth! Go forth! United sons of many lands, / Proclaim the year of jubilee to all the world." After chanting, Meaker shouted, "The Thrill, Abe, I got it! I got the Thrill!" And he held out his arm to show off his goose bumps in the candlelight.

During the time of Terry's visit, doctors' offices proliferated on the street—if not the most elite practitioners. At no. 66, a man calling himself Professor Hoffman offered hair removal for one dollar. A newspaper ad read, "All hair on face and arms permanently removed." Isrial Menchell caused a sensation when he opened a garishly outfitted candy and soda shop at no. 13. The doctors frowned on Menchell's entrepreneurialism. The problem was Menchell's flamboyant signage, which included "a large rose with red and green petals lighted by electricity. . . . Inside the shop blazed and flickered till it looked like the house of a thousand candles with every candle lit."

Menchell's neighbor Dr. Sussman moved out in a huff, and a Dr. Korowitz moved in, solving the neon-sign problem by erecting a twelve-foot-high brick wall in front of the building, obscuring Menchell's gaudy storefront and thwarting the thirsty. The only trace of Menchell's signs now was a pitiful little note outside the wall that read, "Sodas For One Cent." Though Menchell moved, the doctors' victory was short-lived. Establishments peddling worse vices than candy came to dominate the block.

One character who would have delighted Terry was a tall, mustachioed redhead named Harry Kamen, who had graduated from Columbia Dental School in 1921. He rented space on the second floor of no. 4 and set up a two-chair office. In a small back room he installed a beat-up upright piano, which he played in between treating patients, who reached his office via an outdoor flight of wooden stairs. He also had a day bed for naps, and for when he caroused too late to return to his parents' home on Audubon Avenue. Kamen called himself "Handsome Harry" and bet on horses. Sometimes to avoid his creditors he would ask a patient to answer the phone and say the dentist wasn't in.

With the eye of an anthropologist, Terry noted that between First Avenue and Avenue A, Polish and German families filled the tenements, and some remnants of German dominance still lingered, including a beer garden, Aristocrat Hall (no. 69), and a German Methodist Church (no. 48). He also noted that around the corner on Second Avenue, Tammany and Polish Republicans kept nicer apartments.

Grocers hawked their wares on First Avenue. One man sold pretzels out of a baby carriage. "Pennies have power in this mart," Terry wrote. "The odors are strong, the noises are loud. . . . Six-year-old children and eighty-year-old women compete for trade in the selling of matches and paper market bags."

The *WPA Guide to New York City*, published in 1939, said of the neighborhood: "Crowded, noisy, squalid in many of its aspects, no other section of the city is more typical of New York. The district is best known as a slum, as a community of immigrants and a ghetto; yet not all of the district is blighted, not all of its people are of foreign stock, and not all are Jewish."

Russian, Romanian, Polish, and Hungarian restaurants sold stuffed pig and *bigos mysliwski* (cabbage and game). The Jewish intelligentsia met at the Café Royal, where out-of-work actors waited for a road manager to call with a last-minute spot to fill. Stars like Fanny Brice and Jacob Adler (whose daughter Stella would go on to earn fame as an acting teacher and the namesake of an NYU theater program) starred in shows along Second Avenue's Jewish Rialto.

The Charleston reporter, accustomed to more greenery, bemoaned the meager foliage on St. Marks Place—completely absent save for a lone, frail tree propped precariously against a brick building. Terry approved of the greener land up by Guthrie's festively painted church. Peacocks strutted past the Stuyvesant vault and through the churchyard, which thanks to Guthrie's renovations now featured a fountain shaped like a champagne glass.

Terry watched as neighborhood children poked sticks through the hedge and asked their mothers the name of the magical blue birds with shining green plumage. Hurrying the children along, their mothers replied, in the exasperated tone many people still take with mystical rebels like Guthrie: "It's a *boid*."

8

MR. ZERO SAVES THE WORLD

Political revolutionaries of Trotsky and Goldman's model held their ground on St. Marks Place as the national economy took a dive. But in the 1920s one agitator named Mr. Zero emerged as one of the most charismatic, and unfairly lost-to-time, characters in Lower East Side history. He is arguably the first example of an East Village type that endures today: a man selling a colorful myth about his role in the world that's more fun than the reality.

In Union Square Park, half a mile northwest of St. Marks, radicals ranted from atop soapboxes in front of the surrounding bargain stores and burlesque houses. Activists often addressed crowds of workers who had come for concerts and socializing. But if Union Square was the arena of political dialogue, St. Marks was where agitators transformed ideas into action. Workers International led May Day parades from Union Square, but they ran a food pantry down on St. Marks Place at no. 60.

One man mastered the arts of both soapbox lecture and food pantry praxis. The strong, gray-eyed Urbain J. Ledoux served hot meals and grandiose rhetoric with equal enthusiasm. Born on August 13, 1874, to a poor French-Canadian family of cotton mill workers, the ambitious Ledoux grew up speaking French and took jobs at various mills during school breaks. Ledoux, who read his Bible so often it fell apart in his hands, enjoyed serving breakfast to the mill workers. He went through seminary twice, but then entered public service and became a young consul in the American Diplomatic Service. By his twenties, he was a rising bureaucrat with three children.* A series of glamorous appointments followed: Three Rivers, Québec; Bordeaux, France; Prague (then in Bohemia), and Brazil.

During World War I, Ledoux worked for the Government War Camp Community Service taking care of returning soldiers. He found it appalling that these men who had survived mechanized warfare should return to find no jobs waiting for them. Even worse, in some cases they fell victim to homelessness and hunger. Once-proud soldiers now slept at the St. Mark's Baths or in the park, shivering in the winter and rummaging in trash cans for their meals.

Ledoux began to preach at St. Mark's Church-in-the-Bowery and elsewhere about the universal brotherhood of man. He gave up his prestigious position. For money, he worked odd jobs and did fundraising. And in 1921 he gave himself a new name: Mr. Zero. He had been sleeping with a group of unemployed veterans at the south entrance to Central Park. The former diplomat sent a man out with a little money to buy the group food, but the man returned with only denatured alcohol. Even that, Ledoux reports, was not readily sharable, as it was "well wrapped up in [the man's own] frolicsome body." Mr. Zero struck a deal with a cheap restaurant by Penn Station called Blake's Hell of a Place, and took the men there for a hearty meal. So began Mr. Zero's regular feeding of the homeless.

When one of them asked what his name was, Ledoux closed his eyes as if in prayer and said, "I am . . . I am . . . I am *nothing* to you but bread and water. You were athirst [sic] and I gave you to drink; you were hungry and I gave you to eat. *That's all!*"

* Urbain Ledoux's daughter Yvette would grow up to marry surrealist painter George Malkine; they were photographed by Man Ray.

"I've got your number," a tall Irish bum named Mike said in his brogue, "nothing . . . nothing. Why, you're Zero. That's nothing."

Soon after, Ledoux was distributing donuts in Bryant Park when a reporter asked if anyone knew the benefactor's name. "Yes, I do!" called out Irish Mike. "He's nothing. He's Mr. Zero."

From then on, the press referred to Ledoux as "Mr. Zero." He rather liked the sound of it, although he did not mind either when the *New Republic* referred to him in a 1921 feature story as "Urbain Ledoux—Prophet" and as "the shepherd of the shorn lambs of labor." "When I give them food to eat, they say I am a Christ," Ledoux told *Reality* magazine in 1922, "But I am only a Bahai—a child of the light."

Ledoux cobbled together and self-published a revealing autobiography he titled *Mr. Zero?*. In it, he explains that Mr. Zero is "his other self—his fourth dimensional or cosmic conscious self." (Mr. Zero borrows some of this language from the esot eric—and at one point, Theosophical—writer P. D. Ouspensky.) Like the gospel writer St. Mark, who explored the mystery of Jesus's divinity, Mr. Zero knows that he will "be misunderstood by many and be understood by few." In New York, he often declined to provide what he called his "third-dimensional" name.

Ledoux is featured in a 1930s documentary short, *The Street of Forgotten Men*. A narrator describes characters on the street as "sidewalk scavengers." "This sodden soul wonders what the income tax blank is for," the narrator says. Bums in the film wait for sandwiches on the St. Marks Place breadline of Mr. Zero, who "deserves his name, for he is the last hope of the street of forgotten men." The year the movie appeared, Ledoux was living in a little back-room apartment at no. 26 St. Marks Place.

Ledoux stood out from the street's traditional army of charity workers. He was a maverick, and shamelessly theatri-

Urbain Ledoux "auctioning off" an unemployed veteran. From Ledoux's self-published book *Mr. Zero?* (1931). Library of Congress.

cal. He brought World War I veterans to Trinity Church and elsewhere to ask for help on their behalf. The men, he told the congregation, had seen the brutality of war; now that they were home, they needed work and compassion. In Boston, he staged an "auction" of those he referred to as "shorn lambs." The point he made was that strong, hard-working men were so desperate for employment that they would offer themselves up to the highest bidder. "Here is an ex-soldier," Ledoux said from onstage, pointing to a shirtless veteran who flexed for the audience. "He was with the Sixth Marines in France. He was wounded. He is a carpenter. Who will bid?"

On September 19, 1921, at Cooper Union, Ledoux filled a truck with coffee and donuts and led a delegation up to the New York Public Library, where he planned to give a speech and then auction off men in Bryant Park. He brought a body-guard with him: Kenneth Chase, a former chemical-warfare serviceman who was out of work. The *Times* reported: "If any one tries to hustle Ledoux about, or if the police try to interfere, Chase will sing 'The World Is Dying for a Little Bit of Love' as an antidote."

That strategy failed. On the city's orders, the library cancelled Ledoux's speaking engagement, and in front of thousands of onlookers, the police chased his homeless men from the park before they could be given donuts. A strange odyssey followed as the army of homeless men marched for hours through the city to Central Park, followed by a crowd of the curious. "Hurrah for the army of the unemployed!" they called out cheerfully at around midnight. Also: "When do we eat?"

The police called in hundreds of reserves. One zealous officer clubbed a marcher. Eventually the demonstrators dispersed, and the remaining fifty or so ended up sleeping on benches in Madison Square Park. "Liberty is dying in America," Ledoux concluded.

A few days later, Ledoux went to Washington, D.C., announcing that he would camp out in front of the White House for as long as it took until he was allowed to speak with President Warren G. Harding. The next day, the president granted him an audience. He denied Ledoux's request to publish a list of those who had profited most from the war, but he did listen respectfully to Ledoux on the homeless issue and invited him to participate in hearings.

Ledoux set up shelters and breadlines around the city, including at St. Mark's Church and at nos. 12, 26, 29, and 33. Upstairs at no. 26 he kept an office called his "social laboratory." In the basement of no. 33 he ran a restaurant called "The Tub"—so named because once when he was climbing over a pile of coal in the cellar a baby's bathtub fell on his head, and he considered it a nice name for a place for "a group half naked of clothes and completely naked of money." He hung the little tub up over the door. There the homeless could purchase a large meal for five cents, or receive it for free if they were

Tickets Mr. Zero distributed, ca. 1928, to homeless men, who could redeem them for a meal on St. Marks Place. Courtesy of Bryan Kuntz, NYCDreamin Archives.

disabled. A tablet over the fireplace read, "To Bring a Greater Measure of Love and Beauty Into the Life of the Long Denied."

At the Tub, the long denied could also avail themselves of a tailor and a barber, as well as free clothes. By the winter of 1928, Mr. Zero was operating a five-floor shelter at no. 12, where he said he fed two thousand and housed half that many. He called his charges members of the "Old Bucks and Lame Ducks Club." When a snowstorm hit, he handed out hundreds of pairs of wool gloves and sent the homeless all over the city to shovel snow.

As word of Ledoux's works spread, used-clothing peddlers began posing as bums to cadge free outfits. Ledoux then began printing up tickets entitling the holder to all he could eat for free. His wife, Mary, would distribute the tickets between 5 and 6 a.m. to men sleeping on benches and floors at the Bowery missions.

A 1929 newsreel shows Mr. Zero presiding dramatically over a Thanksgiving dinner of Mulligan stew and roast turkey wearing a crisp white shirt over his paunch and a short striped tie, his hair combed back. In a booming, aristocratic voice, he gives a talk about how after the meal there will be contests upstairs for best song, dance, and recitation. "We need," he says, "to have a song in our heart!" Some dazed-seeming elderly men wave their turkey bones to the music.

"Are you filled up to the gizzard?" he cheerfully asks an eighty-three-year-old war veteran in one scene. In another, he says in an upbeat voice to a series of grumpy looking tramps, "And you—what do you need?" They all reply, "Work." Finally he prompts them to say an article of clothing. Several reply, "Overcoats." "And you shall all have overcoats!" he says triumphantly, as though he had just cured all the world's ills. The homeless men look confused, but Mr. Zero cheerfully tells them they are warm and full and grateful, and he beams with pride and satisfaction.

In 1931, Mr. Zero decided his time was up on St. Marks Place. The New Deal was taking care of his Old Bucks and Lame Ducks just fine, he reasoned, leaving his charity redundant. His decision to leave may also have had something to do with the fact that his long-suffering landlord, Anna Brindell, was taking him to court for $7,345 of unpaid rent (about a million dollars today). According to court records, he had only thirty-seven dollars in the bank.

And so, Mr. Zero vanished—along with his wife, a vixenish Shakespearean actress, Mary W. Hall—to South America, in order to write and direct movies about universal peace and brotherhood. Six years later, he was dead. The photograph that ran with his *New York Times* obituary was captioned, "Friend of Poor."

The obituary also should have called him the first St. Marks Place hustler. He was an artist as much as an activist, a showman as much as a savior. He did plenty of good, but not nearly as much as he talked about doing it, and he achieved some glory, but not nearly as much as he radiated. He was, in short, the first instance of a St. Marks Place type that can be seen on the street today: the self-made, self-deluding genius, a man who creates an identity from scratch and rides it for all it's worth, a man who by every established standard of success is always losing, and yet somehow convinces himself and the world that he has won.

PART III

"THEY ALL ENDED UP ON THAT BLANKET ON THE CORNER."

1951–1974

Corner of St. Marks Place and Third Avenue, 1963, looking north.

Slide by unknown photographer. Collection of the author.

9

THE NIGHT PEOPLE

In 1955, the city dismantled the massive Third Avenue El. For decades, Greenwich Village had been the city's hippest neighborhood, home to eccentrics and social experimentation. Now artists streamed east along Eighth Street, and onto St. Marks Place. "The walls of Jericho came tumbling down . . . extending New York's Bohemia from river to river," said the *New York Times*. In June 1956, the Greenwich Village Merchants Association took out a full-page ad in a Village paper that read, "Visit the Booming East Village!"—one of the first uses of the term "East Village" in print.

The neighborhood blinked in the brightness. "The old Italian, Jewish, Polish and Ukrainian neighborhoods began experiencing new sights and sounds—art galleries, espresso cafes and the throb of bongo drums," the *Times* said. Two blocks north of St. Marks Place on Tenth Street, painters like Jackson Pollock, Mark Rothko, and Willem de Kooning took up residence. The influx turned the diverse, industrious community into a debauched, anarchic scene. To the extent that they were aware of them at all, the bohemians displayed flashes of contempt for the old residents' staid sensibilities.

A radio star named Jean Shepherd served as the self-appointed voice for this growing underground. In 1956, Shepherd, a World War II veteran from Indiana, began broadcasting for WOR AM 710, a major New York City news, talk, and music station. From midnight to 5:30 a.m., Shepherd provided "a slow, casual, laid-back, free-floating association of ideas, philosophy, and bemused commentary." He was speaking, he said, exclusively to the "Night People," those who had "that wild tossing in the soul that makes them stay up till three o'clock in the morning and brood."

For youths who had grown up on *Howdy Doody*, Shepherd's trippy intellectualism was a revelation. In one classic show, he took ten minutes to describe the act of buying a cup of coffee. With high-low references to writers like Jack Kerouac and Nathanael West and to the uniform slacks of workingmen, he painted colorful portraits of characters in the café, and then told the story of the fights that broke out among them. In the process, he made societal observations like "College kids today are always on the side of drunks."

Too many Americans were followers and phonies, Shepherd said. To prove his point, he asked listeners to go to their local bookstore and ask for a nonexistent book called *I, Libertine* by one Frederick R. Ewing. When asked for the publisher's name, they were to respond, "Excelsior, you fathead!"

Soon, his listeners reported, those silly day people were banning the book or raving about it, though no such book existed. Because of the hubbub, Ballantine Books rushed out a trashy novel with that title, thrown together by Shepherd and science-fiction author Theodore Sturgeon.

One night in mid-August 1956, as a gag, Shepherd started doing commercials for Sweetheart Soap, which was not actually a sponsor of the show. His boss did not appreciate the prank and fired Shepherd mid-broadcast. But before he went off the air, Shepherd told his listeners to meet for a "mill"— a proto–flash mob—at the recently burned-out Wanamaker Building near Astor Place. The once-bustling store, built in 1862 by A. T. Stewart—whose body was stolen from St. Mark's churchyard in 1876—was now an empty shell.

A St. Marks Place resident named Ernie Hurwitz arrived at the Wanamaker Building at the appointed time. "Many, many people went," says Hurwitz. "So many people showed up that the soap company called and asked the radio if they could actually be a sponsor and if they would hire him [Shepherd] back."

Hurwitz had moved to the ground floor of no. 51 in 1951, splitting the monthly eighty-five-dollar rent with two friends from Far Rockaway High School. One went to NYU and one to Cooper Union. Hurwitz worked as an office boy in Queens during the day and took engineering classes at NYU in the evening. On top of their TV, the young men propped a sign: "Television is chewing gum for the eyeballs." They played softball in an empty lot and sometimes drank coffee all night at the Limelight Coffee House. "When you're young," Hurwitz says, "sleep just gets in the way."

The Night People's soundtrack was jazz. The hot Second Avenue nightclub Stuyvesant Casino, where Dopey Benny Fein and other gangsters had spent late nights in the 1910s, had hosted Dixieland bands throughout the 1940s, and now was where the Night People went to see new forms of jazz. Hurwitz and his friends called the neighborhood the East Bank, but their slang term never caught on. They invited a drummer from another nearby jazz club, Cooper Square's the Five Spot, to practice in the basement, and they let friends serving in the Korean War store their belongings next to the drum kit.

When these friends returned from war, they came to St. Marks to pick up their things and often stayed to party. Whenever the Hurwitz house ran low on booze, the roommates would invite over everyone they knew: "Everyone would walk in with wine or beer, and whatever the fourth person brought would go into the oven, which was our private stock." When the cops were called to the scene to tell them to quiet down, Hurwitz would invite the officers to come over after work for a drink. Sometimes they did.

On Friday nights, the Polish National Home, or Dom (nos. 19–23), hosted dances. This community hall, once the site of German reveling and then of gangster warfare, was now home to mazurka music and buffets of stuffed cabbage. "The mothers of the young ladies would stand on the stoop," recalls Hurwitz. "If they saw a young man walking down the street, they would say, 'Come in! We have good food and dancing!' Every time anyone said 'good food,' we were there in a minute. The downside was the chubby young ladies we then had to dance with. So we only did that a couple of times."

A music student named Jerome Schwartz lived a few doors down from Hurwitz on the second floor of no. 73, and he too listened to Jean Shepard's show. He frequented the Sagamore Cafeteria on the corner of Third Avenue, a Night People hangout. "People just sat there all day, twenty-four hours," says Schwartz. "It was like that Hopper painting."

Poet Ron Padgett writes about the Sagamore in his memoir of poet Ted Berrigan: "Nobody bothered anybody, so it was a good place to sit if you wanted to talk for hours, which we usually did. Good, that is, if you could ignore so much human misery around you." Jack Kerouac referred to it as "the respectable bums' cafeteria."

Schwartz shared a floor and bathroom with a dentist. Upstairs lived the building's owner with his son. "[The son] played this scary, dynamic piano music right through the night," says Schwartz. "He was slightly psychotic. He'd play these arpeggios and real serious, gruesome, ghost-story music."

Downstairs lived a pair of Martha Graham dancers. Two doors down lived a couple Schwartz always marveled at: "These two gentlemen with long coats and hats walking arm in arm around the block—such a picturesque couple. It was like they stepped out of the nineteenth century."

The men were poet W. H. Auden and his partner Chester Kallman. By that point Auden had been famous for some twenty years. Born in York, England, in 1907, he studied Old English verse at Christ Church, Oxford. Wise and playful, he wrote in a huge variety of poetic forms and in a singular voice simultaneously funny and profound. His 1930 book *Poems* was hailed as the voice of a new generation.

Notoriously slobby, the great poet had moved into the roach-infested second floor of no. 77, a former abortion clinic, in 1952 and hung a Blake watercolor over the green-marble fireplace. When neighbors dropped by the filthy apartment for drinks, Auden served martinis in jelly jars.

Down the block, Slavic immigrants opted for vodka and beer, and lots of it. "Upstairs and all around it the older and younger guys would get falling-down drunk and come out swinging and taking their shirts off," says Schwartz. "It was an entertainment zone. We'd go watch the fights. They'd have these massive feasts [at no. 57]. They'd all get very, very happy. They'd fall down the stairs. They never had any hot water. These heavy, greasy dishes—twenty, sixty people at a party—they'd have to wash them in cold water."

To the Night People, the older residents registered as no more than colorful, anonymous people to rent from, to walk by, and to replace. When the Night People were sleeping off their hangovers, the day people were sweeping the stoops, taking out the trash, and heading off to their full-time jobs. In the Night People's movie, the day people were extras.

And yet, the day people had many-layered memories of the street. At no. 57, for example, where the Poles had their hilarious parties, a fire had broken out just a few years earlier. On a warm June day in 1935, an orchestra was playing by the front windows as preparations were made for a wedding. About 250 people were milling around waiting for the ceremony to start. Some children were dancing and others were

Northeast corner of St. Marks Place and the Bowery one midnight in 1942.
Photograph by Marjory Collins for the WPA. Library of Congress.

racing up and down the stairs. Someone flicked colored lights on and off. A spark shot out, and the *chuppah*, under which sat the bride-to-be, Miss Pearl Sokolower of Houston Street, went up in flames.

Pandemonium ensued. Mothers ran to find their children. The bridegroom made a mad dash for the bride and carried her to safety. The orchestra threw their instruments out the window in an attempt to save them, and a fleeing bridesmaid was hit by a falling bass drum. Several people jumped out the second-floor window. Those lucky enough to land on the first-floor awning were not seriously injured. A twenty-one-year-old guest from Brooklyn rushed in and out of the building through the flames saving children. He died from injuries sustained during his rescues.

The Night People saw no. 57 as a clown car—a place of light-hearted drunkenness and chaos. The day people looked at the same building and remembered that gruesome day in 1935. When the day people passed by no. 82, they recalled how in 1938, emergency workers carried eighty-seven-year-old resident Toney Scavoni out of his collapsing home and into the Men's Emergency Shelter at no. 63. When they looked at no. 102, they remembered it in 1946, when the police caught three hold-up men with eight robbery victims lined up in the back of a candy shop, a stolen car idling out front.

The Night People knew none of this history. To them, the buildings represented only cheap, raw space for poetry readings and art galleries, plenty of room in which to be young.

Nor did the Night People take particular notice of the children they passed on the street. Now seventy-one, Bert Zackim moved to no. 126 in 1944 and as a boy attended P.S. 122 on First Avenue. He kept the apartment, which originally rented for $37.15 a month, for fifty years. During his childhood the block was full of bars, along with assorted small businesses like a fur shop, candy store, plumber's, and a grocery store at no. 99. Once, Zackim and his father were hired to evict a tenant from no. 13. The tenant's apartment was like nothing Zackim had ever seen. It had a four-poster bed with a red canopy and huge candlesticks. In the kitchen were two huge Afghan dogs, finches—"bird shit all over the place"—and a religious calendar showing Jesus raising Lazarus from the dead. The neighborhood, Zackim says, was "Russian, Ukrainian, Jewish, Italian, some Puerto Ricans or blacks. . . . They all had something in common: poverty."

Arnold Feinblatt, of Romanian and Russian Jewish heritage, now a senior citizen and history teacher who has come out of retirement to teach immigrants, also attended P.S. 122 in the forties. His parents had moved from Brooklyn to Sixth Street after he was born. After the death of his father, Feinblatt landed in a children's home until he moved in with his grandmother on Seventh Street. When his mother was able to care for him again, she rented an apartment at no. 10, in 1944, for twenty-three dollars a month. The family went on public assistance, and she eventually got a job working as a secretary for the health department. Once in a while Feinblatt's mother would drop him off at a synagogue to say a prayer for his dead father. Mary's Grocery, between Second and Third Avenue on the south side of the street, would cash their welfare checks and keep a tab when they went to pick up butter or bread.

"I remember the terrible smells in the summertime," Feinblatt says.

> On Third, there would be alcoholics stumbling along the avenue throwing up. There were no real parks nearby. Tompkins was about it. As a little boy I would go to Cooper Union. There was grass and trees there and a statue of Peter Cooper. I was reluctant to eat, maybe because of the children's home. But for some reason if my grandmother took me to the statue I would eat. There was open space and I could chase the pigeons. One day, while we were there, a policeman came by. He was drunk. He took the crate my grandmother had brought to sit on and threw it into the street and chased us out of the park.

Polish boys on St. Marks Place read about world events, probably in front of no. 104, 1939. Collection of the author.

Walking home from school, Feinblatt says, "I had a choice between getting beaten up by the Italian kids or the Polish kids":

> You'd just run like crazy. Once my brother came home from a fight with a kid named Walter covered in bruises. Because I was the big brother, I went and found Walter and beat him up. I remember I was pounding his head into the sidewalk when he said to me, "You dirty Jew." I

froze. I didn't even know until that moment what religion Walter was. That kind of anti-Semitism came out every once in a while. After Christmas, my grandmother would tell me not to go near the Christmas trees. The other kids would start them on fire, and she was afraid I'd be pushed in.

Another P.S. 122 boy, Joey Dick, was born in 1941 at no. 54 to Manny and Bea Dick. He remembers Gypsy knife fights in the middle of the street, and constant danger. "I was the short fat kid," says Dick. "I took my life in my hands to walk to Sixth Street for Hebrew School." Classmates at Junior High School 60 made zip guns out of antennas they'd break off parked cars. The aerial would be bent around a wooden frame, to which would be added a thumbtack, a rubber band, and a .22 bullet. The zip guns had to be fired from a distance using a trip wire, because otherwise they had a tendency to explode in the shooter's hand. The young militias of J.H.S. 60 would bring their homemade weapons over to Stuyvesant, the elite math and science high school on Fifteenth Street, to hold up its students for their lunch money.

Dick's parents had started their sewing factory at no. 27 but moved a block over around the time he was born. They expanded into fabricating coffee filters and other products, like the "lemon wedge bag" for tea. The company, called the Royal Urn Bag Company (today, Urnex), lasted at no. 54 into the 1970s. Dick shopped at Chester's grocery store at no. 40, went to Dr. Silverman at no. 57, and played stickball in the empty lot at the corner, where a Chase Bank now stands. "When the police came, you'd hide the bat in the sewer," he says. "Otherwise they'd hit you with it and break it. Same with playing cards on the stoop—if they caught you, they'd smack you with a billy club. And your parents thought that was perfectly okay. It was a different time."

Children ran through the streets without supervision, peeking through the windows at the local bars and pool halls. "We played in the street all the time," says Feinblatt. "One winter, maybe '48, a blizzard buried the cars in snow. We walked the length of the street on top of the cars, because the snow had filled in the space between them."

If they got injured, the kids would visit Estroff Pharmacy on Second Avenue, where the pharmacist, with his big, bushy, white mustache, white hair, and long white coat, would patch up the child and then make a note to charge the parents for the cost of the bandages the next time they shopped there.

Thanks to the underground tunnels dug by gangsters in the twenties, the children of the forties had caves to explore. Feinblatt remembers: "Many buildings were connected underground. You could go from one basement to another." And from one roof to another, too: "The Polish National Home had fire escapes. Once when I was ten or eleven we climbed up the fire escapes and in through the window to the bar. We drank beer. But it was warm, and so not as much fun as we thought it would be."

Movies at the St. Mark's Cinema cost sixteen cents. Feinblatt and his brother went there to watch hours of Westerns, cartoons, and Abbott and Costello movies. His mother called St. Mark's "The Itch," because there were vermin in the seats. Nicer was the Loews Commodore (later the Fillmore East), where patrons watched twenty-five-cent second-run movies like *King Kong*.

Al Jolson even performed there. Feinblatt and his family waited in line for hours. "We sat down in the orchestra," Feinblatt recalls. "Al Jolson came out. I said, in too loud a voice, 'But he's not black!' People around me laughed. I didn't know why they were laughing. To me, Al Jolson was a black man. I didn't know about blackface."

The Feinblatts ate waffles at the Second Avenue Griddle

diner on the corner of St. Marks and Second Avenue, and on summer days they killed hours at the Sagamore over a single piece of watermelon because the eatery had air conditioning, advertised in giant letters on a banner out front.

A few doors down, the Aesthetic Press printing shop at no. 10 would sometimes throw out boxes of irregular paper. "We'd grab piles of this stuff," says Feinblatt.

> You could make airplanes or draw on it. But I decided we should sell it. So we'd take stacks and approach people on St. Marks: "Do you want to buy some paper?" we'd ask, holding out these ragged stacks of ill-shaped paper. They would look at us, these little urchins, and they would give us a nickel or a penny. We thought we were entrepreneurs, but of course we were really begging. When we'd made enough, we would buy a Spaldeen ball on Second Avenue, and we would play until we lost it down the sewer. Kids can make a playground anywhere.

Between the Day and Night people, there were endless resentments and fights over who deserved to be there. "The city has never been so uncomfortable, so crowded, so tense," wrote E. B. White in 1949. Schwartz says control of the neighborhood started shifting more rapidly in the fifties, as the old working-class Slavs lost ground to the poets and artists. Counterculture groups of the East Village and the pretenders who arrived daily to join the party jockeyed for space. "They all ended up on that blanket on the corner of St. Marks Place," Schwartz says. "We called them all 'Beatniks.'"

10

THE BEATS SHALL INHERIT THE EARTH

World War II army veteran Norman Mailer had become a celebrity with the 1948 publication of his war novel *The Naked and the Dead*. Born to Russian Jewish immigrant parents in New Jersey in 1923, Mailer had grown up in Brooklyn, on Cortelyou Road near Flatbush Avenue, and graduated from Harvard. When the Japanese attacked Pearl Harbor, Mailer's first thought, he confessed, was whether it was more likely a great war novel could be written about Europe or the Pacific.

Now living on First Avenue, four blocks south of St. Marks, and a champion of the Beatniks, Mailer was writing his Hollywood novel, *The Deer Park*. Next door lived Dan Wolf, an aspiring novelist who had grown up on the Upper West Side. They sometimes met on the roof for drinks. On October 26, 1955, Wolf and Mailer, along with Mailer's friend, psychologist Edwin Fancher, founded the *Village Voice* (Mailer came up with the name), a hipper version of the *Villager*, which had been around since 1933. The *Voice* examined the passions of the Village's Beats, including civil rights, poetry, drugs, and sexual freedom.

The word "Beat" was a carnival term, referring to carnies' poor income, and a drug term, meaning one who had been cheated in a deal. Itinerant writer, poet, and drug addict Herbert Huncke, thinking the word evoked the state of having been beaten by the world, introduced it to some writer friends, including Jack Kerouac and Allen Ginsberg. (Huncke him-

Author Norman Mailer (right) speaks with journalist and *Village Voice* cofounder and editor Daniel Wolf in Wolf's office, April 17, 1969. Photo by Fred W. McDarrah/Getty Images.

self was the ultimate Beat, always hustling: "He'd beg off of you," says author Arthur Nersesian. "You'd treat him to some pierogi at [Avenue A diner] Leshko's.") To those outside the movement, "Beat" became the pejorative "Beatnik" after a *San Francisco Chronicle* columnist compared the far-out poets to the Russian *Sputnik* satellite.

World War II had created a desire for a new way of being. For some of the war's survivors, that meant a safe and domestic suburb where they could forget all about what they'd seen. For others, it meant living more intensely. The term "Beat" caught on when Kerouac was quoted using it in the 1952 *New York Times*

Magazine article "This Is the Beat Generation," and again once Kerouac's novel *On the Road* came out in 1957.

The *Village Voice* was ostensibly designed to attract the Beats. But after four months, the paper still hadn't distinguished itself and was losing money at the rate of a thousand dollars a week.

Mailer put in a new infusion of ten thousand dollars, and in January 1956 began writing an abrasive weekly column called "Quickly: A Column for Slow Readers." (The name eventually changed to "The Hip and the Square.") The partners fought. "They wanted it to be successful," Mailer said of Wolf and Fancher; "I wanted it to be outrageous." Among his suggestions: the paper needed more interviews with murderers.

Mailer considered his first column a declaration of war: "I will become an habitual assassin-and-lover columnist who will have something superficial or vicious or inaccurate to say about many of the things under the sun," he promised. The *Village Voice* evolved into a speed-addled, anything-goes cacophony of editorials, profiles, and often very funny essays. Its contributor list included Jean Shepherd, who encouraged readers to stop listening to "third-rate poets shout above fourth-rate jazz groups" and turn on the radio instead.

Mailer quit four months later because he was furious a word in one of his articles had been mistakenly changed—from "nuance" to "nuisance." "Why don't you get your finger out of your ass?" he screamed at the editor. Staff members whom he had constantly berated for not being hip enough were happy to see him go. But the *Voice* he helped create served as the progenitor for weekly alternative newspapers around the country.

As much as anything else, the *Village Voice*'s classified ads made the paper the Village's go-to source of information and adventure. The heroine of *Looking for Mr. Goodbar*, a popular novel about sexual predation largely set on St. Marks Place, notes that nearly every page of the *Voice* offered some life-changing opportunity: "You could learn an instrument, meet people, stop smoking, go back to school, join a group, buy a farm, learn to belly dance, move your furniture cheaply . . . scan 5,000 photos to find your new mate, get an abortion, furnish your entire living room in Brazilian leather for six hundred dollars . . . learn Tai Chi or King Fu, palmistry or urban conversational Spanish, or get in early on the grooviest pad in Kismet."

Village apartment hunters grabbed the listings the second they hit the stands at Astor Place and headed straight for the pay phones. Word on the street was that a certain drop-off spot somewhere downtown carried the *Voice* the night before everywhere else. No such magical kiosk existed, but New Yorkers' persistent desire for the perfect apartment kept the urban legend alive for years.

Not everyone was as adventurous as Kerouac or as wild as Mailer, but the East Village's new generation tapped into the energy of St. Marks Place. They redefined the neighborhood as a literary scene, creating an idea about the East Village—as misfit refuge, as proudly un-American, as the most modern place on earth—that would last for decades. The fifties' East Village thought of itself as the opposite of suburbs like Levittown, which were then becoming popular throughout the country. Most of those who came to the street never made names for themselves as writers or artists, but they contributed as readers and audience members, friends and fans. Together, the scene's heroes and their admirers could sit all day in cafés and all night in each other's decrepit railroad apartments. They could smoke cigarettes and write poetry and have adventures—some of them illicit.

Poet Allen Ginsberg, who lived on Seventh Street east of Tompkins Square Park, was out for a car ride with friends one day when he realized the police were tailing them. He might have chalked it up to pot-induced paranoia had the car not been stolen. After a chase through Queens, they were pulled over and charged with grand larceny. Ginsberg cut a deal, and in 1949 went to a mental hospital to avoid jail.

Soon after Ginsberg arrived at the Columbia facility in upper Manhattan, he saw another man being carried down the hall on a stretcher. Emerging from an insulin-shock coma, that man, Carl Solomon, turned to Ginsberg and asked him who he was.

"Prince Myshkin," said Ginsberg, referring to the saintly fool in Fyodor Dostoyevsky's *The Idiot*.

"I'm Kirilov," said Solomon, referring to the nihilist in Dostoyevsky's *The Possessed*.

And the two decided they were meant to be friends.

Carl Solomon was born in the Bronx on March 30, 1928. His father sold smoked fish. A young Marxist and adventurer, he joined lefty groups while at City College and became a Merchant Marine after World War II. He jumped ship in Paris, where he discovered the work of Henry Miller and attended a reading by Antonin Artaud. Artaud claimed that psychiatry stole the clear—if inconvenient—ability of mental patients to see the world as it really was.

When Solomon returned to New York, he struggled with life outside the hospital. He stole a sandwich from the cafeteria at Brooklyn College, confessed to a security guard, requested a lobotomy, and was duly sent to the hospital where he met Ginsberg.

The pair spent their few months of incarceration talking about literature and comparing notes on their analysts. When they were released, Ginsberg introduced Solomon to the Beat inner circle (as an editor, Solomon would publish William S. Burroughs's *Junky*), and Solomon introduced Ginsberg to the East Village.

mishaps, perhaps

carl solomon

Cover of Carl Solomon's book *Mishaps, Perhaps*. Copyright © 1966 by City Lights Books. Reprinted by permission of City Lights Books.

Solomon married a woman named Olive Blake in 1950, and they lived together at what was formerly painter Henry Sexton's apartment at no. 7. Nicknamed the "lunatic saint" by his friends, Solomon played pranks, such as throwing potato salad at a lecturing novelist and impersonating poet W. H. Auden at parties.

"Preposterous that they should talk to me of being demented," Solomon later wrote. "I, who am in the first place the most saintly and idealistic of anybody in this raving world at the present time. . . . And who are you, you ugly skunks with your phony respectability. You punks in police uniforms, with your paranoid asses."

When Solomon was recommitted—this time from 1956 to 1964 at Pilgrim Psychiatric Center on Long Island, the very place where Ginsberg's mother had received a lobotomy in 1947—Ginsberg wrote *Howl* (originally titled *Howl for Carl Solomon*), one of the most famous poems of the past century.

Fifties bohemians like Solomon dismissed money, power, and the mainstream dream of a quiet life in a white-picket-fenced suburb. Electrified by art and music, they drank and slept and collaborated together late into the night, something that could be difficult in what was in the 1950s still a quiet neighborhood. The artist Franz Kline told a visitor to his studio on Tompkins Square Park, "It's terrible in Tompkins Square. Everybody is in bed by eight o'clock at night. You could be in northern Vermont." The painter Joan Mitchell—famous today as the top-selling female artist of all time—often hosted poet Frank O'Hara and his partner Joe LeSueur at her place (no. 60), and yelled at them if they tried to cut the party short by falling asleep before dawn.

Young poets who'd discovered the Beats, usually via *On the Road*, came to the East Village to be near them, or just to walk the same streets they had. "The reason I left home at seventeen was because of Kerouac," says actor and poet Phil Giambri, who now lives on St. Marks between First and Second Avenues. "Growing up in a very restricted, racially charged environment, everyone hated everyone. I subscribed to the *Village Voice* when it came out. I listened to Jean Shepherd every night. New York to me was freedom."

Giambri was a Beat, not that anyone could agree on exactly what that meant. Op-eds were written; panels were convened. On November 6, 1958, Brandeis University sponsored a debate called "Is There a Beat Generation?" at the Hunter College Playhouse. Though he would express ambivalence about having coined the phrase, Kerouac helpfully broke down what he saw as the two types of Beat hipsters: the *cool*, whom he said were "bearded, sitting without moving in cafes, with their unfriendly girls dressed in black, who say nothing"; and the *hot*, whom he described as, "crazy, talkative, mad shining eyes, running from bar to bar only to be ignored by the cool subterraneans."

Not surprisingly, Kerouac sided with the hot. "When I walk into a club playing jazz," he said, "I still want to shout, 'Blow,

Man, Blow.'" *New York Post* editor James Wechsler turned to Kerouac at this point on the panel and responded, "Life is complicated enough without having to make it into a poem."

Some American bohemians of the 1950s considered themselves heirs to the original bohemians, Roma whom the medieval French believed came from the Central European lands of Bohemia in what is now the Czech Republic. These Bohemians' clothes and mores set them apart and provided the model for an unconventional life.

In the first half of the nineteenth century, when industrializing France didn't provide enough work, well-educated, artistic young people arrived in cities and turned their anger and poverty into a Roma- (back then called Gypsy-) inflected style. "They came to starve and to rebel against their fate and society," writes Albert Parry. These early French bohemians developed "into witty circles of half-starved misfits or theoretical rebels, of improvident drinkers in the name of arts and conquered hearts."

Soon, even people who hadn't been shut out of the Industrial Revolution began acting out these glamorous visions of bohemianism. Typically, they spent a few years living the chic life of the educated poor, and then returned to the working world. The Gypsy-like non-Gypsies included, in the words of Parry, "penniless and carefree writers, poets, journalists, artists, actors, sculptors, and other members of that wide group which later the French and the Russians so aptly labeled 'intellectual proletariat.'" In other words, some of the very first bohemians were poseurs, too, acting out a French caricature of Gypsy culture. "Authentic" bohemianism was a dubious claim from the start.

In the winter of 1962–1963, writer John Wilcock hosted a *Village Voice*–sponsored "Greenwich Village Scholarship," a so-called "Emptybright," the Beat version of a Fulbright, which brought a twenty-year-old Swarthmore coed named Amy

Jack Kerouac Avenue A across from Tompkins park 1953 New York, his handsome face looking into barroom door — this is best profile of his intelligence as I saw it sacred, time of Subterraneans writing. Allen Ginsberg

Jack Kerouac on Avenue A, across from Tompkins Square Park, 1953. (Kerouac was staying at an apartment on East Eleventh Street and Avenue A that summer.) Photo by Allen Ginsberg. Reprinted courtesy of the Allen Ginsberg Estate.

Stone to the Village for a weekend of nonstop partying. At the end of her stay, Stone concluded that the bohemian life was alive and well: "It's all true. People really do run around smoking weird things, leading surrealistic sex lives, and never venturing north of Fourteenth Street except for a David Amram concert."

Beat women often shopped at a warehouse called the Ridge Trading Company on Great Jones Street, where one could find a used fur coat for ten dollars. "So we all went around wearing the craziest things," says former Kerouac girlfriend Joyce Johnson, "like monkey fur or rabbit or beaver." (She opted for raccoon.) The Trading Company coats weren't especially sturdy. "One night at the Cedar Tavern [the famous Abstract Expressionist and Beat hangout a few blocks west and north of

St. Marks Place], I made an expansive gesture during a conversation and a sleeve went flying off."

Johnson often ate at the tiny vegetarian restaurant B&H Dairy (which still serves pierogi, potato pancakes, and borscht on Second Avenue around the corner from St. Marks Place) with her best friend, Hettie Cohen, a petite Jew from Laurelton, Queens, the daughter of a sign-maker and a homemaker.

Over her family's protests, Cohen went to the Village determined to be a writer. She became the subscription manager of a magazine called the *Record Changer*. In March of 1957, a handsome young black man named LeRoi Jones arrived to apply for the shipping manager job. "You're reading Kafka!" he said to her with delight when he saw the book in her hand. An hour later, they were still talking about books when Cohen's boss walked in to ask how the interview for the shipping job was going.

"The job?" Cohen said, blushing and raising a hand to her open mouth while Jones grinned.

Within a few years, Cohen and Jones would be married with two daughters and living on Cooper Square in an apartment that had become a bohemian headquarters, alive with parties and poets crashing on the couch. They published a magazine together, *Yugen*, a Japanese word for a sense of the universe so profound that words fail.

Cohen took the girls to Tompkins Square Park to play. "Around us all the Ukrainian, Polish, Jewish, and Italian *babushkas* gathered, and their querulous men who'd glare at us from the benches," she wrote in her memoir, *How I Became Hettie Jones*. From the old ladies she bought vegetables, scarves, and socks. "I liked the quick park exchange, that moment where old and new took equal offense and I could measure our cultural strengths, our freedom against their overdressed babies and angry toddlers, all those longing teenage eyes lured by our sexy lives."

LeRoi Jones was born Everett Leroy Jones in Newark, New Jersey, in 1934, the son of a postal supervisor father and social worker mother. He studied art and played piano, drums, and trumpet. At Howard University, he changed his name to LeRoi and complained that at the school "they teach you to be white." He was expelled and joined the Air Force, from which he was dishonorably discharged on the suspicion that he was a Communist. In the Village, he befriended Beat poets like Allen Ginsberg and the New York School's Frank O'Hara. O'Hara once suggested in a letter that he and Jones were like the Bobbsey Twins of Greenwich Village.

In the early sixties, Jones wrote the influential "Apple Cores" column in *Down Beat* magazine. In his columns, he described a magical world in which free jazz pioneers like Sunny Murray, Albert Ayler, and Cecil Taylor hung out until all hours playing music in smoky rooms, and Archie Shepp organized free Sunday afternoon concerts in the St. Mark's churchyard. According to Jones, these musicians proved that music was part of a revolution in political and social thought, and the headquarters of this new revolution were the jazz clubs of the East Village. The West Village had Chumley's, the San Remo, the Cedar Tavern, and the Village Vanguard. But the East Village had the Jazz Gallery (no. 80), Slugs (242 East Third Street), and especially the Five Spot.

The Termini family's Five Spot bar sat near Cooper Union at Five Cooper Square for more than twenty-five years before local bohemians talked brothers Iggy and Joe Termini, World War II veterans, into offering nights of live jazz. It would become one of the most important jazz clubs in history, hosting the likes of Billie Holiday, Thelonious Monk, Ornette Coleman, Charles Mingus, John Coltrane, and Miles Davis. In 1962, the Five Spot and its long bar moved around the

Poet and playwright LeRoi Jones (later known as Amiri Baraka) leans against the door of a bathroom stall the day his play "The Toilet" debuted at the St. Mark's Playhouse, December 13, 1964. Photo by Fred W. McDarrah/Getty Images.

corner to less dingy digs at no. 2 St. Marks Place. The old club was torn down and replaced by middle-income housing.

Journalist Martin Williams spent a long night there in 1964 and reported that the El train's disappearance had cleaned up the neighborhood and driven away the winos. The skid-row Bowery had given way to a pleasure palace for martini drinkers, *The New Yorker* readers, and mink-coat wearers. Off-Broadway theaters were prospering. Pawnshops had given way to bookshops, music stores, and a nice restaurant with seventy-cent burgers. The stigma of the Lower East Side was fading away, and most people no longer used air quotes when they called the area the "East Village."

The new Five Spot on St. Marks Place was classier, too, Williams noted: "The walls are painted a warm red, and the effect of contemporary décor is spoiled only by a couple of square columns in the center of the room that are encased in mirrors and look rather like surplus props from a 1936 Ruby Keeler musical."

"A young man in a heavy, black turtle-neck sweater and olive-drab corduroys crosses the room earnestly," he went on, "searching for the men's room door, snapping his fingers as he goes." Between sets, "beards, bulky sweaters, and Brooks Brothers suits begin shuffling around the room, table-hopping, men's-rooming, and telephoning." Having watched one too many waiters shush patrons trying to order drinks during stirring performances, the Terminis made a point of hiring only non–jazz fans as wait staff.

The music critic Robert Christgau recalls sitting on the garbage cans at the Valencia Hotel next door and listening for free. He had first seen St. Marks Place in 1958, when he was fifteen and on a school theater trip. "It was snowing," he says. "It was very romantic. And I kept thinking it was just so *cool*." He moved to the neighborhood as soon as he could and has never left.

But the police often intruded into this utopia. Mayor La Guardia had instituted new cabaret laws in 1941. Performers with a police record couldn't get a license to work. The police could crack down on musicians for drug use or obscenity and essentially end careers. The laws gave the cops an excuse to monitor the radical clubs and keep the Beatniks in line.

In a 1953 letter to the New York Liquor Control Board, jazz great Charlie Parker pleaded the case for his cabaret card's reinstatement: "My right to pursue my chosen profession has been taken away, and my wife and three children who are innocent of any wrongdoing are suffering. . . . If by any chance you feel I haven't paid my debt to society, by all means let me do so and give me and my family back the right to live."

Jazz musician Thelonious Monk (left) and his patron, British Baroness Pannonica ("Nica") de Koenigswarter, get into her Bentley outside the Five Spot Cafe, 1964. Photo by Ben Martin/The LIFE Images Collection/Getty Images.

He did get his card back, but even then it was hard for him to get work and he died two years later.

Another famous victim of the cabaret laws was Thelonious Monk, who was unable to make a living for several years. His Rothschild-heiress patron, the British "Jazz Baroness" Pannonica de Koenigswarter, helped support him during that time. In 1957, she helped him reinstate his cabaret card, which allowed him to play a famous series of shows at the Five Spot.

Billie Holiday, also known as Lady Day, lost her card for narcotics use in 1947. Even though she played at concert venues like Carnegie Hall after her release from jail, she couldn't legally perform in nightclubs where alcohol was sold. Through the 1950s, she suffered from drug addiction and a series of abusive relationships. In the depths of her misery, she went to the Five Spot to see her pianist, Mal Waldron, perform with the poet Kenneth Koch. Joe Termini asked her to sing, and she said she couldn't because a policeman was in the room. Termini said the policeman wanted her to sing too, and so she did. When she died soon after, as a result of cirrhosis of the liver, Frank O'Hara memorialized her in the poem "The Day Lady Died" about that night at the Five Spot, when she "whispered a song along the keyboard to Mal Waldron and everyone and I stopped breathing."

Policemen from the Ninth Precinct caught the "hip messiah" Lord Richard Buckley's act at the Jazz Gallery one night in October 1960 and cut short the show on the grounds that his cabaret card wasn't in order. The pot-smoking, pith helmet–wearing Beat comedian's most famous routines were "God's Own Drunk" and a Beat version of the life of Jesus called "The Naz," in which he describes Jesus as "a carpenter kitty . . . so sweet and so strong and so with it, that when he laid it down, *wham*, it stayed there."

At a hearing shortly thereafter, Police Commissioner Stephen Kennedy revoked his card. Buckley, devastated, died the following month of a stroke at the age of fifty-four.

If the Beat world was under attack from conservative laws on the right, it was also being torn asunder by radicals on the left. Inspired by a 1960 trip to Cuba, LeRoi Jones became more political. In 1961, he cofounded the New York Poets Theatre. After a few productions on Tenth Street, the group moved in 1964 to no. 4, where they began performances at the New

Bowery Theatre. The space would later be a site for "Happenings," created by Claes Oldenburg, Jim Dine, and Robert Rauschenberg.

At the St. Mark's Playhouse on St. Marks and Second Avenue, Jones debuted his play *The Slave*. Larry Rivers designed the collapsing scenery. On opening night, Jones's wife Hettie was in the audience. She quietly watched the show, which was set in the future amid a race war. While bombs burst outside, a black radical confronts his white ex-wife. She is dead by the final curtain. The last sound you hear is the screaming of the couple's children as they presumably die as well. Some of the dialogue was straight from Hettie and LeRoi's private conversations. The actress playing Grace, the white wife character, had the audacity to send Hettie a note saying, "Thank you for Grace." ("That drove me *nuts*," Hettie says.)

"I had read the script and everything," says Hettie, "but it was different to see it." She stumbled out into the lobby, fully in shock. "I adored my mother-in-law. My own family had disowned me. After the play, I looked at her and started sobbing. I collapsed in the ladies' room in tears on her shoulder. I can laugh about it now, but I wasn't laughing then. The great racial divide pulled everybody apart at the end of the sixties, even from people they loved."

When word came on February 21, 1965, that Malcolm X had just been assassinated, LeRoi and Hettie were at a party at the Eighth Street Bookshop and had just had their picture taken by Fred McDarrah. It would be the last photo of them as a married couple.

LeRoi handed Hettie his champagne flute and walked out with his new, all-black entourage, into a life that did not include her. He divorced her soon after and castigated his former friends in the downtown poetry scene as part of the problem of racial tension in America. "My first wife," he later wrote of Hettie, "was one spearhead of continuous rancor and bullshit, both privately and publicly." He would call her memoir "lies and self-legitimizing martyr stories."

When Frank O'Hara ran into Leonard Bernstein, Lauren Bacall, and Jason Robards at a bar on St. Marks Place, Bernstein launched into a rant about how Jones had betrayed them all by writing poems about the hypocrisy of white East Village bohemians. O'Hara cut him off and said he loved Jones and couldn't bear to talk about it. O'Hara's partner LeSueur has said that he was glad O'Hara never heard that Jones had belittled his friendship with O'Hara and LeSueur by saying, "I was just pissing in their beer."

One night at the Five Spot, Hettie Jones encountered a group of LeRoi's old friends, including the artist Larry Rivers. They quoted lines from his poetry to her and asked, heartbroken, "Why did he write that?" Hettie tried to explain that the poems—like the one about his wanting to kill them all as they slept in their beds—were metaphorical.

"It was hard," Hettie says, "for all those people who were his very good friends and thought of him as such a fine poet and felt that he had turned on them. If you think about it in another way, he hadn't turned on them. He was pulling people into some independence." Hettie had left her own family to find herself, and so she identified with LeRoi's need to strike out on his own, even though the break was painful for her and for their friends.

Also, she said, she was willing to make personal sacrifices for the cause of black power: "I have two black children. No one was 'multiracial' then. I thought anything that was going to make their lives more possible, so they didn't have to go to school just to become somebody's functionary, I had to be for—even if I had to suffer or lose the love of my life. I accepted [his leaving]. People have said to me ever since my memoir was published in 1990, 'Why aren't you angry?' Why would I be angry? I was hurt. That doesn't mean I have to be angry."

The Beat movement in its purest form only lasted a couple of years in New York before it dissolved into self-parody. *Village Voice* photographer Fred McDarrah put ads in the paper for a fake company called "Rent-a-Beatnik." He received calls from some of the Beats up for making quick cash, and so the joke became real. The black poet Ted Joans, who opened an art gallery called Galerie Fantastique in the storefront of no. 108, became one of the Beatniks who could be ordered for uptown parties. Photos of such parties show amused uptown types fawning over pontificating Beats—a Disneyland version of Kerouac's wild-eyed vision.

The Beats of Pamela Moore's trashy and morose 1961 novel *Diana* (alternate title, *Pigeons of St. Mark's Place*) propagated the familiar beret-wearing, paint-splattered stereotype. The book, set in a few apartments on St. Marks in the late fifties, describes bed-hopping and tension among four groups: Polish families, Jewish families, Puerto Ricans, and newcomer Beats.

When the Beats' café window is smashed, a bohemian makes known his dislike of the neighborhood's Slavs: "'Like, these Goddamned insensitive sacrilegious squares did this to us! Just because they don't like our way of life! Well, you mother f—,' he shouted over to the Poles, 'like, we're artists and we can sleep with whoever we want! You aren't gonna stop us!'"

Police harassment of the Beats for their "way of life" extended to a special squad of Beatnik imitators that infiltrated the scene, reading their poetry in coffeehouses, growing beards, and scoring drugs. Narcotics detective George Bermudez was particularly successful as an undercover operative who went by the nickname "Gorgeous George." He loved his time on the scene, where he played bongos in coffeehouses. He also wrote original poetry that was championed by Beat poet

Ringo Angel and even published in an anthology. Having befriended a number of addicts while undercover, he hated to turn on them, but he had to do his job. A citywide crackdown in November 1959 led to ninety-five arrests all over the city, including thirteen of Bermudez's coffeehouse friends, and the seizure of an estimated million dollars' worth of heroin.

After the bust, Bermudez, clearly sad to be leaving the Beat world, described their endearing habits to a reporter. "Why you can't get in practically if you can't recite Oscar Wilde's whole 'Ballad of Reading Gaol,'" he said appreciatively. "It's their sign, sort of." Bermudez had learned the poem by heart. With feeling, he recited it. And as he talked, his hands fluttered through the air, tapping out the rhythm on invisible bongo drums.

11

VASELINE AND CASTANETS

Poets John Ashbery and Kenneth Koch, who would rise to prominence in the 1950s as leading figures in the New York School of poetry, were playing pinball at a Harvard café one evening when their hero, the British poet W. H. Auden, walked through the door. Ashbery had written his senior thesis on Auden and worshipped him like a god. After finishing his coffee, Auden left. Ashbery was incensed that the great man hadn't said hello, says New York School historian David Lehman. "But we don't even know him and we haven't published anything," said Koch. "Well, you'd think that he would know," said Ashbery, sulking.

Auden served as a superhuman figure to the Beats and other young writers of the fifties and sixties for many reasons. Though he didn't give Ashbery anything that day in the coffee shop, Auden was famous for his generosity. He spent summers in Europe and let young writers stay in his apartment at no. 77. In 1958 his subletter was *Esquire* literary editor Gene Lichtenstein.

"One hears about how inhibited society was in the fifties," says Lichtenstein, the nephew of Ray Euffa, who ran away to live on St. Marks Place in the twenties, "but people I knew were having affairs or going to parties where they would put their keys on the floor and pick them up and go home with someone they weren't married to. Anyway, it wasn't all that inhibited. At least in the East Village."

W. H. Auden with the owners of his local hardware store, 1971. Published in the *New York Times*, March 18, 1972. Photo by Karl Bissinger. Reproduced courtesy of Bissinger's son, David Fechheimer.

Lichtenstein and his wife, Cynthia, were divided on the merits of Auden's apartment. "It was very large and very dirty. It was fine for me. I liked it," he recalls. He enjoyed living close to friends like artist Paul Jenkins, who stayed across the street in the painter Joan Mitchell's apartment. But he says Cynthia, a law student at Yale who would come down on

Friday night from New Haven to spend the weekend, hated the place.

He says they had a laugh, though, one day when a box fell from a closet shelf. It was full of photographs of Auden's partner Chester Kallman in compromising positions. "At that time, it was shocking," says Lichtenstein. "Gay life was really closed and quiet." Another house sitter of Auden's recalls opening the bedside table and finding nothing but a jar of Vaseline and two pairs of castanets.

Auden and Kallman were a prominent gay couple in the neighborhood at a time when most gay culture was underground. Most of the Village's gay gathering places were semisecret and Mafia-run. At one such spot in the fifties and sixties, Club 82, four blocks south of St. Marks Place, men sang songs by female stars like Judy Garland and performed elaborate group numbers with high production values. Much of the club's audience was heterosexual, looking for an exciting night out. Stars like Milton Berle, Elizabeth Taylor, and even Judy Garland herself reportedly caught shows there. Legend had it that Errol Flynn once whipped out his penis and used it to play the house piano. (The club later hosted punk acts like the New York Dolls, fronted by David Johansen in a slinky sleeveless dress.)

Gay hook-ups along St. Marks Place in the fifties were generally negotiated via what Edmund White describes as a vocabulary of furtive over-the-shoulder glances and "Got a light?" codes. Auden's partner Kallman was a master at this game. Joe LeSueur recalls a story Kallman once told at a bar about bringing home a well-hung hustler to the St. Marks apartment and Auden calling out, "Ches-ter! Is that you?" To which, Kallman called back, "Yes, Wystan."

"Ches-ter?" Auden said. "Are you alone?"

At which Kallman said, "No, Wystan, go back to sleep."

While telling this story, Kallman mimed oral sex on an

obscenely large phantom penis. When LeSueur got home, he told O'Hara, "If you ever catch me talking the way Chester did tonight, get a gun and shoot me. Don't ask me if I want to be shot, just shoot me."

Once when Lichtenstein was house-sitting, there was a knock at the door. A Merchant Marine asked to speak to Chester.

"They're off the coast of Italy," Lichtenstein said.

"Well, I left some things here," the man said. "Can I come and get them?"

He looked around and chatted. "Can I use the bathroom?" he finally asked. He came out and his pants were around his knees.

"He was hanging out of his drawers," says Lichtenstein. "He was essentially asking if I wanted to go to bed with him. I said, 'I think you better leave.'"

Postcard of Club 82, a drag club on Second Avenue and Fourth Street, ca. 1959. Collection of the author.

That weekend Cynthia visited from Yale and came out of the bathroom saying, "Did you see my perfume? It's missing. Has there been a woman here?" Lichtenstein had to explain that the likely thief was not another woman but rather a disappointed Merchant Marine.

Auden considered himself married to Kallman, and they continued to live together after they had stopped sleeping with each other. It was a monastic arrangement suited to Auden, possibly the most devout Christian ever to reside in the East Village. His acts of charity were legion: When an elderly fellow parishioner suffered from night terrors, he took a blanket and slept in the hallway outside her door to make her feel safe. He paid for war orphans to attend college and stealthily arranged to pay for a friend's operation. When he was asked to marry Thomas Mann's daughter in order to provide her with British citizenship and thereby protection from the Nazis, he cabled back "DELIGHTED." While he suffered from Kallman's escapades, Auden lived by this line in his 1957 poem "The More Loving One," which now adorns a plaque on his former building: "If equal affection cannot be, / Let the more loving one be me."

Auden revered Dorothy Day of the *Catholic Worker*, whose headquarters were a few blocks south at Thirty-Six East First Street. Day had been born into a middle-class Brooklyn home in 1897. Her family moved to Chicago, but when she was of age she moved back to New York on her own, settling on the Lower East Side. She was influenced by the writing of Emma Goldman and lived a life of free love and political agitation.

In 1924 she wrote an autobiographical novel, *The Eleventh Virgin*, which describes, among other things, a young woman's abortion. She later found Catholicism, after which she became devoted to charity work and tried to destroy all remaining copies of her bohemian novel. In 1933, she cofounded the Catholic Worker Movement.[*]

Onetime St. Mark's assistant rector Reverend Tom Pike recalls visiting Day's Lower East Side soup kitchen. A rich Park Avenue socialite who had ladled out soup for a few days approached Day and grandly removed a big, dazzling ring from her finger. She patronizingly presented it, saying, "Dorothy, it's been wonderful being with you these last few days. Please take this ring, *for the work.*"

Day said, "Thank you," and then called out, "Gertrude! Please come out here!" A wizened old woman emerged from the kitchen. "This is for you," Day said, and handed her the ring.

"Oh!" the Park Avenue woman said, turning pale, "Dorothy, that *ring* . . . it's very *expensive.*"

"I know! Isn't it wonderful?" Day said smiling. "It's probably the nicest thing Gertrude owns. She could never have afforded it otherwise."

Auden had met Day at a meeting of the ecumenical group Third Hour. He admired her as a fellow Christian living in the proudly godless heart of bohemia. They two were keeping alive the flame of organized religion, though most of the people around them had fled their religious childhood homes and reinvented themselves in New York as sophisticated agnostics. Auden had contributed a poem to the *Worker* and seen Day lecture, but they were little more than mutually admiring acquaintances.

So when Auden appeared in front of Day's Chrystie Street

* In 2012, conservative New York Archbishop Cardinal Timothy M. Dolan nominated Day for canonization in spite of her abortion and sympathy to the Communist Party. See Sharon Otterman, "In Hero of the Catholic Left, a Conservative Cardinal Sees a Saint, *New York Times*, November 26, 2012.

Dorothy Day fights closing of House of Hospitality at 221–223 Christie Street. Day holds a vacate notice issued by the Department of Buildings. Photo by Ken Korotkin/*New York Daily News* via Getty Images.

building early one cold morning, she didn't recognize him. Day had opened the door and unhappily headed for the subway. She was on her way to answer charges that her House of Hospitality, a homeless shelter, was a firetrap. The charge carried a $250 fine, the equivalent of thousands today.

As she went, planning to throw herself on the mercy of the court, she passed Auden, who stood there in his rumpled tweed suit. Day assumed he was one of the men who arrived in the mornings for handouts. But he handed her a slip of paper and walked away. It wasn't until she was on the subway that she saw that it was a check for $250 and that it was from Auden. He'd seen an article about the fine in the *New York Times* and walked down from St. Marks Place in time to catch her on her way to pay it. When the fine was commuted, she tried to return the check to him, but he told her to keep it. Later she told the press that she was embarrassed she hadn't recognized him, but she added, "Poets do look a bit unpressed, don't they?"

Auden's quiet generosity produced many such stories and his presence helped attract a new generation of writers to the street. That summer of 1958, when Auden's house sitters were the young couple Gene and Cynthia Lichtenstein, Gene was editing, among others, a twenty-five-year-old Philip Roth. By coincidence, Lichtenstein and Roth were both in Europe that summer. Cynthia was staying behind in New York, working at a Wall Street firm. She took as her roommate Roth's then-girlfriend, Maggie Williams. The women fought all summer.

Life overseas was much nicer. "I ran into Philip in Paris," Lichtenstein recalls. "We sat down in a café, and he said, 'Too bad there's not a war on. We could send the girls letters about how hard life is here in Europe.'" When Lichtenstein returned, he found a chilly reception from Cynthia but didn't blame her. While he'd been hanging out with Doris Lessing and Kingsley Amis, "she'd been with a terrible woman in a filthy apartment in a sweltering city."

The relationship between Williams and Roth would prove one of the more famously unhappy marriages in literary history. Three years into it, Williams confessed that in order to pressure Roth into marrying her, she had lied about being pregnant. To falsify her pregnancy test, in February 1959 she had paid a black pregnant woman three dollars to pee in a jar for her. She told the woman the urine was required for "a scientific experiment." The arrangement was made a block away from the Auden apartment, in Tompkins Square Park.

Gene Lichtenstein says that things changed radically on St. Marks Place just in the time he was there. In 1953, in his twenties: "I had a girlfriend, Marie, and we lived together. One day, a female friend came to visit. I went to collect my laundry and the elderly woman there glared at me. She thought I was cheating. She spoke in a frosty way and said, loudly, when I was leaving, 'And say hello to *Marie* for me!' The neighborhood belonged to them [the Eastern Europeans]. We were being let in and tolerated. Then five years later it looked as though the neighborhood belonged to us [the bohemians] and *they* were being tolerated."

One thing that hadn't changed, though: "In 1953, everyone said, 'You should have been here during the thirties! It was so great. It's terrible now.' And when I came back in the sixties, everyone said, 'You should have been in the Village in the fifties!' And I said, 'Hey! I was!'"

12

THE NEW RELIGION

Three blocks away from W. H. Auden's apartment, St. Mark's Church-in-the-Bowery was struggling. Despite the relative calm following Father Guthrie's rebellion in the 1920s, the Episcopal Church had all but given up on the parish. "There's nothing you can do," priest Michael Allen recalls the bishop telling him in 1959. "That place is dying." But Allen had never put much stock in his superiors' opinions.

As a seminary student, Allen was taught that unconfirmed people shouldn't be allowed to receive Communion because it was up to the clergy to "protect the Holy Table." Father Michael rejected that logic. "God doesn't need to be protected," he said, "and when we act in those ways I'm not sure we're all worshiping the same God." Between his defiance of church policy and his aggressive support of civil rights, Allen was labeled a troublemaker. It was a reputation he cultivated.

"[My wife] Priscilla and I went to a very fancy Episcopal gathering, very pompous—people in dinner jackets and all that," says Allen. "Out of the blue, this big guy with a clerical collar came up to me in this huge, booming voice, and he said, 'The trouble with you, Michael Allen, is you love Negroes. You identify with the poor and you have no respect for respectability.' I said, 'Amen, brother. Amen.' I think that's the greatest compliment I've ever received."

Allen had inherited a church suffering financially and culturally. The last of the Stuyvesants, Augustus Van Horne

Augustus Van Horne Stuyvesant, displeased, standing in the St. Mark's churchyard with his sister in front of the statue of their ancestor, 1955. Collection of the author.

Stuyvesant, a difficult man with a shrill voice and few friends, had died in 1953, six years before Allen arrived. By that point, he had fallen out with St. Mark's, and had made few donations to the church aside from strange, self-serving ones. One of the last things he'd done before abandoning the place altogether was to have electric lights installed in the Stuyvesant vault.

(He was, in the carefully chosen words of the polite St. Mark's archivist Roger Jack Walters, "a wacko.")

In his will, the last Stuyvesant denied the church any bequest, instead donating his wealth to St. Luke's Hospital. His will also had two strange requests. The first was that when he was interred in the family vault a truck of concrete be backed up to the door and dumped in after him, sealing the vault for eternity (leaving open the question of whether the lights are still on down there). Reverend Tom Pike, who for three years served as Allen's assistant, says that Stuyvesant did this because he was racist and feared otherwise black people might someday be interred around him.

The second directive in his will was that every last photograph or likeness of the Stuyvesants be destroyed. The New-York Historical Society sued. The judge agreed that if the last Stuyvesant had wanted to destroy all those photos, he could have done it himself when he was alive for the price of a book of matches.

If Augustus Stuyvesant—now dead and sealed in the crypt below—was the church's past, Michael Allen was its future. One of his early orders of business was to be seen drinking at McSorley's Old Ale House. Allen wanted to be the pastor for everyone who lived in the neighborhood, even those who never attended church. The neighborhood bohemians largely skipped services—with the exception of Auden. Every Sunday, the poet slipped into a back pew, wearing slippers on his feet and a rope for a belt, and prayed alongside the old ladies who had been attending services at St. Mark's their whole lives and a few young idealists whom Allen recruited to enliven the aging congregation.

A longtime civil rights activist, Allen had marched with Martin Luther King, Jr. When he arrived in New York City, he was shocked by the tension he found between those who lived in the Alphabet City tenements and law enforcement.

"If it wasn't for the good work of you and all the clergy in this community," he recalls a police captain telling him, speaking of the projects' minorities, "we'd have to go out and conquer them."

Allen saw in such exchanges a parallel between the 1960s United States and the world that Jesus inhabited. "Imperial Rome was pressing down hard on the people," Allen said. "It was confiscating their land, trying to destroy their culture. The Jewish leaders weren't a hell of a lot better. So what was Jesus' secret? Well, I think part of it was that the healings and exorcisms were signs of this coming age, but he didn't want it to become a circus." At a time when young people felt the country was spinning out of control and the people in charge

Michael Allen officiates at the wedding of playwright Sam Shepard and actress O-Lan Johnson (today, O-Lan Jones) at St. Mark's Church-in-the-Bowery, November 9, 1969. Photo by Michael Evans/*New York Times*.

had lost their minds, Allen offered love as the answer. "When Jesus is called the Son of God, it's St. Paul saying, 'You Romans think that Augustus is the Son of God. I'm telling you that Jesus is the Son of God.' Paul is using that language to say, 'No' to the false theology of the state; to say, 'No, the empire that Jesus speaks about is not one of terror. It's not one of war and violence. It's an empire of peace.'"

One of Allen's early decisions as pastor was to merge the 9 a.m. and 11 a.m. services into one 10:30 a.m. service. This amounted to integrating the church, because black parishioners had traditionally attended the earlier service and whites the later.

Allen's goal was to stay true to what he saw as his theological responsibility to honor prophecy wherever he found it, even in avant-garde theater and political revolt. "Prophecy is truth-telling," he said. "It isn't crystal-ball gazing. Certainly at that period in the sixties, a lot of the truth, a lot of prophetic speech was taking place in the artistic world. . . . What I was trying to do was make it possible for these prophetic voices to be heard or seen. . . . That is the role of the church at its best." For him, the future of religion lay in jazz and poetry.

In his book *This Time, This Place*, Allen gleefully recounts referring to a baby as a "whore" at her baptism and brags, "You have no idea what kind of pornography we showed in our parish hall." "The arts were raw, *raw*," says Pike.

When heavy chain sculptures went up in the churchyard, neighbors called to complain that it looked like a taxi wreck. During this period, Allen sold off much of St. Mark's vast land holdings, ten buildings around Tenth Street, for a total price of about three hundred thousand dollars. A shopkeeper named Kristina Olitski bought one of these buildings, a brownstone, for forty thousand dollars, which she says even then was cheap. When Winnie Varghese, the current rector of chronically underfunded St. Mark's Church, discusses the sale of all that now extremely valuable property, she puts her head in her hands.

But Allen never regretted his choice to surrender all that real estate. He believed that the church shouldn't be a landlord. Time after time he declined to exercise authority over the people of the parish, even when his leniency allowed some to take advantage of the church. Allen's secretary, Nell Gibson, once looked out the window and saw a junkie running down the block carrying the church's antique silver cross. The parish replaced it with a rough-hewn crucifix made of floor beams salvaged from a demolished tenement.

Allen tried to court both the poor of Alphabet City and the bohemian artists, but he sometimes misunderstood the lower classes' desires. When he promised to remove what he saw as an ostentatious silver tea service and an exclusionary iron fence around the churchyard, the poorer parishioners protested. "You had one of these growing up; we didn't!" they said of the tea service. Parents pointed out that the only reason they brought their kids to play in the cemetery by the church was that iron fence, which kept out the Village riff-raff.

The church was sometimes overwhelmed by its community's capacity for violence. In the summer of 1963, when Allen was on vacation, Tom Pike hosted a youth dance at the parish hall. A fight broke out. While trying to turn the lights up, Pike accidentally turned them off. "All we could hear was furniture crashing, and screaming," he says. "And the police wouldn't come in. They just drove around and around the church with the siren on. The lights came up on blood. It was like *West Side Story*."

But Allen, Pike, and others at St. Mark's Church were committed to integration at any cost. East Villagers watched on television as fire hoses and police dogs were turned on protesters in Birmingham, Alabama. On November 22, 1963, John F. Kennedy was shot. Pike was in the office at St. Mark's Church when the secretary came and told him. They felt the urge to do something, but they didn't know what. Finally, it occurred to Pike: ring the bells. He and the secretary climbed up into the bell tower. The bells had not rung for many years, perhaps not since the death of Lincoln. Pike grabbed the ropes, which still miraculously worked, and tolled the bells again and again.

In 1965, a civil rights activist named Pauli Murray moved to 245 East Eleventh Street. Her apartment overlooked the courtyard of St. Mark's Church, where she sang in the volunteer choir. Murray went to the pound and adopted a black-and-white mutt watchdog, which she alternately called Doc and "Black-and-White-Together-We-Shall-Overcome." With him at her side, she strolled through the Lower East Side and dropped in for visits with her neighbor and close friend Eleanor Roosevelt.

Born the fourth of six children in Baltimore in 1910, and raised by her aunt and grandparents in Durham, North Carolina, Murray was in her time one of the most brilliant legal scholars in the country. The NAACP had used her 1950 book *States' Laws on Race and Color* to formulate its case in *Brown v. Board of Education*. Thurgood Marshall called it "the bible for civil rights lawyers." Now, in New York, she was preoccupied with the sexism she saw in the civil rights movement. She delivered a speech entitled "The Negro Woman and the Quest for Equality," in which she criticized the lack of women in the leadership of the 1963 March on Washington. In October 1966, she helped found the National Organization of Women, but like other lesbians of color in NOW, she faded into the background as the straight, white activist Betty Friedan became the group's figurehead.

Michael Allen appointed Murray's companion, Renee Barlow, to the traditionally all-male vestry. He also asked a woman to read the epistle during church services. But these small concessions only stoked Murray's frustration that men alone could serve as priests. One Sunday morning in March 1966, during the celebration of Holy Eucharist, Murray watched in increasing fury as she saw the women singing in the choir while men swung the incense, carried the cross, and handled the sacred vessels. She stormed out. "I wandered about the streets full of blasphemous thought," she wrote, "feeling alienated from God." She fired off a letter to Allen that afternoon, and he quickly convened the vestry to take up the issue. Her letter was sent up the chain of command and influenced the central Episcopal Church's decision to allow women not just into the lay ministry, which is what Murray was agitating for, but into the priesthood. In 1977, Murray herself would be made a priest.

In 1964, Ralph Cook started Theatre Genesis at St. Mark's Church. Genesis was an edgy, macho company that staged challenging political work. "Personally I have little hope for the survival of our civilization," Cook said around that time. "But whatever hope we have lies with our artists. For they alone have the ability (if we do not corrupt them) to withstand the onslaught of the mass media and the multitude of false gods. They alone have the ability to show us ourselves."

Reverend Tom Pike once took three nuns to St. Mark's to see Theater Genesis wunderkind Sam Shepard's *The Rock Garden*. In the one-act play, men playing father and son sit on opposite sides of the stage. The father drones on while the son nods off to sleep, rousing himself occasionally to say sexually explicit things like, "When I come it's like a river." Pike worried that his guests would be offended, but as the lights came up, the nuns told him they saw it as an exploration of alienation between generations, and quite liked it.

The head of the vestry, however, told Allen that he had brought sin into the church. Allen had to defend the play publicly. He said, "I believe this whole generation of young people is saying to us in effect, 'Look, you use beautiful words and do ugly things; we'll take ugly words and make beauty out of them.'" Later, Allen presided over the marriage of Sam Shepard to a nineteen-year-old actress named O-Lan Johnson. At the ceremony, Allen said, "In a broken world and a polluted land, nothing could be more beautiful than a marriage." The Holy Modal Rounders passed out purple tabs of acid to the antique lace-clad guests.

Artists filled the church with their music and poetry and film, and Allen applauded even the most debauched and nonreligious among them. "Is God Dead at St. Mark's in-the-Bouwerie?" asked a *New York* magazine article dated February 6, 1966. The author quotes Allen saying, "Hell, yes, the church is in its grave, the church as an instrument of social power, that is. The Way lives on." The article's author seemed convinced that the death of the establishment was a good thing: "Read St. Mark's in-the-Bouwerie as a work of art," he suggests, "and love it in its new octopus form."

In 1968, parishioners ripped out the pews, just as St. Marks Place resident James Fenimore Cooper had advised 168 years earlier. Ever since, services have been held more or less in the round. (Today, fragments of the finely wrought old pews can be found tucked into various corners of the narrow archive room upstairs.)

W. H. Auden, who had complained when the linens on the altar changed, was aghast at the lack of furniture and even more appalled by Allen's insistence on modernizing the liturgy. In November of that year, Auden sent Allen a letter in protest that began: "Dear Father Allen: Have you gone stark raving mad?" Pike recalls Auden's misery while serving on a committee to revise the psalms. Of his fellow parishioners' liturgical edits, a distressed Auden said, "It would have been better to put them back into Latin." Auden's plea for Allen to stop "improving" upon the ancient church service closed with the line, "I implore you by the bowels of Christ to stick to Cranmer [the Book of Common Prayer] and King James."

Allen ignored the aging poet. St. Mark's Church experimented with folk music, mariachi music, and protest songs. One service featured a rock number performed by the proto–Christian rock group Mind Garage. Today, a recording of that service sounds like a lost track from *Hair*, which was about to give a nationwide face to the hippie movement. The church's modernization was part of a broader attempt by evangelicals to bring young people back to the church with rock music. But most of those who came to the area seeking spiritual succor went not to St. Mark's Church but to St. Marks Place. They created their own brands of spirituality and their own churches.

Down on St. Marks Place, Jeremiah Newton, a teenager who attended Quintano's School for Young Professionals in back of Carnegie Hall, three miles north of St. Marks Place in Midtown, came to the East Village to explore a world where every day brought some new and strange occurrence. Once, for instance, Timothy Leary paraded down St. Marks Place followed by hundreds of people, popping into stores and handing out free acid.

Newton sometimes smoked pot in a mysterious space on the third floor of a St. Marks apartment building. "Nobody was ever there," Newton says. "There were psychedelic projections on the wall, but I could never see how to get into the projection room, like a door or any type of opening. It was very curious. Nor could I ever find out who managed it, who was in charge."

This mysterious secret room devoted to art and drugs was called the World Church. Drugs, sex, and art had become the new religion on St. Marks Place. Michael Allen didn't mind this heresy a bit. "God's truth is not limited to the church, that's for sure," said Allen. "If it were—boy, God would be in trouble."

13

THE SLUM GODS AND GODDESSES
OF THE LOWER EAST SIDE

A block south of St. Marks Place, on the corner of Seventh
Street and Avenue A, stood one of the cheapest, best-loved
coffee shops in a city full of cheap and well-loved coffee shops.
Policemen walking the beat enjoyed Leshko's food, as did
hippies who were starting to make the officers' lives difficult.
Families ate there. Homeless people ate there. The counter of
Leshko's was a microcosm of the neighborhood.

Leshko's restaurant on Seventh Street and Avenue A, ca. 1984. Photo by Susan
Fensten, who was a child at no. 7 St. Marks in the mid-sixties.

Leshko's restaurant's omnipresent sentries were Theodore and Stefania, the family's charismatic patriarch and matriarch. Stefania was known around the neighborhood as funny and no-nonsense. According to her granddaughter Adriana Leshko: "She didn't have time for machinations."

The Leshkos lived two blocks away, on St. Marks Place between First and Second Avenue. Like thousands of other Slavic immigrants, they had come in the 1940s and '50s after fleeing Communist regimes. Other Ukrainians had paved their way in the beginning of the twentieth century, setting up a church and other institutions in what was then the northern part of the Lower East Side. The Leshkos bought the regal brownstone no. 66 St. Marks in 1950 and turned it into an unofficial Ukrainian settlement house. Family, friends, and friends of friends arrived from Ukraine to a hot meal and a bed in the Leshko building.

One evening, Stefania arrived home to no. 66 from a day at the restaurant. She was giggling. "What's so funny?" Mrs. Leshko's son, Jaroslaw, asked his chuckling mother.

"Today at the counter," she said, "one hippie turned to the other and said, motioning to the menu, 'After the revolution, *this will all be free.*'"

"Yes!" she said to her son, laughing so hard tears came to her eyes, "I'm going to get up. I'm going to go to the restaurant. We are going to cook for them, wait for them to come so we can feed them—for nothing!" She dissolved again into giggles.

Leshko's served policemen for free, but the family was not inclined to subsidize the hippie movement, too, especially when its philosophy was so antithetical to the Ukrainians'.

The hippies of the 1960s flaunted their Communist leanings. A city kid named Jim Carroll took a break from snatching purses uptown to attend a Communist Party meeting in the winter of 1965 with a Marxist friend named Bunty, "in this sleazy place on Eleventh Street called Webster Hall. . . .

Everyone moans a lot and plays folk songs," Carroll wrote of the East Village far left, "one of the requirements seems to be that you have to be ugly. I was wearing my seediest clothes and I still came off looking like Arnold Palmer."

"You will never meet a pro-Communist Ukrainian from [Stefania's] generation," says Jaroslaw Leshko. He notes that his parents' cohort had suffered starvation and totalitarianism at the hands of the Communists, and that they were understandably appalled that the young people moving into their neighborhood found this barbarous political system so appealing. The young people's presumption that bringing about world peace—and squelching materialism, jealousy, and individualism—would be easy and painless enraged the older Slavic residents, who felt their suffering was being dismissed, or worse: mocked.

"They were very anti-Communist," says then–Regional Director of Students for a Democratic Society Jeff Jones of those Ukrainians who owned the restaurants where he and his friends ate. "There was always tension."

Mike Hodder, who lived at no. 81 from 1967 to 1971, agrees: "The locals didn't care for us newcomers until we began spending in their shops. Then we were tolerated, but still not really welcomed."

The young people didn't much care that the older people didn't understand them. They were swept up in a national tide of youth-driven progressivism. Twenty-one-year-old Joyce Hartwell moved to Alphabet City in 1960 with her Great Dane named "County Kerry." A red diaper baby and proud graduate of Greenwich's Village's famously lefty Little Red Schoolhouse (her parents met at Columbia University's Teachers College), Hartwell pledged her life to social justice. In a storefront on Tenth Street and Avenue B, Hartwell founded a business called Lady Carpenter, where she offered manual-labor classes for women. Riding around on her bike, she would pick antiques out of the trash and take them back to her shop to refurbish.

Soon after arriving in the East Village, she started a relationship with a Puerto Rican man and helped him take care

Joyce Hartwell's Lady Carpenter headshot, ca. 1970. Courtesy of Joyce Hartwell.

Joyce Hartwell (right) teaching Evelyn LaFontaine (left) and Cynthia Singleton how to use a power saw during an All-Craft workshop. Photo by Nancy Kaye. Originally published in the *New York Times*, December 6, 1987. Reprinted with permission of Nancy Kaye.

of his six children. When Hartwell's mother, head of welfare for a machinists' union and a Smith College graduate, visited and saw Hartwell tending to all those babies, she burst into tears. According to Hartwell, her mother cried, "I thought I'd gotten rid of all this poverty in my life!"

The teenage Hartwell was recruited by a leading modeling agency, but she turned them down when they asked her to diet. A man who owned the deli down the block bragged about how back in the old country he'd been chauffeured around. "It took me a little while," she says, "but eventually I realized that he was trying to pick me up by telling me that he had been a Nazi officer."

That tack was unsuccessful, but Hartwell did find love—with Stanley Tolkin, who ran the bohemian-friendly bar Stanley's on Twelfth Street and Avenue B. "Stanley was very welcoming of all types," says Hartwell, "not like a lot of the Polish and Ukrainian immigrants there."

Tolkin was bald, sturdy, and instantly likeable. He was Polish, and his parents had run a speakeasy in the neighborhood back in the thirties. During the Depression, his pregnant mother swam out into the East River to a coal barge to steal coal for their fire. He adored his mother but dreaded ending up like his father, who died of alcoholism in a state institution.

Stanley's served as a hangout for poets and artists. "I used to watch Stanley hooking the new hip population of the East Village," writes literary theorist Ronald Sukenick, "working them with free beers and sympathetic talk at a time when the rest of the locals regarded these strange guys with beards who didn't work, and their bra-less girls who looked like they wore nothing under their skirts either (and often didn't), with at best mild contempt."

A young art student named Andy Warhol, born in 1928 to Slovak immigrants living in Pittsburgh, showed early work at

Stanley's. Warhol had sublet an apartment for the summer of 1949 on the top floor of a roach-filled six-floor walk-up on the north side of St. Marks Place, a couple of doors from the park, with his friend, painter Philip Pearlstein.

Stanley's also hosted young poets who came to New York in the 1960s following the siren call of their heroes, the stars of Grove Press's epic *The New American Poetry 1945–1960*, published in May 1960.

Poets gravitated to the East Village. When Frank O'Hara died in a freak accident on Fire Island in 1966 (he was hit by a dune buggy), Koch eulogized his friend at Columbia by reading O'Hara's "Rhapsody," a poem that describes lying in a hammock on St. Marks Place.

Of this new generation, poet Ted Berrigan—author of 1964's *The Sonnets* and editor of mimeographed poetry magazine *C*, published from 1963 to 1966—was among the coolest. "You could extrapolate everything worthwhile in the universe from thirteen issues" of *C*, wrote punk musician and author Richard Hell, and "you'd have a great time, giggling."

An army veteran, experienced, older, and charismatic, Berrigan dominated the East Village poetry scene and seemed to get away with an awful lot. More than once, he slept with the wives of other men on the scene. One poet recalls charging into Berrigan's apartment in a murderous rage to confront him about one such indiscretion, only to find Berrigan sitting in a rocking chair holding one of his infant sons. Unable to hit a man holding a baby, the poet screamed in frustration and stormed out.

In an article called "In the Berrigan Era," one critic wrote, "To read the poems of Ted Berrigan is to be socked with evidence of how it is to be alive right now and full of Self and feelings. . . . It's scary to think what our literature and literary life would be like without him."

"That was a time when people would re-form their entire

identities overnight," that critic says. "They would go to sleep as one person and wake up as someone else. Everyone wanted to be Ted Berrigan, so they would become him. Ted Berrigan was like a mother duck who would walk through the East Village trailed by his baby ducks."

And yet, to the Eastern Europeans, Berrigan looked like just another obnoxious Beatnik. On a hot summer afternoon in 1960, Berrigan and his friend Ron Padgett stopped into a bar on St. Marks between Second and Third Avenues for a cold beer. "It was a lazy, quiet bar with some neighborhood people," recalls Padgett. "It was not trendy. It was rather dismal. As soon as we walked in, the people uniformly turned to stare at us with an unblinking, inscrutable dourness that stopped us in our tracks. It was partly because we were strangers, but also because Ted had a little beard at that time. We didn't look right. These people were all Ukrainian immigrants. One of us said to the other, 'I think maybe we should find another bar.'"

Soon after, in 1964, Stanley Tolkin bought that same bar from the Polish National Home (nos. 19–23). As a link to the former owners and his own Polish heritage, he kept the former name: "The Dom." There were two entrances to Tolkin's downstairs Dom bar at no. 23: one led to a relatively quiet gathering place for Stanley's regulars, the other into a dance club. At the top of the stairs, another entrance opened into a party space that would become an epicenter of art and rock music.

Most nights until four in the morning, Joyce Hartwell (who was now living with Tolkin on Third Avenue between Thirteenth and Fourteenth Streets) worked the door at the disco end of the downstairs Dom. She had decorated the place in red and orange, and Tolkin had artists he knew from Stanley's repaint the eighty-foot-long bar in vibrant colors, sprucing up the older generation's dive. As the space came into its moment in history, Hartwell greeted celebrities including Leonard Bernstein and Jackie Kennedy. During lulls, she read books about the black experience, like Malcolm X's autobiography, as if studying for a test that the whole neighborhood was about to take.

14

HIPPIE HEAVEN

According to Joshua White, the "Sixties" actually started in 1964, the year of the "Freedom Summer" civil rights movement, Muhammad Ali beating Sonny Liston, the New York World's Fair, and the Beatles' arrival in America. That was the year when White, who came from a prosperous uptown family, dropped out of college and started hanging out on St. Marks Place. "Hippies were not nice people," he says. "It was not a time of beautiful design and freedom and flowers. That was the media take on it. It was a lot of people barefoot and letting their hair grow out and looking for something and needing something. If you had long hair, you were cool. If you had short hair, you were a narc. If you were under thirty, you were cool. If you were over thirty, you were not. If you had a blissed-out smile, people left you alone."

White perfected his smile—"a kind of rictus"—and had a wonderful time. "I was cute! And I was single! And I had a car!" He hung out with Andy Warhol and others at a Christopher Street loft, playing with slide projectors, a mirror ball, a wheel of colored bulbs, and blinking Christmas lights—a revolution in multimedia design that would soon make its public debut on St. Marks Place.

The street had become the Champs-Élysées of the counterculture, teeming at all hours with bright young people. In his 1966 book *The New Bohemia*, John Gruen wrote: "Walking on St. Marks Place on a weekend night, you become aware of a rhythm. It has an imperceptible underground beat and you feel it increasing as the night wears on. . . . It can take you to a bottle-party in a $15-a-month loft (records by Bob Dylan only), to an underground poetry reading, to a wild 'happening,' to a way-out theatrical production. It can lead you to encounters with dope addicts, free-love cultists, Swedenborgians, or white chicks looking for noble savages." According to Gruen, the artists of St. Marks Place were "all of them bent on the demolition of the past."

Writer Paul Krassner, who ran the satirical magazine *The Realist*—a highlight was the often-reproduced cartoon poster "Disneyland Memorial Orgy"—lived on Avenue A between Sixth and Seventh Streets and says St. Marks Place in the mid-sixties was magic. "Walking from Tompkins Square Park to Astor Place, you could smell marijuana coming out of windows. You'd hear a Beatles song on the radio and you could hear it continue as you walked on—the same song, coming out of all the windows." St. Marks Place's landmarks provided a constellation of delights. At the romantically named newsstand Gem Spa on the corner of Second Avenue, you could browse obscure magazines all night. In Tompkins Square Park, you could take your shirt off and lie in the sunshine all day.

In 1966, Father Michael Allen invited the East Village's poets to congregate at St. Mark's Church, a more sustainable space than the nearby Café Metro, which didn't seem thrilled to have them and to that end had instituted a twenty-five-cent per person minimum purchase (coffee was a dime). At the new St. Mark's Church Poetry Project, newcomers could appear at the same podium as Allen Ginsberg. On Fridays, Ted Berrigan led poetry workshops. Paul Blackburn led the Reading Committee. Anne Waldman, the Project's first secretary, and then its director, reviewed submissions for a journal called *The World*.

Funding for the Poetry Project came from an unlikely place: a Department of Health, Education, and Welfare grant Michael Allen secured through a New School sociology professor named Harry Silverstein, who wanted to use the group to gain access to the neighborhood's juvenile delinquents so he could write an academic paper about them.

The poet Bob Rosenthal says that, when he was first married, he answered an ad for an apartment at no. 31: "Even though I came to be in the poetry world, I didn't know that I was so close to the Poetry Project. We took the studio, and when we looked out the window, facing north, there was the weathervane of St. Mark's Church. And I realized, 'Oh, we're *right here.*'"

Berrigan's friends George Schneeman, a painter and sculptor, and his wife Katie lived at no. 29 with their three young sons. (They'd landed the apartment thanks to five hundred dollars borrowed from Ron Padgett, for the common move-in bribe known as "key money.") The Schneemans hosted episodic parties, and in his studio looking out over St. Marks Place, George painted nudes of their poet friends.

Two doors down at no. 33, Anne Waldman and her husband, Lewis Warsh, hid a time capsule under the floorboards in their apartment that contained the staples of life on St. Marks Place in the sixties: a hit of acid, a joint, a Valium, and a poem. Artists Martha Diamond and Donna Dennis lived across the street. Everyone was always dropping in on everyone else, collaborating on magazines and chapbooks and collages.

Poet Sam Kashner would come to New York from his parents' Long Island home and call his hero, Allen Ginsberg, from the pay phone on the corner. The poet would pop his head out the window and throw down the key. Kashner thought of the East Village, where he'd been coming since high school, as "something out of the *Arabian Nights* romances." Walking to a New Year's Eve party at Waldman and Warsh's apartment, he writes, "I had the feeling in this bitter cold that the rest of the world had gone away."

Ted Berrigan and Dick Gallup co-wrote a poem that begins:

It's 2 a.m. at Anne & Lewis's which is where it's at
On St. Mark's Place, hash and Angel Hairs on our minds

Katie Schneeman and her friend Tessie Mitchell wrote a pornographic novel, published by Grove Press in 1973 under the pseudonym Katie Mitchell. "Elio [the Schneemans' middle son] was seven years old, and he said, 'What's it about?'" Schneeman recalls. "And I said, 'The adventures of two girls.' And he said, 'Why don't you call it *Two Suspicious Girls*?' And we did. It's so dirty. We were just wildly sexy. We didn't wear clothes, all that. We did have a good time."

The St. Mark's Church crowd partied, drank, and played "musical beds." One of its members says that parties back then were aggressively liberated: "On St. Marks Place in the sixties, not wanting to do something wasn't a good enough reason not to do it."

Padgett and Berrigan often walked back and forth on Eighth Street from Sixth Avenue to Tompkins Square Park. "You'd often see people walking along talking in this very interesting way," says Padgett. "Ted and I had an idea to walk up and down the street with a hidden tape recorder to record these snatches of conversation. People we passed would say things like, 'How about Kierkegaard's nightshirt?' Ted and I would raise our eyes at each other like, 'Whoa!'"

At night, Padgett and Berrigan would stand out in front of the Five Spot, too broke to go in, just listening to jazz greats like Monk and Mingus filtering out onto the street: "Poets," Padgett says, "standing there like children looking through a knothole to watch a baseball game."

For a while, the Five Spot was the only "hip" place on the street. But one by one, the old shops on St. Marks Place, sleepy Ukrainian- and Polish-run travel agents and printing presses, closed, and bright new shops opened to meet the needs of this new group. In 1963, Kristina Gorby (who would go on to marry the abstract painter Jules Olitski and take his last name) lived at no. 4 and opened an eponymous boutique on the block at no. 7. She specialized in Greek and Indian clothing and accessories and custom-made clothes for musicians, including the stretch-velour outfit Janis Joplin wore at Woodstock.

"I was living in Forest Hills, Queens, at the time," says Nancy Rubin, who worked as a salesperson at Kristina Gorby. "I couldn't stand the cliqueyness in the schools, so I took the train every day into Manhattan. I couldn't breathe in Queens." She fondly recalls wandering in and out of the street's hippie boutiques: Queen of Diamonds (no. 33, run by Mary Kanovitz), Something a Little Bit Different (no. 8, run by Helaine Clark), and the Owl and the Pussycat (no. 34, run by Amelia Varney and Edward Felton). At a store called Gussie and Becky at no. 20, a designer named Ruth Graves offered a short satin dress with a swimsuit top and an ostrich-feather hem for eighty-five dollars (the equivalent of more than six hundred dollars today). At no. 28, the gay rights activist Randy Wicker's Underground Uplift Unlimited sold pot paraphernalia and "Make Love Not War" buttons.

After work, Rubin would go meet up with the guys from the clothing store Limbo, and they would head to Union Square–area nightclub Max's Kansas City, where Andy Warhol and his entourage held court. She says it was the time of her life.

Celebrity hairdresser Paul McGregor opened a salon at no. 15, and for years the shop was a star magnet. The May

26, 1975, issue of *People* magazine opened with a photograph of McGregor wearing a beret, giving dancer Susan Hunt a "Babylonian-style Ziggurat." Two pages later, in a tank top and chain, he is giving actress Margaux Hemingway what the magazine identifies as a "bleached Afro."

Many other salons followed, but the famous flocked to McGregor's. In a time when a hamburger was one dollar and the bus was fifteen cents, only the most fashion-forward would spring for his ten-dollar haircuts. McGregor gave Jane Fonda the revolutionary shag, a look she made famous in the movie *Klute*. His daughter Paula says he tried out the shag on her first, making her the toast of fourth grade. "I believed the story that Paul McGregor invented it," says his friend, musician and DJ Johnny Dynell, "knowing how crazy he was. If everyone was going to the left, he would go to the right."

McGregor's wife and six children lived on Long Island, while he worked five or six days a week on St. Marks. Paula loved the days when she was taken to work with her father. "If we spent Saturday there, you knew it would be exciting. The hair salon had lots of mirrors and colored floor tiles—lots of white, and blue, and green. The sinks were in the back. We'd make a game out of it. 'Jump on the red tile! Now the blue one!' It was a checkerboard for us. Real colorful." Her father she describes as "a hippie, a butt smoker, and fun-loving guy. He taught us to appreciate the block and everything that went with it."

St. Marks between Second and Third Avenues would sometimes close to traffic on weekends, and the neighborhood children would roller skate up and down the middle of the street. Paul McGregor loved skating and for a time converted his hair salon into the world's smallest roller rink.* "It made no sense

---

* McGregor's roller rink lasted until a teenager broke his arm trying to do a trick and sued; McGregor settled for twelve thousand dollars and turned the place into a bar, which he then converted into the gay club BoyBar.

at all," says Dynell, "except that he really liked to roller skate. He was so St. Marks Place, such an East Village character."

One of St. Marks Place's all-time most successful entrepreneurs is a man named Charles Fitzgerald, now eighty years old and still on St. Marks between Second and Third, in a building that bears the engraved insignia of a nineteenth-century German shooting club. "I didn't want to move there," says Fitzgerald, who came to St. Marks Place in 1959. "I got an apartment on Minetta Lane in the Village years back from this girl there, and moved in and spent two weeks renovating it, and then woke up at five o'clock in the morning to a knock on the door. A marshal threw me out on the street, because she hadn't paid the rent for two years. So I was out on the street with a few belongings and someone mentioned this guy who had a little van that could move my stuff. He was a sensitive poet who looked like a longshoreman.

"So I sat there on the street, trying to protect my stuff from being stolen. He picked me up, brought me over to St. Marks, and said, 'I've got a room in the back for five dollars a month.' That was the beginning of the saga of St. Marks Place. I eventually took over his apartment because he woke up one night and there was a rat sitting on his chest, eating crumbs out of his beard. And he said, 'That's it, I'm moving out.'"

Fitzgerald took advantage of the cheap rents on the block and opened a series of businesses, starting with the Pas de Dieu ("There Is No God") Gallery and the handmade wooden goods shop Bowl and Board, which lent an earthy, Vermontian aroma to the block for decades. Poet Ron Padgett describes Fitzgerald's Bowl and Board as the epitome of a new kind of hippie chic: "People were starting to tear off the plaster and show the bricks and hang up ferns. [Fitzgerald] sold kitchen knives with nice wooden handles, and natural hardwood salad bowls."

The economics of the time made it possible to open shops with little overhead. In the early sixties, rent for Fitzgerald's apartment with the store in it was twenty-eight dollars a month. He made sixty-eight dollars a week teaching English as a second language in Midtown and extra money renovating apartments. His VW Beetle, which he drove to Vermont to buy bowls, cost fifty dollars. At the Five Spot jazz club, beer was fifteen cents. Buildings cost about ten thousand dollars. Fitzgerald says he lost property to the bank a couple of times, but the bank decided it was so worthless that they gave it back to him.

At one point, Fitzgerald ran seven stores on St. Marks Place at once. He would open new ones overnight. One of the big moneymakers was a fur shop: "I discovered old fur coats. You could go to the felt-maker Gelbwachs down under the Brooklyn Bridge and there was a guy there. You could buy old fur coats for two dollars apiece and run them up to St. Marks Place and sell 'em as fast as you could for twenty dollars." Fitzgerald let neighborhood children run around the store and roll in the furs.

Uptown wealth helped sustain the Village's bohemian lifestyle. "It was the throwaway era," says Fitzgerald. "I mean, all I had to do was trundle my way up to Park Avenue on Wednesday night and pick up beautiful furniture being thrown out and bring it back down here and sell it."

One of Fitzgerald's tenants was the "dean of black designers," Arthur McGee. St. Marks Place was becoming a street-style runway. People paraded in their beads, bell-bottoms, flowing prints, and Sergeant Pepper jackets. Ethnic clothing and black fashion were particularly popular on St. Marks, which was becoming known as a safe space for interracial couples and a gathering place for black-power activists. "There was always something nice happening there," McGee says of St. Marks. Some days he'd get someone to cover the shop and he'd take off walking. After work each day he closed up and went to the Five Spot.

One of McGee's apprentices was Khadejha McCall, who opened up Khadejha Designs down the block from him at no. 5 selling African prints. "The Velvet Underground came to my store and sat," says McCall. "I wanted to dress them, but they wore jeans and leathers and that kind of thing." McCall went on a macrobiotic diet, which was easy to maintain given all the hippie restaurants in the neighborhood. She loved the vibe of the street. "All people wanted was to be loved," she says. "We got it wherever we could find it. I wish it were like that now."

In spite of all the love and smiles, crime was a serious problem: "People used to come out of [the Dom] at night and break down my storefronts and walk away with the entire contents of the stores," says Charles Fitzgerald. "I had guns and knives and everything under the sun held on me."

Once, a local drunk named Pablo stood in the street waving a gun.

"Pablo!" Fitzgerald yelled. "Put that thing away!"

Pablo drunkenly held the gun to Fitzgerald's chest. The men heard police sirens. "Pablo, just give me the gun," Fitzgerald said. Pablo relented. Fitzgerald ran to no. 11 and threw what he thought was an unloaded weapon down the corridor. It hit a radiator and fired.

Another time, Fitzgerald recalls, "A guy was coming out of the building with a big pile of clothing. I opened the door to let him out, and then suddenly something clicked and I recognized that it was my clothes. He had broken into my apartment and he had my TV in the clothes. He was sneaking out with it."

Fitzgerald's employee, Arthur Ohnewald, would call him when a shoplifter was in the store and say their code word: "Schweinhund." Fitzgerald would run over and deal with it. The cat burglars were harder to catch. "My warehouse at no. 12 was being robbed every night," Fitzgerald recalls. "I finally borrowed a .22 rifle from a friend. I stayed all night long in the sheepskin rugs. All of a sudden I heard the windows coming up. I jumped on this card table and said, 'Don't move or I'll shoot!' The card table collapsed and the lamp on it broke. Now it was pitch black and I was alone with these two criminals. I started shooting—not at them, at the ceiling. I had twenty shots. I'd shoot and say, 'I've got nineteen more shots!' And I kept counting down. When I was almost through, Arthur came in with an old Luger automatic my father had gotten in the First World War, and we held them up until the cops came."

"The drag queens had the longest arms," recalls shopkeeper Marty Freedman. His store, Limbo (first at no. 24, then no. 4), an anchor of the neighborhood, sold army surplus and secondhand jeans. "They would reach back over the counter and grab the most expensive stuff." Freedman and his partner, Freddy Billingsley, sold what they called "carefully selected dead man's clothing." After rag-picking all morning, they often opened at 2 p.m. to long lines out front.

"One winter, everyone on St. Marks Place wore the same exact Afghani wool-lined coat from Limbo," recalls Judy Garrison, who now runs a shop upstate. "I wore mine outside the city once and everyone looked at me like I was insane."

The writer Paul Krassner remembers once buying a derby hat and a long overcoat at Limbo while on acid. He realized once he came down that he'd made a mistake on the coat. Luckily, on St. Marks Place in the sixties that was a fully acceptable excuse. Krassner says the clerk told him, "Oh, of course, if you were tripping, you can return it."

Musician Peter Stampfel, of the band the Holy Modal Rounders, had arrived on the Lower East Side in 1959 and found St. Marks Place to be a haven. "It was possible to live a life that was almost magically excellent—by nineteenth-century standards," he recalls. "You could live very, very comfortably on very, very little money. In 1962, there was a feeling that anything was possible, anything could happen."

Stampfel was part of a new movement of young cultural revolutionaries who came together around drugs and music. "Like a lot of so-called hippies, I've always not liked the label hippie," he says. "That was pejorative. It meant phony wannabe. Countercultural types back then called themselves freaks. We were freaks." Freaks lived boundaryless, liberated lives that scandalized older generations. "The scene was 'the set,'" Stampfel says, translating the slang of the time. "You got kicked off 'the set' for being 'a dickwad.'"

Stampfel's friend, musician John Townley, who often gigged with the Holy Modal Rounders, lived at no. 73. Townley recalls that a woman who lived at no. 75 put her birdcages out on the fire escape, and he could spend hours communicating with them: "My parents would say you couldn't understand *Finnegans Wake* unless you were drunk. So, too, if you're smoking the right thing, it's really easy to speak to animals."

One evening Stampfel and his wife were visiting Townley, who had moved to St. Marks Place in part because his father (who'd partied with Henry Miller and F. Scott Fitzgerald in Paris in the twenties) had lived on the street a generation earlier. Townley told his guests that he'd learned the teenage boys in the group home across the street could see through the windows. They had seen plenty, Townley said, "and enjoyed every peek!"

Armed with this knowledge, Stampfel's wife, Antonia, and his bandmate Steve Weber decided to put on a show. "There was a couch against the window," says Stampfel. "Antonia and Weber arranged themselves on the couch with legs and arms sticking out as if in wild sexual congress. They were just making a tableau. The kids from the home gathered at the window, dozens of them, ogling."

The Holy Modal Rounders were one of the emerging Village bands who sang dirty and quite funny songs about drugs, sex, and crash pad life. The Rounders had a song, "Bad Boy," about a Village heartthrob who sold hearts on St. Marks Place in glassine envelopes. The Fugs, a like-minded band, was started nearby by Ed Sanders and Tuli Kupferberg and named after Norman Mailer's euphemism for "fuck" in *The Naked and the Dead*. The Fugs's first album included songs like "Boobs A Lot" (chorus: "Do you like boobs a lot? / Yes, I like boobs a lot!"). "Her dildo is made out of a petrified paper snout," the Fugs said from the stage when introducing their song "Slum Goddess" to an East Village crowd. "Around her neck, is an amulet made from onyx-colored tit wax."

Among the Fugs's big songs was "Kill for Peace," a video of which shows Kupferberg running around sixties New York City in a pith helmet, wielding a toy gun that he then pretends to jack off by the highway. Poet Ted Berrigan provided the Fugs with this lyric for "Doin' All Right": "I'm not ever gonna go to Vietnam / I prefer to stay right here and screw your mom."

It was a period when The Fugs's Ed Sanders wrote that "the roots of revolution were going to lift the concrete away from the field of truth, after which Bread and Roses and the utopian place I called Goof City would grow up afresh in a warless world—Goof City on the hill, Goof City in the Lower East Side, Goof City shining."

15

THE EXPLODING PLASTIC INEVITABLE

Starting in April of 1966, Andy Warhol occasionally hosted shows upstairs from Stanley Tolkin's Dom bar. The upstairs space was called "The New Mod-Dom." Warhol created a trippy multimedia show with live music, along with elements of dance, theater, and video. He sat in the balcony with a film projector, which sent images to the opposite wall. He called these nights "The Exploding Plastic Inevitable."

"The counterculture, the subculture, pop, superstars, drugs, lights, discotheques—whatever we think of as 'young-and-with-it'—probably started then," Andy Warhol wrote in his book *The Philosophy of Andy Warhol*. "There was always a party somewhere: if there wasn't a party in a cellar, there was one on a roof, if there wasn't a party in a subway, there was one on a bus; if there wasn't one on a boat, there was one in the Statue of Liberty." He loved the Velvet Underground song "All Tomorrow's Parties" and invited Nico to sing it on St. Marks Place.

The film director John Waters, having been expelled from college for smoking pot, found the trippy, speed-freak scene at the Mod-Dom welcoming. "It was amazing," says Waters, who went several times and recalls paying a two-dollar admission fee. "It was the full Velvet Underground. They were shooting up onstage. It may not have been real, but it looked real! Andy was in the back with projectors. He would spin color wheels onto the band when they sang. It was sort of an anti-hippie thing. And outside on St. Marks Place was like the hippie

The entrance to the Dom (from "Polski Dom Narodowy" or "Polish National Home"), no. 23 St. Marks Place. A banner advertises Andy Warhol's Exploding Plastic Inevitable, March 31, 1966. Photo by Fred W. McDarrah/Getty Images.

aorta. The Exploding Plastic Inevitable was mocking that. It was punk before there was any such thing as that."

On St. Marks, social boundaries seemed to fall away. A debutante and a juvenile delinquent could dance together. Anything was possible, and free love and sex were everywhere. The dawn of this new era gave young people hope. "Drugs helped," Warhol noted.

The second time Warhol staged a multimedia night at the club, he called it The Balloon Farm (according to legend, Bob Dylan coined the name; if so, he might have been describing Warhol's 1966 exhibit of silver helium "cloud" balloons at the Leo Castelli Gallery). The lights and the drugs helped distill all that was wild and good about the sixties into a beautiful, intense dream. Warhol only staged a few shows in the course of a few months, but the evenings became iconic, and in many people's memories they went on for years.

Nico, "that white, white creature," in the words of journalist Lucian Truscott IV, was up on stage, and "outside the street was a confusion of limousines . . . tall ladies in the first silver lamé mini-dresses, men with long sideburns and mustaches, and the crazy, crazy, crazy Warholoids freaking out the columnists and art elite with long eyelashes, white cake make-up,

Village Voice ads for Warhol's Velvet Underground shows: one in fall 1966 and the other, with Nico highlighted, in February 1967. Reprinted courtesy of the *Village Voice*.

and casual conversation about drugs, needles, and rushes." Truscott writes, "Everything was just so fabulous, dear, just *fabulous*. The way they talked. My god. You'd think that was all they did—go out at night and talk like that."

The music journalist Richard Goldstein, in his 1966 article "A Quiet Evening at the Balloon Farm," concludes a description of a sexy, grinding dance with "Wow—you don't see that on *Hullabaloo*." In Goldstein's story, Warhol sits in the balcony by the video projector "looking haunted" in his mirror shades and leather jacket. He describes Nico as "half goddess, half icicle. If you say bad things about her singing, she doesn't talk to you. If you say nice things, she doesn't talk to you either. Onstage, she is somewhat less communicative."

Consensus among the cognoscenti was that the Exploding Plastic Inevitable was one of the coolest things to happen anywhere, that Nico was a goddess with vacant eyes and Warhol film star Gerard Malanga, dancing with a long, comic book–style whip, was a god in leather pants. But as a business venture it was a disaster. (While countless former East Villagers remember attending these events, only a few seem to remember paying.) "The Warhol crowd was high most of the time and dysfunctional," says Joyce Hartwell. Famously fond of speed, they were often coming or going from their "poke." Shooting galleries lined St. Marks Place. Within the year, an even trendier new nightclub culture was on its way in.

In 1967, the year of the Summer of Love out west, an ambitious Brooklyn-born promoter and former William Morris agent named Jerry Brandt took over the upstairs space at the Dom and reinvented it as The Electric Circus. Brandt claims he promoted the Electric Circus as an "East Village" club rather than a Lower East Side one, because: "'The Lower East Side' reminded me of immigrants. I didn't find it appealing."

St. Marks was a developer's dream back then. "Every store

A typical night at the Electric Circus. Collection of Joshua White.

was for rent on the street," Brandt recalls. "It was like fifty dollars a month. It was virgin territory and that's what I wanted. My biggest mistake was I didn't rent the whole block. I should have bought everything in sight. But I was only twenty-seven or twenty-eight. What did I know?"

The Electric Circus took the multimedia experience even farther than Warhol had. Revelers encountered fire-eaters, tightrope walkers, and actors in gorilla suits. Every once in a while, a performer might race onto the floor and fight his way out of a straitjacket to applause. The door people wore white karate uniforms. Liquor wasn't served, only drinks like egg creams and milkshakes, but everyone was on something.

The Electric Circus's opening night might well be the most legendary party in East Village history. Among the guests: Gloria Vanderbilt, Yves St. Laurent, Tom Wolfe, Truman

Capote, Diana Vreeland, George Plimpton, Phil Ochs, Muhammad Ali, Mary McCarthy, Jon Voight—even the Prince of Laos. At one point, Brandt recalls Bette Davis stopping him on the stairwell and saying, "You know, son, getting old ain't for sissies."

The venue boasted three hundred thousand dollars' worth of flashing strobe lights and projectors, but there was no air conditioning, so the dance floor was like a furnace. "It got so crazy I had to go out on the fire escape and watch it from the outside in," says Brandt. The sweaty crowd swirled, intoxicated with the energy of the gathering.

"[The Electric Circus] did feel decadent," says novelist Carole Rosenthal, who lived at no. 37½ for many years. Anything could happen there. Rosenthal remembers walking down St. Marks and being waved in off the street for free cake because the famous hippie singer Wavy Gravy was having a birthday party and the guest list included anyone who happened to walk by.

"I was astounded people were drawn to that flashing of the klieg lights," says photographer Larry Fink, who hung out there often. "It was the same light they used at the police station to break down hipsters so they would spill the beans, the same lights at the Electric Circus under which they would spill their sexual beans across the floor."

Many locals failed to see the appeal. Joey Dick, for example, heir to the Royal Urn Bag Company, loathed what the street had become. Dick's grandmother, Beatrice, had grown up with her grandparents at no. 22 and married a boy across the street named Manny. Manny was the son of Regina and Havy, a tailor who moved to no. 27 from a small town in Poland after World War I. The Dicks had been on St. Marks Place longer than just about anyone. Joey remembered the St. Marks Place of his youth, a street where, while grocery shopping with his mother as a little boy, he'd seen the old-world butcher smack

Fillmore East. Crowd for Crosby, Stills and Nash tickets, May 1970. Photo by Amalie R. Rothschild.

huge slabs of liver on the counter, where at the fish store the little blue crabs had pinched his fingers, and where while studying to be a dentist, he had borrowed extracted teeth from Dr. Walter Halpern (no. 44) for practice.

When Joey moved back to his childhood neighborhood with his wife in 1966, after college, he hardly recognized it. Now, when he passed Warhol on the street, he glared at the man whom he believed had killed his St. Marks Place.

Warhol and Brandt had made the neighborhood into a club scene. But an entertainment professional operating on a far grander scale eclipsed them both. In March 1968, promoter Bill Graham opened the Fillmore East rock club on Second Avenue, a couple of blocks down from St. Marks Place. In the three years of its existence, Fillmore East hosted the major bands of the day, including John Lennon, Jefferson Airplane, and Jimi Hendrix (who recorded *Band of Gypsies* live there on New Year's Day, 1970). Tickets, also available at the St. Marks Place clothing store Limbo, cost between three and five dollars.

Bill Graham had suffered. He escaped the Holocaust while other members of his family, including his mother, did not. In a Pleasantville, New York, orphanage, he lined up for prospective adoptive parents in front of his perfectly made bed day after day only to be passed over for other children. Eventually he was taken in by a family in the Bronx, served in the military, and grew up to be a combative, intensely ambitious man with a love of live music and a preternatural gift for event planning. His rock club in San Francisco had been a sensation, and he arrived in New York a confident success. From his time dealing with hippies and cops in California, he'd learned a few tricks for preventing trouble.

On opening night of the Fillmore East, he found a few thugs hanging around the marquee, including a redheaded kid kicking the front door. "Hey!" he said. "I just bought this place. My name's Bill. What's your name?" The kid said it was Rusty. "Rusty. Let's get something straight," Graham said. "That shit don't go down here." Within fifteen minutes, he had hired the kids to help him unload the trucks and provide informal security for the block. Rusty and his gang worked for Graham for three years and came to almost every show.

As a teenager, Richard Blum thought the Fillmore East was the coolest place on earth. He and his friends took the train down from the Bronx to see bands. After the shows, Blum and his friends bought greasy food on St. Marks Place at a hole in the wall called Pizza Pazza before taking the train back home. Blum was required to keep his parents (his mother was a civil servant and his father a shoe salesman) informed about his whereabouts.

"I remember calling my mother up when I was tripping on mescaline," he says.

If I didn't call my mother up when I was coming home, she would call all my friends' mothers up and they would all say, "Richie, tell your mother to stop calling us at two in the morning." Once I was at a Dead show, and after about two hours, [British singer-songwriter] Dave Mason came on, and I got on the phone to my mom. "Dave Mason showed up!" I told her. She didn't know who Dave Mason was. "When are you going to be home?" she asked. "Late," I said. "But I'm with six guys. We'll all take the train together. Please don't worry." She was an unbelievably classic neurotic Jewish mother worrier.

The revolutionary lighting designer Joshua White describes the Broadway-caliber Fillmore as the perfect venue for a moment when great bands were coming out of London and the Bay Area. The Fillmore East gave New Yorkers their first real taste of those exploding scenes. Once White had tried to create a transformative light show to accompany such ultra-sincere music as Peter, Paul, and Mary's "This Land Is Your Land" or The Lovin' Spoonful's "Do You Believe in Magic?" Now he was able to take people for a ride with Janis Joplin and Big Brother and the Holding Company doing "Summertime." He also did lighting for Led Zeppelin ("when they weren't coked out and still very good musicians"), Country Joe and the Fish, and Steve Winwood. In 1975, Zeppelin would use a photograph of nos. 96–98 St. Marks as the cover of their album *Physical Graffiti*. The building is now the home of Physical GraffiTea, a tea shop.

The Fillmore East, White says, fulfilled the promise of the Balloon Farm and the Electric Circus, which now seemed contrived by comparison: "I saw the Fillmore and everything in my life after that was about making light shows and being as close to the best music as possible."

By the late sixties, the Fillmore, Electric Circus, and Dom

had transformed St. Marks Place into the kind of debauched playground it had been during Prohibition. The once-poor neighborhood was getting richer. It had proved itself marketable in a mainstream way—a destination not just for freaks, but also for faux freaks who were willing to pay for the privilege of being around real ones. "There would be no East Village or St. Marks Place without me," the Circus's Jerry Brandt says by phone from Miami. "Someone's got to kick it off. . . . I don't want to say 'without me, blah-blah-blah,' but . . . *blah–blah–blah*."

16

A TREE STOPS TRAFFIC

During the sixties, St. Marks Place came to feel more and more like a separate planet. Here, it was groovy: sex and drugs were readily available. Out there, it was chaos: Politicians were being assassinated and Freedom Riders beaten. On St. Marks Place, open rebellion seemed to be an appropriate reaction to a nation that had lost its mind, especially as the Vietnam War escalated. In February 1965, President Johnson authorized the bombing offensive Operation Rolling Thunder. The hippies of St. Marks Place embraced the spirit of the antiwar protest movements sweeping the country—though they put their own freaky spin on activism.

One night in 1965 the Fugs performed the "Night of Napalm" at the Bridge Theater at no. 4. Flyers promised "songs against the war, rock n roll bomb shrieks, heavy metal orgasms. Watch all the Fugs die in a napalm raid." The band played a tape of patriotic songs and then a regular set, at the end of which they staged "The Fugs Spaghetti Death." That afternoon they had filled a garbage can with spaghetti. Now they flung it all over the theater, slid around in it, and made sure plenty got on the audience—especially Andy Warhol, who was seated in the front row wearing a leather tie.

Around that time, a native New Yorker named Joey Skaggs graduated from the High School of Art Design and became a student at the School of Visual Arts. He moved to 199 Avenue B, which he describes as "like living in a really cheap dorm, a

Cover of *The East Village Other*, April 15, 1966. Joey Skaggs, twenty-one, with his sculpture *The Very Last Day*, on Easter morning, in Tompkins Square Park. Courtesy of Joey Skaggs.

slum dorm, and all of your roommates are artists." Love was free. Drugs were cheap. Skaggs's Southern Baptist, Kentucky-born father had been in the military and his New York Italian mother was a Roman Catholic. He found a new, far less conservative family in the East Village and had his first art show at Stanley's.

Skaggs was mostly a painter, but in 1965 he decided to make a sculpture that expressed how he felt "about the war in Vietnam and mankind and religion and God and the church and hypocrisy." He made a cross and a body to put on it, topped with a real skull with mannequin eyes, haloed in barbed wire, its jaw open in agony. The sculpture didn't fit in his apartment, so he worked on it in the hallway. A homeless Russian man who had been sleeping on the landing upstairs got freaked out by the sculpture and found somewhere else to live.

On Easter Sunday, Skaggs paraded the statue through Tompkins Square Park before an impromptu audience that included art-world types like Yoko Ono, Hispanic families out for a stroll, and a dog eager to pee on the artwork. The police soon arrived and took Skaggs to jail.

Father Michael Allen, who considered the defense of anti-war protesters to be part of his job as head of the parish, went to the Ninth Precinct to argue for Skaggs's release. The Irish policeman, assuming Allen would be on the side of the law, ranted about how awful the sculpture was. He concluded his diatribe with, "And, Father, the Jesus had a *penis*."

Allen looked below the officer's belt and said, "Well, you have one, don't you?"

The policeman went, in Allen's words, "berserk." But Skaggs was released shortly thereafter.

Skaggs also shot films, some of them with his then-girlfriend, musician Debbie Harry. She would later go on to become a queen of CBGBs but was then living at no. 113 St. Marks Place and singing in a folk band called The Wind in the Willows.

In one Skaggs film, his character was a hippie vampire, but instead of sucking blood to survive, he had to suck breasts, so his apartment was full of bare-breasted young women.

Over on Second Avenue, the charismatic artist Larry Rivers, also known as "Libertine Larry," was filming his adolescent daughters naked and making them talk about their emerging sexuality on film. (The avant-garde of the time was oddly dependent on young women taking off their clothes.) This spirit of playful, often sexual, and sometimes disturbing experimentalism found its fulfillment in a new political group: the Yippies.

From 1967 to 1968, young people were constantly streaming in and out of the basement apartment Abbie and Anita Hoffman rented at no. 30. On a street known as an activist thoroughfare—you couldn't throw a rock on St. Marks without hitting a radical—Abbie and his collaborator Jerry Rubin raised the stakes with a more aggressive and stunt-driven hippie protest movement. Their group threw real and fake money down to the floor of the Stock Exchange in 1967. The next year, they were arrested for antiwar protests at the Democratic National Convention.

Paul Krassner says he coined the term "Yippie" (for Youth International Party) on December 31, 1967, at Abbie and Anita's house, with Jerry Rubin and another six to twelve friends in attendance. "One thing about the Yippies was that we would do pranks or stunts or various things in order to get media attention," Krassner says. "So it was a mutual manipulation. We gave good quotes. [The media] gave free publicity for a demonstration."

"The first time I was on St. Marks," recalls Yippie Judy Albert, also known as Judy Gumbo (a name given to her by Black Panther Eldridge Cleaver),

> I had just arrived from Canada after getting divorced from my first husband. I saw soul food restaurants with these amazing smells. The traffic was noisy. There were

Activist Jerry Rubin holds a toy M16 assault rifle above his head on the corner of St. Marks Place and Second Avenue, September 28, 1968. Photo by Fred W. McDarrah/Getty Images.

head shops with posters of Jimi and Janis. Beautiful filigreed earrings. Guys sitting out selling paperback books, making a living any way they wanted. I was there with Stew [Albert, of the New Left Movement]. He was taking me to Gem Spa. This voice came out, "Stew, c'mon over here!" It was Abbie [Hoffman]. I went to Abbie and Anita's apartment. Abbie had a color TV. We sat down to watch Walter Cronkite.

Many former freaks have stories like this of being waved into the Hoffmans' apartment to watch one of the neighborhood's only color television sets.

One of the stunt events held at Abbie and Anita's apartment

was a press conference for a fake drug called Lace. Hoffman said Lace was a combination of the hallucinogen LSD and the skin-permeable pain reliever DMSO. He claimed that it was absorbed through the skin and functioned as a powerful, fast-acting aphrodisiac.

The Hoffmans invited the press to their home, where they had laid mattresses on the floor of the living room. The plan was to spray Lace on people who would then pretend to become uncontrollably aroused. They would immediately start having sex on the mattresses while the journalists took notes. Soon, the Hoffmans announced, there was going to be a protest at the Pentagon. The building would be levitated by mind control, and the Yippies would use water guns to spray gallons of Lace on the Washington, D.C., police and the National Guard. "Even people who may not have been anti the war in Vietnam, would come just to see the slogan 'Make Love Not War' come true," said Krassner.

Krassner was supposed to attend the Lace press conference posing as a reporter. His job was to be accidentally sprayed and to immediately start making love to a redheaded teenage hippie girl who was in on the prank: "I would put down my pad and pen and disrobe. I was kind of excited about it. It was a blind date where you knew you would get laid. But when I checked my calendar, I found I had to go to the University of Iowa literary conference, so I had to back out. I told Abbie and he said, 'There are a lot of farms in Iowa. Would you get some cornmeal so we can encircle the Pentagon with it? We could use it as a pre-levitation rite.' The guy who took my place [in the Lace prank] got accidentally sprayed, did what I would have done, and ended up living with the redheaded girl. Even though I'd never met her, I felt jealous."

Hoffman and his Yippie entourage once showed up to a coffee hour at St. Mark's Church. "He started cursing the church, in general, organized church, organized religion, fiscal church, and on, doing it up," recalls church administrator Stephen Facey, who was standing next to Father Michael Allen at the time, "Michael looked at him and said, 'You fancy yourself an organizer, right? Do you know how easy it is to take over this little church? All you have to do is come to church, bring your friends, run for the vestry.'" Hoffman left and never came back. He had a more theatrical revolution in mind.

On the night of August 12, 1967, at around 10 p.m., five hundred hippies led by Hoffman and Rubin gathered in the middle of St. Marks near Third Avenue to "plant" a five-foot-tall evergreen. They danced around it while a band called the Group Image played music and a singer named Sheila the Slum Goddess sang. The Diggers, a hippie sect famed for giving things away at their "free stores," handed out yogurt.

Ninth Precinct Officer Joe Fink, known as the "hippie cop," looked on. Smiling, he told a *New York Times* reporter, "They're just 'doing their thing.'" At midnight, the tree planters marched off toward Tompkins Square Park with their tree, and the street was clear again.

The son of a Lower East Side Polish immigrant tailor, Fink was a middleman in charge of "preventative enforcement." He invited hippies to come in and "rap" with him about their concerns and gave them concert tickets. He picked his battles.

That summer was a low point for community relations. On August 25, 1967, hippies shut down St. Marks between Second and Third Avenues for a "psychedelic block party." Merchants sponsored the party to call attention to a proposal they'd submitted to Mayor John Lindsay for that stretch of St. Marks to be car-free every night from 7 p.m. to midnight, creating a "night mall." The Electric Circus provided the electricity and music. A projector cast colored lights onto the St. Mark's Baths at no. 6, as down below, Baths manager Jerry Polk muttered, "I'm too old for this stuff," as he handed out towels. "This is the destruction of the twentieth century," added a woman at no. 10. "The merchants aren't speaking for the average person on this block."

In Fink's 1974 book, *The Community and the Police—Conflict or Cooperation?*, he describes a scuffle that took place in Tompkins Square Park on Memorial Day in 1967 with assimilated immigrants from Ireland, Italy, Eastern Europe, and Puerto Rico on one side and the "young, uninhibited" hippies who "desired no assimilation" on the other. The hippies romped naked through the park, singing and dancing. The older residents called the police. The cops tried to enforce community standards—the traditional ones. Scores of people were arrested, and several were injured. Fink said, "No attempt was made to include the hippies in the definition of community and the result was, inevitably, increased community tension."

The Yippies sometimes played pool with Officer Fink, but that didn't make them immune from arrest. Right after dropping powerful acid, Hoffman and Krassner heard that some black and Puerto Rican kids whom the Yippies considered allies had been busted. The Yippies went to the Ninth Precinct to see what they could do. Hoffman was protesting loudly. Fink asked Krassner to take Hoffman away so he wouldn't have to arrest him. "Abbie saw us talking and knew it was about him. He kicked back into a trophy case and broke the glass," Krassner said. "*Now* you're under arrest," Fink said wearily.

"It was one of Abbie's favorite arrests," says Krassner, "because it was a spontaneous impulse. He hadn't planned it. There was something bizarre about it. They didn't want to arrest him. One of the officers who arrested him said, 'The captain really liked that trophy case.'"

17

UP AGAINST THE WALL, MOTHERFUCKERS

In October 1967, a teenage socialite from Greenwich, Connecticut, named Linda Rae Fitzpatrick was found naked and murdered in a boiler room and known drug den at 169 Avenue B, outside of which hung a sign reading "Free Love." She had been raped multiple times. Next to her lay the body of her boyfriend, James Leroy "Groovy" Hutchinson, a happy-go-lucky twenty-one-year-old from upstate who was known around the neighborhood as someone who helped runaways find shelter. He had been killed with a brick while trying to defend Fitzpatrick. Two men—Donald Ramsey, a Black Nationalist ex-convict who lived upstairs with his wife in an apartment with a black panther drawing on the front door, and Thomas Dennis—were sentenced to prison for the murders.

The musician Peter Stampfel says that with the Groovy murders, the East Village took a turn: "After that, it was a very fast slide. The scene was attracting fuck-tons of ex-con types and human garbage attracted by drugs and girls. . . . Things started getting bad in '67 when the flower power bullshit made the whole country aware of sex and drugs and young girls who were sexually active. It was a powerful sleaze magnet." Stampfel retreated inside: "My old lady and I took fuck-tons of amphetamine and stayed home and played music." Poet Ron Padgett says that before 1967, everyone walking up and down St. Marks Place was carrying books. After that, they didn't carry books—"just joints or something." If the peace-and-love sixties really only lasted from 1964 to 1967, the violent seventies began in 1967.

Soon after the murders, the Avenue B building's "Free Love" sign was amended to read, "Hate." That strip of Avenue B from Tenth to Twelfth Streets had been called the "Sacred Via," a road for hippies in search of intoxication and mind expansion, but from then on it was, in the words of the Fugs's Ed Sanders, "Via Terroris—waypath of terror and desolation."

A Pulitzer-winning *New York Times* story, "The Two Worlds of Linda Fitzpatrick," told how a girl who rode horses, took family vacations to Bermuda, and lived near a Connecticut country club was drawn to an East Village scene "whose ingredients included crash pads, acid trips, freaking out, psychedelic art, witches and warlocks."

After the murders, many suburban kids were no longer allowed to visit the Village. Shops like Limbo suffered and the streets grew emptier, increasing the ratio of hooligans to innocents. Crime rose. Nationwide, there was a sense of looming apocalypse. On St. Marks, a survivalist store opened selling gas masks. The *Whole Earth Catalog* offered strategies for life post-annihilation.

The cops tried to keep order, but often failed. "The Ninth Precinct had a special squad lurking around St. Marks Place looking for drug users," shopkeeper Kristina Olitski says. "We all knew who the cops were." They had paunches and wore black socks, whereas the real St. Marks Place dealers were lean and barefoot. Olitski thought it was absurd to police drug use on a street where it was so ubiquitous. "I said to them, 'What are you going to do, arrest the whole street?'"

Olitski says the social revolutionaries were determined to bring about the end of the world, or at least to provoke serious showdowns. The people who ran the Bridge Theater downstairs from her apartment once asked if they could use her six-year-old son on stage for a show. She said sure. "He went down on stage and did whatever they did," she says, "then he came back upstairs and went to bed."

At eleven-thirty that night, the doorbell rang. It was the FBI. "They accused me of promoting anti-Americanism," says Olitski. "I said I didn't even know what had happened." The agents informed her that with her son onstage, the performers had burned the American flag. Her response to the FBI: "Oh my God, they [the theater people] are idiots."

Olitski says St. Marks Place made her children cynical. She, too, found it depressing as more and more people on the street overdosed. She recalls that more than one kid coming down off acid at the Valencia Hotel believed it was possible to fly off the roof. She started keeping a bulletin board on the wall of her store where worried parents and their runaway children could exchange notes. She tried to refer them to the mental health clinic at no. 70. But death was everywhere, even among the scene's stars.

"She was tiny," Olitski says of Janis Joplin. "Nobody thinks of her that way. You think she's a [size] twelve. She was like a four or six. She had a ten-year-old boy's body. One day she came by to get something. I was fitting something on her, and she felt like a rock—like stone. I said, 'You feel hard.' She said, 'It's the drugs.' A week later she was dead. She went to California and that was it."

Many of the few children who lived in the neighborhood walked around in bare, filthy feet. The Fenstens, an artist couple, lived with their two little girls at no. 7 from 1965 to 1967 and hung out with Joplin. During that period, their bare-bones apartment was robbed nine times. When their mother, who had worked as a waitress at the 1964–1965 World's Fair, complained, the policeman told her he wouldn't file charges unless she slept with him. Instead, the family fled for the relative civility of Spanish Harlem. "When I look at photographs of me and my sister in the St. Marks apartment," Susan Fensten recalls, "I think, we're cute, but so dirt broke it could be Appalachia."

The Peñas, a Puerto Rican family, lived on the second floor of no. 11. The mother, Carmen, sat in the east window, watching her children play outside and keeping an eye on the fighting cock the family kept on the fire escape for fights they hosted in the basement. "Every morning it would crow at 6 a.m.," recalls Paul Schneeman, who grew up at no. 29 and still lives there. A girl living across the street at no. 8, who had a crush on Paul's little brother Emilio, sometimes saw dead roosters in Tompkins Square Park on her way to school. That girl, now *New York Times* lead film critic Manohla Dargis, had a sister named Trishka who spent so much time with the Peñas and other Hispanic neighbors that she developed an impeccable Puerto Rican accent. *"Mami!"* the little white girl would chirp. If they stayed up late enough, the girls could hear drunks singing "God Bless America" at McSorley's last call.

When Dargis started attending the competitive Hunter High School uptown, she realized that not everyone lived the kind of bohemian life she and her neighbors did. "When I was twelve, I went to a birthday party in Forest Hills [an upper-middle-class neighborhood in the borough of Queens] and there was a maid in a uniform." At a time when, for her, a pack of candy was decadent, this house had "a bowl of M&Ms on the table—a *bowl* of M&Ms."

By 1968, the East Village had end-times fever. "It was like the San Francisco Summer of Love had moved east, but not so much love," says Students for a Democratic Society's Jeff Jones. In fights with police, bottles were thrown. After one particularly violent scuffle, someone said it looked as if blood were flowing out of the pavement of St. Marks Place.

The street began to attract the homeless, both the truly poor and the poor by choice. "There were sleeping bags lined up end to end," says Carole Rosenthal. "There were bodies everywhere." And the neighborhood had a creepy vibe. Rosenthal recalls two well-dressed, middle-aged Italian sisters with dyed-black hair who collected stray cats around St. Marks. "They would lure them into boxes," says Rosenthal. "It took me a long time to figure out what they were doing. But once I was trying to get rid of kittens and put an ad in the *Voice*, all these medical students started calling me. I realized the sisters were more than likely selling the cats for vivisection."

One by one, new rebels replaced the Night People. Young people who had read Norman Mailer's *Village Voice* and answered Jean Shepherd's call to gather at the Wanamaker Building for a "mill" were approaching middle age. The Beatniks' bohemianism seemed quaint in the face of the new revolution: "Beneath the surface emaciation and phony glitter of St. Marks Place, hate, resentment, and alienation transform themselves into thrusts of liberating energy," wrote an anarchist in the East Village zine *Rat*. Ernie Hurwitz of no. 51 met a teenage runaway who was living near Tompkins Square Park, and they fell in love. He decided it was time to leave the East Village for good, a decision he now regrets. "Probably the worst thing I ever said to anyone," he says, "was, 'Let me take you out of this neighborhood!' But she was a queen, so we moved to Queens." Squatters, drug dealers, and radicals continued their colonization.

One winter night in the late sixties, Kenneth Koch was doing a Poetry Project reading at St. Mark's Church-in-the-Bowery. A tall, skinny, scuzzy man—someone said he was a poet from Detroit—stood up, held out a handgun, yelled, "Koch!" and fired at him three times. The man was Alan Van Newkirk and the mastermind behind the attack was anarchist Ben Morea. To Morea and his Black Mask group, a Dada-inflected street gang that sought to destroy capitalism, Koch was a symbol of what Morea described as "this totally bourgeois, dandy world."

Koch staggered back, waiting to be dead. Some people screamed, thinking he'd been murdered. But the bullets were blanks. Black Mask members rained down leaflets from the balcony where Peter Stuyvesant's slaves once sat. The leaflets showed a photo of the poet LeRoi Jones—who by this point had converted to Islam; moved back to his hometown, Newark; and changed his name to Amiri Baraka—with the caption "Poetry is revolution."

Once everyone realized what had happened, the reading resumed.

Weren't people freaked out? Didn't anyone call the police?

"Nah," says one frequent Poetry Project attendee. "Back then that kind of thing happened all the time."

"Reactions after the event were split," Morea has said, "between people who thought it was the greatest thing they'd ever heard and those that thought we were a bunch of sophomoric assholes." Black Mask was, in Morea's words, "all about pushing people to decide, 'Do I belong with this group of people or this one?'"

Black Mask would evolve into a group called Up Against the Wall Motherfuckers (also known, simply, as "The Motherfuckers"), named after a line in the Baraka poem "Black People!" The group handed out flyers on St. Marks Place—or, as they called it, "St. Marx," an homage to Emma Goldman's and Leon Trotsky's Hail Marx Place.

According to Paul Krassner, "The Lower East Side Motherfuckers were an anarchist group who wore black until they got influenced by the hippies and started wearing beads. But they were black beads." They fought incessantly with the police. "When a cop politely suggested [a Motherfucker named] Carole could find a more private place to breastfeed than the corner of Second Avenue and St. Marks Place," Osha Neumann recalls, "she whipped out her tit and squirted him full in the chest with breast milk."

The Motherfuckers claimed St. Marks Place between Second and Third Avenues as their turf. "It would take half an hour to walk that one block, we'd hand out so many copies of the newsletter," recalls Jeff Jones. (Jones later decided that he wanted "more organization, strategy, and discipline—and less anarchy." He went on to become a founder of Weatherman.)

One Motherfucker leaflet about Lower East Side outlaw life, written by Johnny Sundstrom, inspired the 1968 Jefferson Airplane song "We Can Be Together." Their August 19, 1969, performance of the song on the Dick Cavett show marked one of the first uses of the word "motherfucker" on American television.

Some of the Motherfuckers ran a Free Store on Avenue A that from about 1967 to 1970 was an activist meeting spot. "We did such things as collect clothing, food, and we ran a mimeograph machine, and all of these were services to the runaway street people community," says Sundstrom. "Tompkins Square Park was home to all kinds of people. There were always drum circles all day long. There was one group of guys that adopted us and who we allowed into our Free Store in the cold weather: the Wine Group for Freedom—black veterans, proud winos. They could have their meetings in our Free Store when it was cold outside. They'd pass wine and talk politics. They were quite politically astute. They were back from Vietnam and not going to buy into the system."

One morning in late 1967, calling it "culture exchange," the Motherfuckers and those they'd enlisted via flyers brought trash bags from the streets of the Lower East Side uptown on the subway and dumped them in the fountain at Lincoln Center. Just three years earlier, construction of the Center had leveled the Italian part of Hell's Kitchen where one of the group's members had grown up; the trash dump was payback.

Another time, the Motherfuckers released stink bombs at a Dada exhibit at the Museum of Modern Art, believing the artists would have appreciated the gesture. They also cut the fences at the Woodstock Festival in August 1969 so people could enter for free.

The Motherfuckers menaced the owners of East Side Books and other businesses, but they went full force against Bill Graham's Fillmore East. Graham had made peace with the local Hell's Angels, led by Sandy Alexander, after they had hit him with a tow chain while trying to fight their way in for free. But now the Motherfuckers showed up demanding a free night at the Fillmore once a week. In his own theater, recalls Joshua White, Graham stared down people chanting, "Music should be free!"

"What are you going to do to me with your berets and your fake military crap and your black leather jackets?" he asked the Motherfuckers. "If you want the music to be free, go liberate the Metropolitan Opera House."

But the Motherfuckers had a specific reason for targeting the Fillmore: they were indignant that other people—fake people from foreign lands, such as California, New Jersey, or above Fourteenth Street—were profiting from their authentic countercultural lifestyle. There was some truth to that. The East Village's reputation as the epicenter of hippie depravity brought tour buses full of normal-looking folks who gawked at the freaks.

"You'd see a bus pull up. I'd be out in front of the store in my bare feet, and I had long hair and a beard," recalls Charles Fitzgerald. "I'd be sweeping the sidewalk and then someone on the bus would point out, 'There's one!' And I'd make a face."

Turning the tables, in 1968, artist Joey Skaggs arranged a "Hippie Bus Tour to Queens." Sixty hippies boarded a rented Greyhound bus at St. Marks Place and Second Avenue, by Gem Spa, armed with cameras. On the way to Queens, they stopped at a White Castle for hamburgers and at a Howard Johnson's for ice cream. On a random street in Queens, they snapped pictures of suburbanites mowing their lawns and reading the Sunday paper, and asked them lifestyle questions like, "Hey, what do you do at night around here?" The reply, from a grandmother on 181st Street: "Not much. We go to sleep early."

But the Motherfuckers weren't content with cheeky stunts like Skaggs's bus tour.

"The Motherfuckers' ideology," says Sundstrom, "was that the reason [Graham] was thriving and people came from Long Island to go there [the Fillmore] was because it was in the cultural hub of the so-called hippie population and activity. Bill Graham was making money off the image created by the runaway street people, where ten to twelve people would live in crash pads in tenements and get busted. All those kids were the draw for his audiences to come down and stare at the hippies and be hippies for one night a week. So, we asked for one night a week to put on free concerts for that community. We were met with insane outbursts of resistance. It was a showdown."

Some Motherfuckers attempted an alliance with a biker gang. "They wanted to take over the Lower East Side," Sundstrom says of the bikers. "We said, 'No way. You'll just sell drugs and scare people. We represent the people already here.' We made a truce in which we divided up the Lower East Side in terms of territory. One night some of us went into a meeting with them, no guns allowed. We told our people around the meeting area, 'If we're not out by 8 p.m., come in and get us.' There were six of us—three from each side. We were having a great time, until we realized no one in the room had a watch." Any second, the lookouts outside would get nervous and storm the place with guns. "We ran out into the street waving our arms, saying, 'Don't shoot!'"

Paul Krassner went along with an activist named Tom Motherfucker to negotiate a plan to get Bill Graham to hand over the keys to his theater. Graham said, "What do you want to do on those nights?" Tom Motherfucker replied, "Bomb! Shoot! Kill!" Krassner said, "He's just kidding. They're just going to raise money for the United Jewish Fund."

Another time, Ben Morea held a sit-in on the Fillmore stage after a Living Theatre performance.

In the end, Graham decided he was fine with a free night. "Sure, if the bands will play for free, I'll do it, sure," he said, according to Joshua White. He quickly regretted it. Graham reported that on that first night, four or five hundred people showed up and wrecked the place: "They messed up the floor and peed on the walls and put their feet on the chairs and brought in their cooking utensils so it became like an overnight shelter for the homeless."

Sundstrom would stand up with the microphone and call out, "It's *freeee* night at the Fillmore! If you have something in your pocket, pass it around!" The group handed out free marijuana, featured bands like the antiestablishment Detroit rock band MC5 (best known today for "Kick Out the Jams"), and did goofy, ranting commercials for the revolution that offended just about everyone.

"I was an atheist, but when the Motherfuckers took the stage, they started criticizing all religions," Krassner says. "I yelled, 'There are Buddhist nuns and monks burning themselves! You have to judge people by what they do, not what they believe!' The Motherfuckers were hard to deal with, because they had so much anger. They were the dark side of the antiwar movement."

Ben Morea says the free nights ended because the NYPD wrote Graham about all the free dope. But Graham said they ended when the Motherfuckers broke the concession display case, at which point he also started to think seriously about getting out of New York altogether. Graham was secretly pleased when MC5, advertised as the "people's revolutionary band," discovered after a Fillmore gig at which they'd burned an American flag on stage that all their equipment had been stolen—"by the *other* people, I guess," he quipped.

In 1968, a young actress moved to New York. Having been raised mostly in Texas by overbearing parents, she couldn't get over the freedom and delights that New York City offered. She walked into a deli in the Village and, pointing to a sign in the window that read "Coffee Rice and Beans," enthusiastically said, "One pound of coffee rice, please!" The man behind the counter laughed her out of the store.

For her day job, she worked as a receptionist at the famous Kenneth Salon. On June 3, Warhol superstar Viva was at the salon getting her hair done in preparation for a role in *Midnight Cowboy* and talking on the salon's phone to director Paul Morrissey. Viva was treating the salon to a running commentary of her conversation. When Morrissey left to use the bathroom, he put Warhol on the phone in his place. "Andy says that bitch Valerie just walked in," the receptionist recalls Viva announcing.

Radical feminist and friend of Ben Morea Valerie Solanas had been hanging around Warhol's Factory, although she made people there nervous. "Life in this society being, at best, an utter bore and no aspect of society being at all relevant to women," Solanas wrote in her *SCUM Manifesto*, "there remains to civic-minded, responsible, thrill-seeking females only to overthrow the government, eliminate the money system, institute complete automation and destroy the male sex."

In the salon, Viva held out the phone receiver. Those assembled heard *crack, crack, crack*. "Listen," Viva said to the people around her at the salon, "they're playing with that bull whip I brought back from South America."

In fact, Solanas had shot Warhol and art critic Mario Amaya. Warhol lay bleeding on the floor of the Factory until the ambulance came; he reached the hospital clinically dead. Doctors opened his chest and massaged his heart, then performed five and a half hours of surgery. Solanas surrendered herself to a cop near the Factory, saying that she'd shot Warhol because he had been exerting too much control over her life. Warhol survived, but he was never the same. And this wasn't the only major shooting that year—not by any means.

The same year, Martin Luther King, Jr., was assassinated. "That was when the country moved from 'We shall overcome' to black power," recalls Nell Gibson, a black parishioner at St. Mark's Church. As a radical activist, she was not surprised when she picked up her phone and heard the clicks of phone taps, or when the police came to the door asking to search her apartment. According to parishioners, there were often "phone company workers" asking to do "routine maintenance" in and around the Church; sure they were FBI agents, Church workers denied them entry.

That year, Bill Graham saw a young black man punch a young white one in front of his San Francisco club for what seemed like no reason. "Why'd you hit that guy?" Graham asked the attacker. "He killed my brother, man," the young man said. "He killed Martin Luther King. All you white bastard motherfuckers. You killed *Martin Luther*, man."

Law enforcement targeted St. Marks Place. Detectives monitored stores like East Side Books (no. 34), which sold underground comics like the explicit *Zap Comix* (featuring characters such as Captain Piss-Gums and his Pervert Pirates). A nationwide crackdown on lurid comic books in the fifties had resulted in the relative sanitization of the medium for children. But the sixties saw a surge in next-level perverse comics for adults. The bookstore was raided the same day as at least two other lefty bookstores, including City Lights in San Francisco, for selling *Zap Comix* no. 4—August 25, 1969.

In *Zap* no. 4, page after page of cartoon orgies give way to a strip about a father and mother who rape their daughter and son, then celebrate when the son and daughter have sex with each other. One line: "The family that lays together, stays together." On other pages, a girl persuades a cow to perform oral sex on her by covering her vulva with salt, and beasts with multiple penises ejaculate profusely. It's about as lurid as anyone could imagine, which was more or less the point.

"I was not even really at work that day," recalls then–East Side Books employee Terry McCoy. "I hadn't sold it to the undercover cop. It was a Wednesday and I stopped in to get the *Village Voice*. This bearded guy pushed the door open aggressively and said, 'Okay, this place is closed down!' I thought he was a street guy. I instinctively blocked the entrance. 'Hey, buddy,' I said, trying to calm him down and get him outside, 'what's the problem?' He said, 'You work here?' I said, 'Yes,' and he said, 'You're under arrest.'"

McCoy and another employee were taken over to the Ninth Precinct and then to the Tombs. The owner of the store, Jim Rose, showed up in a huff, McCoy recalls, saying to the police, "See here, now!" They threw him in jail, too.

In San Francisco, the lawyer defending City Lights had employed celebrity expert witnesses, so Allen Ginsberg offered to testify on behalf of East Side Books. But the New York lawyer tried another tack and argued that bookstore employees couldn't be expected to know what was inside every book they sold.

The judge was not persuaded. The Court decided: "It is material utterly unredeemed and unredeemable, save, perhaps, only by the quality of the paper upon which it is printed. . . . It is what Dr. Benjamin Spock characterizes as 'shock-obscenity,' representing a brutalizing trend in our society." In the end, McCoy got off on a technicality and the charges against Jim Rose were dropped, but Peter Dargis (Manohla

Dargis's father) was convicted of promoting obscenity and fined five hundred dollars.

In this late hippie period, a black steel cube sculpture, eight feet long on each side, tilted on one point on which it could rotate like a playground roundabout, appeared on a traffic island in the center of Astor Place. Installed in 1967, Tony Rosenthal's sculpture *Alamo* became a meeting place where new waves of young and damaged free spirits could smoke pot and make out. The heavy black cube offered a nicely ominous backdrop as the sixties' playful creativity was beginning to yield to the seventies' debauchery and rage.

The young people of the early seventies Village soon made their way into fiction. In James Leo Herlihy's 1971 novel *Season of the Witch*, set in part on St. Marks Place, one of the main characters is a teenage draft-dodger who has renamed himself Roy. Roy is mugged but won't turn in his muggers. He feels more allegiance to them than to the police, and he says to his friend, who calls herself Witch, "Witch, you know what I really hate about this revolution? It makes you think about *sides*. You always have to think about which one you're on."

In Harold Franklin's 1970 novel *Run a Twisted Street*, a teenager named Freeman runs away after learning that he was adopted and winds up crashing at 35 St. Marks Place. He's the anti–Horatio Alger character: lazy, aimless, and unlucky. A charismatic pseudo-cult leader named Gee takes "Freem" under his wing, and while they walk around Tompkins Square Park says things like, "You scream 'murder,' get my attention, and you still need to hug your pain to you like a money belt."

A late sixties change in the drug culture—from pot and acid to cocaine and heroin—changed the street's vibe. "Everyone thought cocaine was amazing," says Joshua White. "The tragedy of cocaine was not clear for many years. When you came down off it, you were mean."

"I saw kids who were sweet acid-heads in 1969 drop out," writes the professor and historian Marshall Berman, "and come back as angry, snarling junkies panhandling on St. Marks Place in 1971."

On March 6, 1970, the Weather Underground's headquarters on West Eleventh Street was destroyed when a bomb went off by accident. On March 22, 1970, another bomb exploded on the dance floor of the Electric Circus, injuring seventeen people. Former owner Jerry Brandt claims he's not sure whether it was "a stink bomb or a bomb-bomb," but when asked if the rumor that it was planted by the Black Panthers was true he says, "I doubt it, but you can say that if you want. It's good press."*

No matter the nature of the explosion, the Circus was already losing its cachet. Jerry Brandt's partners redesigned the space, and Joshua White says it "completely lost its spirit. They were very precious. It's a lovely idea to put AstroTurf on the walls. It's kind of groovy. But when people spill Coca-Cola on it, which they do, it is disgusting."

Downstairs, the Dom had become a hangout for the Negro Ensemble Company, which performed around the corner, and for college students from Harlem. The white upstairs crowd and the black downstairs crowd rarely mixed.

On Christmas 1969, a West Point cadet and reporter named Lucian Truscott IV went to a free event at the Circus and wrote it up for the *Village Voice*. He documents a series of unsuccessful hippie moments, interrupted by, for example, a cry of "Up Against the Wall Motherfucker!" during an activity in which everyone was to tell one another "Merry Christmas." A geodesic dome was constructed in the space to promote "'dome consciousness, togetherness, love' and the like." Straw was placed in the dome's center and babies were placed on the straw. The

* The man has a memoir to sell: *It's a Short Walk From Brooklyn, If You Run: A Conversation with Jerry Brandt*.

The scene at Dom dance hall at no. 23, July 13, 1967. Photo by Larry C. Morris/*New York Times*.

group was to "zap" them with love. But two men took all their clothes off, freaking out some of the parents.

"One infant showed up, cradled in the arms of a somewhat frightened looking mother, who sat as directed in the hay where she was immediately surrounded by other 'infants' who averaged about seven to 10 years old and came equipped with every undesirable and obnoxious trait of that age," Truscott wrote. One of the organizers asked that a spotlight be put on the children. Big mistake. "Violation one in dealing with the brats that age: never put them in the center of attention. Hay began to fly, most of it directed at the two naked men, who threw it back, much of it going past the kids and landing on the now irate mother of the infant."

After Truscott's story ran, it was clear that the Electric Circus had become a joke. St. Marks Place's love-zapping days were over.

Stanley Tolkin, meanwhile, had used some of the money he'd made from the Dom to buy an old motorboat. Each night after they closed the bar, Tolkin and Joyce Hartwell would take the boat out into the dark stillness of the East River and drift until dawn. One night in 1968, Tolkin accidentally set a fire while trying to make coffee on board. "He was concerned we would all be killed," recalls Hartwell. "He put out the fire with his hands. The Coast Guard had to come to get us. When the two boats pulled next to each other, he grabbed a chain with his raw hands."

His hands were slow to heal, and that wasn't his only health issue. He also had a weak heart. Not long after the boat fire, the couple was at home when Tolkin suffered a full-blown heart attack. "Where's your medicine?" Hartwell remembers screaming at him. He died in her arms.

Tolkin's son tried to keep the Dom going, but without his father, the space couldn't sustain the warm, open vibe that had drawn both the creative class and students. Hartwell notes that she wasn't particularly popular with Stanley's son, as she had been Tolkin's mistress, and so she stayed away. In the summer of 1974, an announcement was made that the Dom, now all but deserted, would briefly become, of all things, a country-Western bar with sawdust floors called The Cow Palace.

The Electric Circus closed in August 1971. One of the last shows featured Iggy Pop covered in glitter. Johnny Ramone was in the audience with a tape recorder. The Fillmore East closed the same year. Joshua White recalls that the beginning of the end was when "someone died at a Vanilla Fudge concert from inhaling too much Whippets from a whipped cream canister."

Bill Graham's personal assistant desperately tried to revive the short-haired, twenty-one-year-old man, but he expired in the back of the theater.

That summer, the Truscott reassessed St. Marks Place and found that it had changed "from a hippie haven to Desolation Row." He encountered a group of four young men sitting in front of no. 26 passing around a switchblade. John, "the dirtiest of the group," wearing "dirty Levi's and a vest festooned with bits of leather, seashells, and long curls of human hair," went over to Gem Spa to accost passersby with "whatever scrap of mindless hustle his fizzled-out brain could muster." St. Marks Place had ceased to be original and surprising. The clothing store Limbo had moved from no. 24 to no. 4, and wearing the clothes it sold now provoked a sneering "I bet that came from Limbo," rather than a wide-eyed "Where did you get that?"

"The street had its finest hour during the days of the Balloon Farm and the Five Spot," wrote Truscott, "before a massive influx of boutiques, antique fur stores, hairdressing shops, and pizza and ice cream beaneries turned the block into a limp Times Square. Back then, the street had a fleeting sense of glamor and importance." Truscott says that the end of St. Marks Place as a destination was imminent. "Residents of the area, in fact, give St. Mark's Place a couple of years. Outside estimates say five."

Meanwhile, tension was growing within the civil rights movement. James Forman was among the black activists shifting the movement away from the pacifism of Martin Luther King, Jr. Forman, who had been threatened with lynching at the age of eight while growing up with his impoverished grandparents in Mississippi, was tired of being told to take the high road. "If we can't sit at the table of democracy," he said, "then we'll knock the fucking legs off."

That more extreme approach appealed to a lot of St. Marks Place's heroes, including Amiri Baraka. In an essay about the assassination of Malcolm X, Baraka wrote, "Black people must have absolute political and social control." He advocated for a sovereign Black Nation with its own laws. "And there is only one people on the planet who can slay the white man," he wrote. "The people who know him best. His ex-slaves."

In April 1969, at the National Black Economic Development Conference in Detroit, Forman outlined a manifesto for eliminating racism by means of "an armed confrontation and long years of guerilla warfare inside this country" and by "assuming leadership inside the United States of everything that exists . . . total control of the U.S." As a start, Forman demanded "$500,000,000 from the Christian white churches and the Jewish synagogues." One item on the manifesto's budget was thirty million dollars for "a research skills center, which will provide futuristic research on the problems of Black people." In May 1969, Forman brought his demands to Riverside Church in Manhattan, where he interrupted services to make the case for reparations. Several parishioners at St. Mark's Church took Forman's words to heart.

On the morning of Sunday, October 5, 1969, in the middle of Father Michael Allen's service, a group of six black and Latino parishioners rose from their seats. For weeks, Allen had suspected that his secretary, Nell Gibson, and his newly appointed assistant minister, David Garcia, just out of divinity school, had been up to something, but until that moment he didn't know what it was. Now he would find out.

John Clarke, who had grown up in the parish, announced that those who were standing were called the Black and Brown Caucus, and that they had a list of demands, including thirty thousand dollars as "reparations" and the replacement of the American flag at the front of the church with the Black

Nationalist flag. Demand number three: "That the whites of this parish cease and desist this WASP service, conceived solely by whites to help themselves over their white middle class hang ups." Number six: "That the words, 'Go, serve the lord you are free,' be immediately deleted from the service, because we are not free." Number seven suggested replacing that phrase with "Power to the people."

The Caucus protesters had practiced their presentation and prepared for various reactions. They expected Allen to reject their demands, and they thought it possible that parishioners would also attack them physically, at which point they were prepared to resist. Nell Gibson, who still attends services at St. Mark's Church, says that her fellow Caucus members had sensed weakness in her because she cared about Allen. They'd made her swear that if it came to an armed conflict, she would be prepared to kill him. Seven months pregnant at the time, she'd taken an oath before them, promising to do whatever it took, even that. "For me it came down to Michael or the future of my unborn child," she said.

But violence proved unnecessary. Allen waited a beat and then followed the Caucus out of the church. "That was a hard moment," says Allen. "I had heard men and women whom I loved, and who had loved me, judge me, judge us all. And I wondered what I should do. . . . I followed the blacks and the browns, because to do anything else would have denied every-thing I had lived and believed for ten precious years of my life."

In fact, the congregation overall reacted far more positively than the Caucus had anticipated. One white woman came up to Nell Gibson outside the church holding the American flag. "I took it down," she said. "What do we do next?"

Father Tom Pike says he wasn't there that Sunday, but that he heard about it from an elderly white lady named Mrs. Morton, the wife of a former warden. "Sunday was wonderful!" she told him. "Michael got up to preach and David stood up and said, 'I'm not sitting for this!' and everyone walked out! What a marvelous little play!"

Soon, though, Mrs. Morton and her friends realized that it was no play. In a letter dated October 6, 1969, Allen wrote to ask members of the vestry to step down to make way for Caucus members (the Caucus's list of demands included four spots on the vestry). "Please consider that the nature of every crisis is to stretch the imagination, the dignity, and the freedom of men to the utmost—and then leave them the better or worse for it," Allen wrote. "I think we could be better." He authorized a check for thirty thousand dollars (about two hundred thousand dollars today), payable to the Caucus.

The group's members worked with the Black Panthers to form a prison law library that became a model for such libraries around the country. The service changed as well. Soon, the liturgy emphasized, in Gibson's words, "the strong sitting with the weak."

The Gibsons say it took months of hard conversations to sort through what had happened. The theme of that year's Lent was finding ways to come back together as a congregation. "We made public confessions," says Gibson. "I had to tell Michael that I had been prepared to kill him." Reconciliation began, she says, when Allen baptized the Gibsons' son, Bertram Maxwell III, a few months later and took on the role of his godfather.

"Little black baby," Allen said in that ceremony, "we're going to baptize you now. We're going to bury you in your grave like the people Israel were buried in the water. . . . We're going to let you die now so you can begin to live." Turning now to the congregation, he said, "You could teach him, if you believed it yourself, that at the center of this universe there is justice, there is love, there is dignity."

"Our three-month-old baby was the only person in the church not crying," Gibson says.

Allen went even further in his efforts to bring about racial reconciliation. In June 1970, he left St. Mark's Church, taking a position at New Haven's Berkeley Divinity School. Before he left, he recommended to the bishop that David Garcia be made the next rector of St. Mark's Church.

In some ways, Garcia and Allen were similar. A half-Mexican, half-white son of a strict, strategic air command officer, Garcia had grown up struggling with his racial identity and rebelling against those in authority. And yet, in other ways Garcia and Allen were polar opposites. Where Allen was patient and a famously good listener, Garcia was irascible and prone to filibustering. Where Allen wanted to appeal to the better angels of the community's nature, Garcia wanted to wage war until justice as he saw it was done.

"Mike was a wonderful, radical guy," says former assistant rector Pike, "but he was also an old white WASP. David's takeover was personal. It was a mixture of ideology and emotions. It was racial and it was Oedipal."

Garcia won the day, but the church he inherited was not what it had been. Around the time of the October Sunday revolt, two hundred people regularly attended services. When Garcia took over the pulpit, just a few months later, there were approximately twelve.

In 2013, after a coffee at Grand Central Terminal, Garcia stopped in the hallway. As commuters streamed around him, he said, "You know, Michael could have been bishop. But he's a tragic figure. A great tragedy. The Episcopal Church said to him, 'You help those spics, niggers, and lesbians, and we'll never forgive you.' But he can die complete, because he did the right thing. He is a great man."

Garcia's words were an unexpected eulogy. On September 4, 2013, a week after that conversation, Father Michael Allen died in St. Louis, Missouri, at the age of eighty-five, less than a month after being diagnosed with pancreatic cancer and just six months after the death of the Rev. Priscilla Allen, his wife of sixty-three years.

During his post–St. Mark's time as rector of St. Louis's Christ Church, Allen had turned the cathedral basement into a homeless shelter, fought for abortion rights, and conducted outreach to recruit transgender parishioners. He retired in 1998, but continued to act as a substitute preacher at various churches. In one of his last sermons, he spoke on prophecy in Ezekiel. Later that day, he said that he'd been thinking a lot about St. Mark's: "What I was trying to do there," he said, "was make it possible for these prophetic voices to be heard or seen." He hoped his legacy would be an example of acting through love rather than fear. "All the world religions, the great ones," he said, "agree that at the heart of that which is transcendent, that which is holy, is compassion. And compassion is the heart of what holiness means."

On a rainy day in October 1974, a couple came to Father David Garcia to see about getting married. He was a poet and she was an actress. They'd been living together on St. Marks Place for a year, and while lying in bed sick from the flu had decided that they should go ahead and make it legal.

Garcia asked them about their "sexual menu" and enthusiastically handed them examples of the modern-language vows he preferred. One line read, "My body worships your body."

"We'd just like the *Book of Common Prayer*," the man said.

"Are you sure?" Garcia said. "What about these?" He proffered mimeographs of vows promising marriages of friendship, social awareness, and world peace.

"No, thank you," the woman said.

Garcia hesitated.

"The first time I was married," the man explained, "I laughed through the ceremony and then cried for five years. This time I want to be scared."

Bishop Paul Moore, unknown child, poet Anne Waldman, Rector David Garcia, and Stephen Facey in St. Mark's Church's yard, summer 1978. Collection of St. Mark's Church. Reprinted with permission of St. Mark's Church and Stephen Facey.

Garcia had to hunt for the book. It was the first time he had performed the traditional liturgy, he said. (Unbeknownst to the couple, Father Michael Allen had recruited the young priest right out of divinity school, and rather than apprentice himself to scripture, Garcia had staged a revolution.)

The wedding was beautiful, by all reports, although some said that Father Garcia's hands shook throughout the ceremony, especially when the text referred to "the dreadful day of judgment, when the secrets of all hearts shall be revealed." The woman wondered in retrospect if her cute brown suit didn't make her look rather like an airline stewardess. For the party that followed, they miscounted the number of bottles per case of champagne and ended up with more than one bottle per person, all of which vanished. Calls came in the next morning from gay men waking up next to straight girls.

That couple—Peter Schjeldahl, the art critic who had witnessed the fake shooting of Kenneth Koch, and Brooke Alderson, the actress who had heard the *crack-crack-crack* through the phone receiver at Kenneth Salon when Andy Warhol was shot—lived together in a four-flight walk-up at no. 53. The three-bedroom co-op apartment, not far from the former site of Nicholas W. Stuyvesant's Bowery House, cost two hundred dollars a month. They lost touch with friends at the Poetry Project. He worked as an editor at *Art in America*. She began acting in TV commercials and theater. In two years they would have a daughter—me. Everyone had been so sure the world was going to end in the late sixties that when it didn't, no one quite knew what to do with themselves. "We woke up in a time that wasn't supposed to happen," Schjeldahl says. "The good news was we were still here. Everything else was weird."

PART IV

"IT WAS LIKE IF YOU TURNED THE LIGHTS ON AND ALL THE ROACHES RAN."

1977-1991

Bernard Rosenthal's sculpture *Alamo*, at Astor Place, ca. 1971.

*Photo by Donal F. Holway/*New York Times.

18

STUPID ON PURPOSE

One bright spring afternoon, Carole Rosenthal, a professor who lived at no. 37½, saw a former student of hers named Artie walking through her neighborhood. Artie had taken her freshman English class at Pratt, and she remembered him as a diligent student and art lover. Today Artie was wearing blue hot pants and high heels. His companion, a skinny man about the same age, was in red hot pants. Both men wore clothing covered in rhinestones and tights that matched their shorts. They passed a paper bag back and forth and drank from it as they ambled along, obviously sloshed, stumbling into each other in a friendly way, deep in conversation.

Rosenthal was shocked that Artie, whom she'd known as a quiet art student, had devolved into a flamboyant degenerate. "Artie was very sensitive and sweet," says Rosenthal. "His mother had just died when he started college. I hadn't seen him for years. I thought, *My god! What's happened to him?* I said, 'I'm going to pretend not to see him. This is so embarrassing.' And then I found out about the Dolls."

"Artie," Rosenthal soon learned, was in the process of metamorphosing into a star of the lower Manhattan music scene: Arthur "Killer" Kane, bass player for a loud, funny new band called the New York Dolls. The man with whom Kane had been sharing a bottle that day was the lead singer and songwriter David Johansen. The band performed catchy songs about garbage and personality crises that managed to be at once silly and romantic, to capture the scuzziness of seventies New York as well as its dark humor. Often drunk, the men in the band were willfully sloppy. With their unique look—they were sexy straight men with shaggy hair wearing feather boas and high heels—they seemed to be playing a clever joke on the homophobic rock world.

"There has never been a band—not even the Velvets—who have conveyed the oppressive close excitement that Manhattan holds for a half-formed human being the way the Dolls do," wrote Robert Christgau in 1973. "The careering screech of their music comes right out of the Cooper Union stop on the Lexington IRT."

When Artie became Killer Kane, one of the first things he did was move onto St. Marks Place, a couple of doors down from his former professor. After recovering from her initial shock, Rosenthal became proud of him and would stop and talk to him when they ran into each other on the street, though she declined his offers to hang out at his apartment. She didn't want to know the details of his new rock-star life.

Members of the Dolls lived at various places on St. Marks (Sylvain Mizrahi at no. 13), and their first album's back cover was shot in front of Gem Spa—where legend has it members of the band, supported by bouncers from Max's Kansas City, once brawled with a homophobic West Village gang using the newsstand candy counter's long strings of licorice as their weapon of choice.

Musician Jeffrey Lewis, who grew up—and still lives—near St. Marks, says that when the New York Dolls appeared on the scene in 1971, they defined the moment "when stupid on purpose became the new smart." Critic John Rockwell says the band was "hated by the rest of the country, and their records sold zilch." They had a savant-like capacity for self-sabotage that helped make them a quintessentially St. Marks Place band.

The Smiths' Morrissey, who started a New York Dolls fan club as a teenager, has affectionately called the Dolls "probably the unluckiest band in the history of the world."

The Dolls, like the Ramones—a far more successful group—were bridge-and-tunnel kids. Most of the Ramones were from Forest Hills, Queens. David Johansen was from Staten Island. Arthur Kane was from the Bronx. Johnny Thunders, the Dolls's guitarist, and drummer Billy Murcia were from Queens. Their next drummer, Jerry Nolan, was from Brooklyn. They all came to the East Village as scrawny outerborough kids—the Ramones carried their instruments onto the Manhattan-bound subway in shopping bags—and redefined New York City cool.

The headquarters of this new music scene was CBGB, a bar a few blocks south of St. Marks Place on the Bowery, that old Lenape trail and Mr. Zero recruitment ground. For a long time the only people who hung out there were old Bowery drunks, and no one in the neighborhood even knew what the letters on the awning outside stood for. Officially, they signified "country, bluegrass, and blues"—what those things could possibly have to do with the 1970s Lower East Side was anyone's guess.

"People talk about CBGB as the height of cool when it opened," says Jeff Roth, who lived at no. 30, the same building as several stars of the scene, including, briefly, Iggy Pop. Roth insists CBGB wasn't the louche Valhalla people describe. "It wasn't cool at all. I was there. Look at this," Roth, who now manages the *New York Times* photo archive, says, calling up some mid-seventies photos from the *Times*. On stage at CBGB are a sincere-looking group that includes a maxi-dressed singer, a harpist, and a flutist. Crowd photos show a bunch of aging flower children in big glasses, frumpy jeans, and long sideburns sitting around tables covered with garish flower-printed oilcloth. "Look at those mooks," says Roth with a smirk.

The Ramones played their first shows at CBGB on August 16 and 17, 1974, and went on to appear twenty times more that year. "It was just an old, dumpy little bar on the Bowery," wrote Johnny Ramone, who wore New York Dolls–style silver lamé pants for the occasion. "It was like a practice in front of ten people." They broke strings, trailed off, and yelled at each other. But they soon perfected their sound—loud, fast, strangely transcendent paeans to drugs and misfit-dom that made them the biggest band on the scene. Gradually, kids with ripped shirts and grimaces started edging out the winos at CBGB. Before long, the Dead Boys's Stiv Bators was onstage pretending to strangle himself with a mic cord, and the place was packed.

While CBGB was becoming a world-class dive, St. Marks Place—whose hippie haven had yielded to a decrepit mall of black-light posters, fringe vests, and incense—became the daytime hangout for kids calling themselves punks, and a place for them to assemble a new wardrobe. The punk look was, first and foremost, anti-hippie. Younger kids mocked the pastel and psychedelic prints of the preceding youth culture by dressing in black and ripping up their clothes.

From the vantage point of the early seventies—when the economy was a disaster and violence was everywhere—the hippies' idealism looked like a bad joke. Punks inverted the "rictus grin" that Joshua White perfected in 1964 and went around with perpetual sneers. The name "punk" caught on as a description of the scene's loud music and disaffected look thanks to the comic book–inspired *Punk* magazine. Its creators were Legs McNeil and John Holmstrom, who for a time lived at the corner of St. Marks Place and First Avenue. The debut issue featured an interview with Lou Reed at a CBGB Ramones show and an editorial by John Holmstrom that began: "Kill yourself. Jump off a fuckin' cliff. Drive nails into your head. Become a robot and join the staff at Disneyland. OD. Anything. Just don't listen to discoshit."

The punks hated disco and anything else that seemed fake. The hippies had tried to bring about the Age of Aquarius. They'd wanted to end war, racism, and bad vibes. It hadn't gone so well. Punks were realists. By keeping their expectations at rock bottom, they were able to elude disappointment.

The UK punk scene, generally considered the original and more "authentic" one, was about anger—against Margaret Thatcher, against class hierarchy, against unemployment. New York had rage, too—against the tanked economy and conservative politics of a nation that would elect Ronald Reagan to the presidency in 1980. New York's punks were proudly DIY, believing that it wasn't necessary to get signed to a major label to make a record or even know how to play an instrument to start a band. Dingy clubs like CBGB gave a generation full of loners a way to be alone together, pressed up against each other in the dark.

St. Marks was the punk clearinghouse for new fashions, new albums, and new ideas. Collaborative Projects, Inc., known as Colab, opened the New Cinema on St. Marks Place. They showed Super 8 footage of the Sex Pistols, the first time many of those on the New York punk scene had seen the group perform. Vintage shop the Late Show (no. 2), where the workers had mythic nicknames—Johnny Rotunda, Frenchy, and Champ—served as a hangout for the Dolls. Once at the Late Show someone bought the jacket that writer Luc Sante's friend had taken off and set down while they were shopping. Sante drank at the Center Bar, at no. 29. "If you stayed long enough," says Sante, "the owner would heat up some Beefaroni and feed everyone." He knew a drug dealer named Jerry who

Trash and Vaudeville and Valencia Hotel, 1980. Photo by Michael Sean Edwards.

lived on the street and in addition to drugs sold vintage shoes. "I bought Quaaludes—and a pair of shoes once," says Sante. "When I came in, Jerry was always ironing. That to me was so St. Marks Place."

On Jerry the drug dealer's block, a vintage clothing store called Trash and Vaudeville opened at no. 4 in 1975. Ray Goodman owned the shop and hired a neighbor, Wells Moore, to design the store's logo in exchange for one month's rent: one hundred dollars. One room of Moore's apartment was covered in phone lines, all waist-high—the sure sign of a former bookie joint. Her apartment was bookended by the Valencia Hotel, a nonstop prostitution hub, and the St. Mark's Baths, a gay-sex mecca.

"My roommate would take a Quaalude and roll next door and then roll back at five in the morning," says Moore. "I never knew who I would see for breakfast. It was before AIDS. Everything was different. There was sex in the streets. When I went up to the roof, I'd be looking into the Baths at what looked like a dorm room with iron beds—like fifty beds. I would look in the window and the guys would wave. It was always crowded."

But the most important shop for punks was Manic Panic.

Growing up in the Bronx, two sisters—Eileen (nicknamed Snooky) and Tish Bellomo—had watched their single mother struggle. "Never be poor," their mother told Snooky as she put up curtains with a string to save money on a rod. But they thought the curtains looked just fine, and they decided

Snooky and Tish of Manic Panic, 1977. Personal collection of Manic Panic's Tish and Snooky Bellomo. Photo by their mother, Estelle Bellomo.

they were okay with being broke. They started playing music in bands together when they were sixteen and eighteen, and eventually formed a punk band called the Sic F*cks. Fellow rockers liked their music and loved their style, which—conveniently, given how broke everyone was—involved repurposed secondhand clothing. They became the go-to peddlers for punk accouterments, from vinyl pants to Johnny Rotten T-shirts. Thinking of themselves as "punk pirates," they went to England with suitcases of sixties sunglasses and came back with suitcases full of Beatle boots. They just needed a shop to sell them in.

"We didn't think we could afford St. Marks Place," says Tish. "St. Marks has always been the coolest street, with the coolest vibe." But by 1977, the city had gone broke. Services everyone had taken for granted, like fire departments and trash pickup, were compromised. Many St. Marks storefronts sat empty or had been turned into dingy, makeshift apartments after the post-hippie crash. The Bellomo sisters rented their place at no. 33 for $250 a month and opened what they called (and what very well may have been) the first punk store in America.

The Bellomo sisters' mother, an art therapist at a Bronx psychiatric center, gave the store its name. She thought the term for when manic-depressives go into a panic was catchy. The only problem with the name was that the store sometimes received calls from people in crisis saying, "Is this the manic panic hotline?" The sisters would say, "I'm really sorry! You'll have to call someone else. We're a clothing store."

The street's poverty gave the sisters the freedom to do what they wanted, but it also created danger. "It was like if you turned the lights on and all the roaches ran," says Tish. "There were a lot of people with no places to go—junkies, homeless. It had a real desperate feel." Shoplifters were a problem. "I was there alone one day. Some guy went in the dressing room and he was in there too long and I had a feeling he was up to something. He had ripped the curtain and was in our back room." Tish started screaming at the man. She made him take his clothes off and empty his pockets. All she found was a syringe. "He didn't get anything."

Half the people who worked for the Bellomos also worked at CBGB. "We'd say, 'Go see Hilly [Kristal, the owner of CBGB],' and they would," says Snooky. "It went both ways. Neither of us paid much, so they had to work at both."

After gigs, Tish and Snooky would often sleep in the store with their friends—sometimes seven people, lined up on the floor, sprawled on ratty secondhand fur coats, surrounded by roach nests. When they awoke, they'd look out the window and see "a lot of Polish and Ukrainian and very conservative people who still looked like it was the sixties, mixed in with people who had green and purple hair. It was such a combination. And further east was all the Puerto Ricans—or, as our friend put it, Punkaricans. They loved our go-go boots."

On one side of Manic Panic was the St. Mark's Cinema, which they could hear through the walls. On the other side was a huge Roma family. "They couldn't read, most of them, so they would ask us to read things for them," says Snooky.

They and all their relatives were coming in all the time. And when we got robbed they 'never heard anything.' There was a big hole through the cement wall in our hallway. A thick wall! It must have taken hours to break through. They went through and took all our leather jackets. And the gypsies said they never heard anything. This guy Ricky, who looked all of fourteen, was always playing in the street outside. Then one day he came in all dressed up and said, "I'm getting married today!" And the next day he was back playing ball out in the street with his friends.

The band Television on St. Marks Place, 1977. Photo by David Godlis.

As the seventies went on, punks like Patti Smith began overtaking both the old Slavic neighbors and the hippies. They turned it into their own playground. Where the Slavs had dined on hearty pierogi and the hippies had patronized cleansing macrobiotic cafés, Richard Hell and Tom Verlaine of the bands the Voidoids and Television talked late into the night as they smoked unfiltered cigarettes, drank beer, and ate ice cream from Gem Spa.

The New York City punk world had barely become known outside the island of Manhattan when some of those within its ranks decided the time had come for the end of music. Punk was being commercialized and corrupted, they reasoned.

Poppy bands like Blondie, with its intimidatingly gorgeous lead singer Debbie Harry, were making punk popular with normal people. Where had the danger gone? And so punk music's self-appointed angel of death appeared in the form of a sex-crazed, five-foot-four teenage girl from upstate New York, a wrecking ball in thick black eyeliner and a miniskirt.

Singer Lydia Lunch caught her first glimpse of the street at age fourteen at home in Rochester, looking at the back cover of the first New York Dolls album. Later that year, she ran away to New York and met Stiv Bators, lead singer of the Dead Boys, walking down St. Marks. From that moment on, she says, "My path was clear." She left Rochester for good at the age of sixteen and started hanging around the Lower East Side, playing gigs at places including CBGB. In 1976, she became the abrasive lead singer of Teenage Jesus and the Jerks, and the queen of "No Wave," an aggressively anti-form genre that came across to the uninitiated as between-the-radio-stations static.

Joey Ramone on St. Marks Place, 1981. Photo by David Godlis.

Lunch gleefully slept her way through the scene. "She was the welcoming committee," says Jim Marshall, who claims that Lunch was the first person many people had sex with upon arriving in New York City. Jim Sclavunos, a fan of Teenage Jesus, heard that sax player James Chance was about to leave the band. He asked if he could take Chance's place. "Lydia told me there were certain conditions," recalls Sclavunos. "One was that I play bass instead of sax. The other was that I lose my virginity to her. I thought about it for about three seconds and then agreed. But I did negotiate. She wanted to do it in the club bathroom between sets, but I insisted it be in her *boudoir*."

Experimental film director Nick Zedd, who shopped at Manic Panic, met Lunch at the rock club Tier 3. "I told her I was interested in putting her in a movie called *Bogus Man*," says Zedd. "She was very businesslike. She told me she would take me to her office. Her office was the hallway."

The No Wave movement was an attack on what a normal audience had come to expect from rock, like rhythm and melody. For Teenage Jesus and the Jerks shows, Lunch would deliver an atonal guitar track, and her drummer would pound out a military beat with one drumstick. The lyrics, too, were caustic, like: "Little orphans running through the bloody snow." Lunch's nickname was "the tiny terror."

"A good show for Teenage Jesus would be they'd clear the place out," says David Godlis, who photographed their early shows and says he often found himself shooting pictures up front surrounded by a crowd, only to turn around soon after to find he was the only person still there. Sets rarely lasted more than fifteen minutes.

Though it's sometimes conflated with punk, No Wave was resolutely anti-punk. "Sex Pistols has Chuck Berry in it," says J. G. Thirlwell, who performs as Foetus. "This didn't have Chuck Berry in it." Its goal was to save music by killing off everything in it that was familiar, and safe, and pleasing. No

Wave found its home on St. Marks Place in part because one of the Jerks, Bob Quine, lived at no. 73. Quine played on what many consider Lydia Lunch's best album, *Queen of Siam*. When he wrote songs with other musicians and couldn't find time to meet, they communicated by hiding cassette tapes for each other in a drop behind a brick in his building's façade.

No Wave also belonged on St. Marks Place because, perhaps more than any other street in the country, it has for so long provided a home for cultural death and rebirth, like a pop-culture version of India's burning ghats. "St. Marks Place really did seem kind of like the graveyard that always accepts more ghosts," says Lunch, "and always regurgitates more life, and you just can't kill it."

19

RAIN-WET ASPHALT HEAT

For the punks of St. Marks Place, the East Village was the greatest haunted house in the world. Richard Blum, the Bronx kid who had grown up going to shows at the Fillmore, had by the mid-seventies reinvented himself as Handsome Dick Manitoba, lead singer of the Dictators. He was happy to see the street become seedy: "The danger kept people away, and kept this neighborhood for *us*: the black sheep, the artists, the bohemians, the ne'er do wells, the druggies."

"It was a slum," writes Richard Hell, "but it was where we wanted to live because it was cheaper than anywhere else while also hosting the best bookstores and movies and drugs and people and music."

"In 1975, I lived on St. Marks with four rooms and a fireplace for $125 a month," says bookstore owner Bob Contant. "We were getting $2.50 an hour. You could afford your own apartment. There were cheap restaurants where you could go on a date. There wasn't a stigma about being poor. Everybody was poor. The neighborhood was an exciting place to live."

The journalist Joel Millman describes that time on St. Marks as heavenly. He was driving a cab between roadie gigs. His perfect day was rising at noon, going to the Baczynsky Meat Market for ham on rye with a pickle, to St. Mark's Cinema to eat his sandwiches while watching a movie and drinking a beer, and maybe to Gem Spa for a hard-to-get UK music magazine. Then he'd pick up his cab and work until 6 a.m.

But while the decrepitude of the neighborhood was an aesthetic plus for the new arrivals, for the mostly working-class Polish, Ukrainian, and Puerto Rican families who had been there for decades, it was a soul-crushing grind. They tried to scratch out a living in the decaying, filthy city living alongside this nightmare in black leather. For once the Slavs and hippies and Beatniks were on the same side: the neighborhood was turning into a horror show and the addition of drunk, bespiked new neighbors was not helping.

"The punks were out on the street with boom boxes late into the night and we had two little kids who had to go to school in the morning," says Libby Forsyth, whose apartment overlooked the Holiday Cocktail Lounge. "I was the crazy lady with her raincoat on over her nightgown: 'I'm going to smash that radio!'"

Homeless people slept in lobbies. When night fell, muggers lurked behind seemingly every mailbox. Where once Angela Jaeger had attended a child's birthday party at the Electric Circus and walked down St. Marks Place with her sister holding their father's hand and coming across "kids sitting in a circle holding daffodils," now she saw drug dealers, hookers, and muggers. The closest thing to the hippies now were the Hare Krishnas who paraded down St. Marks Place to their holy place in Tompkins Square Park: the tree where the Hare Krishna mantra was first chanted in the West on October 9, 1966, with Allen Ginsberg in attendance. With their shaved heads and jangly trips up and down the street, they were still working toward peace on earth. Everyone else was preoccupied with day-to-day survival.

On December 23, 1974, a thirty-year-old man named William Connell took two hostages at his three-room, second-floor apartment at no. 102 St. Marks, where he'd lived for the better part of a decade. The hostages were William Muller, a spring-water deliveryman, and Andrew Sach, the building's agent. In the apartment Connell held five rifles, a shotgun, six handguns, a mortar, more than two thousand rounds of ammunition, and four hand grenades. Detectives believed that Connell was an illegal arms dealer and that he planned to blow up the Statue of Liberty. He was killed in a shootout at the apartment.

Around this time, the writer Luc Sante moved into the front apartment on the sixth floor of no. 109 and stayed for a year and a half. He felt lucky to have his own bathroom; the back apartment's toilet was in the hall. When it rained, the apartment flooded. A robber somehow climbed through a tiny window from the airshaft—miraculously missing the rent money sitting out in cash, but stealing Sante's cameras. And one windy day in March, a window flew right out of the frame. "I knew my building might fall down at any moment," says Sante. "But so what? I was twenty-three."

Outside of the East Village's borders, the national news was bleak: inflation, serial killers, American hostages in Iran, Pol Pot, the killing of student protesters at Kent State. The stock market crashed in 1973 and 1974. The United States suffered a gas crisis and President Nixon was forced to resign in August 1974. In cities, crime rates soared, and those who could afford to leave fled to the suburbs. During this period, New York City lost more than eight hundred thousand residents.

Contributing to the Lower East Side's emptiness may have been a longtime isolationist immigration policy. "'White flight' wouldn't have been so bad if they'd been letting in the white immigrants who desperately wanted to come here," says immigration expert and former East Village resident Joel Millman, who now works in Geneva as the press officer for the International Organization for Migration. Between 1945 and 1965, hundreds of thousands of Europeans had been denied entry to the United States because of quotas.

In Congress, Newark's Peter Rodino, a hero of the Watergate hearings, worked to reform the immigration quota system and allow in more Southern Europeans. But reform came too late for the Lower East Side, which by the late sixties was emptying out. And the work New Yorkers did was undergoing a fundamental change. Various industries—including the Garment District a couple of miles uptown, to which gangster Dopey Benny Fein had repaired after his St. Marks Place shootout—went into steep decline.

"It is no coincidence that the period when the cities began to fall apart was the same period during which immigration hit its lowest level," says Millman. "There was no new demand to occupy the empty apartments, so they burned. There was no one to buy the things in the stores, so they closed. There were 260,000 Italians waiting for visas. Can you imagine what [even] 20,000 Italians could have done to the Lower East Side?"

Formerly elegant Astor Place, the site of the fatal 1849 riot and the unofficial plaza for Cooper Union, became something out of Bosch. Crack dealers, burglars selling TVs on dirty blankets, recently released mental hospital patients, New Wavers with huge hair—they milled around the foreboding cube of the *Alamo*. Tompkins Square Park was off-limits to children. It was full of junkies shooting up and sleeping out, prostitutes, criminals, and desperate people trading their food stamps for money—seven dollars cash bought ten dollars of groceries.

Punk-fashion icon and Trash and Vaudeville store manager Jimmy Webb, spirit animal of St. Marks Place, came to the city in 1975 from a little town in upstate New York near Troy. A serious heroin addict at the time, he lived on Fourth Street and Avenue D. There were camps in empty lots all over the neighborhood, Webb recalls: "makeshift shanties out of cardboard boxes which became a whole culture. They had windows, TVs."

Drug addicts commandeered the bathroom at the Leshkos' coffee shop and chased the Ukrainian seniors from the Tompkins Square Park benches. And yet, Webb says, there was something seductive about the junkies' world beyond just the drugs.

"Even amongst us, your drug addict culture or your thief culture or your criminal culture, everyone thrived off of what everyone else was," says Webb. "There was such an explosion of beauty and art and culture. The Puerto Rican men on the Lower East Side, with all the religious candles on the ground, Christmas lights up all year in the window, playing dominos—*everyone* was welcome, everyone. If you were a white boy or a tranny and they were cooking rice on a barbecue, you were welcome to come eat. The biggest words in the streets were *todo bien* [all clear, no cops]."

Webb worked at a gay bar and sometimes went to the St. Mark's Baths: "I never had sex in there in my life, it just wasn't my thing, but sometimes I would go there to sleep because I was kind of homeless at times."

Homeless people on St. Marks Place would take any unlocked door as an invitation to camp out. They often turned vestibules and doorways into toilets. "We cleaned up after the four homeless people on our corner every day for five, six, seven years," recalls Anthony Scifo, who has run a shoe store at St. Marks and First for the past thirty-five years.

At the age of twenty-two, writer Arthur Nersesian, whose family was from the Lower East Side, got a job as an usher at the St. Mark's movie theater on Second Avenue. "It was a crash pad for all the junkies and alcoholics," he recalls. "It was a difficult job. There were lunatics with weapons. I got $3.35 an hour to hoist psychotics jerking off out of the theater. There were fights breaking out during the movie. I was living with my girlfriend, a Cooper Union student, on Eleventh between

Jimmy Webb at Trash and Vaudeville, ca. 2013. Photo by Rick Edwards.

First and Second. I threw one guy out and went home to find
him sleeping in my lobby. I had to throw him out at work and
then at home."

The St. Mark's Cinema, October 1978. The St. Mark's Playhouse, housing the Negro Ensemble Company, was on the second floor. Photo by Ann Sanfedele.

The panhandlers multiplied and became a familiar cast of characters in each block's drama. One homeless man in the neighborhood, a former prizefighter, wore colorful, feminine clothes and called out to passersby, "Little bit change?" The drunkest and most charismatic was Vincent, who claimed to be from a Native American tribe in Canada.

One evening, Al Forsyth, who'd moved with his wife Libby to St. Marks between First and Second in the mid-seventies (they now live in the building with their two grown daughters and grandchildren), came home to find Vincent and his girlfriend in his vestibule, finishing up a meal and getting ready to go to sleep. Forsyth kicked them out, only to hear Vincent mutter, "I'll just burn this building down." Forsyth decided to befriend him. "Hey Vincent," he said the next time they met,

"I know you're drunk, but when you're sober, can you keep an eye on the building?"

For years, Vincent would take his watchman job seriously, reporting to Forsyth on the state of things. One winter in the middle of a snowstorm, Forsyth found Vincent almost completely concealed by snow, wedged into a nook in the side of a building on Second Avenue. "Can I get you some coffee?" Forsyth asked, to which Vincent responded, "No, get me a drink!"

You couldn't walk more than a few blocks without seeing at least one junkie nodding out. Columbia University sociologists embedded themselves in a storefront for three years in the late seventies to write a detailed account of the culture of Alphabet City and the logistics of the drug trade, whereby young people from the projects serviced the drug appetites of the young people from around the city who came to the Village to play. The most eloquent contributor to the resulting *Hispanic Study Report* writes about how the drug dealers on the corner were "slowly revealed to us as the most visible and vulnerable extensions of struggling households."

She describes how the boys enthusiastically rode bikes into oncoming traffic, their reckless vitality in contrast to "the dead-end setting of the street . . . the cool stench yawning from peeling entrance ways and the hum of biting insects, spawned in stagnant backyards and cellars."

Between the poor dealers and the desperate addicts, theft was rampant. "We parked on the east side of Tompkins Square Park," says Al Forsyth. "Once I got into the van and started it up and there was something dragging on the bottom. I went out and took a look. Someone had propped up the car on milk crates and taken off two tires. Everyone back home loved that story."

The seventies East Village provided a grimy backdrop for books and movies. Theresa, the doomed heroine of the novel

Looking for Mr. Goodbar, moves in with her older sister on St. Marks Place. Their neighbors in the building include three androgynous fashion plates with shoulder-length blonde hair and jeans worn tight in the back, who have "that look that was just becoming commonplace on the streets of New York—of having been someplace that made them realize that earth was a two-bit town."

In Yuri Kapralov's 1974 novel *Once There Was a Village*, an aging Russian artist in a mental ward avoids "The Kid," "a totally flipped-out hippie they dug up somewhere on St. Marks and brought here along with his one hundred thousand lice." Kapralov's seventies East Village is full of predators like Jack, who kidnaps and drugs young runaways, then sells them to houses of prostitution.

In former St. Marks resident Michael Brownstein's novel *Self-Reliance*, Roy describes the street he sees out his window as: "Poverty-stricken Puerto Ricans and paranoid Ukrainians, dazed hippies resentfully aging, venomous bikers and junkies, desperado Vietnam veterans with shaved heads and cancelled eyes—these were the residents of the era." Nihilists wore "Let's Do It" T-shirts, commemorating the last words of murderer Gary Gilmore before he was executed by firing squad in 1977.

Piles of trash bags accumulated on street corners. Excavation for the proposed Second Avenue subway had begun in 1972, but with no money to continue, the work was abandoned, leaving booby-trap pits along the avenue. Mayor Abe Beame appealed to President Gerald Ford for help making payroll for the city's policemen and garbage men. Ford declined to send aid, prompting the infamous *Daily News* headline, "Ford to City: Drop Dead."

To the east of St. Marks, fires burned nearly every night. Buildings were torched for the insurance money. Landlords who couldn't afford to heat or repair their buildings just walked away. Windows were boarded up. Pigeons colonized century-old brownstones. Graffiti covered subway cars. Dog feces befouled the streets, as this was in the days before the so-called "pooper scooper" law, which required owners to clean up after their dogs. In the blackout of 1977, chaos reigned and stores were looted. The Son of Sam serial killer terrorized the city in 1976 and 1977 with his random murders and his letters to the press promising more mayhem.

"It wasn't just the criminality that kept you radar-alert, the muggings and the subway-car shakedowns," writes James Wolcott, "it was the crazy paroxysms that punctuated the city, the sense that much of the social contract had suffered a psychotic break." Wolcott moved into a rent-stabilized studio on St. Marks Place in 1979, when, according to his memoir *Lucking Out*, the street was still "the Sunset Strip of bohemian striving and slumming."

Allen Ginsberg, living just a few blocks away, could often be seen walking down St. Marks Place to buy a newspaper at Gem Spa, which showed up in poems written by him and others throughout the seventies. "Rain-wet asphalt heat, garbage curbed cans overflowing," Ginsberg wrote in a poem about a night of fruitless cruising beneath a chemical vapor. It ends: "Back from the Gem Spa, into the hallway, a glance behind / and sudden farewell to the bedbug-ridden mattresses piled soggy in dark rain."

"Shots rang out in the neighborhood somewhere," wrote Edmund White of New York in the '70s. "Traffic lights blinked out of sync with each other. Old people on chromium walkers were mugged."

People expected to be mugged, and some carried decoy "mug money" of five or ten dollars in various pockets, the idea being that the mugger could be given a small amount while the rest remained safely in your sock. Theatre 80 on St. Marks was held up repeatedly at knifepoint and gunpoint. Citing fear of crime, W. H. Auden left New York in 1972 and died the next

Allen Ginsberg in front of Gem Spa, winter 1978–1979. Photo by Harvey Wang. Courtesy of Harvey Wang and the Allen Ginsberg Estate.

year, on September 29, 1973, the same week my parents moved to St. Marks Place.

In July 1978, near the end of a renovation that had cost half a million dollars, a young summer worker with a welding torch sparked a massive fire at St. Mark's Church, destroying nine of the church's stained-glass windows and causing part of the roof to collapse and fall into the main sanctuary.

The violent East Village made national news. In 1981, a criminal named Jack Henry Abbott, who had charmed his way into the literary establishment by sending eloquent letters to Norman Mailer from jail, moved into a flophouse not far south of St. Marks Place on the Bowery. Six weeks into his stay, at the end of a night of uptown literary parties, he stopped in to the twenty-four-hour hangout the Binibon three blocks below St. Marks for breakfast.

The Binibon's co-owner was Paul Delaney, who'd been hanging around St. Marks Place since childhood. His mother was an actress and singer who performed as Lori Jon. His godfather was the director Robert Altman. As a teenager, Delaney had smoked joints with his actor father on the patio of a fish and chips place on St. Marks and Second Avenue. His father also, he recalls, dosed him with acid at the Electric Circus during a Jefferson Airplane concert. Delaney's fifth stepfather was the jazz bassist Billy Popp, who played at the Five Spot.

Delaney had just finished two degrees on the GI Bill. Since then, he'd worked for UPS, driven a taxi, and sold African jewelry. Eventually he ended up in the restaurant business,

St. Mark's Church-in-the-Bowery on fire, July 27, 1978.
Photo by Steve Kagan, a photo intern at the *Village Voice* that summer.

opening the Binibon on a lonely stretch of Second Avenue full of men's shelters and refrigerator warehouses. But business was looking up: the rock club CBGB had opened nearby, and guys from the band Earth, Wind & Fire were dating his waitresses.

On that early morning in July, Jack Henry Abbott went to the back of the restaurant to use the bathroom. A twenty-two-year-old, newly married waiter named Richard Adan told him the men's room was for employees only, and that customers had to pee outside against the wall by the dumpster. This was, in fact, protocol at the Binibon, but Abbott thought Adan was teasing him. They got into a fight, which quickly escalated. Outside the restaurant, Abbott stabbed Adan, killing him.

"I was packing my kids in the car to go to Canada that morning," says Delaney. "My partners had been on vacation three times. I hadn't been once. My partner was supposed to be on that shift. He put his brand-new son-in-law on the shift instead. [Adan] had only been there once before for an hour for training. He came off hard, told Abbott to get out. He foolishly went outside with the guy, and the guy pulled out an eight-inch blade."

By coincidence, the very next day, a review of Abbott's first book, *In the Belly of the Beast: Letters from Prison*, appeared in the *New York Times*. It was a rave: "awesome, brilliant, perversely ingenuous." The critic also wrote: "His prose is most penetrating, most knife-like, when anger is its occasion."

20

ONE BIG INVITATIONAL

The St. Mark's Baths, a four-story brownstone at no. 6 St.
Marks almost indistinguishable from the surrounding
buildings except for its fairly grand first-floor dimensions, had
been a disreputable bathhouse and rooming house for generations of locals lacking hot water or a permanent residence.
When the Baths, an unofficial homosexual meeting spot for
decades, went formally gay in 1979, it remained modest on
the outside. A black door read "The New St. Marks" in simple
white block letters on one side and "Six St. Marks Place" on the
other. But inside, the space was a pornographic palace.

Owner Bruce Mailman* spared no expense redecorating
the "New St. Mark's Baths"—a gay pilgrimage spot nicknamed
"Our Queen of the Vapors"—in primary colors with spotlights
and elaborate tile work. In one pool room on the ground floor,
walls were lined with sparkling white tiles accented with pale
green ones. Men could rent a locker for seven dollars for eight

---

* Mailman also owned popular gay disco The Saint, which opened in the
old Fillmore East in 1980 with a 4,800-square-foot dance floor under
a ceiling filled with a planetarium-like star projection. Men met on the
dance floor and then repaired to the balcony to have sex. Early in the
AIDS epidemic, some called the illness "Saint's disease" because many of
those infected were regulars at the club. (Randy Shilts, *And the Band Played
On* [New York: Macmillan, 2007], p. 149; "Rich Wandel: A Brief History
of the Saint," OutHistory.org; David W. Dunlap, "As Disco Faces Razing,
Gay Alumni Share Memories," *New York Times*, August 21, 1995.)

hours, or a private room for a few dollars more. Then they could cruise the various rooms for partners. In his poem "The St. Mark's Baths," Tom Savage writes about trying to find the men who are "not too old to be repulsive; not too young to be conceited." "Guys would be lined up around the block to get in," recalls St. Mark's Bookshop's Terry McCoy—even celebrities. One neighbor recalls seeing the dancer Rudolph Nureyev "duck-footing in there." Different rooms catered to different sexual proclivities. On the top floor: "You could pretend you were in jail, and of course the jailer was for sale," says one former patron. "You could have sex in the cab of a truck!" says another, his voice turning wistful. "I never knew how they got that truck cab up there."

The narrator of the novel *Eighty-Sixed* goes there on New Year's Eve 1980. "I managed to come at the stroke of midnight with my third companion of the night," he says. "I took the

THE LARGEST BATH HOUSE IN THE COUNTRY
6 SAINT MARKS PLACE (8TH ST. AND 3RD AVE.) NEW YORK. 212-473-7929.

Ad for the New St. Mark's Baths, ca. 1979. Reprinted with permission of Boris Vallejo, illustrator.

subway home at two in the morning, the car littered with beer cans and streamers."

According to gay nightlife impresario Scott Ewalt, one short, hairy, older regular at the Baths was always naked except for a leather mask over his face. People joked that the masked man was New York City's bachelor mayor Ed Koch.

In 1969, less than a mile to the west of St. Marks, a group of gay-bar patrons at the Stonewall Inn defied a police raid. The gesture spurred a protracted battle between the gay community and law enforcement that's often hailed as the start of the gay rights movement. Throughout the sixties, gay bashing had been a regular occurrence even in the supposedly progressive East Village. A reporter profiling transgender Andy Warhol superstar Jackie Curtis wrote, "Walking down St. Mark's Place at midnight with Jackie offers a revelation about the long-haired political activists who regard themselves as street guerillas of the new people's revolution. They jeer at and threaten Jackie with the backlash zeal of a bunch of uptight goons." Curtis strode through the mob, chiffon scarf waving like a banner, "with the confidence of one who knows that she is riding the wave of the future."

Novelist Perry Brass found similar homophobia among supposedly peace-and-lovey hippies at the St. Mark's Free Clinic (no. 44), which treated "hip people problems," like bad acid trips and sexually transmitted diseases. "I was dating this guy who's still a friend of mine—it's been forty-five years—and he told me that he felt he had gonorrhea. The two of us went to the clinic. The doctor who came in to treat us went into a rant about how homosexuals were like promiscuous women. He said, 'You use your asshole like women use their vaginas! You don't know what's been in there before you. You have to stop doing this!' Here was this guy who was in early middle age with a ponytail, thinking he was so hip. I thought he was a jerk."

As the seventies went on, gay sexuality thrived more openly

on the street. In his 1978 novel about gay nightlife, *Dancer from the Dance*, set largely on St. Marks Place, Andrew Holleran wrote that instead of Poles and hippies, "St. Mark's Place now belongs to hair stylists, pimps, and dealers in secondhand clothing." In the novel, Holleran depicts a young gay heartthrob named Malone who lives above the former Electric Circus. Each night, Malone (a man, though he sometimes takes a feminine pronoun in the book) changes clothes countless times before having a meal and then, "just as the Polish barbers who stand all evening by the stoop are turning back to go upstairs to bed, she [Malone] slips out of her hovel—for the queen lives among ruins; she lives only to dance—and is astride the night, on the street, that ecstatic river . . . down into the dim, hot subway, where she checks the men's room."

In the book, Malone and his friends hook up throughout the city, cruising clubs, bathhouses like the New St. Mark's Baths, and outdoor areas like Stuyvesant Park a few blocks north on Second Avenue and Fifteenth Street. The primary consequences are heartbreak and exhaustion. Journalist Carl Swanson (who lives on St. Marks between First Avenue and Avenue A) calls the book "*Gatsby* for the cusp-of-AIDS era."

Many of those who indulged at the Baths were also part of the new East Village art scene, a do-it-yourself movement that Craig Owens nicknamed "Puerilism" in a 1984 essay. Storefront galleries and improvised performance spaces were filled with the work of artists like photographer Nan Goldin (her subjects: those who stayed up late, Peter Schjeldahl said, "to fit into each day its maximum number of mistakes") and performance artist Karen Finley.

With the Dom, Balloon Farm, Electric Circus, and Fillmore East gone, young artists created their own funhouse-mirror versions, acting out their fantasies of what St. Marks Place once was and could be again. The art scene became a playground modeled on Andy Warhol's St. Marks Place and peopled by artists like Jean-Michel Basquiat, Kenny Scharf, Joey Arias, Wendy Wild, John Sex, and Keith Haring.

Gallery owner James Fuentes was born on the Lower East Side before moving to the Bronx. Fuentes, who now runs his own gallery on Delancey Street, liked the DIY ethos of the eighties galleries: "They were taking matters into their own hands. They were rejecting the minimal and conceptual art of the sixties and seventies. There was a very strong feeling of activism and socially engaged work. It was an art world pre-commerce, before the boom time when Wall Street guys were buying. This was a sliver of a moment of social awareness." The scene rallied in opposition to President Reagan and the conservative America he represented. East Village artists identified with one another in opposition to the rest of the country—a land that in their eyes was full of homophobes willing to let New Yorkers die by the thousand.

Keith Haring grew up in Kutztown, Pennsylvania, as the oldest of four children. His mother was a housewife and his father worked for AT&T. Haring studied at New York's School of Visual Arts from 1978 to 1980. He drew TVs, dancing people, penises—all of them in a distinctive, radiant style; and he drew them everywhere—on subway cars, building walls, posters, discarded furniture, and on the singer Grace Jones's body. He campaigned against drugs—his "Crack Is Wack" mural survives on a handball court along the Harlem River Drive—and for gay acceptance.

Mostly he was known for his prolific images of cartoon babies. "The reason that the 'baby' has become my logo or signature," Haring once explained, "is that it is the purest and most positive experience of human existence. . . . The feeling of holding a baby and rocking and singing them to sleep is one of the most satisfying feelings I have ever felt."

Though a relatively new arrival, Haring felt at home in the East Village, which had evolved an identity scruffier and scrappier than the comparatively wealthy, clean-cut, and muscle-bound gay scenes in the West Village and Chelsea. Haring admired William S. Burroughs and loved that the author of *Naked Lunch* had lived for a time on St. Marks Place at the Valencia (no. 2). He defended the East Village as a special place with an important history. In 1980, Haring used a stencil to spray-paint the phrase "Clones Go Home" on the western borders of the East Village. He hoped to scare away those whom he felt weren't true East Villagers. (Some called it apt when, in 2015, the foot of a large green Keith Haring sculpture installed at St. Marks Place and Third Avenue was accused of clonking a texting NYU student in the head.) "We felt the East Village was a different kind of community," he said, "which we didn't want too cleaned up in the way of the West Village." Note that he was a white, middle-class college student from the suburbs who had been in New York for just two years when he decided the East Village's integrity was his to protect.

Haring felt at home at Club 57, a punk-art venue at no. 57 inspired by Dada, Godard movies, exploitation films, and vaudeville. Entrance fees were two to five dollars for theme nights like "Putt-Putt Reggae," "A Night at the Opry," model-plane making, lady wrestling, and a prom for people who didn't go to their own proms. The mistress of ceremonies, actress Ann Magnuson, lived on St. Marks and Avenue A from 1979 to 2003 after having fallen in love with St. Marks Place the first time she saw Tish and Snooky's Manic Panic. "They had a poster of Farrah Fawcett in the window," Magnuson says. "It had been defaced in a hilarious way. I think she had a paper bag on her head. I thought, 'I want to know those people.'"

Haring hosted a "Club 57 Invitational," at which everyone was welcome to make art. "[The Invitational] was typical of the scene," says Magnuson, "inclusive, encouraging, and open-minded." Nick Zedd's favorite regular event was "Monster Movie Night": every Tuesday they would show the worst monster movie they could find. Magnuson started the "Ladies' Auxiliary of the Lower East Side," her take on the Junior League to which her mother had belonged. "It was part of a sincere desire to bond with the gals of the scene," she says.

One night, a poet who goes by the name Sparrow (and who a decade later would run for president, campaigning in front of Gem Spa with signs like, "Don't eat Pez; Sparrow for Prez" and "Sparrow, fly to the Oval Office") walked into Club 57 just as a performance of *The Wizard of Oz* was concluding. Holly Woodlawn, the transgender Warhol actress whom Lou Reed immortalized in the song "Walk on the Wild Side," stood center stage. Surrounding her, Sparrow says, were "the Tin Man, the Scarecrow, the Cowardly Lion, and a few Munchkins singing 'Somewhere Over the Rainbow.' It was your basic high-school production–plus-transvestite. As Holly pronounced those sacred words: 'And the dreams that you dare to dream really do come true,' we all felt beacons of hope."

On "Elvis Memorial" night, someone (Magnuson thinks it was one of the "juvenile delinquents" from the home down the street) sprayed beer on the air conditioner, causing a short that started a small fire and sent dozens of people dressed as Elvis streaming out onto St. Marks Place. "Everyone started getting on the fire trucks in their rockabilly outfits, singing and doing Elvis impersonations," recalls Magnuson. "When the police arrived it wasn't as much fun, but the firemen seemed to enjoy it."

The mood at Club 57 and related clubs around the Lower East Side in those days was highly sexual. Artist Kenny Scharf has said that sometimes he'd look around and realize he'd slept with everyone in the room. At the Lower East Side space ABC No Rio, naked performers once chased the audience down the street while flinging horse manure at them. John Bernd's tighty whitey–clad Go-Go Boys danced for raucous crowds at a performance space in the former elementary school P.S. 122.

Club 57's resident opera-singing performance artist Klaus Nomi lived at no. 103. Kenny Scharf lived at the back of 418 East Ninth Street, and could hear Nomi's voice carry through the courtyard when he practiced. Nomi was, in the words of former St. Marks resident Mark Howell, "a little guy with a mystery and beauty about him, a ghostlike presence in his Kabuki makeup." Howell says he always loved seeing him "the next morning at the grocery store with no makeup on and his hair plastered down."

It hit this close-knit community especially hard when several people on the scene, including Nomi, began to get very, very sick. "It certainly freaked the hell out of everybody," says Magnuson. More and more artists grew weak and some began to die. Most of the stricken were gay.

Performance artist and Club 57 performer Klaus Nomi in 1980, three years before he died of AIDS. Photo by Harvey Wang.

In January 1982, the strange "gay cancer" gained a new name, GRID ("gay-related immune deficiency"). That summer, the disease was renamed "acquired immune deficiency syndrome," or AIDS. Doctors had little information about what the disease was and exactly how it spread. Fear fed homophobia. The nightly news reinforced East Villagers' sense that they were living on an island that the rest of the country wished could be cut loose and pushed out to sea.

New Yorkers were outraged by national apathy in the face of the plague killing their friends. Worse, they were terrified by the Reagan administration's seeming disregard for their lives. Some in the city at that time believed that the government was on the verge of setting up internment camps for those who'd been diagnosed.

Playwright Larry Kramer held a meeting and asked half of those in attendance to stand up. "You're all going to be dead in six months," he said. "Now what are we going to do about it?" In March 1987, he founded the activist group ACT UP, the AIDS Coalition to Unleash Power. ACT UP held fierce "Silence = Death" marches. Another group, Gay Men's Health Crisis, paired those dying of AIDS with "buddies" who volunteered to take care of them.

One of the most public victims of AIDS was the New Jersey–born artist David Wojnarowicz, who lived at 189 Second Avenue. A former hustler, Wojnarowicz made work largely about alienation, but he also had a sense of humor. Once the artist collected an army of East Village cockroaches, pasted little triangle ears on their heads and cotton tails on their backs, and dropped them off at an art gallery to wobble around. He called them "cock-a-bunnies."

Tom Rauffenbart has said that the first time he met Wojnarowicz was when they had sex in the bathroom of the Bijou Theater on Third Avenue in 1985. The first words they spoke, after having sex, were about how Rauffenbart had lived in the East Village since the 1960s. "You must have seen a lot of changes," replied Wojnarowicz.

St. Mark's Baths worker Jay Blotcher kept a diary. "I meet my guest at the foot of the steps, bearing two towels and a cup of Lube, and take him to his personal fuck cubicle," writes Blotcher of his first day of work, on February 25, 1983. "Sometimes a 50-cent tip, more often not. The most unattractive part amid all this glamor is cleaning the rooms. In the Age of AIDS can I really afford to handle cum-and-crap stained sheets and overturned bottles of poppers? Eight lonely hours of this dirt and darkness, and I was finished!"

Bruce Mailman struggled to be a responsible bathhouse owner in the AIDS era. He started a policy of handing out free condoms and safe-sex literature to patrons. He told the *New York Times*, "Am I profiting from other people's misery? I don't think so. I think I'm running an establishment that handles itself as well as it can under the circumstances."

And yet, misinformation about AIDS flourished. Responding to a reader letter, downtown scene queen Cookie Mueller said in her *East Village Eye* column "Ask Dr. Mueller" that AIDS was nothing to worry about. "If you don't have it now, you won't get it," she wrote. "By now we've all been in some form of contact with it. . . . Not everybody gets it, only those predisposed to it." She herself would die from AIDS a few years later.

Klaus Nomi died of AIDS in 1983. "We didn't know who Klaus Nomi was," says Barbara Sibley, who followed her NYU-student sister, *Widow Basquiat* author Jennifer Clement, from their home in Mexico to no. 13, and today runs the Mexican restaurant La Palapa at no. 77. "To us then he was just the creepy guy who was dying next door. That's when you didn't know what AIDS was yet. It was pure Russian roulette. I was flirting with people who had AIDS then. All dead."

Keith Haring at an ACT UP rally protesting Mayor Ed Koch's inactivity on AIDS, ca. 1989. Photo by John Penley. Reprinted courtesy NYU's Tamiment Labor Archive.

When Wojnarowicz died of AIDS at home on Second Avenue and Twelfth Street at the age of thirty-seven, an ACT UP affiliate group called The Marys staged the first political funeral of the AIDS crisis. The procession started at Wojnarowicz's loft and wound east through the East Village to Avenue A, then west to Cooper Union. Neighbors joined in until there were hundreds marching in the parade. They showed slides, including one of a dead body on the White House steps, and ended by burning an American flag with Wojnarowicz's name on it and throwing flowers into the pyre. (A more subdued memorial took place at St. Mark's Church that September.) When one member of The Marys died, he was given an open-casket wake in Tompkins Square Park.

In a way, Magnuson says, the anxiety around AIDS "made everyone burn brighter. People worked even more furiously. Certainly Keith Haring did. He was going gangbusters until the end." Haring died on February 16, 1990, at the age of thirty-one.

Some artists raged against the specter of death with glitter and posturing. Lavishly costumed performance artist Leigh Bowery was resplendent in blinking light bulbs, head-to-toe makeup, wigs, elaborate body stockings, and huge heels. The British raconteur Quentin Crisp (who moved to Fourth Street and Second Avenue at the age of seventy-two) walked through seas of punk kids with safety pins stuck in their jackets looking aristocratic in his lipstick, silk scarf, and jaunty hat.

Meanwhile, the East Village gay community's sparkly nightlife, a complex and defiant response to AIDS, was being packaged for sale around the country, minus the anger. Promoter Scott Ewalt says New York City's gay nightlife was trying to overcompensate for the horror of AIDS, but that the aesthetic was co-opted for mass culture without preserving any of that original awareness and energy.

"Madonna is the worst thing to ever come out of the East Village," says Ewalt. "You had Cristina, Debbie Harry, Phoebe Legere, and Cherie Currie from The Runaways playing with sex in a cynical type of way, and then Madonna just came along like a playground brat and took the best elements from those people and lost the irony along the way. It wasn't like she was mimicking a pop tart. She was a pop tart. When the eighties went mainstream with Madonna, it lost that edge and just became about rubber bracelets and lacquered bangs."

In 1983, Madonna went platinum. Two years later, by order of the New York City Health Department, the New St. Mark's Baths was shut down for good. The East Village art scene effectively ended with the stock market crash of 1987, which was also the year Warhol died. A few years after that, Baths owner Bruce Mailman died of AIDS. At his Astor Place Theatre memorial service, a slide projector clicked through images of Mailman and his friends from the days before any of them had become sick—a time that suddenly seemed very long ago.

21

THE PARABLE OF ARNIE AND FRITZ

Like any other nation, St. Marks Place has its favorite fairy tales. One is the story of a rich man named Fritz and a poor boy named Arnie.

"I hated that place," Arnie Weinberg (no. 70) says of Club 57, which he considered loud and lawless when he moved onto the street as a young man from upstate. "I called the cops on them all the time, and if they were there late at night I would pour industrial-grade ammonia on the steps right behind them and start cleaning."

A product of foster homes, Weinberg became a resident of the boys' home Kaplan House at no. 74 at the age of seventeen. He found work as an electrician and plumber. Lorcan Otway's mother hired him to work on no. 80. Weinberg moved into no. 130, which he says was "not a very nice place." He started bartending, but didn't like the "angel dust idiots." If St. Marks Place was paradise for most young people who landed there, for some, like him, it was a punishment.

As Weinberg walked down the street one morning, he saw a distinguished, if slightly potbellied and bestubbled, older man perched in a second-floor window of no. 68, sipping coffee from a red cup. A scion of the Duponts from Wilmington, Princeton class of 1947 graduate, and a onetime Marine drill sergeant who had served tours in Germany and Korea, Brokaw owned several buildings, including nos. 70, 50, and 40½.

"Looking for someone to work?" Weinberg yelled up to Brokaw.

"Yes, I am!" Brokaw called back. He immediately hired Weinberg to paint the building's railings.

"The rest," Weinberg says with a smile, "is history, or infamy."

Within a few years, Weinberg was Brokaw's right hand, handyman, and superintendent. "He would see me coming down the street a block away and call my name," Weinberg recalls. "His voice was so loud you could hear him over on Third Avenue."

Brokaw treated real estate as a game, and mentored others in the rules of play. Tom Birchard owns the popular Ukrainian restaurant Veselka, which recently celebrated its sixtieth anniversary on Ninth Street and Second Avenue. (He inherited the place from his ex-wife's parents.) Birchard says that when he was looking for a building to buy, Brokaw "jumped right in. He had me over to his apartment a few times. He had setup sheets from brokers . . . he'd show me what to look for, pitfalls."

Brokaw was always looking to move people into or out of buildings on the block. Weinberg recalls how an old Italian woman lived on the top floor of no. 68, paying next to nothing in rent. Brokaw was eager to take over her apartment and was often heard mumbling as she tottered in and out of the building with her groceries, "Any day now. . . . " Then he would shake his head and say, "That woman's going to outlive me."

"He said outrageous things but didn't mean them," says Brokaw's across-the-street neighbor Al Forsyth. For example, Brokaw delighted in cat-calling women he knew. Myrna Hall, who moved to St. Marks between First and Second Avenues in 1963, and still lives there, says when she walked by Brokaw would always lean out his window and whistle at her. "It was very embarrassing," Hall says. When medical problems caused his voice to falter, a neighbor gave him a thoughtful gift: a megaphone.

"Fritz had a formal Christmas party every year," Al Forsyth recalls. "He had these high ceilings and he'd have to go under the West Side Highway to buy a tree tall enough to touch the ceiling. He'd decorate with antique ornaments and big, old-fashioned bulbs. The ladies were told to wear long dresses. Arnie Weinberg would show up in tails, a turtleneck sweater, and combat boots, or a suit with a bow tie, ruffled purple shirt, and sneakers. The party started late and would be crowded. Brokaw liked good food and fancied himself a good cook, and he was a Francophile. He made Christmas pudding, which he would flambé and parade around over his head, calling, 'Wassail! Wassail!' Someone in the crowd would shout, 'Wassup!'"

Weinberg, now a shy, heavyset middle-aged man, can usually be found standing outside on St. Marks Place between First and Second Avenues—talking with friends in the neighborhood, taking out the trash, or walking his dog. Weinberg prides himself on his command of street lore. "That's where an accountant for the mafia was executed about twenty years ago in his apartment," he says, pointing to the top floor of no. 44. "This is where a baby got thrown out the window," he says, pointing to no. 57. "Here, at no. 51, with the flowers, is where the guy used to masturbate in his window. We took photos of him and said, 'Get off the block or we'll lynch your ass.' He moved." He points to a terrace and laughs. "That's where you'd see the woman Fritz called 'Udders,' because she was always sunning herself in a bathing suit that didn't stay on." The printer at no. 77 pulled a double-barreled shotgun on punks who peed on his property. "Give me a gun and I would have shot them myself," says Weinberg. "They were disrespectful."

Lorcan Otway of Theatre 80 describes Brokaw as a Goldwater Republican. "He was a great believer in the Horatio Alger story," says Otway. Republicans, of course, often cite the late-nineteenth-century novelist (who lived on St. Marks when Brokaw's oldest property was brand-new) because his rags-to-riches stories suggest that the meritocracy delivers wealth to people according to their hard work and talent rather than their class. "I would explain to him that just doesn't happen," said Otway. Brokaw insisted that it did, and went to great lengths to win the argument.

When Brokaw died unexpectedly on August 5, 1991, while on vacation in Europe, his will decreed that one of his buildings (no. 40½, which today houses Porto Rico Coffee) should go to his longtime handyman. Weinberg—a man who had arrived on the street as a poor, surly teenager—now held the deed to an expensive piece of Manhattan real estate.

"Fritz told me he was going to leave it to me," Weinberg says, "but I didn't believe him. He was that kind of a person. He treated me like I was his son, and I treated him like my dad. I also earned it. I worked for him twenty-one years."

"Fritz basically created a Horatio Alger story to prove that it could happen," says Otway. "Not to mention the fact that he was an extraordinarily nice guy."

22

THE ALL-CRAFT CENTER

Photographer Roberta Bayley, who lives between Second and Third, has every punk credential there is: she worked the door at CBGB, dated Richard Hell (who fondly describes her breasts in his memoir), and took iconic images of several bands at their peak, including Debbie Harry and Joey Ramone in bed together for a legendary *Punk* magazine comic strip. She also has, to this day, flawless two-tone hair. When she arrived on St. Marks Place in April of 1975, she found a five-room apartment for $125 a month, and was very happy there. But one summer morning in 1986, she looked out the window of her apartment and did not like what she saw.

Once again, a film crew had invaded. That in and of itself was nothing new. In the late seventies, the title song of the musical *Hair* had blared beneath her window for days. That had been pretty bad. The *Desperately Seeking Susan* shoot hadn't been fun either. Right across the street, they had shot the scene in which Madonna pulls a copy of *USA Today* out of a sidewalk kiosk—as *if* something as mainstream as *USA Today* would take root on St. Marks Place—and the pop star learns from the paper that a character played by none other than Richard Hell is dead.

Bayley had grudgingly accepted all of that. But this was a new circle of hell: having rented the basement of nos. 19–23, pop singer Billy Joel was filming the video for his 1986 hit song "A Matter of Trust."

"The song played for twelve hours straight at full volume," Bayley says. "You woke up at 8 a.m.: it was playing. And when you got home at 8 p.m.: it was still playing." Smiling, sweaty Billy Joel, with his peppy piano music and supermodel wife, was the antithesis of the sullen, black-clad punk ideal.

"Nothing against Billy Joel," Bayley said, noting that a guy who cashed his checks at the corner deli was thrilled to be cast in the video. But Joel's presence undermined the East Village's identity. There was nothing remotely cool about Billy Joel. When he commandeered the street for a full day of singing about the joys of long-term romance built on a solid foundation of mutual faith, it proved to cynics—those who identified St. Marks instead with Ramones values like "I Wanna Be Sedated"—that the commodification of 1980s music and culture was complete.

For the punks, Billy Joel was not the only annoyance to emerge from the new All-Craft center (nos. 19–23), a twenty-four-hour sobriety center. "You're happy about the motive behind it," says Bayley. "I'm sure some people were helped. But I liked the block better when it was very quiet."

A few years earlier, Joyce Hartwell had rented space at no. 20 from Charles Fitzgerald to offer Lady Carpenter home-improvement classes for women. Soon, it became an accredited college course at The New School. In 1976, a grant allowed Hartwell to offer classes to black and Latino women on welfare and with children to support. The program moved to nos. 19–23 not long after. Hartwell added a day-care center and called the complex the "All-Craft" center. Women coming out of Rikers Island prison, among others, could receive a range of social services and training for manual-labor jobs.

Hartwell had many successes. She placed some of the first women ever in the notoriously exclusive and male-dominated New York unions of building trades, including plumbing and

The Rev. Joyce Hartwell in front of All-Craft ca. 1998. Photo by Marilynn K. Yee/*New York Times*.

construction. In 1978, a woman on welfare from the Lower East Side became the first female carpenter with the Metropolitan Opera House. In 1976, Hartwell was featured in *Time* magazine's "Women of the Year" issue. Those she helped remember her with great fondness.

But Hartwell was a polarizing figure. Many of her former neighbors—even normally friendly and placid people—describe her as abrasive. She made enemies in the neighborhood, beyond those who resented her for attracting addicts and ex-cons to the street. Officers in the Ninth Precinct groaned when they were summoned to All-Craft, sure that Hartwell would greet them with vitriol. "I think she did a lot of good," says Charles Fitzgerald, "but she certainly didn't treat those of us around her on the street very well."

Hartwell's hostility toward her neighbors had roots in the

1960s, when she'd witnessed the dark side of the street's hedonism. As Stanley Tolkin's mistress, she had helped turn nos. 19–23 into an anchor of the hippie lifestyle, and even then she'd deplored the drug use she saw there. Now she hoped to undo some of the damage she believed the neighborhood's nightclubs, including the Dom, but especially the Electric Circus, had done. Where once young people had dropped acid and had sex in stairwells, they could now get sober.

All-Craft offered one hundred meetings a week, along with sober dances and social services. One of Hartwell's major legacies was her care for children who otherwise might have fallen through the cracks. At times, Hartwell housed more than fifty children on the top floor of no. 23, legally adopting many of them.

One of the young people who gravitated to All-Craft was a bright thirteen-year-old named Saretha "Sherry" Sotomayor, who lived at Fourteenth Street and Avenue B in an apartment with the bathtub in the kitchen.

"Drugs were everywhere," Sotomayor says of the neighborhood back then. "It was hard to walk anywhere and not see that taking place: addicts nodding out, someone making a sale, a cop stopping someone. Avenue B was really on fire when it came to drugs." The beefy cop known as Rambo (Michael Codella, who would write a memoir of that time, *Alphaville*) patrolled regularly, thanks to Operation Pressure Point—an NYPD anti-drug crackdown that put cops on the corners of Alphabet City. "He was friendly," says Sotomayor, noting that she would never have gone to the cops for help, but that it was still nice to know he was there.

After attending P.S. 61 on Twelfth Street between Avenues B and C, Sotomayor went to J.H.S. 60—the same school Joey Dick had attended in the 1950s. Sotomayor skipped eighth grade but began to struggle with depression. After attempting suicide, she was admitted to Bellevue Hospital, a mile up First Avenue, which had its own high school and mandatory weekly therapy sessions.

One of All-Craft's most popular events was an all-night alcohol- and drug-free disco. Sotomayor wanted to go, but there was a catch: "You had to attend teen group meetings in order to attend the disco, also known as the How Club. You'd have to sign in. Otherwise you couldn't go. Music was a big thing, and so was dancing. They had these major celebrations. There was a great big disco ball and a DJ booth on the top. It had a section where you could sit and relax. All kinds of music: Spanish, English, hip-hop, spaced out."

Wanting badly to attend the dance, Sotomayor went to a teen meeting. The first one was a shock. Here were kids from Alphabet City sitting in a room discussing their lives in a safe space where they were sworn to secrecy. Helped by a counselor and their peers, they talked about living with parents who smoked crack, of stealing, and of sexual abuse. "We were sharing experiences, getting feedback, and not worrying about what we said," says Sotomayor. "Most of our parents had some sort of addiction to drugs or selling drugs. Some had addiction to sex and abusive relationships. At that time it was taboo to tell anyone what you were going through."

The All-Craft teens knew that honesty outside of that safe space could have dire consequences. One kid said: "If my parents had cancer, I could ask for help and get it. But because they're addicts, if I ask for help, they go to jail and I go to a group home."

"Everyone considered her their godmother," says Sotomayor of Joyce Hartwell, who in the 1990s became a Unitarian minister and had people address her as Reverend. "If someone would introduce her it was as, 'my godmother, Joyce.'" Rev. Hartwell, once the Dom's door girl, now provided food and clothing for an army of children, going with them to appointments and making sure they went to school. Prostitutes, addicts, and assorted lowlifes still cycled in and out of the Valencia Hotel at no. 2, but the teens hanging out in front of All-Craft, Sotomayor recalls bitterly, were the ones who felt the brunt of neighbors' not-in-my-backyard hostility.

"We weren't perfect," says Sotomayor, "but All-Craft was an escape from the madness outside. We were a family. We were there for one another. We dealt with strong issues as kids—even a member finding out they were HIV-positive at such a young age. We grew up fast. Having one another made it easier."

In 1983, Hartwell introduced Narcotics Anonymous meetings to the Northeast. Crack addiction plagued Alphabet City, especially among women. One rumor was that it helped you lose weight. "A mother wouldn't think of putting a needle into her arm," says Hartwell, "but a five-dollar crack cigarette at the kitchen table? That seemed okay." Her counseling staff was primarily Latino women who had grown up on the Lower East Side, and she encouraged them to get tested for HIV. "The majority came back positive," says Hartwell, "which was heartbreaking for everyone. They were all mothers. It was horrendous. I went to all those funerals with their children. I started Positives Anonymous, a twelve-step program for people with AIDS." She also brought the All-Craft women to meet Larry Kramer, the head of ACT UP, and took groups of them and their children down to protests in Washington, D.C. She encouraged them to tell reporters how it felt to know they were dying and leaving their children behind, in the hopes that Ronald Reagan would listen to young mothers in a way that he had not listened to gay men.

All-Craft stayed open all day, every day. "If you got out of prison and you wanted to stay drug-free and your neighborhood or friends and family were in trouble, you came to St.

Marks," says Hartwell. "Midnight Miracles" meetings ran from midnight to two in the morning, when "Recovery After Hours" convened. On summer nights, with the windows wide open, passersby heard post-sharing applause pour out into the dark street.

One of many neighborhood people who got sober there was punk rocker and junkie Richard Manitoba, lead singer of the Dictators. "It was crazy!" says Manitoba of All-Craft. "It was old-school Spanish drug addicts, which I needed to see. As an obsessive IV drug user, I needed to see these guys from Avenue D saying, 'I sold heroin. I did eighteen bids in jail.' I was on my way there. You could get a hot cup of coffee and smoke a cigarette. It was a social thing. There was a fun aspect to getting clean and having a place to go."

When Marky Ramone finally convinced Joey Ramone to go with him to an AA meeting in 1990, the meeting was at All-Craft, in the former home of the Electric Circus, where Marky's band had played in high school. "Look, *Merk*," Joey said on the way out, "I'm not into this God crap." The band broke up in 1996 and Joey died of lymphoma a few years later, at the age of forty-nine.

Safe spaces were few and far between for children growing up in the eighties East Village. Jessica Forsyth says that every time she asked if she could go to the candy store alone, her mother would mention Etan Patz. (In 1979 the SoHo boy went missing on his first day of first grade and was never found.)* Outside, punk and hip-hop thundered from boom boxes. As a young girl, Forsyth kept the clock radio in her room turned to the easy-listening station. "When you live in a war zone," she explained, "you retreat to somewhere safe."

---

* In 2014 a man confessed to Etan Patz's murder, though as of this writing the body has never been found.

Ann and John Tyson moved to the Leshkos' building and had a daughter, Rachel. Rachel recalls setting up a lemonade stand on the block when she was nine. "I made $250 in two hours," she says, but she earned it. A bag lady with long blonde hair in a ratty ponytail and a broom handle she wielded like a wizard staff demanded that police shut down the stand. Instead, the officers bought lemonade. Hells Angels bikers also seemed to have Rachel's back, though they insisted on calling her "Sweetie Tits."

Ted Berrigan's sons Anselm and Eddie recall Mayor Ed Koch showing up once in the eighties in front of their home at 101 St. Marks to film a "Let's Clean Up New York" commercial. In the most famous of such public-service advertisements, from the late seventies, a man on a crowded subway drops a candy-bar wrapper and is glared at by his fellow passengers until he picks it up. Initially excited that they might get on TV in such a spot, the Berrigans were disappointed to find that Koch had brought in child actors to portray the neighborhood kids and hauled in his own trash.

"It was Upper East Side trash," says Eddie. During the filming, a neighbor yelled out, "Why don't you go somewhere *dirty*?" When the crew finally packed up and left, it left the garbage on the street—an unwitting echo of the Motherfuckers' dumping of East Village trash into the Lincoln Center fountain a generation earlier.

In the 1980s, there was a heightened fear of pedophilia. On St. Marks Place, rumors had it that predators were drawn to the street by the boys' homes. One alleged procurer of victims for pedophiles lived at no. 59. An *Eyewitness News* report estimated that in the late eighties, possibly a dozen boys trafficked by him were murdered. Hartwell learned that a superintendent between Second and Third Avenues was sexually abusing a number of neighborhood children and buying their silence. She also discovered that another neighborhood figure would sexually assault boys and then keep them from telling anyone by pointing at trash bags and saying, "Those are full of dead kids."

One local cop answered a call at an East Seventh Street apartment and found it filled with photo books of homemade child pornography. The resident—"a dirty sleaze"—was having a heart attack. The officer's superior, already on the scene, said, "This man is having a heart attack. Hurry and call an ambulance." And out of view of the gasping man, the superior shook his head while delivering the verbal order, as if to say: *For this slimeball, don't rush to get help.*

At the peak of the predation in the 1980s, a boy named Ben Laurence lived with his mother in an apartment on Stuyvesant Street. His mother worked from nine in the morning until five-thirty in the evening, making him a latchkey kid from junior high on. Down the block, the new NYU building Alumni Hall was going up, one of the first buildings to break height restrictions in the neighborhood.

One spring day, returning from sixth grade at a private school where he was a scholarship kid and miserable, Laurence arrived home and found out he'd misplaced his keys. (He was easily distracted and often lost things.) He walked down to Seventh Street, but his friends who were usually there weren't home. He went back and rang the super of his building, but the super wasn't there either. So he went to St. Marks Place and played video games. Having blown through his two dollars in quarters, he went back to his front stoop to wait the remaining hours for his mother to get home.

After a little while, a sleek black town car with tinted windows pulled up and double-parked in front of the building. It sat there for twenty minutes. Then a man in a suit and dark sunglasses got out and started staring at him. "Every once in a while, he would lean in and confer with the driver," recalls Laurence, "and then go back to watching me. After a while I started to get pretty nervous. I thought: *It's probably nothing, but it can't hurt to run.*"

He performed a calculation kids often made in the eighties: run against traffic so the car couldn't follow, risking a pursuit on foot; or run with traffic, hoping that the pursuer would get back in the car and get stuck at a red light. Laurence bolted off with the traffic toward Second Avenue. Sure enough, the man jumped in the car and gave chase.

Laurence raced onto St. Marks Place and ducked into a shop. "They had a few popular arcade games in the back that usually drew a crowd that was older and a little rough for my taste," he says. "But this time I didn't care. I wormed my way deep into a bunch of teenagers watching some aces play a game. I stayed there until I was sure my mom was home."

Besides dodging pedophiles, kids on the street had to run gauntlets of street hustlers. One of the rougher video gamers at the St. Marks arcades was John Spacely, a scrawny blond junkie with an earring, pointy white boots, and an eyepatch who was always on the block shaking down tourists. He lived for a while in an apartment at the corner of St. Marks and Second but seemed always to be outside, striding or skateboarding down the street, seeking a fix or a few dollars.

A punk scenester named Peter Nolan Smith who often drank with Spacely says Spacely once told him he knew who had really killed Nancy Spungen. Spungen was punk singer Sid Vicious's girlfriend, famously murdered at the Chelsea Hotel in 1978. Vicious was suspected. Spacely promised to tell all for just two dollars. Smith paid. They went to the Holiday Lounge at no. 75 and Spacely talked and talked—about everything but the murder. When at last Smith pressed him to reveal the killer's name, Spacely said he wasn't a snitch. Another day, another hustle.

"Here, come see my movie," Spacely said when handing out

pink flyers for the 1987 Lech Kowalski film *Gringo*. A more dramatic advertisement for the movie—a two-story-tall mural of Spacely, his cigarette dangling from his lips and through the *o* in "Gringo"—loomed on the side of no. 5. Local artist Art Guerra had designed the image and done the brushwork. During the job, Spacely, looking like an extra in a pirate film, frequently climbed the painter's sixteen-foot ladder to ask Guerra to buy him something, usually a large can of Budweiser. "I'd do drawings of him while he sipped his beer and sat there looking at me," says Guerra.

Dealers sold from a constellation of different apartments all over Alphabet City, as well as social clubs and bodegas. In *Gringo*, also known as *Story of a Junkie*, Spacely roams the neighborhood scoring and shooting heroin—something he also did when the cameras weren't rolling. The film opens with footage of Spacely reading a comic book on the street with a magnifying glass while in a voiceover he describes junk sickness: "It's like a chill you can't shake, like an ache you don't know where it comes from. It's like a good love affair: it's nice when it starts. Then it becomes fucked. Just like everything else." The movie shows him scoring and shooting up again and again, in various apartments and in Tompkins Square Park.

Spacely stops on the corner of First Avenue in front of the St. Marks Bar and Grill—a setting for the 1981 Rolling Stones video for "Waiting on a Friend"—and peers inside. Working the bar around that time was the comic Colin Quinn, later a cast member on *Saturday Night Live*. "It was rough," Quinn says of the bar. "You'd have to throw the junkies out of the bathroom. Then the Puerto Ricans would come in and fight, and when they left the Hells Angels would come in and fight. Everyone tipped in quarters. It was a lot of quarters, but it still didn't add up to much."

A later movie by the *Gringo* director, *Born to Lose*, shows Spacely engage New York Doll Johnny Thunders in a fistfight onstage

The *Gringo* mural of John
Spacely, painted by Art Guerra,
on the side of no. 5 ca. 1987.
Photo by Keith Meyers/*New York Times*.

at downtown hotspot the Mudd Club. It also shows him talking on his deathbed, his bleached hair grown out a flat brown.
One of the film's final shots finds Spacely on a metal slab. A
mortuary worker pushes the corpse into a cabinet and shuts
the door.

Throughout the eighties, violence hummed in the background
like TV static. On New Year's Eve 1982, Officer George Ackerman, the neighborhood's beloved, baby-faced beat cop, was
working in a radio car. He and his partner for the night picked
up a "psycho." Ackerman waited with the guy at Bellevue,
letting his partner take off. He was getting ready to call it a
day when he received word of a bombing at One Police Plaza.
Suddenly two fellow officers were brought in—one had been
blinded and the other had a serious injury to his leg. Ackerman, put into scrubs, had to sign for their guns and badges

and spend the night in the hospital with them, seeing a doctor enter with a saw to remove the one officer's leg. He learned that the small Puerto Rican nationalist group FALN had set five bombs around the city that day. The one that had taken his comrade's leg had been concealed in a Kentucky Fried Chicken box. Ackerman says leaving the hospital after dawn on New Year's Day 1983 was the low point of his time as an officer. And for the first time in all his years on the force, he started the day in search of a drink.

Ackerman was no stranger to death—"You'll never forget that smell," he remembers a veteran cop telling him after he had found his first dead body, the victim of an adventurous S&M sex act gone wrong. Every night seemed to bring another gruesome death to the East Village. Some cops took to calling it the "E-VIL."

One senseless tragedy occurred in the summer of 1985 at no. 32. At around 10:30 p.m. one night, a waitress at the Afghan restaurant Café Kabul at no. 34 found herself without the keys to her apartment next door. She asked Asamat, the twelve-year-old son of her boss, Shah Rahni, if he would help her get into her apartment. Asamat agreed, and they went up on the roof. There she tied one end of a clothesline around his waist and the other around a chimney. As she lowered him to her fifth-floor window, the line snapped, and he fell sixty feet down the airshaft. He died of his injuries at St. Vincent's Hospital.

In the Gringo mural building, no. 5, there was a restaurant called Sandra's and a punk clothing store called Enz, which sold clothes by designer Vivienne Westwood. The store was one of the many between Second and Third Avenues with an entrance a few steps down, providing a partially secluded area for homeless people to huddle or drunks to pass out. Enz's owner, Mariann Marlowe, lived on Sixth Street. Around

Memorial Day 1987, Marlowe was taking the day off when she got a call from one of her employees, Steve Firestone, complaining of a horrible smell. "They thought it was a dead dog," Marlowe says. She told Firestone to call the police. "When they came, they found that a man's head was in one garbage bag and the rest of him was scattered through other ones."

"The first bag they opened had a foot," says Firestone. "After that everything changed rapidly. We were ordered to stay in the shop, which stank something awful for hours. The street was immediately blocked off with tape. Loads of police cars came and the forensics guys came to continue the search through the bin. They came up with multiple body parts in different bags, which they were lining up on the sidewalk in front of the shop."

"My store didn't make any money for two months after that," says Marlowe. "Everyone was so spooked."

That wasn't even the worst East Village decapitation story of the decade.

In 1989, Daniel Rakowitz made the tabloids' front page. A long-haired, charismatic man who looked eerily like Charles Manson, Rakowitz hung around Tompkins Square Park with a pet rooster on his shoulder. The son of a Texan sheriff, he smoked copious amounts of pot, carried around *Mein Kampf*, and told everyone he was, according to one news report, "Christ or the antichrist, and sometimes, just the 'God of marijuana.'"

Community activist Curtis Sliwa, who lived across the street from the park, remembers him: "David Rakowitz would sit in the park with a chicken on his shoulder and he would come into the apartment building on Avenue A and knock on my door. He was like a male yenta. He would talk all kinds of nonsense. I would simmer him down. I would go out and sit on the steps with him and administer verbal Prozac."

In 1989, Rakowitz met a young dancer named Monika Beerle in Tompkins Square Park. They moved into an apart-

"Butcher of Tompkins Square Park" Daniel Rakowitz, with chicken, 1989. Photo by John Penley. Reprinted courtesy NYU's Tamiment Labor Archive.

ment together on Ninth Street and Avenue C. A month later, she disappeared. It came out that when she'd tried to evict him from their apartment, he slit her throat and cut her into pieces. He then reportedly cooked her into a stew and fed her to the homeless in the park. A squatter claimed to have found a human fingertip in his bowl.

In 1991, Rakowitz, nicknamed the Butcher of Tompkins Square Park, was found not guilty by reason of insanity. The killer's public defender was Denis Woychuk, who now owns the KGB Bar on Fourth Street and who wrote the book *Attorney for the Damned: A Lawyer's Life with the Criminally Insane*. Rakowitz responded to the verdict by telling the jury, "I hope to some-day smoke a joint with y'all." He's still imprisoned in the maximum-security mental hospital on Wards Island.

In this context, it's not surprising that the children of St. Marks in the 1970s and 1980s, myself included, tend not to have much nostalgia for the street of those eras. They grew up witness to an endless parade of murderers, pedophiles, and drug addicts. They were groped in movie theaters. They found used condoms and weapons in playground sandboxes. At random intervals, their homes incurred break-ins. It seemed that every night on the news, they learned of horrendous crimes happening right outside their front doors.

Their parents taught them to carry their keys poking out between their fingers in case they needed them for self-defense, to look both ways before entering vestibules, and to avoid walking too close to the buildings, lest they be grabbed into a darkened doorway—but also not too close to the parked cars, in case someone tried to throw them in the back of a van.

The romance of poverty and chaos held less glamour for native New Yorker children of that generation than it had for their parents. Some were perfectly happy when that particular St. Marks Place died and yuppies and generic businesses took over. Chain clothing stores may have been bland, with their crisp stacks of denim, racks of floral dresses, and arrays of plaid flannel shirts, but plenty of us who grew up in the East Village were almost intoxicated by this blandness, as if by an exotic new perfume. As a little girl there, I nurtured dreams of leaving New York and becoming a farmer. I would lie in my bed by the top-floor window at no. 53 that framed the scream-ing below and read books about permaculture.

As the nineties approached, freaks began to leave the street corners. Some just disappeared. One skinny, punked-out musician had performed in front of the bank on the corner of Second Avenue, next to the best quarter toy and gum-ball machines in the neighborhood, for what felt like years. He played the same few tones again and again—something vaguely resembling the harmonics in *2001: A Space Odyssey*—on an amplified instrument he seemed to have made himself. He would play for hours. Sometimes a child was with him, looking bored. Then one day I realized the man hadn't been there for years, and that his child was probably grown. But other East Village eccentrics did not slip away quietly. They went down fighting.

23

THE BOTTLE BRIGADE

In March 1988, the Gap set up shop on the corner of Second Avenue in a space vacated by Steve's Ice Cream and St. Mark's Cinema, reportedly paying a staggering $33,000 a month in rent. The store's Middle American sensibility was perceived by some as a direct threat to the neighborhood's culture of independence and weirdness. "When the Gap opened there, we were all dumbfounded," says Matthew Kasten, who had been directing drag shows around the corner.

The Gap soon had bricks hurled at its windows and feces deposited at its entrance—whether by a protesting anarchist or an apolitical homeless person, no one knew. Anarchists spray-painted anti-yuppie symbols on the glass. The 501 Gang, known for their mob-theft of pants around the city, rushed in and stole stacks of jeans.

A typical response to such bougie intrusions as the Gap was a screed in the *East Villager* newspaper by one Jonny Xerox, in both English and Spanish, addressed to the residents of the Lower East Side and titled, "The Danger Is Here! What Are You Going to Do About It?" "You've heard the name of the problem before—Gentrification," the writer warned. "You've seen the effects of the problem before—rents climbing higher and higher, art galleries replacing bodegas, strangers armed with briefcases and business suits crowding the streets where once your friends and neighbors stood. And you all know what is happening—you are losing your neighborhood."

WHERE THOUSANDS OF FAMILIES ARE "DOUBLED-UP" AND TRIPLED-UP" . . . WAITING FOR YEARS ON HOUSING LISTS!

WHAT GIVES YOU THE RIGHT TO JUMP TO THE FRONT OF THE

LOS SQUATERS SOMOS DE LA MUJERES Y HOMBRES COMO TU, QUE LUCHAMÓS PARA CONSEGUIR UN BARRIO SEGURO JUSTO Y DIGNO PARA TODOS ¡¡UNETE!!

SHAME ON YOU, "PUNKS"! LOOK BEHIND YOU, ON AVENUE "D" WHERE THOUSANDS OF FAMILIES ARE "DOUBLED-UP" AND TRIPLED-UP" . . . WAITING FOR YEARS ON HOUSING LISTS!

WHAT GIVES YOU THE RIGHT TO JUMP TO THE FRONT OF THE LINE?

Lower East Side residents protest against squatters, ca. 1988. Photo by John Penley. Reprinted courtesy NYU's Tamiment Labor Archive.

Xerox identified two threats: "real estate developers" and "uncaring artists." He outlined a future in which "white middle-class people who do not come from this area, who do not understand you, and whom you do not understand" will invade and "change your neighborhood rather than be changed by it."

"Yuppies go home!" signs proliferated. No one wanted the Village to get rich—except, ironically, those families who had emerged from the apocalyptic seventies and eighties with a shot at prosperity. Some Latino families protested "Los Squatters," who in the name of taking back the neighborhood from The Man were actually taking housing opportunities away from Hispanic people who had been in the neighborhood for decades. Those families now had to cope, too, with a whole new counterculture that somehow managed to be more obnoxious than the punks.

The new crowd listened to hardcore rock. After nights spent in mosh pits at Avenue C's C-Squat (today the home of the Museum of Reclaimed Urban Space), they patrolled St. Marks Place like a skinhead army in bomber jackets and combat boots. Most of the big hardcore bands, like Bad Brains and Black Flag, came out of Washington, D.C., or Los Angeles, but New York contributed its own thrash-y groups, which filled CBGB with angry young white guys slamming their bodies into one another.

Youth Defense League, one of the hardest of New York's eighties hardcore bands, sang about the plight of the workingman. One slogan was "Blue Pride." Another was "Rock Against Communism." They aligned themselves with America's white poor and sang songs like "Skinhead 88" and "Old Glory." There was an air of neo-Nazism to the band—a swastika showed up now and then in their stage sets. One night, they drunkenly sprayed "YDL" graffiti all over St. Marks Place.

YDL expressed a new counterculture that defined itself as musically and politically distinct from the punks who had ruled the neighborhood in the seventies and much of the eighties. They seemed, if it was even possible, angrier than the punks and physically a lot scarier. Where the punk look was a Rimbaud-inspired wastrel, sun-deprived and heroin-slimmed, the hardcore gods were pumped-up, shirtless, and emboldened by beer and blunts.

The band's guitar player, a tattooed teenager who went by Nicky Dirt, actually had working-class credentials. (And still does. Today, he works construction down south and has four children.) He spent his first few years on Avenue B surrounded by biker gangs like the Hells Angels and Gypsy Jokers and, he says, an organ grinder with an actual monkey. He read comics at East Side Books.

Dirt was glad when friends of a friend invited him to join their band. It was 1985. "We only did a few shows a year: CBs, parties," says Dirt. "We didn't do many shows, so when we played it was an event. A lot of people would show up." After hours, from 4 a.m. to 8 a.m., they would head to the underground club Save the Robots on Avenue B and Second Street.

By the end of the eighties, there were still occasional Mohawk- and safety pin–bedecked punk-punks, but they were remnants of a vanishing tribe. Though outsiders sometimes had trouble telling them apart, the punks hated the hardcore kids. New York hardcore offended even D.C. hardcore musicians, who were known for being extra offensive. "To me, it was Archie Bunker with guitars," says Henry Rollins, lead singer of Black Flag (their first show was at the club 7A, a block south of St. Marks Place). Of New York hardcore bands like CBGB-regular Agnostic Front, Rollins says, "They gay-bashed, et cetera. I don't remember anyone I knew in D.C. having a second for any of those bands."

The feeling was mutual. New York hardcore kids took every opportunity to antagonize anyone who wasn't in their tribe, especially the punks. "[Punk] was a genre that we were no longer connected to," says Dirt, who like many people in that scene presents the city of that time as a nonstop battle for survival. "We got chased, things stolen from us. Then it was our turn to do it to someone else. It's like a food chain." The Cro-Mags's Harley Flanagan has said his physical aggression was born of a desire to protect his neighborhood from gentrifiers: "I used to beat up the artsy-fartsy faggots. But it wasn't because they were gay, it wasn't because they were arty. . . . In my own child-like way I felt like I was trying to save the neighborhood from turning into what it finally turned into. I was wrong, but goddamn if my intentions weren't good."

Of the right-wing stuff, Dirt says, "It was a time when everything was anti-American, so to be rebellious, we rebelled against the rebels and became patriotic. We were so nonconformist we conformed." Their reputation could make it hard for them to book shows, and so the hardcore crowd often just partied outside, smoking weed and drinking beer at Tompkins Square Park and on the corner of Avenue A and St. Marks. Sometimes harder drugs made the rounds. "By then I'd already been through my drug problems," says Dirt. "Recently, I heard from someone I used to know back then and I was asking, 'How's this person? How's that person?' They were all dead, all drugs. It wasn't shocking, but it was sad."

One of the guys who survived is Danny Martin, a writer and barber who now works at Royal Unisex Hair Style (no. 16)—a shop that has been in the same location for nearly a century, run by a series of immigrants: Italians, then Polish, now Russians. The cozy leather President-brand barber chairs have been in place for more than fifty years. Martin, who in the hardcore era was a short-story writer who read at open-mic nights and was a fan of bands like the Cro-Mags and YDL, started coming to St. Marks from Long Island when he was about twelve.

"St. Marks was hella wild," he says. "Something was always going on—lots of fights. It was all bars, goth shops, porn shops. This is where you hung out when you cut school. People would be like, 'Let's break a window and start some shit.'"

Rock clubs like Continental and C-Squat became roiling mosh pits on skinhead nights, full of high, angry teenage boys. There were so-called "neg" bands with thuggish German names like Krieg Kopf (from Astoria, Queens). One local musician recalls asking one band member what the initials "P. P." on his jacket stood for. The response: "Pussy Patrol."

Overlapping in unexpected ways with the hardcore crowd,

the Hare Krishnas often passed out food at Tompkins Square Park, where to this day their sacred elm tree is often ringed in flower garlands. For a while the Hare Krishnas rented a space in the Little Missionary building. "The neighbors hated it," says their former landlord, "because they'd chant on the weekends."

Sometimes the group set up a table near Gem Spa and handed out literature. One devotee, Jai Nitai Holzman, was at the table when members of the band Born Against threatened him. Another hardcore musician—the Cro-Mags's John Joseph—stepped in and defended his brother in animal rights. Joseph, author of the book *Meat Is for Pussies*, was fiercely vegan. Luc Sante remembers the vegan thrashers as a walking contradiction: "They beat people up, but didn't touch animal products. The guy from the Cro-Mags would say to Leshko's breakfasters, 'Do you realize you are eating the menstrual cycle of a chicken?'"

The hardcore guys were disillusioned and cynical, high and wild. "There was no anti-bullying campaign bullshit," Danny Martin says nostalgically. "If someone messed with you, you jumped the guy. It was the last roughneck era."

When Louise Teiga, a substance-abuse treatment nurse at Bowery Residents' Committee, moved into no. 109 in 1986, she had fond memories of the street from twenty years earlier. In her youth she'd worked for Charles Fitzgerald, driving his van in a dress and platform shoes for two dollars an hour. Back then, when an old college friend had seen her in one of Fitzgerald's stores, the friend had asked, sincerely, "How could you be any cooler than to be working at Bowl and Board on St. Marks Place?" As a Bronx teenager, Teiga had been taken on a date to the Electric Circus, where she did the Twist, and then to Astor Place, where she spun the *Alamo*.

There was much she loved, too, about the new late-eighties

incarnation of the street. She was happy to spend time with transvestites at the Pyramid Lounge. A video shot by the film-maker Nelson Sullivan on July 17, 1986, shows drag superstar RuPaul across the street from Teiga's house, wearing an elaborate outfit made of white plastic bags and asking for quarters to buy pizza.

"Sometimes I'd wake up and there'd be a bagpiper on the street," says Teiga. "I thought that was so romantic." But the neighborhood was not always fun: "A street person made it into the building and I saw him peeing down the stairs. I thought, *I'm not in Kansas anymore.*" And Teiga hated the skinheads, especially after a particularly brutal fight among them left a trail of blood on the sidewalk in front of her building. She heard shots coming out of the park some nights. Once, she thought she saw a dead body under a blanket in front of All-Craft. After a while, she felt the street was no longer the one she had loved for so many years: "I had PTSD living on St. Marks. I was so totally traumatized."

Miserable residents wished someone would come in to clean up the streets. And then someone tried. In February 1979, Curtis Sliwa, a Canarsie and Brownsville kid working as a Bronx McDonald's night manager, started a nonprofit, volunteer neighborhood watch group called the Guardian Angels.

Sliwa had decided the police weren't doing a good enough job protecting average citizens. Not short on ego, he offered to personally take up the slack. He gave his patrollers red berets and jackets, making them look a little like a tribe in *The Warriors,* Walter Hill's 1979 cult film about a city run by gangs. Mayor Koch, who had been elected largely because he promised to be tough on the kind of crime that had broken out during the '77 blackout, disparaged the group as vigilantes.

Sliwa still wears the beret and jacket, even when doing his AM 970 The Answer talk show in front of the huge window

Guardian Angels founder
Curtis Sliwa, 1993. The LIFE Picture
Collection/Getty Images.

of an otherwise abandoned ground-floor lobby space in the
Pennsylvania Hotel, across the street from Madison Square
Garden. On a break between shows in 2013, fans waved and
took photos of him through the window, and he smiled and
waved back.

As a teenager, Sliwa had taken the subway into the Village
to see shows at the Fillmore East and shop at record stores.
"I always got ripped off," he says of the records he bought
there. "There were scratches, and junk recorded in the bathroom." He would browse the underground magazines at Gem
Spa. One published photos of undercover cops. Others were
Trotskyite. "You'd stand at the counter for a month of Sundays.
No one would wait on you. It was a strange retail environment,
not very customer-friendly. No one had a smile. 'What do you
want?' they'd say. 'Here's your change. Get out of here.'"

Around the time he started the Angels, Sliwa moved to Avenue A, into his girlfriend Lisa Evers's cold-water flat opposite Tompkins Square Park. She had been curator of the gallery Bushido. They paid $125 a month.

"What I remember most was a falafel store," says Sliwa. Iraqis ran the place and displayed a framed picture of Saddam Hussein on the wall. "They simmered the garbanzo beans in the back kitchen. It was a horrible smell. It would waft right up to us on the second floor. We had a rooftop we could walk on and we could look into the park. There was nonstop traffic," says Sliwa, "eclectic, eccentric people; emotionally disturbed people; anarchists; homeless people. Four in the afternoon was like four in the morning, no change in the traffic whatsoever."

One park regular was a guy who went by the name Ugly George. He dressed in aluminum foil, like a DIY astronaut, and had a cable TV program for which he would try to get women to flash the camera. Another was Aron Kay, a hippie who threw pies at people's faces. "He tried to clobber me with a cherry pie, but I ducked," says Sliwa. According to Sliwa, producers from *The Morton Downey, Jr. Show*—the abrasive TV program that is credited with ushering in the age of such "trash TV" as *The Jerry Springer Show*—recruited guests in the park.

Rumor has it the Clash wrote the song "Red Angel Dragnet" about the Guardian Angels after an Angel was shot in 1982 while patrolling a housing project. Some old Eastern European and Italian residents of the neighborhood also expressed support for the Angels. "In their *schmattas*, they would give me all the grief about how [the drug dealing and chaos] would never have been permitted in the old Soviet Union," says Sliwa. "So why'd you come here?" he would respond.

He and Evers ate at Leshko's. "I would have the bowl of mushroom barley," he says. "It would grow hair on your chest. It stuck to your ribs. When we were really down and out and we didn't have two nickels, Lisa and myself would get rye bread and mushroom barley soup, and you were good to go for the whole day."

Sliwa says that one day the owner of Stromboli Pizza (no. 83) complained to him about the dealers in front of the St. Marks Bar and Grill. So the Angels took on that corner. "One day, about noon, there were twenty drug dealers on one side, four of us Guardian Angels holding down the corner opposite," says Sliwa. "We didn't let a seed or a stem get sold or used. We held it down!"

According to Sliwa, an undercover cop told the Angels to back off. "How come you're so friendly with these guys?" Sliwa asked. The cop, he says, told him, "We depend on snitches. These guys are small time. They turn in rapists, assaults, guys dealing pounds." After the cop left, Sliwa says, the dealers attacked the Angels: "These dealers are pouring out of nowhere. We took our lumps. We took a beat-down. But we held the line—battered, bruised, bloody, missing teeth, busted heads."

Sliwa caught it from all sides, fighting at various points with the cops, the Hells Angels, and the hardcore kids who filled Tompkins Square Park. One warm weekend night in 1988, a hundred skinheads were playing music, drinking beer, and smoking pot in the park. "[The Guardian Angels] figured they needed to get involved," says Nicky Dirt, one of the partiers that night. "Sliwa sent a few of his favorites to surround the park. We taunted them and called them names."

Eventually, the Angels—under a barrage of flying bottles—fell back. "Guardian Angels were not exactly tough guys," says Dirt. "They were the weak guys who got picked on and couldn't be an actual gang. I got a lot of respect for Sliwa, what he was trying to do, but as far as trying to regulate us in our neighborhood? That was a bad call."

Activist Bill DiPaola, who grew up in the Bronx and Long Island, then went to Hunter College, was one of those who spent nights in Tompkins Square Park playing loud music and earning the wrath of Sliwa. Starting in 1988, DiPaola, founder of the anarchist group Times Up, hung posters up and down St. Marks Place on what he calls "the good lampposts." Prime posting real estate was the corner of Third Avenue and St. Marks.

"A lot of kids came from New Jersey, hung out in Tompkins Square Park, and then went back on the PATH train. The idea was to use the corridor of St. Marks to let them know that they were getting into a political zone, to open up their minds," he says.

Times Up–focused organizers agitated for bike lanes, environmental protection, rent regulation, and neighborhood gardens, where residents could convert empty lots into sources of food and points of assembly. One of the group's posters shows a woman walking with an umbrella. The sign reads, "Stop acid rain. There's still time." Another advertised an "awareness dance party." Another key issue was squatters' rights.

Squatter Jerry Wade (also known as Jerry the Peddler) has estimated that East Village squatters at one point controlled thirty buildings, a newspaper, and a radio station. But as the neighborhood grew richer, some squats were converted into luxury apartments. The most famous of the conversions was the sixteen-story Christodora building, built in 1897 at 143 Avenue B. The former immigrant settlement house was rumored to have housed a number of political groups, including the Black Panthers, before becoming yuppie condos. In front of the building, DiPaola and his friends staged an ongoing protest. They chanted and drummed late into the night.

While Bill DiPaola was screaming his political slogans outside of the Christodora, Jerry Saltz, today the art critic for *New York* magazine, was inside wishing that he had never moved in. For a moment before it became an anarchist target, the Christodora had been Saltz's reward for many years spent living a couple of blocks away in a 215-square-foot, five-floor walk-up apartment at 60 Avenue B.

Saltz had paid five thousand dollars to a lawyer for his apartment at no. 60, only to learn that the guy wasn't a lawyer and didn't own the apartment. Saltz lived there for years without paying rent as the building descended into chaos. Drug dealers' German shepherds menaced him on his way in and out, and a woman in the apartment below had extremely loud sex at all hours.

Saltz's apartment was robbed several times. Sometimes he bought back his stuff from junkies who had spread it out on blankets on Avenue A. "The cost of heroin meant junkies had to rob you constantly," says Saltz. "The good thing about crack is, it's so cheap the robberies stopped. Of course, while heroin addicts are comatose, crackheads are insane! But I was ecstatic. The whole time. Always."

Before moving to the East Village, Saltz had been a long-distance truck driver, then a chauffeur. In the East Village, he became a writer and started a new life. "I was reborn," he says, "in that shithole apartment. I will always love the East Village and how it allowed me to pretend to be what I was until I could finally muster enough nerve to finally try and actually become it."

After meeting his wife, art critic Roberta Smith, who in 1986 started writing for the *New York Times*, Saltz decided to move to a nicer place. They moved a couple of blocks to the comparatively nice Christodora, home of Iggy Pop, among other successful East Villagers. Unfortunately, the building had become the symbolic top sail of a new ship on the horizon: gentrification.

"In the minds of others, the transition from 60 Avenue B to 143 Avenue B was like going from being part of a band of

Tompkins Square Park's homeless "mayor" J. R. Hunter practices quick-draw with a toy gun before an eviction by police, 1990. Photo by John Penley. Reprinted courtesy NYU's Tamiment Labor Archive.

brothers and sisters to being piranha, traitor, flesh-eating virus," says Saltz. "Where I used to be kept up all night by drug dealers, the barking watchdog, and the screams of that woman, now I was kept up all night by protesters in front of our building day and night: drums, boom boxes blaring, chants—the whole thing. Going in or out of our apartment was a horrible experience; yelled at, threatened, shoved, followed. We were very scared. We were 'the enemy.' And there was nothing we could do about it. Summers were terrible. Winters weren't much better. We were fried by constant adrenaline."

The line between one-of-us pioneer and gentrifying other was perilously thin. As *Village Voice* critic Gary Indiana wrote in his 1989 East Village gay-romance novel *Horse Crazy*, "Someone dies in an apartment three floors down, a week later the place rents out to a prosperous, starched-looking couple for $1,200 per month. People who sail out the door every morning carrying matching briefcases, dress for dinner, complain to the landlord about the opera singer on my floor who rehearses in the evening, have the hall bulletin board removed as a fire hazard." As sushi restaurants opened and people with real jobs moved in, the anarchists grew angrier.

One hot August night in 1988, there was a roar. Heads poked out of windows up and down the street to see people below running at top speed. Some of the runners knocked over garbage cans and threw things at storefronts. Policemen on horses were charging down the middle of the street. Helicopters with searchlights droned overhead. It seemed that the gates of hell had opened in Tompkins Square Park.

Scuffles with police had erupted many times before. Squatters in tents resisted removal as police tore down their shelters and scattered their belongings. The weekend prior the police had given notice that they were going to start enforcing the park's official 1 a.m. curfew. Protesters had gathered, blowing conch shells and shaking maracas. They chanted, "Whose park? Our park!" and "Pigs out of the park!" There was one arrest, which touched off a storm. Flyers appeared up and down St. Marks that week warning of retaliation. Outreach officers contacted community leaders. Curtis Sliwa was one of those called to One Police Plaza for a meeting. A cop there told him, "Watch what happens on Saturday."

Saturday came. Hundreds of police gathered at St. Marks Place and Avenue A to enforce the park's curfew and keep it empty overnight. At least a hundred demonstrators started marching around the park, yelling at the officers. The protesters felt that gentrifiers had invaded *their* neighborhood. They saw themselves as a native people whose way of life was being threatened by hostile colonists—the Lenape versus the Dutch, redux. One sign read, "Gentrification is class war."

Anselm Berrigan—whose poet father, Ted, had died in 1983—was fifteen and trying to fall asleep in the extreme heat. He heard, over the sound of his fan, the noise of a police helicopter above his building. He and his mother ran downstairs. From their stoop, they saw a crowd of people marching toward the park, where the police were lined up wearing riot gear. The marchers stopped in front of the cops, yelling and throwing M-80s and bottles at the officers and their horses. Anarchists hoarding Molotov cocktails called themselves the Bottle Brigade.

Scuffles exploded into a full-on battle. After realizing that his deputy chief, Thomas J. Darcy, had gone AWOL in the chaos (reportedly to use a bathroom at a station a mile away), Captain Gerald McNamara called in reinforcements via a "10-85" radio distress call, bringing the number of police to 450. Many officers from outside the district had no clear orders. Poorly trained in crowd control, new to the situation, and incensed by the protesters' aggression, they lost their composure. A police officer came by the Berrigans' building, banged on garbage cans with his nightstick, and told them to get inside.

Writer Jason Zinoman was thirteen years old and visiting his sister, who lived on Avenue A. It was only his first or second time in New York. "I looked out the window at an insane face-off between cops on horses and a huge crowd, staring each other down twenty feet away from each other, like some kind of Civil War military battle."

Arnie Weinberg was walking his dog, Cesar, a ninety-six-pound Scottish collie, when a cop came by and almost hit him. "The guy was swinging at people," says Weinberg. "My dog went after the horse."

Louise Teiga lay on the floor of her apartment because she

was afraid a bullet would come through the window. "I was feeling sick and had an anxiety attack thinking about leaving the house late at night to go to the ER. The riots were terrifying. You didn't know what was out there. That surge of squatters—young punkers—marching through the neighborhood scared the crap out of me."

Curtis Sliwa watched the riot from his apartment over the falafel place. "I saw the tactical patrol force with the big ghetto birds—the helicopters," he says. "The anarchists rolled marbles out to trip the horses and sent darts out from behind the kids going to bars. The police launched a charge. The anarchists said, 'They're going to start giving wooden shampoos and concrete facials.' The cast of characters all disappears, and the cops start hitting everyone else! It was a debacle."

One local artist stood in the street wearing his mosaic-ed bike helmet, screaming, "We'll burn your fucking tanks!"

The neighborhood became, according to the next morning's *New York Times*, "something of a war zone." The poet Allen Ginsberg told the *Times* reporter: "The police panicked and were beating up bystanders who had done nothing wrong and were just observing." He said six officers hit a houseguest of his with clubs. Some police officers had taped over their name badges.

Businesses along Avenue A locked their doors. Nine people were arrested. At least fifty people, including thirteen officers, were injured.

The rioting continued until dawn, at which point Bill DiPaola and others charged the Christodora, Jerry Saltz's building, smashing the front doors and chanting, "Die, yuppie scum!"

Commissioner Benjamin Ward later admitted that mistakes were made. Even the *Times* editors later called it a "police riot." There were 115 civilian complaints. Six officers were indicted on criminal charges. The deputy chief who fled the scene was forced to resign. Chief McNamara was relieved of

On Avenue A, by Tompkins Square Park, protesters hurl bottles at police in riot gear. May 27, 1991. Photo by Q. Sakamaki.

his command. He was later made commander of a precinct in Queens.

"One of the most critical shots in my whole riot tape," says Clayton Patterson, who filmed several hours of the riot, "is a white shirt [commander] going like this [trying to give orders with hand gestures] and all the blue shirts [officers] going by, and nobody's listening. They're running down Avenue A. There's no central authority. What you have is this police force that couldn't close a ten-and-a-half-acre-square park on the Lower East Side. Couldn't do it." Cut to a decade later: "2001 comes along, and in two hours they close bridges, airports, tunnels, ferries, subways, trains—everything, all the street traffic."

The city would struggle with the question of what to do with Tompkins Square Park. The morning after the 1988 riot, Mayor Koch lifted the curfew and effectively delayed a decision about the park's fate. Protests continued on and off for three years. The tent city was destroyed and then resurrected. Patterson remembers three main riots, which he refers to as: "May Day, Memorial, and the Police Riot." He also recalls a "tornado" of a riot that erupted around Tompkins Square following the Rodney King trial, though he says those protesters were "outsiders."

Each time squats were evicted in those years, it was amid cries of "Police state!" Comic book artist Seth Tobocman's anarchist imagery was everywhere, as was graffiti of anti-gentrification symbols, like an upside-down martini glass. Once again, St. Marks was called St. Marx. Flyers showed a flying bottle alongside slogans like, "Fly high" and "Hit hard." Squatters mobilized over the years at various nearby head-quarters, including Anarchist Switchboard, ABC Community Center, and Sabotage, an anarchist bookstore at no. 96. On at least one occasion, attendees were asked to set fire to a dollar bill to gain admission—harking back to when in the late sixties Abbie Hoffman had burned dollar bills on St. Marks. "Blacks and Latinos couldn't understand why Abbie burned a dollar bill to make a point," says Paul Krassner. "They didn't have money to burn." Anarchy is a middle-class dream; the poor and the rich are at one in wanting no part of it.

For David Dinkins, who took over from Ed Koch as mayor in 1990, the Memorial Day Riot in Tompkins Square Park was an unwelcome test of his authority. At around five-thirty in the morning on June 3, 1991, with command trucks stationed at each corner, 300 police officers evicted the remaining 150 residents. A huge fence was erected around the park and remained there for a year.

Sliwa says that around four in the morning one night after

the closing of the park, he was beaten up near Ray's Candy Shop on Avenue A. He climbed the chain-link fence "bleeding like a sieve." The cops were called and came to unlock the gate. "They look at me sitting on the grass," says Sliwa, "and they said, 'I guess you're not Superman.'"

To Sliwa, the fence was a lifesaver—both for him and for the neighborhood. To others, it was a symbol of the takeover by those who would turn the People's Park into a corporate playground and St. Marks into a street like any other.

Even though it had once been his home, Jimmy Webb, who was getting sober upstate during the riots, was glad when he heard about the end of the tent city. "You know when drug addicts are taking something over you can basically bet it's based in self-centeredness—mine, mine, mine, mine—with no awareness of anything else around you."

In the end, the anarchists like DiPaola and the upwardly mobile bohemians like Saltz—on opposite sides of the Christodora's walls, and opposite sides in the battle for Tompkins Square Park—both lost. Neither particularly liked the look of the newest group of winners.

PART V

"THE ERA OF FEAR HAS HAD A LONG ENOUGH REIGN."

1992–1999

After a live show by the Varukers, a punk band

from England, at Coney Island High in 1996.

Photo by Teru Kuwayama.

24

THE LIVING MUSEUM

What I remember more than anything else was the noise. Out on St. Marks there were parties—dozens of them— happening on any given night, just beyond my bedroom window. As a child I'd been annoyed by the shouts and screams and trash cans being overturned, especially in the summers before my parents bought an air conditioner, when the windows were wide open and it felt like I was sleeping in the middle of the street.

But when I became a teenager, the noise changed for me: it became the roar of promise. The street seemed suddenly like a grand bazaar of bars and beds and futures. I realized I could join any of those parties, have any of those lives. I could put on this or that outfit, have these friends or those, sleep with this person or that one.

My friends and I walked from river to river, along St. Marks Place and Eighth Street, passing drag queens in front of no. 15, skaters catcalling us at the Astor Place Cube, drug dealers everywhere hissing, "Smoke, smoke," and the grimy, pierced runaways known as "crusty punks" begging. We felt like we owned the city. We had that feeling of being the right age, at the right time, in the exact right place. For nearly a century, that has been what being young has meant on St. Marks Place.

St. Marks Place is like superglue for fragmented identities. The street is not for people who have chosen their lives—the married, the employed, the secure, the settled. The street is

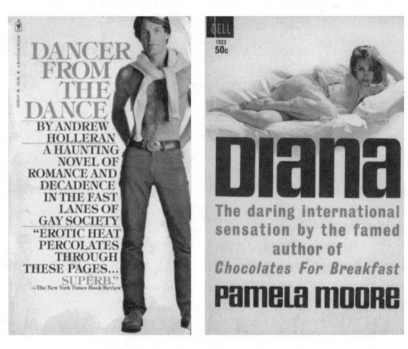

Heroes and heroines of books set on St. Marks Place are often pretty slutty.
See: *Dancer from the Dance*, 1979 Bantam edition. *Diana*, 1961 Dell edition.

for the wanderer, the undecided, the lonely, and the promiscuous. St. Marks courses with sexual energy and opportunity. This perhaps more than any other reason is why people say that the street is lame and dead after they stop hanging out there. Lust is a kind of drug. Once it wears off, you may be left feeling embarrassment, confusion, and wistfulness about how you acted under its spell.

St. Marks Place in the 1990s was many things at once. You could eat challah French toast for breakfast, pizza for lunch, and empanadas for dinner. Friends made each other mix tapes. One neighborhood band that appeared on a significant number of those mixes was King Missile, whose lead singer John S. Hall sang about losing his "detachable penis" (a song he'd written at the Kiev diner on Second Avenue) and having to buy it back from a thieves' market on Second Avenue and St. Marks Place. But the tapes raided from every era: the Beatles, the Violent Femmes, the musical *Hair*, the Velvet Underground, Bob Dylan, Deee-Lite, the Beastie Boys, Led Zeppelin, Madonna, and (not even always ironically) Billy Joel. There was room for anything that would fit into ninety crackly minutes.

After the Tompkins Square Park riots, the police more or less succeeded in conquering the anarchists, the area's most antisocial group. In their wake, St. Marks Place saw the most diverse social scene in its history. It was as if the apex predator had been eradicated, turning the region into a playground for a wide array of beta species. Where once there had been a single "cool" group—the Beats, the hippies, the punks—now there were as many ways to be cool as there were clothing and record stores on the street.

St. Marks in the nineties was a place where you could geek out any way you wanted. You could join forces with the nerds of St. Mark's Comics, the skater kids doing kickflips at the Cube, or the indie kids leaving secret messages for each other in typed, Xeroxed zines at St. Mark's Bookshop. The older bohemians formed an amusing cast of characters—Irving Stettner patrolled the neighborhood selling watercolors and his zine, *Stroker*, made up largely of letters to and from his friend Henry Miller; Adam Purple, aka "Les Ego," biked around the neighborhood dressed all in purple; Jim Power, aka "Mosaic Man," decorated the street's lampposts with broken tiles. A white-bearded man known as "East Village Santa" walked the neighborhood in all seasons wearing red clothes; faced with a curious child wondering if he were *really* Santa, he would pull a bouquet of flowers out of his jacket.

Stores like Sounds, Venus, and Kim's, the one-stop mini-mall for music and movies, allowed every clique to realize its fullest self. If you were a Riot Grrrl, you could find every Bikini

Kill and Bratmobile album. If you loved indie music, you could stock up on Dinosaur Jr., Belly, and Guided by Voices.

And if you couldn't find enough of your kind walking up and down St. Marks Place, you could find them online. The same year Tompkins Square Park closed for renovation, the World Wide Web made its debut. By 1993, St. Marks Place had its first Internet café: @ Café at no. 12.

Writer Dan Oko, who grew up on the Upper West Side and attended the progressive prep school Fieldston, spent his teen years on and around St. Marks, where his friend's older brother had an apartment. "We would roll joints, buy forties [forty-ounce bottles of beer], and sit on the stoop watching the punks and trannies roll by, armed with fake IDs in order to make occasional forays to the Palladium Club, CBGB, or Irving Plaza. But it was the street scene that always captivated me above all."

Oko and his friends went to the famous multilevel, punk-friendly barbershop Astor Place Hair to get "our Jew-fros cut into outlandish reverse-mullets, puffy in the front, shaved in the back. . . . It seemed the height of worldliness at the time to grab a bite at Dojo"—a popular, cheap restaurant at no. 24 where you could get a filling soy burger sandwich for three dollars, four if you wanted cheese—"and discuss the merits of Lou Reed's sobriety and the latest release from Bad Brains."

Uptown kids, drag queens, punk rockers, skaters, book nerds, and ravers loitered side by side on stoops, drinking forties. There was still crime, but not too much; danger, but not too much. Clothing was available at all price points, from cheapo thrift store dresses to upscale punk looks at Trash and Vaudeville. Reporter N. R. Kleinfeld described 1990s St. Marks in the *New York Times* as "a street where you can see a young man with a Mohawk haircut begging for money and see another young man with a Mohawk haircut give him some."

One New York City band exemplified and precipitated this culture-sampling: the Beastie Boys. As teens in the 1980s, Adam Horovitz, Adam Yauch, and Mike Diamond had cut class to hang out on St. Marks, buying music and checking out flyers for bands. "Instead of spending the money my mom gave me to buy lunch, I would eat the absolute bare minimum: a bagel with butter that would cost me thirty-five cents, and then I would pocket the rest and use it to buy records," says Diamond.

The friends thought of St. Marks as the place where things happened. Horovitz and a friend were walking down the street one afternoon when a guy came up to them, pulled out a color Xerox of a red door with a number on it, and said, "*Psst!* I got Sid's door!" Sid Vicious had just died, and this would-be salesman said he'd taken the punk singer's door off its hinges to sell. The pair declined the offer—they only had a couple of dollars on them, and they were scared. "It was this punk-rock grown-up," says Horovitz.

The teenagers often saw the same cast on the street, like Jason from hardcore band the Attack, handing out flyers, saying over and over: "The Attack. CB's. Tomorrow. Be there." Or their friend who conscientiously picked a bloody tooth off an Avenue A barroom floor after a fight and for days afterward went to St. Marks Place with the tooth in a tissue, looking for its owner. It was like the eighties East Village version of Cinderella's slipper.

The friends hung out at Tish and Snooky's Manic Panic and idolized the Bellomo sisters' punk band, the Sic F*cks. "They were older and we were in love with them," says Horovitz of Tish and Snooky. "We thought they were the coolest." The friends started playing music themselves. They drank with a guy named Danny Vegas, whose name they envied, at the Holiday Cocktail Lounge (no. 75)—where a drinking age was strictly enforced: you had to be "tall enough to reach the bar," according to Diamond. "Actually," says Horovitz, "the drinking age was 'confidence.'"

They played video games, ate around the corner at Fun and Burger, and bought records at the Rat Cage, a store on Avenue A that doubled as an independent record label. One of them was shopping there when someone ran in and yelled, "Quick, Johnny Thunders is selling a bunch of his shit!" And they ran over to the thieves' market at Astor Place to see if they could score some of the strung-out New York Doll's record collection.

Another time Diamond ran into their friend Dave Parsons, who managed the Rat Cage. "I was just in a Rolling Stones video," Parsons said. Walking down St. Marks Place, he'd been cast as an extra in the video for "Waiting on a Friend."

The Beastie Boys put out their first two albums on Rat Cage Records. One afternoon, sitting in front of Sounds Records at no. 20, Adam Horovitz and NYU student Rick Rubin worked on lyrics for the song "Paul Revere." That song appeared on the 1986 album *Licensed to Ill*, the first rap album to make it to number one on the Billboard charts.

That album provided the perfect soundtrack for the new, multi-everything era of St. Marks Place: part punk, part hip-hop, part smart-ass, part actually smart. It brought the Beastie Boys stardom and eventually, in 2012, induction into the Rock and Roll Hall of Fame. For many years afterward, teenagers all over the city would brag—falsely, nine times out of ten—that one of the Beastie Boys had gone to their high school.

One of the high-schoolers from outside the city who took refuge on St. Marks Place was Chloe Sweeney McGlade, a proudly punk-rock girl who now bartends at Grassroots (no. 20). Growing up in a Westchester suburb, she hated her vanilla classmates, and the feeling was mutual. "They didn't appreciate my Mohawk," she says. "At my last high school, kids spit on me on the school bus. I graduated early to get away from them."

In the East Village, she felt at home. St. Marks Place was her favorite spot in the world: "It was the block where all the crazies came out." The Metro-North train was her conduit to this heavenly, bizarro world where everything that drew scorn at home made her cool. Here, her punk hair was envied. Here, the lacrosse-playing Westchester it girls were lame. "Walking down the street the dealers would say, 'Smoke?' And I would say, 'No thanks! I don't do drugs!'" recalls McGlade. "They liked me."

In 1991, McGlade moved to no. 34½ (eighty years earlier, the home of a German butcher shop) and says the mid-nineties were the glory years for her and for the street. She started a band called Snuka and worked first at Manic Panic, then at the door of a new club on the street at no. 15½ called Coney Island High, where she also DJed. "When bands played CBGB or Continental or Coney Island High, they would crash with us. We were friends with bands like Nashville Pussy and Supersuckers. . . . We lived in the hub. People would buzz in the middle of the night: 'I got beer!' It was the most exciting time of my life."

That same year, Barry Joseph, as not-punk as they come, also was having the time of his life. An NYU grad student from Long Island, Joseph lived at no. 11, and the following summer he moved to no. 5. "[St. Marks] felt like the center of everything," he says. "It never stopped. I loved sitting on the stoop. St. Marks was young, edgy, dirty, subversive, alternative."

Until that period, a big part of underground communication had been the flyers posted up and down the street, but the police were starting to crack down on the practice. The Internet filled the void. People were talking to each other online

The Gap and Kim's Video, early 1990s. Photo by Barry Joseph.

for the first time, creating whole worlds there. That was when, Joseph says, geek culture became cool. "We [Generation X-ers] were no longer characters in a Richard Linklater movie," he says. "Video games suddenly seemed important."

One businessman who realized there was money to be made on this new generation was a Korean immigrant named Yongman Kim. Kim had immigrated to the Lower East Side in 1979. First he ran a green grocery. Then he opened a dry cleaners on Avenue A. VCRs were just coming into vogue, and video rental promised to be a lucrative business. Kim started offering a few shelves of videos for rent at the front of the store.

"The collection was very small and scattershot, mostly a few new releases and some bad action movies," says Matt Marello, who was put in charge of the videos when he started working there. "Mr. Kim, to his credit, gave me carte blanche with respect to ordering the movies for the store. As the collection started to grow, I decided to arrange the videos by countries, and within each country, by director. Soon after I started putting the collection together and business started booming, Mr. Kim decided to expand the video counter to be more like a store within a store, which did most of its business at night when the dry cleaners was closed."

In 1987, Kim's Video opened as a standalone operation nearby. Movie rentals proved hugely popular, and within a few years, Kim had established a Kim's Video at the corner of St. Marks and Second Avenue, above the Gap. In 1995, he opened an expanded store, Mondo Kim's, at no. 6, the site of the former St. Mark's Baths.

Kim's employees were famously haughty. When someone rented foreign and indie movies like *Run Lola Run* or *Roadside Prophets*, the Kim's workers checked them out without blinking, but a mainstream rom-com on the counter would incite perceptible disgust. While applying to work at Kim's, artist Guy Richards Smit failed the elaborate movie test that he was given with the job application. "Where it said, 'Name two porn stars,' I wrote 'The Sisters Lynn,'" he says. "I was informed by my interviewer that Ginger and Amber Lynn were not related, and that I didn't get the job." In the Gospel of Mark, Jesus withholds the secret of his divinity from outsiders, and on St. Marks Place in the nineties, Kim's clerks withheld the *Three Colors* trilogy from those who couldn't pronounce the name of Polish director Krzysztof Kieślowski.

Smit later worked at the Kim's on Avenue A for about five dollars an hour, plus free rentals. The employees would let bartenders borrow movies for free. In exchange, the Kim's crowd scored free drinks around the neighborhood. "It was a great deal," says Smit, "because they would get a free three-dollar rental, and then we would get thirty dollars' worth of drinks. Although, come to think of it, because they were mostly alcoholics who couldn't get things back on time, there were a lot of late fees that we'd have to waive. Maybe it evened out."

That *mi casa es su casa* practice was called "club courtesy," and among its practitioners were the drag queens of BoyBar.

On Thursday nights in those days, young men dressed as beautiful women made their way to no. 15½, across the street from the former New St. Mark's Baths. The show's director, a recent Princeton graduate from the Upper East Side named Matthew Kasten, worked all week to produce the shows—writing skits, tracking down costumes, and casting songs.

Doors opened at 9 p.m. The show was supposed to start at ten but rarely went on before midnight, by which time there was often such a big crowd on the second floor near the stage that it was hard to breathe. Drag in the early eighties had been campy, with predictable anti-Reagan political references. During the AIDS crisis, the scene took on the rigorously uplifting spirit of, in Kasten's words, "a USO show." BoyBar's Thursday shows provided a release valve for the anger and sadness.

Kasten wrote a whole new show every week, with two or three torn-from-the-headlines production numbers and some coveted solo spots. "We did a First Ladies show—Imelda Marcos, Barbara Bush, Nancy Reagan," recalls Kasten. "Another one was the songs of [performance artist] Diamanda Galas . . . Christmas in July . . . a Hanukkah Pageant, Vampires. . . . Once a year we did *Valley of the Dolls* onstage. It was packed all three floors. People watched on a video monitor."

Backstage, the performers treated BoyBar as a sorority. "If you couldn't do your wig, someone else would do it for you," recalls Kasten. "It was an amazing and collaborative time." The club was run like the studio system. You did your time in the chorus, then got a lead, then you got your own show. Stars

included Sweetie, Candis Cayne, Princess Diandra, Miss Gla-
mamore, Miss Guy, Perfidia, Afrodite, International Chrysis,
and Sister Codie Ravioli. The BoyBar Beauties, as they were
known, performed at other clubs and in countless AIDS ben-
efits all over the city, as well as in Wigstock, Tompkins Square
Park's annual outdoor drag festival started by drag star Lady
Bunny.

BoyBar wasn't quite as avant-garde as Club 57 had been
or as the Pyramid Club on Avenue A still was. The Pyramid
had revolutionized drag in the early eighties. "Before the
Pyramid," Johnny Dynell says, "drag queens tried to look like
women—movie stars like Marilyn Monroe. At Pyramid, they
were trying to look like drag queens." The next-generation
drag queens at BoyBar wanted to look pretty. The club's motto
was "Beauty Now and Forever."

"Pyramid was more kooky," says BoyBar Beauty Steven
"Perfidia" Kirkham, who won Miss BoyBar 1986. Perfidia
did a lounge act inspired by the Peruvian exotica singer Yma

BoyBar regular Perfidia performing at Wigstock, Tompkins Square Park, 1989.
Wig by Matthew Kasten. Photo by Tina Paul.

Sumac, who claimed to be an Incan princess. "BoyBar was more queens from the sixties," says Kirkham. "Our favorite movie was *The Queen*," the 1968 documentary about a beauty pageant. That pageant took place at Club 82, the fifties drag bar on Second Avenue and Fourth Street, which rumor held had since become a sex club.

Drag at BoyBar "wasn't suburban drag; no one was doing *Dynasty*," says Kasten. "Once I got a huge black garbage bag full of dresses from Oscar de la Renta. Summer dresses and suits. We used them for our show *The Harlem Women's Contingent Meets the Hamptons Women's Contingent*."

Celebrities flocked to BoyBar. One Fashion Week, Kasten recalls seeing the designers Jean Paul Gaultier, Thierry Mugler, and Karl Lagerfeld in the audience on the same night. Another evening saw models Naomi Campbell, Christy Turlington, and Kate Moss. The dance band Deee-Lite were regulars. (The group's Lady Miss Kier, who lived on St. Marks Place, sometimes appeared as what was termed "a lady drag queen.") "Cher was there. Cyndi Lauper. Madonna tried to get in but we didn't let her in," says Kasten. "She was a piece of crap. She talks about Lady Gaga stealing! Anything anybody did original in the scene would show up on her." Kasten was particularly galled by Madonna's sense of entitlement. "She once came with twelve people trying to get in for free! Bitch, you're rich!"

Paul McGregor, the club's landlord, was very proud of the show's popularity. On a bright afternoon, he might prance down the block cheerfully playing his flute. He was beloved, and even though he wasn't gay, he loved dancing at BoyBar. He would call to DJ Johnny Dynell from the dance floor: "Play my song!" Dynell would dutifully put on Danny Krivit's ten-minute version of "Love Is the Message," and McGregor would play the flute and dance alone in the middle of the floor.

Many of the queens shopped at the Astor Place thieves' market, which they called "Bumingdale's." Manic Panic gave every BoyBar Beauty a pair of patent-leather heels and dark lipstick for her birthday. "They were the best big sisters," says Kasten of Tish and Snooky. The whole neighborhood was a drag paradise: "You could go to Trash and Vaudeville for Cuban-heeled boots, and then buy a beer at the deli even if you were fifteen. They didn't care as long as you had cash." After the show, the Beauties would walk to 1950s-style diner Stingy Lulu's, where the waitresses were drag queens. By day, many of them would hang out at designer Patricia Field's store a few blocks west. There, Perfidia developed the popular wig bar, where anyone could experiment with new looks.

Kids from the projects were sometimes hostile to the BoyBar Beauties. One former dealer from Alphabet City's Campos projects, east of Avenue D, recalls glowering at the drag queens who hung out at Stingy Lulu's and cruelly teasing a straight friend for working there as a busboy. The kids from the projects had been left out of the East Village's evolution. The counterculturalists ventured over to buy drugs; otherwise, the poorer communities didn't much share in the live-and-let-live paradise. But like an ambassador from the world east of Tompkins Square Park, one teenage skateboarder was about to actualize St. Marks Place's promise of inclusivity.

HAROLD HUNTER OWNS THE CUBE

At the Astor Place Cube throughout the nineties, skater kids held sway. The one with the most flair was Harold Hunter. "He was the Bruce Lee of skateboarding," according to fellow skater Billy Rohan. "He was pushing skateboarding further than anyone in New York. He was an athlete. He was the king of New York. To every girl he saw, he'd say the same thing: 'God bless you, ma. I love you.' When he wanted to make something happen, he'd make it happen. This guy looked like a pug dog, but his charisma and personality took him all over the world."

Hunter bridged the divide between the mostly white, mostly middle-class world of the Village and the mostly black, mostly poor world of the projects to the east, bringing the two together with his humor and skills. His pied-à-terre was the Forsyth home on St. Marks between First and Second.

One afternoon in August of 1990, Jessica Forsyth looked out the window of her family's apartment and saw her thirteen-year-old sister, Priscilla, chatting with two older boys holding skateboards. "I had just come home from summer camp," says Priscilla. "I was with my friends Margaret and Liza. And they're both blonde—one real, one fake. We were sitting on the statues out in front. I was hoping someone would talk to me.

Skater Harold Hunter, in his early twenties, ollies a trash can at the Astor Place Cube, ca. 1996. Photo by Giovanni Reda.

Harold came down the street on a BMX bike and stopped in front of us and said, 'Oh my god! I've never seen blonde girls in New York before!' That was his reason to talk to us. He made us laugh. His whole shtick was hilarious."

The Forsyths and Hunter drank forties in Washington Square Park and wandered on St. Marks Place at all hours. When they arrived home at 3 a.m., the girls would salute the drug dealers out front as if they were doormen, says Jessica: "It was a relief to see somebody there who knew us."

On the next block, another woman had a similar experience of the dealers. A Sarah Lawrence graduate, Miranda Lichtenstein, moved in between First and Avenue A in 1994. She was the daughter of Gene Lichtenstein, who had sublet Auden's place in the fifties, and the great-niece of Ray Euffa, who had lived nearby in the twenties. Resembling her great-aunt in her delicate features, Miranda lived on the street with two or three other girls. "They promised to keep me safe," she says of the dealers who served as her unofficial doormen, "though I would not have phrased it as romantically as that. I suppose I was happy to have them there."

"Those were the Dinkins days—" Priscilla Forsyth says.

"—when you could piss on the street," Jessica adds.

The Forsyth house became the headquarters for a crew of skaters. "A lot of the bohemian white moms were raising biracial kids alone," says Jessica. "We had two parents [Al, who is black, and Libby, who is white], and they owned the building. We were the Cleaver family. The skater guys who would come to barbecues here would say, 'I can't believe this is on St. Marks Place.' We had skaters drinking all of Mommy's orange juice. She started keeping a secret stash of orange juice in a little fridge in her bedroom. [My parents] still decided they'd rather us hang out here."

Highlyann Krasnow of no. 122 spent time with Hunter and the Forsyths in those days—typically on her own front stoop, or on her roof. "I wasn't allowed to go to Tompkins Square Park alone because of the tent city," Krasnow says. "The first time I ever saw anyone have sex was two homeless dudes in the bandshell in the park. I still can't eat Cornish game hens because they remind me of the pigeons they used to roast over garbage-can fires in the park. I remember a lot of rats, a lot of burning buildings, and a lot of dope fiends.

"When I started high school I was a little punk-rock skater chick," she says. "Almost all of my friends were hardcore skater kids. We were either on my stoop, my roof, in the park or at the Pyramid, the Garage, or ABC No Rio. There was a liquor store on Avenue A and Twelfth Street that would sell us hard alcohol—as early as twelve, I remember buying alcohol there. We would steal forties and smoke a lot of weed and trip our balls off on acid."

The three Hunter brothers—Ronald, born in 1972; Harold, born in 1974; and Mike, 1975—grew up in the Campos Plaza housing project on Thirteenth and C. "My whole family was crackheads. The illest crackheads on the Lower East Side," says Ronald. "We got ass whuppings. We'd create strategies to get away. Once we heard our grandmother's slippers, *shush, shush, shush*, we'd run around the bunk bed—jump on the heater, jump on the bed," trying to hide. Ronald recalls, "I was the tallest. I was the easiest to catch. I'd hide under the mattress, between the bureaus."

Ronald spent time in juvenile hall. "I was a really bad kid," he says. "I got a job at one of those stores selling nunchucks. I was only paid five dollars a week, so I robbed his store. I was so stupid. But [my boss] left an eleven-year-old in charge of his store! I took a hundred dollars. I bought white Reeboks."

After he got out of juvie, Ronald opted to go to a group home rather than returning to his grandmother's apartment. But when his grandmother died, he went home to take care of Harold and Mike. He was just eighteen, but he managed to get the family on food stamps even though he still couldn't read. Ronald says a relative reappeared around this time and made life difficult for the boys again: "I got a crazy beat-down," he recalls, "with keys to the face. I still have a scar."

Ronald became one of Joyce Hartwell's charges. "You'd climb into a cubbyhole to go to sleep," he says of All-Craft. "I lived there starting when I was twenty-one for two years." In 1992, Hartwell had gotten two floors of All-Craft at no. 25 approved as a shelter for fifteen people at a time. On a typical night, she housed more like forty. "We put people anywhere we could," she says.

Addiction and legal trouble plagued the skaters' circle. Once, Priscilla Forsyth heard a commotion in front of her building, opened her window, and saw a friend of hers on his knees being arrested. "I opened my window and he smiled and waved with his hands behind his head," she says.

Meanwhile, Ronald's little brother Harold skateboarded up and down St. Marks, past Mondo Kim's at no. 6 and past the ravers around East Village Shoe Repair (no. 1), where Boris Zuborev produced ridiculously high platform shoes. Ravers wore Zuborev's creations to nightclubs like NASA. "They'll dye your pumps hot pink, spray-paint pictures on your sneakers or raise your heels up seventeen inches," said the *Villager* of the shop.

Harold Hunter was a star—the poster boy for skateboarding brand Zoo York and for a new idea of how to live in the city. You could be poor but have access to the richest parts of Manhattan, and you didn't even have to dress up. Videos of Hunter that passed from fan to fan showed him confidently skateboarding all over the island. In one video, Wu-Tang Clan's Method Man and Ghostface Killah rap in the background as Hunter rides from the middle of the day to the middle of the night, from Tribeca to Radio City Music Hall, flying down stairs and gliding sideways along railings, jumping trash cans and landing back on his board as though it were the easiest thing in the world. In his hoodie and with his cocky smile, he makes every corner a stage and every fence a prop to work into his act. At last, he returns to the East Village, back to the Cube.

On his local rounds, Hunter would nod to the guy with the boom box selling "DJ Lenny M's Music World" mix tapes on the corner of Third Avenue, and then coast by the record stores, like Sounds (no. 20) and Venus (no. 13), past St. Mark's Bookshop (no. 12), beloved sock store The Sockman (no. 27), and bars like Sin-é (no. 122), where sensitive singer-songwriter Jeff Buckley had a weekly show in the nineties playing a mix of original music and covers of Nusrat Fateh Ali Khan, Bad Brains, and Bob Dylan.

Hunter inspired a legion of teenagers to adopt his swagger and grin, and to move through the city like they owned it. To relieve any doubt about their range, some members of this subculture wrote their names on buildings and subway cars. On warm days, they took their shirts off and tucked them into the backs of their saggy shorts, underwear bands deliberately showing, whistling at girls, tanning their skinny torsos and not bothering to bandage their battered knees.

Harold was immortalized as a king of the new East Village by a movie called *Kids*.

In the summer of 1994, Harmony Korine was a nineteen-year-old NYU student. In Washington Square Park, he met a high-school senior named Chloë Sevigny. Together with the transgressive, fifty-something photographer Larry Clark, Korine conceived a feature film that would epitomize the life of teens in the Village. They cast it primarily with teenagers who were already hanging around St. Marks Place, including the Forsyths, Harold Hunter, and Rosario Dawson. *Kids* features explicit sex scenes, a violent beating, young boys smoking pot, and a plot that centers on a serial virgin-seducer named Telly, who has given at least one girl AIDS.

The film was scripted, but handheld cameras made it feel like a documentary. Some critics fretted over the sociopathic characters, pointing especially to the skaters' bloody attack on a gay man in Washington Square Park; others accused it of being borderline child pornography. In the opening scene, a barely pubescent girl is seduced by Telly, who lives on St. Marks Place.

When *Kids* was finished, the Hunters and Forsyths went to a friends-and-family screening upstairs at the Tribeca Grill. "That's when we all saw it for the first time," says Priscilla Forsyth. Sitting next to her parents, she squirmed in her seat as she watched her character talk explicitly about sex in a St. Marks Place apartment. Watching her friends play caricatures of themselves wasn't the pure fun she'd anticipated.

Plenty of locals considered the film absurd—a melodramatic, alarmist representation of what was in fact a more or less harmless community. But outside the East Village, it was a hit. Released in 1995, *Kids*, which cost less than two million dollars to produce, grossed twenty million. In the *New York Times* Janet Maslin wrote, "Think of this not as cinema verité but as a new strain of post-apocalyptic science fiction, using hyperbole to magnify a kernel of terrible, undeniable truth."

Nineties Village kids were genuine cosmopolitans, moving easily from dealers' hallways to yuppies' bedrooms. Whatever else it exaggerated, *Kids* faithfully documented this moment of connection between the poor and the rich, uptown and down. Young people around the country saw a street that offered seemingly unlimited freedom. The picture was both horrifying and attractive—a window onto a world where teenagers could be themselves, and where they could get away with murder.

In the wake of *Kids*'s success, some of its actors became stars. Others suffered. Justin Pierce, who played Casper, hung himself in 2000. In 2006, Harold Hunter died at the age of thirty-one from a heart attack after a night of drug use. "That night was crazy," Ronald says.

> We were arguing. My son was about four months old. [Harold] picked up my son and said, "We should stop fighting. The kid is here." I was like, "I gotta go to sleep." [Harold] was wigged. I went and laid down in my room with the girl I was with. Harold knocks on my door and says, "I gotta tell you something." My shorty's like, "Don't say nothing." She was scared of Harold. His mouth was crazy when he got going. "I love you!" he said through the door. He was already drunk. "I just want to give you a hug!" My sister said, "Harold, leave him alone." He stood at my door for an hour. My sister said, "Harold go in your room." I felt bad, like I should have said something, but I didn't want to argue.

Harold passed away before Ronald awoke the next morning. In their friend's memory, the Forsyths founded the Harold Hunter Foundation, which provides support to young skaters. Ronald Hunter learned to use computers, got a good job, and bought a house in Queens, where he lives with his wife and two children. Doctors recently removed a bullet he'd had in his body for more than a decade. "Now when someone gives my kids guns as a present I throw them away," Hunter says. He doesn't like the East Village now. "There's no culture any-more," he says. "I'm driving my car and this lady gets out of a cab in the middle of the street. I yelled at her. She said, 'Fuck you!' I said, 'Bitch, I was born in this city. Don't talk to me like that.'"

In the days when Harold Hunter was skating along the sunny street, upstairs in a dark room of the St. Mark's Hotel sat Kevin Michael Allin, better known as GG. His fans revered him as a quasi-religious figure. Others thought he was the worst thing that ever happened to music.

Born in Lancaster, New Hampshire, in 1956, Allin was a performance artist known for the violence of his stage shows, during which he often took all his clothes off, shoved people, injured himself, defecated on stage, and flung his feces at the audience. Once he slammed a microphone into his mouth, breaking several teeth. Now and then, he rolled on broken glass. Allin's tours typically ended with him in the hospital.

He took the punk-rock ethos of id gratification to its farthest extremes. If the typical conversation around punk was about whether a band was fake or authentic, Allin's nihilism was only too real. He said his bodily fluids were "the blood of rock and roll," something he bestowed as communion on his fans. "GG Allin is an entertainer with a message to a sick society" reads a promotional blurb provided by Allin's friend, the serial killer and rapist John Wayne Gacy, who also painted the poster for *Hated*, the documentary about Allin by *Hangover* director Todd Phillips.

After assaulting a woman in Michigan, Allin did two years in prison. (In *Hated*, Allin yells at the judge sentencing him, "You're trying to kill rock 'n' roll!") He skipped parole to go on tour in New York City, staying at the St. Mark's Hotel (no. 2). "Where other people stop, I accelerate," he once told an interviewer. "Whether I shit on you, whether I cut you up . . . that's what I want to do. I don't give a shit what you want to see. That's what I want to do. If you come to my show and you're disappointed, good." Allin often spoke of a plan to commit suicide, always on the following Halloween. "Why do I want to get old and be nothing, be a boring human being?"

GG ALLIN
and the murder junkies

THE DENIED
BLACK RAIN
HUMYN SEWAGE

Avenue B & 2nd Street
3PM SUNDAY, JUNE 27th
$7.00

at the GAS STATION

The last flyer GG Allin ever posted on St. Marks Place, 1993. Collection of Tony Mann.

he said. Fans asked each other, "Is he really going to do it this year?"

On June 27, 1993, mostly naked, wearing a black dog collar, and covered in blood and shit, Allin walked through the East Village after a show that had ended (as they often did) with a riot. The little East Village club the Gas Station had cut his set short, and a hundred fans poured out into the street, screaming and throwing things. Allin rammed his head into a lamppost several times and then did a backward somersault in the middle of the street, where a city bus bore down on him.

The bus stopped short. Allin got to his feet. "Fuck the police!" some fans shouted when a patrol car flashed its lights and a cop told the group to break it up.

A video camera followed Allin as he walked with a few friends through the Lower East Side, talking about how he was heading for "drugland." Desperately trying to get a cab to stop for them, they discussed the crowd that had followed him for blocks, occasionally smashing bottles onto the sidewalk or yelling, "GG, I love you!"

"I should bring this whole crowd down to St. Marks, have like a fucking parade," Allin says to his friends. "We'll be like Jesus leading the masses."

They continue their walk, full of adrenaline, with no clear plan.

"Wait, where is St. Marks?" Allin asks.

"Eight blocks up and to the right," a friend says.

"Man, then why are we walking the wrong fucking way?" says Allin.

He never made it back to St. Marks Place. Within hours, at the age of thirty-six, he had overdosed and died in an apartment on Avenue B. With him went St. Marks Place's reputation as a home for true depravity. The East Village's new residents were ready for a world without people like GG Allin. A few months later, the people elected a mayor who promised to deliver exactly that.

26

"I WAS A QUALITY OF LIFE VIOLATION"

In 1993 Bill Clinton took office, the first Democratic president in a dozen years. But New York City moved in the other direction. In 1994, aggressive former district attorney Rudy Giuliani became the 107th mayor of New York City, and the first Republican to hold the office in nearly three decades. He vowed to take New York City back for what he called "conventional members of society." "The era of fear has had a long enough reign," he said in his inauguration speech on the steps of City Hall. "The period of doubt has run its course. As of this moment, the expressions of cynicism—New York is not governable, New York is not manageable, New York is not worth it—all of these I declare politically incorrect. Let's not use them anymore."

British sociologist Ruth Glass had coined the term "gentrification" in 1964. Giuliani, together with his police commissioner William J. Bratton, seemed to personify it. The pair subscribed to the "Broken Windows Theory" of policing. It held that people are far less likely to break the window of a pristine apartment building than of a decrepit warehouse. If a community cracks down on smaller crimes, like littering and vandalism, more serious criminal behavior, too, will decline.

Giuliani and Bratton began a campaign against "quality of life violations" and instituted a zero-tolerance policy for minor infractions. The police zealously pursued subway-fare dodgers, panhandlers, small-time drug dealers, "squeegee guys"

The thieves' market, aka Bumingdale's. East Eighth Street between Astor Place and Broadway, ca. 1988. Photo by Jesper Haynes.

(who would "clean" your windshield with a filthy rag when you were stopped at a light and then demand payment for the service), and the other annoyances then rampant in New York.

In the seventies, the St. Mark's Block Association had done

what it could to clean up the neighborhood—they planted many of the trees that now line the street, for example—but they found little support from City Hall. Under Giuliani, that changed. "When Mayor Dinkins was in place, we went to his office to try to get rid of those guys," says Charles Fitzgerald, who as a shopkeeper trying to make a living had little patience for the dealers selling books and junk in the sidewalk thieves' markets. "[Dinkins] didn't want to seem to be against the people selling the books. We were totally frustrated. Right after Giuliani came in, a police lieutenant appeared on the block and said, 'Everybody out!' In a half hour, everyone was gone. It was over. We all breathed a sigh of relief."

In his play "Spare Change," Arthur Nersesian eulogizes the thieves' market. "I loved that shit," says Nersesian. "I collected old inkwells and phones and lighters. I bought my Selectric there to write on. I'm sure some of it was stolen. You had all these mentally unstable people. There would be operas unfolding. A guy would run over there and steal [an item] and then come back. It was a street scene." Luc Sante remembers the same set of writings by Khrushchev passing from one seller to another day after day for months; no one could sell it. "I got to know some of those sellers," says Nersesian. "They're probably all dead. Occasionally, I do see this one lady on crutches who used to sell porn."

One night, Nersesian had received a call from someone who'd found a draft of an unpublished novel with his name and phone number on the title page. "He offered to return it in exchange for a few bucks," says Nersesian. "I declined his offer and said that if he wanted to put his name on the cover and send it around, he'd probably have better luck getting it published."

Once Giuliani's police officers started kicking sellers' blankets, that world evaporated. The police also cracked down on drug dealing, which moved from street buys to delivery services. Gone were the days when twenty-year-olds would sit on the Tompkins Square Park benches with a joint, looking to other people for entertainment. Now people got high at home while watching movies rented from Mondo Kim's.

The owners of St. Mark's Bookshop, located at no. 13 from 1977 to 1987 and then at no. 12 from 1987 to 1993, were among those delighted to see the thieves' market curtailed. "The book tables were the worst for us," says co-owner Terry McCoy. "It didn't only affect us trying to make a living selling books, but there were turf wars. Those were dangerous people out there."

"The depressing part of St. Marks Place has always been how dirty it is," says architect Jonathan Kirschenfeld, who has lived between First and Second since the eighties. "You'd wake up sometimes and it was so distressing to see the garbage on the street and people sleeping on the stoops. I never minded it at night. It was in the morning. It's like when you catch fireflies in the night and put them in a jar and punch holes in it and it's beautiful—and then you wake up and you have a jar of dead bugs."

But many who had been drawn to St. Marks Place by the promise of freedom now felt as though they were under surveillance. As commercial areas like St. Marks Place became more gentrified, the city tightened zoning restrictions. Inspectors zealously enforced the city's old cabaret laws, which had once kept jazz musicians out of work. In the 1990s, the laws were used to prohibit dancing at clubs without an expensive license. This made life far more difficult for East Village partiers. Nick Zedd made a movie called *I Was a Quality of Life Violation*, in which a woman, is played by Rev. Jen Miller, putting up lost-dog signs is arrested for illegal flyering.

Just as during Prohibition, when St. Marks Place speakeasies had created a network of secret knocks and tunnels, bars in the 1990s found ways to circumvent the laws. At BoyBar, Paul

McGregor instituted a system. He painted "No Dancing" in six-foot tall letters on the wall. Anyone coming into the club had to go up one flight of stairs and then down another. In the event of a raid, the doorman would trip a secret alarm alerting the DJ booth, where DJ Johnny Dynell would immediately switch from dance to lounge music. "I would kill the disco lights," Dynell wrote, "and bring up lounge lighting. By the time the police got to the dance floor, the dancing had totally stopped and the crowd was just milling about under signs that read 'No Dancing,' listening to Laura Nyro." Still, BoyBar received noise complaints from neighbors and was shut down early in Giuliani's first term.

Coney Island High took over the space not long after and opened a three-floor, windowless nightclub. There were still occasional drag shows there. The downtown drag king Mr. Murray Hill launched his mayoral campaign at the club while still in art school. A Mr. Zero–like showman, Hill hit the scene calling himself "the hardest-working middle-aged man in show business." But Coney Island High was primarily a temple to punk rock. Those who had grown up listening to the Ramones got the chance to hear Ramones-inspired bands. Better still, they might find themselves on the roof of the club talking to Joey Ramone himself. Punk rockers like Cheetah Chrome of the Dead Boys, Blondie tour manager Mike Sticca, or Iggy Pop could occasionally be spotted at the club, sitting in the audience watching younger people invoking the street of twenty years before.

Like the Club 57 crowd before them, which had revered Warhol's Balloon Farm, the Coney Island High regulars who jammed the sweaty, claustrophobic shows were reenacting the scene that had first drawn them to the street. The club served as a safe, dark space for loud music and debauchery. Bands, many of which aped the sloppy playing style of CBGB circa

1977, typically netted about one hundred dollars a night, plus all they could drink. The four-hour sets grew chaotic as the booze flowed. Punk-show attendees wore the period garb of the original scene and strove for authenticity in all respects, including vomit.

For guitarist Mike Jackson, St. Marks Place hit its ecstatic peak with Coney Island High, where he played in the band Girltoucher. "If somebody didn't know that history, I'm not sure they would have seen it as anything more than a loud, dingy nightclub," says Jackson. "But if seventies and eighties punk rock was your thing, it was the ultimate living museum of it. It was the perfect re-creation of it. And yet it was also the real thing."

But outside the doors of Coney Island High, most New Yorkers were not nostalgic for the grim 1970s. The city was getting cleaner and safer. Beyond St. Marks Place most people thought that was a good thing. Giuliani won a second term by a landslide. After him, Mayor Michael Bloomberg was elected three times. While revelers on St. Marks Place drunkenly sang along with "Blank Generation," the rest of the city opted for money over poverty, and Billy Joel over Richard Hell.

Crime went down and empty buildings filled up with new, employed young people, and with an influx of immigrants. Immigration expert Joel Millman credits the increasing number of eyes on the street, not Giuliani, with the city's increased safety. But most New Yorkers—even if they didn't agree with his draconian methods—gave him credit for the city's turnaround. If it was a culture war, Giuliani won it. And St. Marks Place's rebels lost.

In 1993, Joyce Hartwell had been ordained as an interfaith minister at the New Seminary on Bank Street. To create more gathering spaces—and potential income sources—in the building, she opened the Imami Cyber Café for people in NA, and the New Age Cabaret for everyone else; and she drew up plans for a boutique hotel in the space. It was never built.

All-Craft, populated by seemingly disreputable people who spilled out onto the sidewalk, had never been popular with its bohemian neighbors; it was even less compatible with Giuliani's notion of a cleaner, tourist-friendly Manhattan. In 1995, a judge said Hartwell needed to install separate electrical systems for three tenants who had been living there for free since Hartwell bought the building in 1987.

The judge, skeptical of Hartwell's claim that she couldn't afford the renovations, held her in contempt of court and sentenced her to thirty days on Rikers Island. While Hartwell was in jail, members of Narcotics Anonymous raised the money for the electrical improvements. But it made little difference. In 1996, the *New York Times* reported that Hartwell was more than one million dollars in debt. "Dinkins's people considered our work phenomenal and said that we shouldn't have to pay what we owed the city, and didn't consider us in debt," says Hartwell. "The Giuliani administration didn't want to work with us."

Developer Charles Yassky won control of the building during bankruptcy proceedings. Hartwell was offered eight million dollars for the property but refused to sell. According to Hartwell, the organization covering her liability insurance let it lapse, causing her to lose favor with the bankruptcy court judge and costing her the decision.

Broke, Hartwell had to figure out where to go next. She decided on the state capital. "I felt like for years I had been pulling all these kids one at a time out of the river," says Hartwell. "You finally think, 'Wait a minute. How did all these children get in the river?' I decided that policy in Albany was important to address, so that programs like ours could be supported instead of closed." She packed up and moved to Albany, where she formed the Life Craft Foundation. She still lives there, advocating for social justice. Adorning a wall of her new office is a huge, painted praying-hands cutout that once hung on St. Marks Place.

The same year Hartwell lost All-Craft, Abe Lebewohl, owner of the Second Avenue Deli, was killed at the age of sixty-four while making his weekly drop at the NatWest bank on Second Avenue and East Fourth Street, near the former site of the Fillmore East. He was shot once in the head and once in the stomach, and was pronounced dead at Bellevue Hospital. A Polish immigrant who had survived the Holocaust, Lebewohl was a much-loved neighborhood figure, always giving food—soups, sandwiches, pickles—to the homeless, to strikers, to cops on patrol, to hospital patients. Photos on the walls of the deli showed Lebewohl with celebrities including Bob Hope and Muhammad Ali. Ten years later, the deli moved off of Second Avenue for good.*

In the summer of 1999, Coney Island High, too, closed. Rumors flew about the cause of the shutdown: a drug bust, noise complaints, fire-code violations, or an incoming fast-food restaurant. Most people on the scene suspected missteps by the managers, who were musicians, not businesspeople. In fact, landlord Paul McGregor had taken the partners to court for failing to pay rent. The judge said they had to come up with at least $150,000 or get out. They got out.

Mike Jackson now says it feels like he spent the best years of his life playing music and drinking at Coney Island High, but that in reality the golden age lasted probably only about ten months.

By the end of Giuliani's time as mayor, the major night-life landmarks on St. Marks Place were gone. Not a single

---

* Abe Lebewohl's murder was never solved, though the murder weapon was found in Central Park.

nightclub has opened there since. In 1961, there were 12,000 licensed cabarets in New York City. In 2002, there were 276. Young people making the pilgrimage to New York looking for the mythical St. Marks Place of *Kids* or Coney Island High could no longer find it. St. Marks Place was over—for real, this time—and it would never, ever be cool again.

"HOLD MY HAND.
SQUEEZE REAL TIGHT."

2000–2015

The restaurant Kenka and the clothing
store Search & Destroy, 2015.

Photo by the author.

i.

LITTLE TOKYO

And yet. New York City's public schools let out for summer vacation on June 26, 2014, a hot and sunny Thursday during World Cup fever. By dinnertime, St. Marks Place was full of liberated teenagers looking for places to eat. Near Avenue A, a young woman leaned down and applied mascara while looking in the mirror under Nino's Pizza's ATM. The sound of buzzed, excited conversation poured out of a dozen bars. Karaoke clubs were filling up. For a dead street, it seemed pretty lively.

Young people still flock here. And like those before them, today's visitors grew up hearing of the street's past. Nineteen-year-old Zac Bogus, who grew up on a farm in Pennsylvania, works behind the counter of hot-dog spot Papaya King (no. 3). He is tattooed, wears gauge earrings, loves punk music, and has long been obsessed with the history of St. Marks Place. "I fought to get this job on this street," Bogus says. "Did you know Andy Warhol had a club here? The Velvet Underground played there. *The Ramones* walked down this street." Signs on Papaya King's wall celebrate the neighborhood's history, though they could use some copyediting. Bogus tried in vain to get his bosses to fix the spelling of one sign mentioning "Cindy"—actually, Cyndi—Lauper.

Bogus is thinking about studying at the Fashion Institute of Technology. Meanwhile, even working a low-paying service job, he is ecstatic. Most days for his lunch break he gets a couple of one-dollar slices at 2 Bros Pizza (no. 32) and sits on the steps of Trash and Vaudeville with Jimmy Webb. At that store, Bogus once bumped into a pants-less Dave Navarro of the band Jane's Addiction.

Bogus's Instagram account shows a picture of two Asian men in front of the hot-dog restaurant. One is passed out cold on the street, lying on his back with one arm thrown back over his head. Another is standing over him, throwing up on the splayed one's pants. "Real friends purge on each other's groins," Bogus writes, "#saintmarks #turndownforwhat."

And there are more kids coming in every day, drawn here by images of St. Marks Place in popular culture. The TV shows *Girls* and *Broad City* both filmed scenes on St. Marks Place in the summer of 2014.

And where there are teenagers there are shops to serve them; on any given day, immigrants from China, Africa, and Bangladesh are here peddling sunglasses and bongs and earrings. An older Hispanic woman standing in front of a macaron cookie parlor at no. III sells snacks, including a sweet, hot, rice-and-milk drink out of a cooler set in a shopping cart. "She's got good stuff," says a hip young man buying tamales from her.

The salesmen of St. Marks between Second and Third Avenues commute from the Bronx and Queens. The teenagers they sell to come from all parts of New York City, New Jersey, and Long Island. Their interactions are intimate. Sounds come from behind a curtain in the little jewelry store at no. I, First Rich Body Piercing. "I'm just gonna do it," a girl's voice says. "I'm real nervous. Hold my hand. Squeeze real tight. Am I doing this? I'm doing this. Motherfucker! Motherfucker! Oh my GOD! Oh Jesus Christ!" The street's soundtrack still features cries of teen revelation.

Today, scrappy new theaters typically choose to open in cheaper parts of the city like Bushwick, Brooklyn. But the East

Village—especially the Public Theater's cabaret space, Joe's Pub, just below Astor Place—still stages shows in the cheerfully depraved old-neighborhood spirit. As the hours ran out on 2014, the neo-burlesque headliner Dirty Martini, wearing glittery blue eye shadow, could be seen rushing along St. Marks Place (where she has lived since 1993) to perform in Murray Hill's bawdy annual New Year's Eve show at Joe's.

Japanese entrepreneur Tony Yoshida, who once ran popular local restaurants Dojo and Around the Clock, and years before that could be seen hustling food here in a little cart, arguably started the Asian restaurant craze on St. Marks Place that in the past decade or so has earned it the name "Little Tokyo."

Out in front of the Japanese restaurant Kenka (no. 25), one of the most popular restaurants on the street, there stands a free make-your-own cotton candy machine, a demonic bear with blinking red light-bulb eyes, and a pornographically painted wooden cutout where patrons pose looking out of a woman's anus. Inside, the menus are designed like gaudy movie posters. In a little back garden, sexy naked mannequins lean against a wall.

"St. Marks Place has a lot of chill people," says an Asian Rutgers student who gave her name only as Anna, because she had been drinking on the street for years even though she is only now "twenty-one? I could say I was twenty-five, but you wouldn't believe me."

Standing with her friends waiting for a table at Kenka, she says that on her birthday she waited two hours for a table there, and declared that she owes a lot to St. Marks Place. "I met a lot of my friends just by walking around here. Also, these places are small, so you end up sharing tables with people and talking to them."

Anna rattles off the names of the many Japanese and Korean places now open on St. Marks Place for dinner, dessert, karaoke, and drinks. Boka (no. 9, where there was a gambling raid in 1900), she says, has the best watermelon soju (Korean vodka and watermelon juice ladled from a hollowed-out watermelon), and Iris Tea & Bakery Café (no. 33, where a slave trader was arrested in 1861, Urbain Ledoux hosted homeless men at the Tub in the 1930s, and Poetry Project poets partied in the late 1960s) offers some of the best desserts.

Down the block from Kenka at the upstairs club Sing Sing Karaoke, men and women gather around a long bar. After a few six-dollar cranberry-and-Japanese vodka drinks, they take turns singing songs requested via slips of paper passed to the bartender. Two men in their mid-twenties sitting on barstools by the door wear Japanese headbands reading "Batsu." They explain that they'd just participated in a game show at the sushi restaurant Jebon, which has been at no. 15 since 2003. "Batsu means punishment," they explain gleefully. David, age twenty-six, hails from the Bronx. His friend says that St. Marks Place is full of bargains: the St. Mark's Hotel can be rented for two hours for sixty dollars, the one-dollar pizza place will let you hang out all day, and the yakitori skewers down the block are only two dollars. The men request the Amy Winehouse song "Rehab" but learn that someone at the other end of the bar has already put in for that one. They settle for Seal's "Kiss from a Rose." David sings the song while repeatedly thrusting out his arm, making a fist, and then pulling it back in.

Down the bar, Rick and Antonella of Jersey City, after finishing up a rendition of "Part of Your World" from *The Little Mermaid*, say they are Sing Sing regulars. "I don't like this city," says Antonella. "I only like St. Marks Place." Rick has been coming to St. Marks for karaoke for years, but back in the day, he went to a place downstairs from Sing Sing that he claims was more authentic. "You had to get buzzed in. They had a video camera," Rick says. "We used to make fun of people who came here [to Sing Sing]. We used to say, 'That's not *real* karaoke!' Now we come here all the time."

A block away, St. Dymphna's bar (no. 118) is packed. Skater videos that could have been Harold Hunter's Zoo York mix tape play on a TV screen behind the bar. A Beastie Boys song plays over speakers. An elderly Chinese man comes in hawking light-up souvenirs to the young men and women enjoying a warm summer night on what is still the hippest street in America.

ii.

THE NOSTALGICS

On a rainy night in May 2014, a fire burned in the middle of East Seventh Street on the south end of Tompkins Square Park. Boxy blue 1980s cop cars, their lights flashing, discharged policemen in short-sleeved uniforms. An army of disconcertingly healthy-looking young men and women were dressed as strung-out anarchists. A movie called *Ten Thousand Saints*, based on a novel of the same name about straightedge kids and inevitably starring Ethan Hawke, was filming a scene about the riots.

At around 10 p.m., under a light rain, I stood with *New York Times* writer Jason Zinoman and watched as extras playing anarchists protested—silently, so as not to disturb local residents—the curfew enforcement. We had both witnessed the riots the first time around as children, and so we were giddy seeing it all again, as though a group of benevolent strangers had just offered to dramatize our old home movies.

Then a production assistant rushed past us out of the park and we heard her call out, "Wait! What time does the park close?"

With a laugh, Zinoman turned to me and said, "That's the question, isn't it?"

During developer-friendly billionaire Michael Bloomberg's reign as mayor, several new buildings rose on and around St. Marks Place, including a huge green-glass tower at Astor

Place nicknamed "The Green Monster." For those who loved the street's grittiness, every glittering pane was a shard to the eye. Between 2000 and 2012, the Lower East Side's average rent increased by 42 percent. In 2014 on St. Marks Place, a typical two-bedroom–one-bath was listed for $3,450 a month, a 650-square-foot storefront for $11,500. Corporate chains could afford the high rents. Kmart inhabited the former Wanamaker's annex at Astor Place. National chains proliferated. Most symbolically, the complex at nos. 19–23 that had been Arlington Hall, the Dom, the Electric Circus, and All-Craft was redeveloped as condos and houses chain stores like Chipotle and Supercuts. "That was really a huge turning point in the block's vibe," says musician Andrew W.K., who got his start performing at the Astor Place Starbucks, "and it never really had much of a chance after that."

"I can't tell you my real name," said the famously enigmatic East Village blogger E. V. Grieve over Budweisers at Odessa on Avenue A. Development in the East Village, Grieve says, has killed the counterculture by causing rent to surge and Middle-American businesses, like the yogurt chain Pinkberry, to push out East Village ones, like the famously grungy Mars Bar on East First Street.

Grieve started coming to St. Marks Place as a suburban kid in 1976 with his father, a lover of poetry and a fan of Allen Ginsberg. They trolled bookstores together. Grieve felt intimidated by the street's coolness. "I remember a lot of beards," he says, "and I remember a lot of denim and I remember it was summer and I remember women in . . . I don't know if they were halter tops or whatnot . . ." He looks away dreamily.

When he visited alone a decade later, he says St. Marks "seemed like the most magical place anywhere." Years later, when he moved to New York for college, he was shocked when he walked down the street. "I remember walking it from

Third Avenue and all of a sudden, *Wait, this is it? We're at the park!* I'd remembered it being so much bigger."

Grieve befriended a bartender at Grassroots Tavern (no. 20) and became a regular there. "I like the junky little thrift shops and the kiosks that sell—even if some of it's so cheesy and touristy—the shirts that say 'Welcome to New York. Now leave,' or the silly Travis Bickle T-shirts or the Ramones ones. I like the ticky-tacky shops like that, and I'm afraid that that's gonna go away soon with Fifty-One Astor Place looming large in the background."

On his blog, Grieve calls the sleek, black, thirteen-story building built at Astor Place in 2013, which features a bright-red, fourteen-foot-tall Jeff Koons rabbit sculpture in the lobby, "The Death Star." When it first went up, someone—*New York* magazine suspected the "ghost of the old East Village"—etched scratchiti on the building's brand-new windows. Grieve's readers trade sardonic quips and photos of the good old days when the Death Star was a Cooper Union building—not to mention, when Cooper Union was free. In the fall of 2014, for the first time in a century, the school that educated Milton Glaser and Thomas Edison began offering incoming students a half rather than a full scholarship.

Grieve, who got his start as a journalist and now works at an office job, worries about chain stores taking over. (There were at one point three Starbucks branches and three Chase banks within a three-block radius.) "I was walking on St. Marks," he says, "and there were two people in front of me probably coming from the St. Mark's Hotel. They seemed sort of like European tourists. And they stopped to go into 7-Eleven, and I thought I was saying it to myself—'*Don't*'—but I actually said it out loud. They just looked confused." (The St. Marks 7-Eleven has since closed. It lasted less than two years.)

He has a soft spot for tourists on the street, though. "I still get a kick out of seeing the teenager trying to be a badass, coming in from Port Authority or their mom's car, trying to be cool, maybe getting a piercing or something. Probably terrified—just like I was much, much earlier."

EVGrieve.com continues to mourn closings—the Holiday Lounge, Leshko's, Kiev. Not long after our dinner meeting there, Odessa, the diner where the poor and the young had long gathered to drink beer and eat stuffed cabbage while looking out into the darkness of Tompkins Square Park, shuttered as well.

"Here's yet another of the most important poets of our generation—not that anyone knows it," Bob Holman said on April 15, 2012, when introducing Lewis Warsh at a Bowery Poetry Club reading to benefit a new East Village audio walking tour that devotes a good chunk of time to St. Marks. "But of course that's the way we like it," he added in a classic expression of a particular brand of St. Marks-ian bohemianism: bitterness over lack of acclaim combined with pride in anonymity.

Holman makes up part of a guardian council self-appointed to preserve the value and importance of the neighborhood. From the stage, he said the club could use a financial supporter—"but not a hedge fund manager, who wouldn't 'get us.' "

Not long after, the Bowery Poetry Club closed. Holman skipped the closing party. Some of the regulars getting drunk on the bar's last cases of Pabst Blue Ribbon grumbled a little: "The shit hits the fan, and he's in Africa or something," one said. His whereabouts were a mystery until a reporter tracked him down in Wales, where he was filming a PBS documentary on endangered languages.

The Bowery Poetry Club space is now home to the restaurant Duane Park, which offers a twenty-three-dollar bacon-wrapped trout. It still hosts burlesque shows, but they're a far cry from the Bowery Poetry Club's old variety burlesque show,

Faceboy's Folliez, in which the nudity was rampant, coed, and often enthusiastically vulgar.

The speeches that final night—there were dozens over the course of several hours—implied that the club was too real, too pure to survive in the gentrified East Village. When the beer ran out, the poets walked up to the brand-new Bowery 7-Eleven to buy more.

"The wall of Five St. Marks Place has commercial value," Leslie Ogrin of Sand Realty told the *New York Times* in 2000, when a sign went up advertising the Gringo mural space for a billboard. Soon, the familiar eye-patched junkie vanished.

"When they painted over the mural of Spacely," says Jimmy Webb, "I stood on the stairs in front of the store and cried."

On his blog, Jeremiah's Vanishing New York, "Jeremiah Moss" wrote in 2014, "If hyper-gentrification were a person, it would be a malevolent psychopath—aggressive and remorseless, with a reckless disregard for others and an aptitude for deception." He says that a few years ago he noticed a change: "The streets were getting louder, more crowded with young people who didn't look or feel like the young East Villagers of the past several decades—they weren't punk, queer, creative, or crazy."

"There are a dozen bars, one after another," says Judy Josephs (no. 98) of her block. "There's an outdoor space where the people are drinking and screaming, and all the others where they are smoking and screaming and being twenty years old. It's awful, awful, awful. Even when we drank and did drugs, it was so much more interesting."

Village Alliance tour guide Jane Marx, who during one of her walking tours sported an outfit that was all yellow, except for purple sneakers and tortoiseshell glasses, said: "New Yorkers live in small apartments, where there's no room for a grudge. We talk fast and walk fast. It's spatial. We don't stab people in the back. We stab them in the front." When she saw a group of modern apartment buildings, she shouted, "Look at those *intrusions*! . . . The counterculture is dead," she explained to those on the tour, "because rent is too high. If you have a poetic soul, which I do, you want to keep old buildings. If you're a business, you want to knock them down."

Jimmy McMillan, who lives on St. Marks between First Avenue and Avenue A, agrees. In 2005, he founded the "Rent Is Too Damn High" political party. He ran for mayor in 2005, 2009, and 2013, and for governor and senator in 2010. While driving around in the rain looking for a parking spot in his customized Honda (it is stenciled with silhouettes of his unusual facial hair: a voluminous white handlebar mustache, side beard, and fluffy cleft goatee), he delivered a rant about the neighborhood. He said he may be facing eviction from his apartment. "Rent is the cancer—1,000 percent of the problems we all face today," he said. "You can't ask about hospitals because: the cost. You can't ask me about day care because: the cost. You can't talk about mortgage because: the cost.

"I took an oath in 1966 to serve this country, and I'm still under oath—like a police officer who is always a cop," says McMillan, who says he has no memories prior to a 1966 head injury incurred while fighting in Vietnam. Stopped at a red light, he asked me what I saw when I looked at the windshield.

"Rain," I said.

"That is what you see," he replied. "I don't. I see the tears of all the people who have been hurt, asking me, 'Jimmy, please help me,' and of my brother veterans who I left behind in Vietnam, and of those who are paying $4,700 a month for a one-bedroom apartment."

While we all deserve to mourn our own eras on St. Marks Place—when faced with grown-up problems, I pine for my time there as a wanton teenager—there is a remarkable lack of self-awareness in some criticism of the new East Village.

In his memoir *Poseur*, writer Marc Spitz describes his memories of the 1990s East Village, drinking greyhounds at the Holiday Cocktail Lounge. Of the girl who turned him on to heroin, he says: "Who wouldn't want to kiss a girl that smelled like St. Marks Place?" Spitz says that he doesn't recognize the Lower East Side when he goes there now. He envisions himself as among the last of the St. Marks Place bohemians and muses about what the "hipsters will move in and ruin" next. "If you ask old people like me," says the forty-something music writer and Bennington College graduate—who arrived in the 1990s to play out a junkie fantasy of the Lower East Side scripted in the 1970s—"you know what we're gonna say. It's almost our duty to say it."

"We're lucky," historian and drummer Eric Ferrara told me one day as we walked up the Bowery. Upon finding out that, like him, I had gone to CBGB before it became a John Varvatos store, he nodded approvingly: "We were the last ones," he said, "who were here when it was cool." I was on Ferrara's walking tour, during which he pulled out a binder of laminated old photographs to hold up against a current landscape of glass-and-steel construction. He glared at the people striding in and out of the new buildings wearing yoga pants and suits.

"They don't even know," he said, his voice hard. "That courtyard used to be where people died after drinking carbolic acid. That's when the Bowery was a real *place*. See the people who live there now? They don't even know." He sounded nostalgic for the days when people killed themselves with carbolic acid.

"St. Marks Place was a magic street," poet and artist Bill Kushner told me at the 2014 New Year's Day Marathon Reading at St. Mark's Church—an annual tradition since 1974. "Now it seems like the kids there just want to make money."

In a piece called "The East Village Is Replaced by Its Own Simulacrum"—one of an infinite number of similar nostalgia pieces recently written by men and women in their fifties, sixties, and seventies—writer Bill Weinberg complained about the closing of three businesses in his neighborhood, while acknowledging that he himself hadn't patronized them much in the past fifteen years.

In 2014, several more St. Marks institutions closed, including the Yaffa Café and the last Kim's outpost, on First Avenue and St. Marks. The Kim's chain had been struggling in the era of streaming video and Netflix and had also encountered legal trouble. Ten years before, one summer day in 2005, musician Chuck Bettis was working on the second floor of Mondo Kim's selling DVDs and vinyl when an undercover agent with the Recording Industry Association of America (RIAA) bought a mix tape with a Fifty Cent sample. Police then entered the store and said, "Who works here?" Forty years earlier, policemen had marched into East Side Books just a few doors down asking that same question, only the material then in question was *Zap Comix* no. 4.

Not long after that, Mondo Kim's closed. After hunting for a buyer who would preserve the collection in its entirety, Mr. Kim sold off all fifty-five thousand videos to the village of Salemi, in Sicily, Italy, where they now sit preserved in a cinder-block building.

Most of the remaining East Village squats closed around that same time, including the Cave (no. 120), an artists' collective where "Mosaic Man" Jim Power once lived. Power can be seen today on St. Marks Place, affixing shards of ceramic to lampposts to make his historical mosaics and delivering diatribes just as he has since 1985. "Warhol was an idiot," he recently told me. "He was a jerk. I guess he was an artist. I'm not an artist. What I'm doing is bigger than art. It's bigger than religion. It's bigger than a lot of things out there." After losing his space at the Cave, Power found public housing. An NYU student recently started helping him sell his mosaics online. Jaime Darrow, who works at a hip architecture firm and misses her time living on St. Marks, recently commissioned one. It reads, "Home Sweet Home."

THE CHURCH AND THE RELIGION

On a recent Sunday at St. Mark's Church-in-the-Bowery, now the oldest site of continuous worship in New York City, former Caucus members Nell and Bert Gibson sat in chairs at the center of the church. They looked eminently respectable, with graying hair and formal clothes. Bert is the chief financial officer of the Upper Manhattan Empowerment Zone development corporation. Over the years, the Gibsons have served on the vestry and been wardens of the church. Today their daughter, Erika, is the vestry's clerk. It was the Gibsons

St. Mark's Church, fall 2014.
Photo by the author.

who originally recommended the new rector, Winnie Varghese, a tough, friendly Indian-American priest with a wife and two children, to the search committee. The Gibsons and Varghese share an admiration for former vestry member Pauli Murray. Varghese keeps a photo of Murray in her office.

St. Mark's doesn't have the same hostile relationship with its authorizing body that it had in the past. The Episcopal Church has embraced many ideas that St. Mark's championed early on, such as the ordination of gay priests. As of this year, church attendance has returned to its pre–October 1969 numbers, with some two hundred people regularly attending services.

Still, St. Mark's struggles to survive financially. Had the property that Allen divested in the 1960s stayed with the church, it could have generated substantial revenue. But his legacy is felt positively, too, in the diverse congregation and liturgy centered on racial equality and social justice. On a recent Sunday, Mother Winnie preached a message of equality and fairness to a congregation of men and women of all ages and races. There was a hymn in Spanish. Rather than receiving the Eucharist from the priest, parishioners passed it one to the next, telling each other, "The blood of Christ and the bread of Salvation." It was more or less exactly what Father Michael Allen had in mind when he said, in 1969, "I think we could be better."

The religion of St. Marks Place, the belief that the street is a space for people who are different, endures, and so do plenty of longtime residents. Charles Fitzgerald still lives there, between Second and Third Avenues. Katie Schneeman is still there too, eating meals with her son Paul at the table her husband made fifty years ago from an old St. Marks Place door.

Downtown performer Penny Arcade, cofounder of the Lower East Side Biography Project, often says that New York has not only been gentrified—it's been "colonized." But Arcade, who came to the East Village in 1967 from Connecticut, hung out with the hippie martyr Groovy, and lived at no. 13 in the late sixties, says St. Marks Place between Second and Third Avenues is the one street in the city immune to gentrification. "There's something magnetic and chaotic about it," she says. "Any time of the day or night there are people on it. Somehow you can't gentrify that block."

The Ukrainian Festival is still celebrated in the neighborhood every year. Neighbors gather with unwieldy paper plates full of pierogi, stuffed cabbage, and kielbasa to watch Ukrainian children in full native dress dance on a raised stage to blaring traditional music.

Adriana Leshko lives on St. Marks between First and Second and notes that it's still possible to navigate an entire day in the neighborhood—banking, buying groceries, eating out, reading the newspaper—all in Ukrainian. During the anti-government protests in Kiev in 2014, a bartender at the Sly Fox, a small, old-school bar around the corner from St. Marks on Second Avenue, raised money for the demonstrators. In March 2014, a vigil was maintained in front of the Ukrainian National Home with flowers, candles, and pictures of protesters who were killed. Above them hung a handmade sign that read, "Our Heroes."

Barbara Sibley's Mexican restaurant La Palapa (no. 77), with its plaque to W. H. Auden, has been on the street long enough to qualify as a quasi-landmark. Now Sibley is helping Pirate Booty magnate Robert Erlich with his renovation of the old Holiday Cocktail Lounge at no. 75. In its basement, Sibley recently found showers where dancers cleaned off when the club was a burlesque house called Ali Baba in the 1940s. Prior to that, the Holiday had been a speakeasy. That element of the street's history is preserved at Lorcan Otway's Museum of the American Gangster (no. 80) and is reenacted at no. 113, where an unmarked storefront conceals a secret bar called

PDT (Please Don't Tell). Entrance is via an unassuming phone booth inside the hot-dog restaurant Crif Dogs. (Sorry, PDT.)

In October 2014, a new bar and arcade opened in the ground floor of no. 6, which once housed Mondo Kim's and, before that, the St. Mark's Baths. Barcade co-owner Pete Langway says neighbors have been coming in to check out the space, especially the wall of the original white-and-green Baths tiles uncovered by renovations along the wall behind the bar. "This older guy came in to look at the tile for a long time," Langway says. "He said, 'This whole bar used to be a swimming pool.'"

While this era's primary St. Marks Place story may be about new buildings and higher rents, so much remains unchanged. The negotiation over the price of a bong or bracelet now is identical to the one that would have taken place there fifty years ago. And while they're touted as symbols of a corporate takeover, developments like the "Death Star" at Astor Place actually tend to make teenagers' lives easier, as they provide free public outdoor seating, removing the hassle of being chased from one stoop to another by annoyed residents.

Old St. Marks Place remains tucked in between frozen-yogurt shops and e-cigarette stores. Three 1830s row houses still stand. The barbers at Royal Hair give men buzz cuts just as they have for decades. People continue to order egg creams with their newspapers at Gem Spa. Anthony Scifo and his family sell shoes at Foot Gear Plus, on the corner of St. Marks and First Avenue, as they have for thirty-five years (and as they will for at least another twelve; they just signed a new lease). Bartenders at Grassroots still encourage drinkers' thirst by providing one-dollar bowls of salty popcorn. Kiehl's Pharmacy, founded in 1851, perseveres on Thirteenth Street; they recently replaced the pear tree that was knocked down in the nineteenth century, adding several more for good measure.

In the spirit of the street's progressive era, and in the same school building where Polish boys once learned that World

War II had begun, the George Jackson Academy at no. 104 offers a competitive private education to boys from low-income homes. Across the street, the Little Missionary Day Nursery founded by Sara Curry prospers in its original spot at no. 93. Curry's portrait looks down, mirror-like, on Eileen Johnson, a warm, generous woman so similarly featured that they could be twins, were they not separated by a century. "I always ask," says Johnson, "'What would Sara Curry do?'"

On October 5, 2013, Little Missionary hosted a street fair with a bounce house, a sand-art table, and food booths. In a quiet ceremony, a sign was unveiled at the corner of First Avenue co-naming that block of St. Marks Place "Sara Curry Way." When the cover fell away, Johnson looked at the sign and her eyes welled with happy tears.

One quality-of-life plague has survived cabaret laws and crackdowns: the street kids called "crusty punks." For decades, the police have been chasing off earlier incarnations of this tribe, but again and again they return to St. Marks Place, an army of dreadlocks and piercings, armed with their pit bulls, forties, and crude cardboard signs asking for change.

Even the old punks, who also have tattoos and ripped clothes, who drank and drugged on the same street thirty or forty years ago—and who were themselves despised—scoff at the new rabble.

"They're trustifarians," says Ann Tyson, using a funny word for a common belief, that these young people are only dabbling in poverty.

"They just take," says Jimmy Webb. "They don't add."

"They're filth," says building superintendent Hysen Gjonaj right after he tries to stop two of them from tagging no. 67 in the middle of the day. There is yelling on both sides, but the crusty punks have the last word: "Go do what old people do," one tells Gjonaj, who has lived and worked on the block for decades, "and *die*." The two guffawing hoodlums then swagger down St. Marks toward Tompkins Square Park.

The crusties, though hated, are a mainstay of St. Marks Place. And within their group, they live by a code of loyalty and friendship. They also share a hero: a man who could be called the king of the crusty punks, sometime-poet Joel Pakela, known as LES Jewels, whose distinctive face tattoos included a jewel around his right eye, dots under his left, a star on his left cheek, and a lightning bolt on his right.

For years, Jewels accosted passersby on the corner of St. Marks Place and Avenue A, hit cabs with his cane, and seemed determined to innovate in the field of indecency. He flashed strangers, defecated on park benches, and engaged in pastimes like "trash sledding," which involved picking up a full trash

LES Jewels during one of his many scuffles with the NYPD, 2006. Photo by Lorcan Otway.

bag, running down the street, then sliding on it, leaving trails of empty coffee cups, used tissues, and apple cores in his wake. His preferred title was "gutter pirate."

Blogger Bob Arihood kept a running commentary on LES Jewels's behavior on the blog Neither More nor Less. A sample: "Wednesday night the usual suspect with a cane was again pissing at the infamous 'Pee Phone' at the corner of Seventh Street and Avenue A. . . . Jewels was on his usual drunken rampage . . . smart-mouthing, bad-mouthing, insulting and taunting all. He threatened folks with his cane raised; a cab driver beat him for such behavior. . . . He managed to purposefully rip Ray's garbage bags, spilling the garbage they contained all around on the sidewalk."

Jewels died in September 2013 at age forty-three. A eulogy on the blog "Save the Lower East Side!" was typical: "LES Jewels, the most transgressive man I know: indifferent to safety, security, health, decorum, decency, police, imprisonment, violence, or any protection from all the dangers we fear. . . . The spirit of the old neighborhood lived in him."

Jewels's longtime love interest had him cremated. Then she put his ashes into a series of saltshakers and other small containers and handed them out to his friends. "I got one of the biggest ones," brags a man who calls himself Booshy-Boosh, sitting on the ground in front of no. 30. The most hated group on the street mourns the man who was hated most of all. They cling to his ashes, carrying this relic of their history on St. Marks Place into its future.

Though St. Marks Place will probably always elude true respectability, the street today is safer and more pleasant than at any point in the last fifty years. "Now you walk down the street and people say 'Excuse me' when they bump into you," says Charles Fitzgerald. "I found a piece of old furniture on the street near St. Mark's Bookshop [now on East Third Street and Avenue A], and carrying it back to St. Marks Place, four people offered to help me, including a seventeen-year-old girl. That never used to happen."

When my son turned seven, we threw a *Harry Potter*–themed slumber party at my parents' apartment. The next morning, when he and his friends woke up just after dawn, we fed them pancakes and escorted them the block and a half to Tompkins Square Park, which had been closed to me as a child. Joggers and dog walkers chuckled at the small army negotiating St. Marks Place in Hogwarts robes. And then, not far from the park's nineteenth-century temperance fountain, World War II commemorative flagpole, and *General Slocum* memorial, the wizard children played as sunlight streamed through the trees.

For Richard Manitoba—who came to the street to see shows at the Fillmore East in 1968, to play punk rock at CBGB in 1976, and to get sober at All-Craft in 1983—the East Village is still home. He runs Manitoba's, a bar on Avenue B near Tompkins Square Park. His jukebox is a who's-who of St. Marks Place in the 1970s and '80s. And St. Marks Place is now a street to explore with his child.

"Jake," Manitoba tells his son, "I walked down these streets forty-five years ago, when I was fifteen. That was my greatest period ever. That was my back-in-the-day." But Manitoba is philosophical about the street's changes: "Now my son's going to be fifteen," he says, "and life is going to be thrilling and exciting for him. We're all going to look at the things that are thrilling and exciting for him and say, 'But that music sucks!' Gee wilikers, guess who else said that? Every generation ever."

Asked to name St. Marks Place's golden age, the street's oldest residents—superintendent Hysen Gjonaj of the former Yugoslavia, who lives at no. 131; Ukrainian butcher Julian Baczynsky, who lives at no. 45; Puerto Rican retired special-education teacher Amelia Hernandez, who has lived at no. 24 since 1940—all smiled, and all said the same thing: "Now."

ST. MARKS PLACE IN POPULAR CULTURE

Songs Name-Checking St. Marks Place

"Alex Chilton," The Replacements.

"Angel," Exposé.

"Avenue A," The Dictators.

"Bad Boy," The Holy Modal Rounders.

"The Birds of St. Marks," Jackson Browne.

"The City," Joe Purdy.

"Crooked Smile," Peter Case.

"Detachable Penis," King Missile.

"Downtown," John Waite.

"A Dream," John Cale and Lou Reed.

"East Village/East Berlin," Phoebe Legere.

"Eyes On Fire," Outernational.

"40 Shades Of Blue (For Kevin Wherever You Are)," Black 47.

"Get Me Out," Slapshot.

"Hendershot," Les Claypool and the Holy Mackerel.

"I Went Walking," Rank and File.

"Lower East Side," David Peel and the Lower East Side.

"New York City," Moe.

"New York City Girl," Riot99.

"95 St. Marks Place," The Sharp Things.

"Of Information & Belief," June of 44.

"On the Drag," They Might Be Giants.

"Police Brutality," The Casualties.

"Potter's Field," Tom Waits.

"Roadrunner," Joan Jett and the Blackhearts.

"St. Marks & Third—The Five Spot," The M Jones Project.

"St. Mark's Place among the Sewers," Jaki Byard Quartet.

"St. Mark's Place," Jack Adaptor.

"St. Mark's Place," Ben Paterson Trio.

"St. Marks Place," *Heart's Delight Follies '69*.

"St. Mark's Place," Jasna Jovicevic.

"St. Mark's Place," Jim Lampos.

"St. Marks Place," Kevin K.

"St Marks Place," Lydia Lunch and Jeffrey Lee Pierce.

"St Mark's Place," Kirsty McGee.

"St Mark's Place," Skip the Use.

"St. Marks Place (feat. Martha Davis)," Earl Slick.

"St. Mark's Sunset," Jesse Malin & The St. Marks Social.

"Sally Can't Dance," Lou Reed.

"Sci-Fi Wasabi," Cibo Matto.

"Scowling Crackhead Ian," Jeffrey Lewis.

"So Natural," Jim Sullivan.

"Storytellers," Michelle Lewis.

"Stranger on St. Marks Place," Joe Cahill.

"Stranger on St. Marks Place," John Carey.

"Sunday New York Times," Matt Nathanson.

"Talking Vietnam Potluck Blues," Tom Paxton.

"This Is Not the Time," Hot Rod Circuit.

"Welfare City," Gene McDaniels.

"When a Pretty Face," Adam Green.

"Why Should I Worry," *Oliver and Company*, Billy Joel.

Movies and TV Shows Using St. Marks as a Location
(or about Some Aspect of It)

Ai Weiwei: Never Sorry (2012). The artist photographs the late eighties and early nineties Tompkins Square Park riots in New York City.

Arthur (2011). AA scenes filmed at St. Mark's Church.

The Blank Generation (1976).

Blank Generation (1980).

Blast of Silence (1961).

Born to Lose: The Last Rock and Roll Movie (1999).

Bowery Dish (2005).

Brave New York (2004).

Captured (2010?).

Damn! Is the Price of Fame Too Damn High? (2011).

Desperately Seeking Susan (1985). Scenes filmed on St. Marks Place.

Escape from New York (1981).

Flaming Creatures (1963).

Ghostbusters II (1989). Scene set at St. Mark's Comics.

The Golden Age of Second Avenue (2009).

Gringo, aka *Story of a Junkie* (1987).

The Group (1966). St. Mark's Church location.

Hair (1979). "Hair" song filmed on St. Marks Place.

Hated: G.G. Allin and the Murder Junkies (1994). Allin is interviewed in the St. Mark's Hotel.

Hells Angels Forever (1983). http://www.youtube.com/watch?v=2Y5nOs8qshM.

"History of the Development of Punk on the Lower East Side," Jeffrey Lewis, Pont FMR, Paris, May 15, 2012. http://www.youtube.com/watch?v=GB5bE6XjB3w.

The Holy Modal Rounders: Born to Lose (2006).

House of the Rising Punk (1998).

How to Lose Friends and Alienate People (2008). Looking out the taxi window as he arrives in New York City, Simon Pegg's character sees Times Square, then St. Marks Place, then Times Square, and then St. Marks Place.

I Remember (2012). http://www.joebrainardfilm.com/Watch-The-Film.

Iggy Pop Tour of the East Village (1993). http://www.youtube.com/watch?v=JKGeh4cVRZE.

Joe (1970). Runaway/orgy scene filmed on St. Marks.

Kids (1995). Telly's apartment is on St. Marks.

Knickerbocker Holiday (film made of the 1938 musical by Kurt Weill and Maxwell Anderson). Here is the "September Song" about Peter Stuyvesant sung by Walter Huston: http://www.youtube.com/watch?v=Dy7gWVBiH8Y.

Koch (2012).

Last Call (2014). Brazilian documentary by Ruth Slinger about New York City in the 1990s.

Lenny (1974).

The Lifeguard (2013). The film opens on Astor Place.

Little Stabs at Happiness (1963). Jack Smith cavorts on St. Marks Place.

Mad Men (season 6, episodes 1 and 2, "The Doorway," April 7, 2013; and Episode 4, "To Have and to Hold," April 21, 2013).

Manhattan Melodrama (1934). Opens with the *General Slocum* disaster. (Which is also its own musical composition: Charles Ives's "The General Slocum." One can listen to it here: http://www.youtube.com/watch?v=cR76S6EHGT0.)

"A Matter of Trust" (1986). Billy Joel video shot in All-Craft basement and outside on St. Marks between Second and Third Avenues.

Midnight Cowboy (1969). The "trip" scene is set at the Electric Circus.

Mixed Blood (1984).

Mondo New York (1988).

Moscow on the Hudson (1984) shows St. Marks Cinema.

Mrs. Santa Claus (1996). Set on Avenue A.

New York Doll (2005). Great Greg Whiteley documentary about Arthur Kane, who became a Mormon. St. Marks is just in it for a second: Gem Spa back cover.

News from Home (1977), by Chantal Ackerman.

The Nomi Song (2004).

On the Bowery (1956).

1/3 (One Third) (2006), by Yongman Kim of Kim's Video. The silent film about a teen prostitute and a Buddhist monk is set largely on St. Marks between Second and Third Avenues, where the two are neighbors.

Punking Out (1978). http://www.punkingoutfilm.com/DVD.html.

The Queen (1968). Drag queens at 82 Club documentary.

Rent (2005).

Runaways on St. Marks Place (2006).

Saturday Night Live ca. 2010 opening credits (Cherries).

7th Street (2003).

Sex and the City ("Hot Child in the City," season 3, episode 15, September 24, 2000). Carrie gets her shoes fixed at East Village Shoe Repair and dates a man she meets at St. Mark's Comics.

Sidewalks of New York (2001). Brittany Murphy's character works at Stingy Lulus and is interviewed in Tompkins Square Park.

Silence = Death (1990).

"Step" (official lyrics video), Vampire Weekend. Mentions Astor Place and shows Royal Hair, Astor Place. http://www.youtube.com/watch?v=_mDxcDjg9P4.

Stranger Than Paradise (1984). Jim Jarmusch filmed the poker scene at no. 130.

The Street of Forgotten Men (1925 silent film). Clip: http://www.youtube.com/watch?v=DNdBKubxlV8.

Style Wars (1983).

Nelson Sullivan videos from 1980s. http://www.youtube.com/watch?v=ZVmrewNtsyg.

Taking of Pelham One Two Three (1974). Car speeds up Lafayette through Astor Place.

Trash (1970). Joe Dallesandro scenes filmed on St. Marks Place.

200 Cigarettes (1999). Scenes on and around St. Marks Place.

Vapors is set in the St. Mark's Baths but was actually filmed elsewhere. https://www.youtube.com/watch?v=6DrCyjzwoWw.

Viva Loisaida (1978). http://www.youtube.com/watch?v=3ciVWF2gg-8.

"Waiting on a Friend," Rolling Stones (1981).

The Weather Underground (2002).

"Weekend Explorer: Art and Unrest in the East Village." *New York Times* video (September 13, 2007).

What about Me (1993). Shot around St. Marks, stars Richard Hell, Nick Zedd, etc. By Rachel Amodeo. http://rachelamodeo.com.

What Would Jesus Buy? (2007). Reverend Billy at St. Mark's Church.

The Wonder Ring, Stan Brakhage (1955). Footage of the Third Avenue El. https://www.youtube.com/watch?v=uD7uqs4y7tQ.

ACKNOWLEDGMENTS

William Warder Norton launched his publishing company in 1923 with "Lectures in Print" pamphlets at Cooper Union, at the western end of St. Marks Place. Nearly a century later, his house has given this book the best of all possible homes. My wise and creative editor, Tom Mayer, had me rewrite this book several times without making me hate him. He did this by always being right, and by offering advice like, "Read a few August Wilson plays and think about the structure of one-set drama," which is sort of the opposite of what editors usually say two years into a book project. Ryan Harrington, Tom's assistant, is supersmart, ultra-efficient, and great fun to be around. This book would be a shadow of itself if not for the two of them. Thanks also to the rest of the team there, including designer David High, lawyer Laura Goldin, production manager Louise Mattarelliano, designer Chris Welch, managing editor Nancy Palmquist, and copy editors Tara Powers and Stephanie Hiebert.

Thanks to Peter Steinberg for believing in this idea early on and for introducing me to Tom, and to everyone who helped me make a living through writing and editing assignments, teaching work, and fellowships while working on the book these past three years, including Anthony DeCurtis, Peggy Engel, Sheila Glaser, Daniel Greenberg, Kathleen Hanna, Logan Hill, David Kelly, Andy McNicol, Vanessa Mobley, Julia Pimsleur, Colin Quinn, and Kristal Zook. Thanks also to thoughtful early readers of chapters, including Jami Attenberg, Boris Fishman, Robi Polgar, Lili Taylor, and Jason Zinoman.

Thanks to clutch babysitter Erica Pirchio, inspirational cabal the Invisible Institute, and friends Tara McKelvey and Tim Gunn (who more than deserves his reputation as the nicest man in the world); and to all the places in New York City that let me write there when I had to escape my tiny, LEGO brick–strewn apartment, especially the New York Public Library (Schwarzman, Mid-Manhattan, Jefferson Market, and Ottendorfer branches) and the South 4th Bar & Café.

Endless gratitude to the 2014 Alicia Patterson Foundation Josephine Patterson Albright Fellowship, 2014 Kiplinger Fellowship, 2014 Residency at the New York Public Library's Frederick Lewis Allen Room, 2013 MacDowell Colony Residency, Oasis 2013 Commission Grant, and the Council on Contemporary Families 2013 Media Award for Print Coverage of Family Issues.

Love to my family, in particular the Medlin men: my husband, Neal; stepson, Andrew Blake; and son, Oliver. Oliver was born at the since-closed St. Vincent's Hospital in the West Village in 2006, and the first person to hold him was nurse Rita Devine, who has lived on St. Marks Place for more than thirty years.

Archives

Thanks to all the experts who helped me ransack their amazing collections, especially everyone at the New York Public Library, among them: Maira Liriano (U.S. History) and Matt Knutzen (Maps). Also infinite thanks to the generous souls over at St. Mark's Church-in-the-Bowery, especially Winnie Varghese and Roger Jack Walters. Roger not only let me camp out in the archives, but also read drafts of chapters and offered vital corrections. Other exceptionally helpful archivists: the Allen Ginsberg Archive's Bob Rosenthal; Boo-Hooray Gallery's Gabriel McKee; Cooper Union's Carol A. Salomon (who, thanks to her conscientious review of pages I sent her, saved me from several errors); the NYU Fales Library's Lisa Darms; Little Missionary Day Nursery's Eileen Johnson; Municipal Arts Society's Erin Butler; Museum of the American Gangster/Theatre 80's Lorcan Otway; MoMA library's Jennifer Tobias; Neighborhood Preservation Center's Felicia Mayro; New-York Historical Society's Marci Reaven; NYU Tamiment Library's Sarah Moazeni and Kate Donovan. And thanks to the countless people who went out of their way to provide timely research recommendations, including Rebecca Amato, Harry Kellerman, C. Greg Kirmser, Tony Mann, Molly McGlone, John McMillian, Joel Millman, Annelise Ream, Christopher Rzigalinski, Luc Sante, David Smith, Darcey Steinke, and David Voorhees.

Interviews

More than two hundred St. Marks Place denizens helped with this book. I am grateful to everyone who spoke with me over eggs at Café Mogador (no. 101) or wine at Café Orlin (no. 41), responded to my emails, answered my phone calls, invited me into their homes, or let me stop them on the street. Whether we spoke for five minutes or five hours, your contribution is appreciated. Thank you: George Ackerman; Cey Adams; Judy Gumbo Albert; Brooke Alderson; Adam Alexander; Leslie Alexander; Michael Allen; Tara Allmen; "Anna"; Penny Arcade; David Arnold; Julian Baczynsky; Elliott Banfield; Bill Barrell; Ted Barron; Roberta Bayley; Kevin Beard; Snooky Bellomo; Tish Bellomo; Anselm Berrigan; Edmund Berrigan; Chuck Bettis; Tom Birchard; Zac Bogus; Jerry Brandt; Perry Brass; Peter Brill; Michael Brownstein; Maggie Bullock;

Ambrose Bye; David Cale; John Campo; Nancy Cardozo; Kristin Carey; Kathy Cerick; Lisa Chamberlain; Robert Christgau; David Ciriaco; Christen Clifford; Paula Collery; Bob Contant; "Crusties" Booshy-Boosh, Rokkoe, and Princess; Cary Curran; Nadia Dajani; Manohla Dargis; Lisa Darms; Jamie Darrow; Darla Decker; Paul Delaney; Paul DeRienzo; Danny Diablo; Mike Diamond; Joey Dick; Bill DiPaola; Nicky Dirt; Johnny Dynell; Michael Sean Edwards; John Erdman; James Estrada; Scott Ewalt; Stephen Facey; Arnold Feinblatt; Susan Fensten; Larry Fink; Steve Firestone; Charles Fitzgerald; Al Forsyth; Jessica Forsyth; Libby Forsyth; Priscilla Forsyth; Eileen Freedman; Marty Freedman; James Fuentes; Michael Galinksy; David Garcia; Judy Garrison; Charles Gehring; Phillip Giambri; Bert Gibson; Nell Gibson; Hysen Gjonaj; David Godlis; Daniel Greenberg; John Gregg; "E.V. Grieve"; Art Guerra; John S. Hall; Myrna Hall; Zoe Hansen; Debbie Harry; Joyce Hartwell; Jesper Haynes; Amelia Hernandez; Murray Hill; Mike Hodder; John Holmstrom; Adam Horovitz; Mark Howell; Ronald Hunter; Ernie Hurwitz; Mike Jackson; Jaap Jacobs; Billy Jacobson; Mark Jacobson; Rae Jacobson; Rosie Jacobson; Angela Jaeger; Eileen Johnson; Joyce Johnson; Hettie Jones; Jeff Jones; Thai Jones; Barry Joseph; Judith Josephs; Linda Justice; Milton Kamen; Matthew Kasten; Steven "Perfidia" Kirkham; Jonathan Kirschenfeld; Highlyann Krasner; Paul Krassner; BB Kuett; Bill Kushner; Pete Langway; Ben Laurence; Pamela Lawton; Phoebe Legere; Adriana Leshko; Jaroslaw Leshko; Ross Lewis; Gene Lichtenstein; Miranda Lichtenstein; Annie Lionni; Jessica Loeser; Lydia Lunch; Jenny Lynch; Ann Magnuson; Alyssa Maldonado; Richard "Handsome Dick" Manitoba; Tony Mann; Matt Marello; Mariann Marlowe; Danny Martin; Dirty Martini; Felicia Mayro; Khadejha McCall; Terry McCoy; Arthur McGee; Chloe Sweeney McGlade; Jimmy McMillan; Rick Meeker; Rev. Jen Miller; Joel Millman; Amaury Mondol; Wells Moore; Ben Morea; "Jeremiah Moss"; Mary Nelson; Paula McGregor Newman; Jeremiah Newton; Dan Oko; Kristina Olitski; Lorcan Otway; Ron Padgett; Clayton Patterson; Philip Pearlstein; Rosebud Pettet; Father Tom Pike; Jim Power; Robert Prichard; Adam Purple (aka David Wilkie, aka Les Ego); Colin Quinn; Antonella Rao; Marci Reaven; Henry Rollins; Bob Rosenthal; Carole Rosenthal; Jeff Roth; Philip Roth; Nancy Rubin; Jerry Saltz; Ann Sanfedele; Luc Sante; Robert Sawyer; Kenny Scharf; Peter Schjeldahl; Katie Schneeman; Paul Schneeman; Jerome Schwartz; Anthony Scifo; Barbara Sibley; Gary Simmons; Joey Skaggs; Curtis Sliwa; Ratso Sloan; Guy Richards Smit; David Smith; Peter Nolan Smith; Raven Snook; Raven Solano; Sherry Sotomayor; Sparrow; Peter Stampfel; Johnny Sundstrom; Carl Swanson; Taku; Louise Teiga; J. G. Thirlwell; Kim Turim; Ann Tyson; Rachel Tyson; Winnie Varghese; Anne Waldman; Roger Jack Walters; Lewis Warsh; John Waters; Jimmy Webb; Arnie Weinberg; Susan Wheeler; Joshua White; Elin Wilder-Melcher; Andrew W.K.; Bert Zackim; Nick Zedd; Jason Zinoman.

Photos

Thank you to all the photographers who helped me secure images for this book, especially John Penley, Roberta Bayley, and David Godlis, who were above-and-beyond generous with their time and work. The *New York Times*'s Jeff Roth, a kind soul and ridiculously sharp dresser, mined the paper's photo morgue for treasures like the image of W. H. Auden in his slippers at the hardware store, that without his diligence may have been lost in time.

In Memoriam

A number of people important to the life of St. Marks Place have died since I began work on this book, including Michael Allen, Amiri Baraka, Leee Black Childers, Curly Giambri, LES Jewels, Derek Lloyd, Judith Malina, Paul McGregor, Taylor Mead, Florence Otway, Rosebud Pettet, Tommy Ramone, Lou Reed, Rene Ricard, and Adam Yauch. The neighborhood also lost two people in the horrible March 2015 building explosion on Second Avenue between St. Marks and Seventh Street: Nicholas Figueroa and Moises Locon. Earlier losses also deeply felt while working on this book: Veronica Geng, Jeremy Morris, Elio Schneeman, George Schneeman, and Brad Will. May they all rest in peace.

NOTES

Epigraph

ix **"Visit New York for the first time":** Percy Seitlin, *That New York*, from "About U.S.: Experimental Typography by American Designers," a series of sixteen-page inserts reprinted from *Der Druckspiegel*, graphic-arts magazine, Stuttgart, Germany. Conceived, edited, set in type in New York and produced under the sponsorship of The Composing Room, Inc., 1960, p. 4. Copy available in the MoMA library.

Introduction

xiv **More than forty songs:** See song list in appendix.

xvi **"I came back from break":** Interview of James Estrada by the author, March 13, 2013.

xvi **"Bohemia is always yesterday":** Malcolm Cowley, *Exile's Return*, p. 62.

xvii **"Unto you it is given to know":** Mark 4:11, King James Bible, Authorized Version, Cambridge Edition.

xvii **"The artists and the poets:** Interview of Michael Allen by the author, July 9, 2012.

Chapter 1

3 **the Lenape camped in the forest:** The WCS Welikia (formerly Mannahatta) Project's addictive website shows how New York City looked, block by block, in 1609.

3 **Kintecoying:** Meta F. Janowitz and Diane Dallal, "New Amsterdam: Americans and Europeans, Historical Background," in *Tales of Gotham, Historical Archaeology, Ethnohistory and Microhistory of New York City* (New York: Springer, 2013), p. 3.

3 **this was where Lenape men hunted:** The man who answered the phone at the Lenape's headquarters referred me to Herbert C. Kraft, *The Lenape-*

Delaware Indian Heritage, saying it is the definitive story of this area at this time. This description owes much to that book: Herbert C. Kraft, *The Lenape-Delaware Indian Heritage: 10,000 BC to AD 2000* (Lenape Books, 2001), p. 56.

3   **"monster of the sea"**: Janowitz and Dallal, "New Amsterdam," in *Tales of Gotham*, p. 10.

3   **whales, seals, and porpoises**: According to the Wildlife Conservation Society, these creatures lived in New York Harbor in 1609.

3   **Dutch West India Company**: Edwin G. Burrows and Mike Wallace, *Gotham: A History of New York City to 1898* (New York: Oxford University Press, 1999), p. 19. They also have a good analysis of "The $24 Question" starting on p. xiv.

3   **This tiny, barely defended colony**: Ibid., p. xvii.

4   **"It is the land where milk and honey flow"**: Henry H. Kessler and Eugene Rachlis, *Peter Stuyvesant and His New York* (New York: Random House, 1959), p. 200.

4   **A strict Calvinist, Stuyvesant**: Russell Shorto, *The Island at the Center of the World: The Epic Story of Dutch Manhattan and the Forgotten Colony That Shaped America* (New York: Doubleday, 2004), p. 2.

5   **a total of more than three hundred acres**: "Stuyvesant Farm Grid," oldstreets.com.

5   **Stuyvesant himself owned about forty**: Burrows and Wallace, *Gotham*, p. 49.

5   **Stuyvesant loved fruit trees**: There is no reliable map of the Stuyvesant farm from the 1600s. I went to the library in Albany where the Dutch scholar Charles Gehring has been translating Old Dutch documents for most of his life. When I asked him if there could be any truth to the rumor that St. Marks Place is the site of Stuyvesant's old pear orchard, he told me that it was a decent guess, because Stuyvesant definitely loved pears. The governor named one of his ships *Pereboom*, or *Pear Tree*. And Stuyvesant did bring at least one pear tree from Holland in 1647, planting it on what would become the corner of Third Avenue and Thirteenth Street. "So if you don't find anything better," the affable Gehring told me, "go with that [the pear-orchard theory]."

5   **The men armed themselves**: Fredrika W. Hertel, *A Guide to Historic St. Mark's Church in-the-Bouwerie* (New York: J. Jay Devitt Co. Litho, 1949), p. 4.

6   **The British Articles of Capitulation**: Burrows and Wallace, *Gotham*, p. 77.

6   **who later attended St. Mark's Church with friends**: "St. Mark's Church in the Bowery, New York. The tercentenary of the city of New York and our neighborhood," 1953. Copy in the collection of the New York Public Library.

6   **and in a fit of nationalist forestry**: Washington Irving, *Diedrich Knickerbocker's History of New-York* (New York: The Heritage Press, 1940; 1st ed. 1809), p. 342.

7   **an underground cave with marble shelves**: "As a nice metaphor for the

way history has muddled Manhattan's Dutch period, Stuyvesant's tomb-stone, embedded in the foundation of the Church of St. Mark's-in-the-Bowery, manages to get both his age and title wrong," writes Russell Shorto in *The Island at the Center of the World*, p. 234.

7   **"great exploit"**: Irving, *Diedrich Knickerbocker's History of New-York*, p. 346.

7   **Stanton Street to East Thirtieth Street**: Email reply to the author from Dr. Jaap Jacobs, University of St. Andrews, School of History, October 9, 2013.

7   **now only about half as many dwelled there**: Thomas A. Janvier, *In Old New York* (New York: Harper & Brothers Publishers, 1922; 1st ed. 1894), p. 44.

8   **Each generation of the Stuyvesants**: A good Stuyvesant family geneal-ogy appears in Cuyler Reynolds and William Richard Cutter, *Genealogical and Family History of Southern New York and the Hudson River Valley*, Vol. 3 (New York: Lewis Historical Publishing Company, 1914).

8   **Bancker arrayed the streets**: This likely happened in phases between 1787 and 1807. See http://www.nyc.gov/html/lpc/downloads/pdf/reports/2491.pdf.

8   **the finest Anglo-Dutch aristocrats**: See http://www.smhlf.org/content/sanctuary-parish-hall.

8   **plans for a Trinity-maintained chapel**: St. Mark's was incorporated under the Act of March 17, 1795. "St. Mark's Church in the Bowery, N.Y., A Statement to the Members from J. H. Rylance, Rector" (*New York: Evening Post* Job Print, 1890), p. 27, in *New York City Churches*. Presented at the Memo-rial Service, Middle Dutch Church, Second Ave., November Second, A.D. 1900. New York Public Library Collection.

9   **hedge-flanked path**: According to a map from 1800 and an illustration in the New York Public Library's collection.

11   **"The magnificent opportunity"**: Thomas A. Janvier, *In Old New York* (New York: Harper & Brothers Publishers, 1922; 1st ed. 1894), pp. 57–58.

11   **Eliza Jumel**: According to the *New York Times*, she attended George Washing-ton's inauguration, and Benjamin Franklin called her his "Fairy Queen." Her obituary ("Obituary: Madam Eliza B. Jumel," *New York Times*, July 18, 1865) is a must-read. And it's probably a whitewash of an even more scandalous life story summarized in "The Incredible Story of Eliza Jumel: Once America's Richest Woman, Now a Ghost in Washington Heights," *Gothamist*, August 13, 2014, http://gothamist.com/2014/08/13/americas_richest_woman.php.

12   **James Fenimore Cooper lived at no. 6**: Judith Stonehill, *Greenwich Village: A Guide to America's Legendary Left Bank* (New York: Universe, 2002), pp. 90–91.

12   **"Distinctions in the House of God"**: James Fenimore Cooper, *Satanstoe, or The Littlepage Manuscripts. A Tale of the Colony* (Albany: State University of New York Press, 1990), p. 157.

12   **In 1969, St. Mark's parishioners**: There are photos of the pew removal in the St. Mark's Church archives. W. H. Auden threw a fit about it.

12   **Keteltas family:** William J. Urchs, "St. Marks Place, Manhattan," in
     Henry Collins Brown, ed., *Valentine's Manual of Old New York* (New York: Valen-
     tine's Manual Inc., 1923), pp. 189–90.

12   **These smooth, new roads:** Cobblestones were replaced with concrete
     starting in the mid- to late nineteenth century. Niko Koppel, "Restoring
     New York Streets to Their Bumpier Pasts," *New York Times*, July 18, 2010.

13   **Colonnade Row:** *WPA Guide to New York City: The Federal Writers' Project Guide to 1930s
     New York* (New York: New Press, 1939), p. 121.

13   **took photographs of the moon:** St. Mark's Historic District Landmark
     Preservation Commission Report (January 14, 1969). See http://www.nyc
     .gov/html/lpc/downloads/pdf/reports/StMarks.pdf.

14   **During the riots:** "Remembering New York City's Opera Riots," NPR,
     May 13, 2006.

14   **One slammed into an iron railing:** "Untimely End of the Stuyvesant
     Pear-Tree," *New York Times*, February 27, 1867.

14   **When the wrecks were removed:** "'Stuyvesant's Pear Tree' Replanted on
     13th St.," *Villager* 73, no. 29 (November 19–25, 2003).

Chapter 2

15   **a coach maker:** Edward Mack, *Peter Cooper, Citizen of New York* (New York:
     Duell, Sloan and Pearce, 1949), p. 35.

15   **a sensitive child:** Ibid., p. 27.

15   **he was one of the richest men in America:** Ibid., p. 59, p. 70.

15   **Into its hollow cornerstone:** Ibid., p. 243.

16   **Bible House:** Until it closed in 1956, the Bible House would print millions
     of Bibles a year. Robert Shackleton, *The Book of New York* (Philadelphia: Penn
     Publishing Company, 1920), p. 85.

16   **Cooper Union's idealistic mission:** Mack, *Peter Cooper,* p. 253.

16   **public reading room:** Ibid., p. 268.

17   **the city now had as many prostitutes as Methodists:** Luc Sante, *Low Life*
     (New York: Farrar, Straus and Giroux, 1991), p. 185.

17   **east and west sides of the building:** Mack, *Peter Cooper,* p. 246. Confirmed
     by email to the author from Cooper Union librarian Carol Salomon, Janu-
     ary 13, 2015.

17   **Cooper, they said, was trying:** Ibid., p. 270.

17   **shipping industry along the East River:** The Dry Dock shipping com-
     pany's Banking House, built in 1827, still stands at 143–145 Avenue D. The
     Dry Dock Company bought the land from Nicolas Stuyvesant and built a
     dry dock for ship repair at the foot of East Tenth Street. See http://gvshp
     .org/blog/2011/03/16/from-banking-to-biscuits-part-2.

17   **"on the most conspicuous front":** Mack, *Peter Cooper,* p. 253.

17 **the tension between North and South**: Abraham Lincoln, "Cooper Union Address," February 27, 1860. Available online at constitution.org/csa/lincoln/cooper.htm.

18 **"The first impression of the man"**: "As Lincoln's Friends Saw Him, *The Touchstone*, Vol. 2, New York: Mary Fanton Roberts, Inc., October 1917–March 1918, p. 197.

18 **"In the Lincoln canon"**: Harold Holzer, *Lincoln at Cooper Union: The Speech That Made Abraham Lincoln President* (New York: Simon & Schuster, 2004), p. 3.

19 **When he finished, the crowd**: Mack, *Peter Cooper*, pp. 270–71.

19 **"the king of the slave-traders"**: "Arrest of a Noted Slave-Trader," *New York Times*, August 28, 1861.

19 **"a sweeping assault"**: Iver Bernstein, *The New York City Draft Riots* (New York: Oxford University Press, 1990), p. 3.

21 **"What a wild state he was in!"**: "Letter from Mark Twain," Special Correspondence of the Alta California (August 1, 1869), http://www.twainquotes.com/18690801.html.

21 **"If ever there was an inspired idiot"**: Ibid.

22 **a boardinghouse at no. 7 St. Marks Place**: "Blind Tom's Return: Back in New-York in His Guardian's Hands," *New York Times*, August 18, 1867.

22 **"If he felt the wind blowing"**: "Blind Tom, Pianist, Dies of a Stroke," *New York Times*, June 15, 1908.

22 **$750,000**: "Blind Tom Is Dying: The Musical Phenomenon Now a Pauper Idiot," *Logan Journal*, January 7, 1891.

22 **at the age of fifty-nine**: "Blind Tom, Pianist, Dies of a Stroke."

23 **to feed a family of six for fifteen cents**: John Mathews, "Wealthy Women as Teachers of Cooking," *Leslie's Weekly*, June 11, 1903.

23 **"A servant with this clause"**: Emily Huntington, *Little Lessons for Little Housekeepers*, New York: Anson D. F. Randolph & Co., 1879. See full text online at http://archive.org/stream/littlelessonsfor00hunt/littlelessonsfor00hunt_djvu.txt.

23 **"How do you make hot suds?"**: Ibid.

24 **the Wilson School's administrators cracked down**: "Removed Because of Her Belief," *New York Tribune*, May 1893.

25 **a Theosophist, as was the matron**: "Split on Theosophy's Rock," *New York Times*, June 26, 1893.

25 **with a doctor's wife named Anna R. Emmet**: From 1857 to 1859, at which point it moved to Lexington Avenue. It also maintained a country branch on Staten Island. See http://dp.la/item/c03d613e5d6879412422490199987d7ac.

25 **"The mother must produce evidence"**: Burrows and Wallace, *Gotham*, p. 811.

26 **"Have these children no one"**: Laura A. Perkins, *From Tragedy to Triumph: The Sara Curry Story*, self-published, April 2008.

26 **Revere, Massachusetts**: Burrows and Wallace, *Gotham*, pp. 977–78.

27   **While giving a tour of the city:** Horatio Alger, *Ragged Dick and Mark, the Match Boy: Two Novels by Horatio Alger* (New York: Macmillan, 1962), p. 71.

Chapter 3

29   **"They practiced four to six hours daily":** William J. Urchs, "St. Marks Place, Manhattan," in Henry Collins Brown, ed., *Valentine's Manual of Old New York*, New York: Valentine's Manual Inc., 1923, pp. 187–89.

29   **casting neighborhoods into shadow:** See https://www.youtube.com/watch?v=wyYnVKhRNYk.

30   **On a platform lit by Chinese lanterns:** Laurel Van Horn, "A History of Tompkins Square Park," Lower East Side Preservation Initiative, published online 2009; see http://www.lespi-nyc.org/history/a-history-of-tompkin-square-park.html.

31   **"The street was cleared like magic":** Urchs, "St. Marks Place, Manhattan," p. 187.

31   **By now the area's Irish shipping industry:** In 1904, a middle-aged German named Christian C. W. Grassman who, according to Lower East Side History Project director Eric Ferrara, "always wore a Russian sailor cap" and "was known for handing out candy and coins and allowing children to run around the hallways of his office" put an ad in the paper: "Wanted, steamers of not less than 6,000 tonnage, to have speed of not less than 18 knots and more, and must be made so they can be fitted with armor plate . . . apply to Grassman & Hirtz Company, 94 St. Marks Place." When a reporter investigated, he learned, Ferrara writes, that "Grassman claimed that he was purchasing these ships not for himself, but to sell to an unidentified country which was in short supply of military vessels. During the conversation, he said he had bought and sold five boats thus far, but was hoping to accrue a total of 200." See Eric Ferrara, "Ahoy? The St. Mark's Place Navy," *Villager*, March 1, 2012.

31   **The East River's old, rotting wooden piers:** James T. Fisher, *On the Irish Waterfront: The Crusader, the Movie, and the Soul of the Port of New York* (Ithaca, NY: Cornell University Press, 2009), p. 224.

31   **German immigrants like the Urchs family:** "Peg-Leg Pete's Bouwerie Tour: Gilded Age Edition," St. Mark's Historic Landmark Fund, Neighborhood Preservation Center, 2013.

31   **now dwelled residents like S. C. Lynes, Jr.:** David Thomas Valentine, *Manual of the Corporation of the City of New York*, 1866.

32   **Members wore hats shaped like dolphins:** Christopher Gray, "Streetscapes: 19–25 St. Marks Place; The Eclectic Life of a Row of East Village Houses," *New York Times*, November 8, 1998.

32   **unemployment in New York City hit 25 percent:** Jennifer 8. Lee, "New

York and the Panic of 1873," *New York Times* City Room Blog, October 14, 2008.

32 **With nowhere to play, boys ran wild:** *WPA Guide to New York City*, pp. 108–9.

32 **"one of the boldest and worst":** Edward Crapsey, *The Nether Side of New York: Or, the Vice, Crime and Poverty of the Great Metropolis* (New York: Sheldon & Company, 1872), p. 150.

32 **"constantly exhibited themselves":** Ibid., p. 10.

33 **"New York was a camping ground":** Ibid., p. 7.

33 **the Quarteraros:** "His Brother Surrenders," *New York Times*, October 23, 1988; "By Order of the Mafia," *New York Times*, October 22, 1888; "The 'Mafia' Murder," *New York Times*, March 27, 1889.

33 **"thin pale men in old clothes":** Excerpt from Bernadine Kielty's "Girl from Fitchburg" (1963) in Shoenfeld and Maclean, eds., *City Life*, p. 183.

34 **In 1876, grave robbers opened:** Peter Levins, "Robbery of Stewart Grave— One of N.Y.'s Biggest Mysteries," *Sunday News*, December 31, 1939.

35 **"a scandal in the Parish":** "St. Mark's Church in the Bowery, N.Y., a Statement to the Members from J. H. Rylance, Rector," 1890, pp. 3–26.

35 **"The Lion of St. Mark is not dead":** "St. Mark's Church in the Bowery" pamphlet produced by the church, 1899, p. 25. The New York Public Library has a copy.

36 **Flags fluttered from the masts:** Herbert N. Casson, "The Story of the General Slocum Disaster," *Munsey's Magazine*, December 1904, pp. 37–60.

37 **"two destructive forces":** Edward T. O'Donnell, *Ship Ablaze: The Tragedy of the Steamboat* General Slocum (New York: Broadway Books, 2003), p. 113.

38 **"Terrible affair that *General Slocum* explosion":** James Joyce, *Ulysses* (Ware, UK: Wordsworth Editions, 2010), p. 215.

39 **"New York, What's the Matter with You?":** See Library of Congress, http://www.loc.gov/jukebox/recordings/detail/id/3473.

Chapter 4

43 **"Marriage and love have nothing in common":** "Marriage and Love," in Alix Kates Shulman, *Red Emma Speaks: Selected Writings and Speeches* (New York: Vintage, 1972), p. 158.

43 **"I had a distinct sensation":** Shulman, *Red Emma Speaks*, p. 7.

44 **She tried prostituting herself:** Ibid., p. 10.

45 **"I do not think I shall die":** William Serrin, *Homestead: The Glory and Tragedy of an American Steel Town* (New York: Time Books, 1992).

45 **had a roll of some eight thousand subscribers:** PBS.org. See http://www.pbs.org/wgbh/amex/goldman/sfeature/sf_motherearth.html.

46 **used dynamite to gain attention for their cause:** Dynamite became more ubiquitous around 1914. The Charlie Chaplin film *Dough and Dynamite*, 1914,

shows striking cooks at a restaurant lacing the bread with explosives. See https://www.youtube.com/watch?v=SkAmLdpFLOM.

46 **"In the Ferrer or Modern School"**: Legislative Documents: New York State Legislature, Vol. 18, "Subversive Teaching in Certain Schools," One Hundred and Forty-Fourth Session, Vol. 18, No. 50, Part 2, 1921, p. 1447.

46 **which had since moved to East Twelfth Street**: Per Catherine Rominger, Fernanda Perrone's assistant, Rutgers University's Special Collections.

46 **"On the deck above us"**: Emma Goldman, *Living My Life*. Vol. 2 (New York: Dover Publications, Inc., 1970), pp. 716–17 (an unabridged republication of the work originally published in 1931 by Alfred Knopf, Inc., New York).

47 **A 1903 almanac lists several union headquarters**: "New York Trade Associations," in *The American Almanac, Year-book, Cyclopaedia and Atlas* (New York: New York American and Journal, Hearst's Chicago American and San Francisco Examiner, 1903), p. 895.

48 **Uprising of the 20,000**: Tony Michels, "Uprising of 20,000," Jewish Women's Archive Encyclopedia online; see http://jwa.org/encyclopedia/article/uprising-of-20000-1909.

48 **admiring its combination of intellectualism and action**: Joshua Rubenstein, *Leon Trotsky: A Revolutionary's Life* (New Haven, CT: Yale University Press, 2011), p. 16–21.

48 **"I left Europe wallowing in blood"**: Leon Trotsky, *My Life* (New York: Universal Library Edition, 1973; 1st ed. 1930), p. 271.

49 **"You must always keep your eyes on him"**: Ibid., p. 275.

49 **Yiddish-language daily paper**: http://forward.com/about/history.

49 **"an old man with suppurating eyes"**: Trotsky, *My Life*, pp. 272–73.

49 **"Revolution is brewing in the trenches"**: Dorothy Day, *"From Union Square to Rome*, Chapter 7—Reporting," 1938, Chapter 7, pp. 71–89. Online at http://www.catholicworker.org/dorothyday/daytext.cfm?TextID=207.

Chapter 5

50 **he had picked pockets in order to buy homing pigeons**: "Seizes Armed Boys in a Jewelry Store," *New York Times*, April 8, 1929.

50 **Clean, organized factories**: Albert Fried, *The Rise and Fall of the Jewish Gangster in America* (New York: Holt, Rinehart and Winston, 1980), pp. 33–36.

50 **"nickel museums featuring mermaids"**: Kenneth T. Jackson, ed., *The Encyclopedia of New York City* (New Haven, CT: Yale University Press, 1995), p. 131.

51 **A raid of no. 9 in March 1900**: "Parkhurst Raid Succeeds," *New York Times*, March 9, 1900.

51 **During a later raid at no. 6**: "Gamblers Resist Raid," *New York Times*, May 9, 1912.

52 **most notably, the Five Pointers:** Albert Fried, *The Rise and Fall of the Jewish Gangster in America* (New York: Holt, Rinehart and Winston, 1980), pp. 82–83.

52 **"taken refuge behind his bulky form":** "Chief and Gangmen Held for Murder," *New York Times*, January 11, 1914.

52 **Fein's top soldiers:** Fried, *Rise and Fall of the Jewish Gangster in America*, p. 84.

53 **In 1915, he went to the police:** "Fein, Fence for Gang, Gets 10–20 Year Term," *New York Times*, February 25, 1942.

53 **Dopey Benny Fein claimed retirement:** Fried, *Rise and Fall of the Jewish Gangster in America*, pp. 84–86.

53 **$2.5 million in merchandise:** "Fein, Fence for Gang, Gets 10–20 Year Term."

53 **In 1926, Black Hand panic:** "Black Hand Panics Spread in Schools," *New York Times*, June 18, 1926.

54 **They found a stockpile of dynamite:** "Found with Dynamite, Held in Palmieri Case," *New York Times*, March 6, 1927.

54 **He said he took the dynamite home:** "Not Convincing," *Pittsburgh Press*, March 30, 1927.

54 **At the height of the Prohibition era:** All quotes in this section are from an interview with Lorcan Otway by the author, July 12, 2012.

54 **The Italian Otway family:** Albert Amateau, "Florence Otway, Shoe Designer, Theatre 80 Co-Founder," *Villager*, July 24, 2014.

Chapter 6

56 **"revolution in taste":** Peter Gay, *Modernism: The Lure of Heresy* (New York: W. W. Norton & Company, 2008), pp. 8–9.

56 **An aspiring young painter:** The story of Ray Euffa is based on census records and on an interview with her nephew, Gene Lichtenstein, by the author, June 7, 2013.

58 **Father William Norman Guthrie was tormenting:** "Guthrie Papers Now Available to Researchers," press release put out by the Andover-Harvard Theological Library, Harvard Divinity School, April 16, 2006.

58 ***The Little Lady of the Dew:*** "Nude Statue in Church," per undated scraps of articles found in the St. Mark's Church archives.

59 **"Be thou unto us this World of the senses":** William Guthrie, *Offices of Mystical Religion* (New York: Century Press, 1927), p. 119. Available online at https://ia700302.us.archive.org/11/items/MN41875ucmf_5/MN41875ucmf_5.pdf.

59 **"We inherited a Colonial edifice":** Ibid., p. xxii.

59 **St. Mark's Garth Apartments:** "St. Mark's In-the-Bouwerie: A Vital Expression of Present-Day Religion in New York City: A Statement of Plans and Policies by the Rector, Wardens and Vestry," ca. 1942, p. 6.

60 **"bare-leg, bare-hip affair"**: Dorothy Dayton, "St. Mark's Back within the Fold," *New York City Sun*, February 2, 1932, in the St. Mark's Church archives.

60 **Body and Soul Clinic**: "Row Over Body and Soul Clinic Shakes Historic St. Mark's Church," *Milwaukee Journal*, August 8, 1932. Bishop Manning *hated* the Body and Soul Clinic, as did some in the neighborhood who claimed its doctors were anti-Semitic.

60 **this handsome free spirit**: *Tramp Poet*, WPA Folklore Project, Life Histories, 1936–39, Manuscript Division, Library of Congress, p. 69. Available online at http://www.loc.gov/item/wpalh001640.

61 **"The play stank and so did Clifford"**: Margaret Brenman-Gibson, *Clifford Odets, American Playwright: The Years from 1906 to 1940* (New York: Applause, 2002; 1st ed. 1981), pp. 84–85.

61 **St. Mark's Towers**: Anthony Alofsin, *Frank Lloyd Wright: The Lost Years, 1910–1922: A Study in Influence* (Chicago: University of Chicago Press, 1993), p. 45.

61 **when it built an eighteen-story dorm building**: William R. Greer, "N.Y.U. Acts to Build Controversial Dormitory," *New York Times*, May 5, 1985.

62 **He had to crawl to Bishop Manning**: Dayton, "St. Mark's Back within the Fold."

62 **Actor Walter Huston, playing Stuyvesant**: "St. Mark's Sees Huston in Role of Stuyvesant," January 1939, St. Mark's Church archives.

Chapter 7

63 **"The street is three blocks long"**: Except where noted, the source for details in this chapter is Don Terry, "Three Blocks of Unusual, That Is St. Mark's Place," *News and Courier*, November 1, 1929.

63 **"Gus La Rocco"**: Card found in the basement of no. 53.

64 **"a large rose with red and green petals"**: "12-Foot Wall Hides Once Dazzling Shop," *New York Times*, August 26, 1915.

65 **tall, mustachioed redhead named Harry Kamen**: Interview of Milton Kamen by the author, October 20, 2012.

65 **"Crowded, noisy, squalid"**: *WPA Guide to New York City*, p. 108.

66 **(cabbage and game)**: Ibid., pp. 123–24.

Chapter 8

67 **Urbain J. Ledoux served hot meals and grandiose rhetoric**: "Bowery's Mr. Zero Is Dead Here at 66," *New York Times*, April 10, 1941. Also, there is a great summary of the press about Ledoux on the blog thisaintthesummeroflove .blogspot.com.

67 **took jobs at various mills:** Urbain Ledoux, *Mr. Zero?*, "Published by the author for the Old Bucks and Lame Ducks Club, and the Tub, located at 33 St. Marks Place, New York City. Copyrighted for them by the author in 1931," copy in collection of the New York Public Library, p. A25ff.

68 **Once-proud soldiers:** "Veteran Hangs Himself," *New York Times*, March 7, 1934.

68 **the universal brotherhood of man:** "The Appeal of Ledoux," *Reality* 3–4 (1921): 5.

68 **"well wrapped up in":** Ledoux, *Mr. Zero?*, p. A9.

69 **"the shepherd of the shorn lambs of labor":** Robert Morss Lovett, "Urbain Ledoux—Prophet," *New Republic*, October 5, 1921. Printed in Ledoux, *Mr. Zero?*, 1931 scrapbook, p. 3.

69 **"When I give them food to eat":** Hari G. Govil, "Urbain Ledoux: His Message to Mankind," *Reality* 5, no. 8 (August 1922): 16.

69 **"his other self":** Ledoux, *Mr. Zero?*, p. A6.

69 **"be misunderstood by many":** Ibid., p. B6.

69 **St. Marks Place breadline:** *The Street of Forgotten Men* clip can be found here: http://www.youtube.com/watch?v=DNdBKubxlV8 and is also hosted at the Travel Film Archive, http://www.travelfilmarchive.com/item.php?id=12044. A 1925 silent film of the same name introduced, without credit, a young actress named Louise Brooks as a gun moll.

69 **at no. 26 St. Marks Place:** Excerpt from the *New York Times*, January 4, 1925, in Ledoux, *Mr. Zero?*, p. A36.

70 **In Boston, he staged an "auction":** Alexander Keyssar, *Out of Work: The First Century of Unemployment in Massachusetts* (Cambridge: Cambridge University Press, 1986), p. 243.

70 **"If any one tries to hustle Ledoux about":** "Ledoux Defies Police," *New York Times*, September 19, 1921.

71 **the police chased his homeless men:** "Police Clubs Break Mobs of Idle; Bar Food and Meetings," *New York Times*, September 20, 1921.

71 **"a group half naked of clothes":** Ledoux, *Mr. Zero?*, p. A10.

71 **There the homeless could purchase:** "10,000 Fed by Mr. Zero, *New York Times*, December 26, 1928.

72 **"To Bring a Greater Measure":** Ledoux, *Mr. Zero?*, p. A7.

72 **he fed two thousand:** "Cold Kills 4 Here; Refuges are Filled," *New York Times*, January 3, 1928; "Snowfall a Boon to the Jobless," *New York Times*, March 10, 1928.

72 **When a snowstorm hit:** "12,000 in Snow Gangs Clear City Streets," *New York Times*, January 30, 1928.

72 **His wife, Mary, would distribute:** Ledoux, *Mr. Zero?*, p. A19.

72 **A 1929 newsreel shows Mr. Zero:** "Mr. Zero Gives to the Needy," November 25, 1949. Moving Image Research Collections hosts this video clip online: http://mirc.sc.edu/islandora/object/usc%3A1951.

73 **his long-suffering landlord, Anna Brindell:** "Receiver Debated for 'Mr. Zero's' $37," *New York Times*, June 10, 1931.

73 **"Friend of Poor":** "Bowery's Mr. Zero Is Dead Here at 66."

Chapter 9

77 **"The walls of Jericho":** Edmond J. Bartnett, "'Village' Spills Across Third Avenue: Demolition of El Opened the Way for Bohemia's Expansion," *New York Times*, February 7, 1960.

77 **"Visit the Booming East Village!":** John Strausbaugh, *The Village: 400 Years of Beats, Bohemians, Radicals and Rogues: A History of Greenwich Village* (New York: Ecco, 2013), p. 329.

77 **"The old Italian, Jewish, Polish and Ukrainian":** "Village Scene Spreading East: Colorful Communities, Low Rents Attract Bohemians," *New York Times*, December 31, 1961.

77 **A radio star named Jean Shepherd:** Today, Jean Shepherd is perhaps best known for two things: 1. Getting his listeners to fund the John Cassavetes movie *Shadows*, and 2. writing the 1983 movie *A Christmas Story*.

78 **Shepherd provided "a slow, casual, laid-back":** Eugene B. Bergmann, *Excelsior, You Fathead! The Art and Enigma of Jean Shepherd* (New York: Applause Theatre & Cinema Books, 2005), p. 132.

78 **"that wild tossing in the soul":** Ibid., p. 131.

78 **In one classic show:** "Jean Shepherd Café Incident," https://www.youtube.com/watch?v=7QF8C6tkA7I.

78 *I, Libertine*: Bergmann, *Excelsior, You Fathead!*, p. 133.

78 **Sweetheart Soap:** Ibid., p. 138.

79 **"Many, many people went":** Interview of Ernie Hurwitz by the author, June 3, 2013.

80 **"People just sat there all day":** Interview of Jerome Schwartz by the author, November 12, 2013.

80 **"Nobody bothered anybody":** Ron Padgett, *Ted: A Personal Memoir of Ted Berrigan* (New York: The Figures, 1993), p. 12.

81 **His 1930 book *Poems* was hailed:** Academy of American Poets, http://www.poets.org/poetsorg/poet/w-h-auden.

81 **Blake watercolor over the green-marble fireplace:** Judith Stonehill, *Greenwich Village: A Guide to America's Legendary Left Bank* (New York; Universe, 2002), p. 91.

81 **At no. 57, for example:** "Crowd at Wedding Stampeded by Fire," *New York Times*, June 16, 1935.

83 **Toney Scavoni:** "Nine Persons Routed from Tenement Homes When Wall Cracks, Threatening Collapse," *New York Times*, March 10, 1938.

83   **eight robbery victims:** "Hold-Up Suspects Captured in Store," *New York Times*, January 29, 1946.

83   **Bert Zackim moved to no. 126:** Interview of Bert Zackim by the author, November 1, 2012.

84   **"I remember the terrible smells":** Interview of Arnold Feinblatt by the author, November 30, 2012.

86   **He remembers Gypsy knife fights:** Interview of Joey Dick by the author, March 12, 2014.

87   **with his big, bushy, white mustache:** Per interview with Lorcan Otway by the author, July 12, 2012.

88   **"The city has never been so uncomfortable":** "Here is New York," in Shoenfeld and Maclean, eds., *City Life*, p. 239.

Chapter 10

89   **When the Japanese attacked Pearl Harbor:** J. Michael Lennon, *A Double Life* (New York: Simon & Schuster, 2013), p. 43.

89   **Next door lived Dan Wolf:** See Lawrence Van Gelder, "Dan Wolf, 80, a Village Voice Founder, Dies," *New York Times*, April 12, 1996; Norman Mailer, *Advertisements for Myself* (Toronto: Longmans, Green & Company, 1959), p. 278; and Strausbaugh, *The Village*, pp. 327–28.

89   **Huncke himself was the ultimate Beat:** Interview of Arthur Nersesian by the author, November 8, 2013.

90   **"Beat" became the pejorative "Beatnik":** Steven Watson, *The Birth of the Beat Generation* (New York: Pantheon Books, 1995), p. 4.

90   **The term "Beat":** Ibid., p. 3.

91   **"They wanted it to be successful":** Mailer, *Advertisements for Myself*, p. 277.

91   **"I will become an habitual":** Ibid., pp. 278–79, 280.

91   **"third-rate poets shout above":** Jean Shepherd, "Dig the Folk," *Village Voice* 3, no. 33, June 11, 1958.

91   **from "nuance" to "nuisance":** Michael Clancy, "The Nuances of Nuisance: Why Mailer Quit the *Voice*," *Village Voice*, January 14, 2008, http://blogs.villagevoice.com/runninscared/2008/01/the_nuances_of.php.

91   **Staff members whom he had constantly berated:** J. Michael Lennon, *A Double Life* (New York: Simon & Schuster, 2013), pp. 204–5.

92   **"You could learn an instrument":** Judith Rossner, *Looking for Mr. Goodbar* (New York: Pocket Books, 1975), p. 371.

92   **No such magical kiosk existed:** While working at the *Voice*, James Wolcott got calls from house hunters begging him for the secret drop-off location's address. He describes this in *Lucking Out: My Life Getting Down and Semi-dirty in '70s New York* (New York: Anchor Books, 2011), p. 20.

93   **Carl Solomon was born in the Bronx:** Bill Morgan, *Beat Atlas: A State-by-State Guide to the Beat Generation in America* (San Francisco, CA: City Lights Books, 2011), p. 68.

93   **and Solomon introduced Ginsberg to the East Village:** This account appears in several books, including John Tytell, "The Comedian as Common Denominator," in Carl Solomon, *Emergency Messages: An Autobiographical Miscellany* (New York: Paragon House, 1989), pp. xi–xvii.

94   **apartment at no. 7:** Solomon, *Emergency Messages*, p. 13. Solomon only talks here about the Prince Street apartment, but Bill Morgan also has him at 7 St. Marks Place during this period. At another point they lived at 181 Prince Street, subletting from the writer Anatole Broyard.

94   **"Preposterous that they should talk":** Carl Solomon, *More Mishaps* (San Francisco, CA: City Lights Books, 1968), p. 3.

94   **the very place where Ginsberg's mother:** Ward Harkavy, "The Scary Days When Thousands Were Lobotomized on Long Island," *Village Voice*, October 26, 1999.

95   **"It's terrible in Tompkins Square":** Lindsay Pollock, "Mama MoMA," *New York* magazine, November 10, 2003. Obit of Dorothy Miller.

95   **famous today as the top-selling female artist of all time:** See http://www.bloomberg.com/visual-data/best-and-worst/top-selling-all-time-women-artists; Joe LeSueur, *Digressions on Some Poems by Frank O'Hara* (New York: Farrar, Straus and Giroux, 2003), p. 161.

95   **"The reason I left home":** Interview of Phil Giambri by the author, June 29, 2013.

95   **Hunter College Playhouse:** Marc D. Schleifer, "The Beat Debated," *Village Voice*, November 19, 1958.

96   **"They came to starve and to rebel":** Albert Parry, *Garrets and Pretenders: Bohemian Life from Poe to Kerouac* (Mineola, NY: Dover Publications, 2012; 1st ed. 1960), p. xxvii.

96   **"penniless and carefree writers":** Ibid., p. xxviii.

96   **"Emptybright":** John Wilcock, "The Greenwich Village Scholarship," *Village Voice*, January 10, 1963.

97   **"So we all went around":** Interview of Joyce Johnson by the author, August 10, 2012.

98   **Over her family's protests:** Hettie Jones, *How I Became Hettie Jones* (New York: Grove Press, 1990), pp. 1–2.

98   **Cohen took the girls:** Ibid., p. 188.

99   **LeRoi Jones was born:** Margalit Fox, "Amiri Baraka, Polarizing Poet and Playwright, Dies at 79," *New York Times*, January 9, 2014.

99   **he befriended Beat poets:** Andrew Epstein, *Beautiful Enemies: Friendship and Postwar American Poetry* (New York: Oxford University Press, 2006).

99 **Bobbsey Twins of Greenwich Village:** Ibid, p. 195.

100 **Journalist Martin Williams spent:** Martin Williams, "A Night at the Five Spot," *Down Beat*, February 13, 1964.

101 **The music critic Robert Christgau recalls:** Robert Christgau, "From Minstrelsy to Vaudeville and Monk to Punk, Never Under-estimate Urban Ugliness," *Village Voice*, February 22, 2005.

101 **"It was snowing":** Interview of Robert Christgau by the author, August 9, 2012.

101 **Mayor La Guardia had instituted:** Strausbaugh, *The Village*, p. 213.

101 **"My right to pursue":** Nate Chinen, "The Cabaret Card and Jazz," *Jazz Times*, May 17, 2012.

103 **"whispered a song along the keyboard":** Frank O'Hara, *Lunch Poems* (San Francisco, CA: City Lights Books, 1964), and online at http://www.poets .org/poetsorg/poem/day-lady-died.

103 **Policemen from the Ninth Precinct:** "Lord Buckley Dies," *New York Times*, November 13, 1960.

103 **"a carpenter kitty . . . so sweet":** "The Naz," Lord Buckley, *Lord Buckley in Concert*, World Pacific, 1964.

103 **the New York Poets Theatre:** Diane Di Prima, *Recollections of My Life as a Woman: The New York Years* (New York: Penguin, 2002).

104 **"Happenings":** Stonehill, *Greenwich Village*, p. 91.

104 **At the St. Mark's Playhouse:** This account taken from Jones, *How I Became Hettie Jones*, p. 220–22; and interview of Hettie Jones by the author, October 3, 2012.

104 **"My first wife," he later wrote of Hettie:** Amiri Baraka, *The Autobiography of LeRoi Jones* (Chicago: Lawrence Hill Books, 1997; 1st ed. 1984), p. xxi.

105 **"I was just pissing in their beer":** LeSueur, *Digressions on Some Poems by Frank O'Hara*, pp. 247–48.

105 **"It was hard":** Interview of Hettie Jones by the author, October 3, 2012.

106 **The black poet Ted Joans:** Bill Morgan, *The Beat Generation in New York* (San Francisco, CA: City Lights Book, 1997), p. 130.

106 **"'Like, these Goddamned insensitive'":** Pamela Moore, *Diana* (New York: Dell, 1961), p. 102.

106 **"Gorgeous George":** "Beatniks Turn Square, Put Finger on 13," *Daytona Beach Sunday News-Journal* (AP), November 9, 1959.

107 **"Why you can't get in":** Barbara Bandschu, "'Ballad of Reading Gaol' Helps Police in Fight on Dope Traffic," *Milwaukee Journal* (UPI), October 26, 1959.

Chapter 11

108 **"Well, you'd think that he would know"**: David Lehman, *The Last Avant-Garde* (New York: Doubleday, 1998), p. 137.

108 **"One hears about how inhibited"**: This chapter's account of Auden's sub-letters' experiences are taken primarily from an interview of Gene Lichtenstein by the author, June 7, 2013, with follow-up call December 26, 2014.

110 **Another house sitter of Auden's**: Moira Hodgson, *It Seemed like a Good Idea at the Time: My Adventures in Life and Food* (New York: Nan A. Talese, 2009), p. 170.

110 **fronted by David Johansen in a slinky sleeveless dress**: There's great video online of the band performing the song "Pills" at Club 82 in 1974 at https://www.youtube.com/watch?v=JPS-CJKDPJo. And watch an interview with the manager who booked the gig here: http://bedfordandbowery.com/2014/01/wed-found-this-cave-out-of-time-a-look-back-at-glam-rocks-club-82.

110 **Gay hook-ups along St. Marks Place**: Edmund White, *City Boy: My Life in New York during the 1960s and '70s* (New York: Bloomsbury, 2009), p. 48.

110 **"Ches-ter! Is that you?"**: LeSueur, *Digressions on Some Poems by Frank O'Hara*, p. 39.

111 **Once when Lichtenstein was house-sitting**: Interview of Gene Lichtenstein by the author, June 7, 2013, with follow-up call December 26, 2014.

112 **His acts of charity were legion**: Edward Mendelson, "The Secret Auden," *New York Review of Books*, March 20, 2014.

112 **"DELIGHTED"**: David Martin, "Why Auden Married," Response to Edward Mendelson's "The Secret Auden," *New York Review of Books*, April 24, 2014.

112 **In 1924 she wrote an autobiographical novel**: Paul Bowers, "Introduction to *The Eleventh Virgin*," CatholicWorker.org, undated.

112 **She later found Catholicism**: Dan Wakefield, "Miracle in the Bowery," chap. 4 in *New York in the '50s* (New York: Houghton Mifflin, 1992), pp. 72ff.

113 **"Dorothy, it's been wonderful"**: Interview of Tom Pike by the author, December 3, 2013.

114 **"Poets do look a bit unpressed"**: "Friend of Homeless Helped by Poet," *Toledo Blade*, March 2, 1956.

115 **"I ran into Philip in Paris"**: Interview of Gene Lichtenstein by the author, June 7, 2013.

115 **To falsify her pregnancy test**: The details about Philip Roth and Maggie Williams were confirmed with Philip Roth via an email exchange, January 13, 2015.

Chapter 12

117 **"There's nothing you can do"**: Interview of Michael Allen by the author, July 9, 2012.

119 **"a wacko"**: Interview of Roger Jack Walters by the author, August 15, 2012.

121 **a "whore"**: Michael Allen, *This Time, This Place* (Indianapolis/Kansas City/ New York: Bobbs-Merrill Company, 1971), pp. 40, 80.

121 **"The arts were raw, *raw*"**: Interview of Tom Pike by the author, December 3, 2013.

121 **for forty thousand dollars**: Interview of Kristina Olitski by the author, December 4, 2012.

122 **The parish replaced it**: Allen, *This Time, This Place*, p. 147.

122 **"All we could hear was furniture crashing"**: Interview of Tom Pike by the author, December 3, 2013.

123 **"Black-and-White-Together-We-Shall-Overcome"**: Pauli Murray, *The Autobiography of a Black Activist, Feminist, Lawyer, Priest, and Poet* (Knoxville: University of Tennessee Press, 1989), p. 363 (originally published as *Song in a Weary Throat: An American Pilgrimage*, Harper & Row, 1987).

123 **Baltimore in 1910**: The Pauli Murray Project, http://paulimurrayproject .org/pauli-murray/biography; Murray, *Autobiography of a Black Activist, Feminist, Lawyer, Priest, and Poet*, p. 2.

124 **"I wandered about the streets"**: Murray, *Autobiography of a Black Activist, Feminist, Lawyer, Priest, and Poet*, p. 370; David Bourdon, *Warhol* (New York: Harry N. Abrams, Inc., 1989), p. 230.

124 **In 1977, Murray herself**: In 2009, the Episcopal Church's General Convention nominated Pauli Murray for sainthood. If approved, she could share a feast day (July 1) with Harriet Beecher Stowe.

124 **"Personally I have little hope"**: Quoted in Nick Orzel and Michael Smith, *Eight Plays from Off-Off Broadway* (Indianapolis, IN: Bobbs-Merrill Co., 1966).

124 **"When I come it's like a river"**: Don Shewey, *Sam Shepard* (New York: Da Capo Press, 1997), p. 34.

124 **"I believe this whole generation"**: Ibid.

125 **Allen presided over the marriage**: Ibid., p. 69.

125 **"Hell, yes, the church is in its grave"**: Douglas Davis, "Is God Dead at St. Mark's in-the-Bouwerie?" *New York*, February 6, 1966.

126 **"I implore you by the bowels of Christ"**: St. Mark's Church archives, also available online at: http://thecuratesdesk.files.wordpress.com/2012/05/ auden-letter.jpg.

126 **One service featured a rock number**: Mind Garage, "Processional Kyrie Gloria from the Electric Liturgy," April 13, 1969, http://www.youtube.com/ watch?v=MpwajIkwyHI. The *TV Guide* listing is here: http://www.mindgarage .com/ABC.html.

126 **"Nobody was ever there"**: Interview of Jeremiah Newton by the author, December 27, 2012.

Chapter 13

128 **Stefania was known around the neighborhood**: Interview of Adriana Leshko and Jaroslaw Leshko by the author, October 20, 2012.

128 **"in this sleazy place"**: Jim Carroll, *The Basketball Diaries* (New York: Penguin, 1978), p. 84.

129 **"You will never meet"**: Interview of Adriana Leshko and Jaroslaw Leshko by the author, October 20, 2012.

129 **"They were very anti-Communist"**: Interview of Jeff Jones by the author, October 7, 2013.

129 **"The locals didn't care for us"**: Interview of Mike Hodder by the author, July 17, 2013.

129 **A red diaper baby**: Interview of Joyce Hartwell by the author in Albany, New York, October 7, 2013, and several phone calls in 2013 and 2014.

131 **"I used to watch Stanley"**: Ronald Sukenick, *Down and In: Life in the Underground* (New York: William Morrow, 1987), p. 160.

131 **A young art student named Andy Warhol**: Bourdon, *Warhol*, p. 14.

132 **Warhol had sublet an apartment**: Email exchange between Philip Pearlstein and the author, June 29, 2014.

132 **"You could extrapolate everything"**: Richard Hell, *I Dreamed I Was a Very Clean Tramp* (New York: HarperCollins, 2013), p. 68.

132 **"To read the poems of Ted Berrigan"**: Peter Schjeldahl, "In the Berrigan Era," *Culture Hero* 1, no. 2 (1969).

132 **"That was a time when people"**: Multiple interviews of Peter Schjeldahl by the author, 2012–2014.

133 **"It was a lazy, quiet bar"**: Interview of Ron Padgett by the author, September 17, 2014. All Padgett quotes that follow are from this interview.

Chapter 14

135 **the "Sixties" actually started in 1964**: This idea of when the sixties really started is well articulated in Joe Boyd's *White Bicycles: Making Music in the 1960s* (London: Serpent's Tail, 2010). Thanks to Peter Stampfel for the book recommendation.

135 **That was the year when White**: Interview of Joshua White by the author, August 15, 2014.

135 **"Walking on St. Marks Place"**: John Gruen, *The New Bohemia: The Combine Generation* (New York: Shorecrest, 1966), pp. 7–8.

136 **"Walking from Tompkins Square Park"**: Interview of Paul Krassner by the author, November 8, 2013.

136 **(coffee was a dime)**: Miles Champion has put together "Insane Podium," a wonderful history of the Poetry Project online at http://poetryproject.org/history/insane-podium.

137 **"'Oh, we're *right here*'"**: Interview of Bob Rosenthal by the author, August 9, 2012.

137 **a hit of acid, a joint, a Valium, and a poem**: They went to reclaim it during a later renovation and it was gone. Melena Ryzik, "Chasing Ghosts of Poets Past," *New York Times*, March 30, 2012. Confirmed by Lewis Warsh email to the author, February 19, 2015.

138 **"I had the feeling in this bitter cold"**: Sam Kashner, *When I Was Cool: My Life at the Jack Kerouac School* (New York: HarperCollins, 2003), pp. 243–44.

138 **"It's 2 a.m. at Anne & Lewis's"**: Ted Berrigan, *The Collected Poems of Ted Berrigan* (Berkeley: University of California Press, 2005), p. 167.

138 **"Elio [the Schneemans' middle son]"**: Interview of Katie Schneeman by the author, June 12, 2013.

138 **"Poets," Padgett says**: Interview of Ron Padgett by the author, September 17, 2014.

139 **"I was living in Forest Hills"**: Interview of Nancy Rubin by the author, January 17, 2013.

139 **At a store called Gussie and Becky**: Angela Taylor, "Downtown Boutique for Uptown Crowd," *New York Times*, January 5, 1968.

139 **Underground Uplift Unlimited**: From 1967 to 1971, see http://gaytoday .com/interview/100102in.asp.

140 **making her the toast of fourth grade**: Interview of Paula McGregor by the author, August 12, 2013.

140 **the world's smallest roller rink**: N. R. Kleinfeld, "On the Street of Dreams," *New York Times*, November 22, 1992.

140 **"It made no sense at all"**: Interview of Johnny Dynell by the author, October 8, 2014.

141 **"I didn't want to move there"**: Interview of Charles Fitzgerald by the author, January 8, 2013.

142 **"There was always something nice"**: Interview of Arthur McGee by the author, March 26, 2013.

143 **"The Velvet Underground came"**: Interview of Khadejha McCall by the author, April 30, 2013. Khadejha inspired rapturous praise in several people I spoke to. For example, photographer Larry Fink said: "[St. Marks] was for me not a love affair but a thoroughfare. When Khadejha came, I became more of a devotee of the street. She was an incredibly beautiful, smiling presence, and with a rigor for capitalist invention from the continent from which her people came." Interview of Larry Fink by the author, June 11, 2013.

144 **"The drag queens had the longest arms"**: Interview of Marty and Eileen Freedman by the author, March 21, 2013.

144 **"One winter, everyone on St. Marks Place"**: Interview with Judy Garrison by the author, January 17, 2014.

144 **"Oh, of course, if you were tripping"**: Interview of Paul Krassner by the author, November 8, 2013.

144 **"It was possible to live a life"**: Interview of Peter Stampfel by the author, November 9, 2013.

145 **"My parents would say"**: Interview of John Townley by the author, February 28, 2014.

146 **"The Fugs's first album"**: Some say the Fugs were founded at the Dom (e.g., Sukenick, *Down and In*, p. 166). Ed Sanders (who would know) says they were founded at the Peace Eye Bookstore. Ed Sanders, *Tales of Beatnik Glory* (New York: Stonehill Publishing, 1975), p. 1.

146 **"Around her neck"**: The Fugs, "Slum Goddess," Live from the Fillmore East, 1968, https://www.youtube.com/watch?v=hadRsj4W4qg.

146 **"Kill for Peace"**: See https://www.youtube.com/watch?v=JvA1bKLQtbM.

146 **"the roots of revolution"**: Ed Sanders, *Fug You: An Informal History of the Peace Eye Bookstore, the Fuck You Press, the Fugs, and Counterculture in the Lower East Side* (New York: Da Capo, 2013), p. xiii.

Chapter 15

147 **"The counterculture, the subculture"**: Andy Warhol, *The Philosophy of Andy Warhol* (San Diego: Harvest, 1977), p. 25.

147 **"It was amazing"**: Interview of John Waters by the author, October 28, 2014.

149 **"Drugs helped"**: *The Philosophy of Andy Warhol*, p. 26.

149 **"cloud" balloons**: Mike Jahn, "'Velvet' Rock Group Opens Stand Here," *New York Times*, July 4, 1970; video of *Andy Warhol's Silver Flotations* (1966), by Willard Maas, https://www.youtube.com/watch?v=65obeVlgD9E.

149 **The lights and the drugs helped distill**: Musician Lenny Kaye put it like this: "Reviewers who came drew parallels to Berlin in the depths of the thirties, but they missed the mark. It was New York in the sixties, the essence distilled and brought out, a city splitting apart and loving every minute of it." Clinton Heylin, ed., *All Yesterday's Parties: The Velvet Underground in Print, 1966–1971* (Cambridge, MA: Da Capo Press, 2005), p. 159.

149 **Nico, "that white, white creature"**: Lucian Truscott IV, "A Stockingful of Love, but No Re-Admission," *Village Voice* 14, no. 12 (January 2, 1969), http://blogs.villagevoice.com/runninscared/2010/06/lucian_truscott.php.

150 **"Wow—you don't see that on *Hullabaloo*"**: Richard Goldstein, "A Quiet Evening at the Balloon Farm," *Reporting the Counterculture* (London: Unwin Hyman, 1989), p. 89.

150 **"Every store was for rent on the street"**: Interview of Jerry Brandt by the author, April 26, 2013.

151 **Revelers encountered fire-eaters**: Molly McGlone, "Excavating Experimentalism: Investigating Musical Space, the Electric Circus, and Nineteen-Sixties New York," Ph.D. dissertation, University of Wisconsin-Madison, 2010, p. 8.

151   **Every once in a while:** John Leo, "Swinging in the East Village Has Its Ups and Downs," *New York Times*, July 15, 1967.

152   **so the dance floor was like a furnace:** Jack Newfield, "Hippies and New Frontier on 'Desolation Row,'" *Village Voice*, July 6, 1967.

152   **"[The Electric Circus] did feel decadent":** Interview of Carole Rosenthal by the author, September 19, 2013; and follow-up emails December 4, 2013.

152   **"I was astounded people were drawn":** Interview of Larry Fink by the author, June 11, 2013.

153   **little blue crabs had pinched his fingers:** Interview of Joey Dick by the author, March 12, 2014.

154   **In a Pleasantville, New York, orphanage:** Bill Graham, *Bill Graham Presents: My Life inside Rock and Out* (New York: Da Capo Press, 2004), p. 248.

154   **On opening night of the Fillmore East:** Ibid., pp. 233–34.

154   **"I remember calling my mother up":** Interview of Richard Manitoba by the author, March 21, 2013.

155   **The revolutionary lighting designer Joshua White:** Interview of Joshua White by the author, August 15, 2014.

156   **"There would be no East Village":** Interview of Jerry Brandt by the author, April 26, 2013.

Chapter 16

157   **Flyers promised "songs against the war":** August 7, 1965; see http://www.npr.org/2012/05/05/152029486/fug-you-the-wild-life-of-ed-sanders.

157   **especially Andy Warhol:** Sanders, *Fug You*, pp. 154–55.

157   **"like living in a really cheap dorm":** Interview of Joey Skaggs by the author, April 30, 2012, and follow-ups March 5, 2015.

159   **"Well, you have one, don't you?":** Interview of Michael Allen by the author, July 9, 2012. Joey Skaggs remembers it slightly differently. He says Allen told the officer, "Well, he was a man, wasn't he?"

159   **was then living at no. 113:** Email to the author from Debbie Harry via her manager, March 5, 2015. Also, Interview of John Campo by the author, March 4, 2015.

160   **"Libertine Larry":** Michael Shnayerson, "Crimes of the Art?" *Vanity Fair*, December 2010.

160   **"The first time I was on St. Marks":** Interview of Judy Gumbo Albert by the author, October 16, 2013.

161   **One of the stunt events held:** Interview of Paul Krassner by the author, November 8, 2013.

162   **"He started cursing the church":** Interview of Stephen Facey by the author, July 12, 2012.

163   **On the night of August 12, 1967:** John Kifner, "500 Hippies Dance and Plant a Tree," *New York Times*, August 13, 1967.

163 **"preventative enforcement"**: "Police: Fink's Peace," *Time*, November 8, 1968.

163 **"psychedelic block party"**: The quotes in this section come from "Block Party Held to Create Mall," *New York Times*, August 25, 1967.

163 **"This is the destruction of the twentieth century"**: Ibid.

164 **"young, uninhibited" hippies**: Joseph Fink and Lloyd G. Sealy, *The Community and the Police—Conflict or Cooperation?* (New York: John Wiley & Sons, 1974), pp. 26–27.

164 **"Abbie saw us talking"**: Interview of Paul Krassner by the author, November 8, 2013.

Chapter 17

165 **James Leroy "Groovy" Hutchinson**: Interview of Penny Arcade by the author, October 20, 2014. Arcade told me: "Groovy was super sweet. He was a really, really nice person. He was like a happy-go-lucky guy who came from upstate. He had met Galahad, who was from the Midwest who was older. He got this idea of saving kids. I was raped five times in the East Village before I was eighteen. There were predators. We needed places to stay. Groovy and Galahad started these crash houses. Groovy wasn't an intellectual. He was that kind of person that existed for a short time in the sixties when the walls fell down: 'Were you for real or were you a plastic person?' When Groovy and Linda were murdered, there was a face on the evil that everybody knew."

165 **Two men—Donald Ramsey**: "New York: Speed Kills," *Time*, October 20, 1967; "Hippie LSD Party Leads to Double Murder in N.Y.," *Jet*, October 26, 1967.

165 **the East Village took a turn**: A related April 2013 subplot of HBO show *Mad Men*, season 6, had Betty Draper looking through the 1967 East Village for a runaway teenager in a decrepit squat just off St. Marks Place. The *Times* ran a story about the similarities: Stephanie Goodman, "The East Village of 'Mad Men' versus the Real Neighborhood in the 1960s," *New York Times*, April 10, 2013.

165 **"After that, it was a very fast slide"**: Interview of Peter Stampfel by the author, November 9, 2013.

166 **"Via Terroris"**: Sanders, *Fug You*, p. 274.

166 **"whose ingredients included crash pads"**: J. Anthony Lukas, "The Two Worlds of Linda Fitzpatrick," *New York Times*, October 16, 1967.

166 **"The Ninth Precinct had a special squad"**: Interview of Kristina Olitski by the author, December 4, 2012.

167 **She recalls that more than one kid**: Bernard Weintraub, "For Many Hippies, Christmas Means Emptiness," *New York Times*, December 26, 1968.

167   **"When I look at photographs"**: Interview of Susan Fensten by the author, August 20, 2014.

168   **"Every morning it would crow at 6 a.m."**: Interview of Paul Schneeman by the author, August 11, 2013.

168   **"When I was twelve"**: Interview of Manohla Dargis by the author, September 21, 2013, and email of December 30, 2014. Dargis met her husband in front of Gem Spa. He reminded her, not unpleasantly, of Elvis Costello. She teased him about the fact that in his coat pocket he had a paperback copy of Maurice Blanchot's *Death Sentence*, a book he had bought at St. Mark's Bookshop, which her father, Peter Dargis, had cofounded. "It was part of my pathetic flirting," she said, "though it did work out, after all."

168   **By 1968, the East Village**: Steve Lerner, "The Lower East Side: Radicalization of Hip," *Village Voice*, November 28, 1968.

168   **After one particularly violent scuffle**: Steve Lerner, "The Street Is Bleeding: A Dead-End Pastime," *Village Voice*, October 10, 1968.

168   **"There were sleeping bags lined up end to end"**: Interview of Carole Rosenthal by the author, September 19, 2013.

169   **"Beneath the surface emaciation"**: Editorial, *Rat*, August 1969. Collection of Eileen Johnson.

169   **"Probably the worst thing I ever said"**: Interview of Ernie Hurwitz by the author, June 3, 2013.

170   **"this totally bourgeois, dandy world"**: Ron Hahne and Ben Morea, *Black Mask and Up against the Wall Motherfucker: The Incomplete Works of Ron Hahne, Ben Morea and the Black Mask Group* (Oakland, CA: PM Press, 2011), p. 157.

170   **"Back then that kind of thing"**: Interview of Peter Schjeldahl by the author, August 9, 2012.

170   **"Reactions after the event were split"**: Red Marriott, "Ben Morea: An Interview by Ian McIntyre (2006)," Libcom.org, March 24, 2012.

170   **"When a cop politely suggested"**: Osha Neumann, *Up against the Wall Motherfucker: A Memoir of the '60s, with Notes for Next Time* (New York: Seven Stories Press, 2008), p. 115. Interview of Osha Neumann by the author, October 16, 2013.

171   **"It would take half an hour"**: Interview of Jeff Jones by the author, October 7, 2013.

171   **Their August 19, 1969, performance**: "The Woodstock Show," *Dick Cavett Show*, August 19, 1969. View part 1: https://www.youtube.com/watch?v=abPpq6hQ67I. At the 3:57 mark, Grace Slick sings, "Up against the wall, motherfucker," but it goes by really fast.

171   **"We did such things as collect clothing"**: Interview of Johnny Sundstrom by the author, October 16, 2013.

171   **"culture exchange"**: Thai Jones, *A Radical Line* (New York: Free Press, 2004), p. 182.

172 **Graham had made peace:** Graham, *Bill Graham Presents*, p. 253. Also: Interview of Paul Krassner by the author, November 8, 2013.

172 **Sixty hippies boarded:** "60 Hippies in a Bus See the Sights of Quaint Queens," *New York Times*, September 23, 1968. Also, interview of Joey Skaggs by the author, April 30, 2012, and follow-ups March 5, 2015.

173 **Some Motherfuckers attempted:** See http://www.devilsdiciples.org.

173 **"They wanted to take over":** Interview of Johnny Sundstrom by the author, October 16, 2013.

174 **"Bomb! Shoot! Kill!":** Interview of Paul Krassner by the author, November 8, 2013.

174 **"They messed up the floor":** Graham, *Bill Graham Presents*, p. 254.

175 **"by the *other* people, I guess":** Ibid., p. 257.

175 **In 1968, a young actress:** Interviews of Brooke Alderson by the author, 2012–2014.

175 **"Life in this society being, at best":** Valerie Solanas, *Scum Manifesto* (New York: Verso, 2004), p. 35 (originally printed by London: Olympia Press, 1971).

176 **he reached the hospital clinically dead:** A minute-by-minute timeline of the shooting can be found at warholstars.org.

176 **As a radical activist:** Interview of Nell Gibson by the author, June 16, 2013, and follow-up emails, especially December 26, 2014.

176 **"Why'd you hit that guy?":** Graham, *Bill Graham Presents*, p. 238.

176 **Law enforcement targeted St. Marks Place:** Sanders, *Fug You*, p. 157.

176 **A nationwide crackdown:** David Hadju, *The Ten-Cent Plague: The Great Comic Book Scare and How It Changed America* (New York: Farrar, Straus and Giroux), 2008.

176 **The bookstore was raided:** "Obscenity Case Files: *Zap Comix* #4," Comic Book Legal Defense Fund, September 24, 2013.

177 **"The family that lays together, stays together":** *Zap Comix* no. 4, Apex Novelties, August 1969.

177 **It's about as lurid:** Mike Diana's later comics, which featured, among other disturbing things, a baby being raped by crackheads, were maybe more lurid. They would be available on St. Marks Place in the 1990s. Diana became the first cartoonist ever to receive a U.S. criminal conviction for obscenity. He appeared with St. Marks Place resident GG Allin in the 1996 documentary *Affliction*, and in the 1999 Nick Zedd movie *Ecstasy in Entropy*.

177 **"I was not even really at work that day":** Interview of Terry McCoy and Bob Contant by the author, February 12, 2013.

177 **"It is material utterly unredeemed":** "Obscenity Case Files: *Zap Comix* #4."

178 **a teenage draft-dodger:** James Leo Herlihy, *Season of the Witch* (New York: Simon and Schuster, 1971), p. 218.

178 **"You scream 'murder'":** Harold Franklin, *Run a Twisted Street* (Philadelphia: J. P. Lippincott Company, 1970), p. 59.

178 **"Everyone thought cocaine was amazing"**: Interview of Joshua White by the author, August 15, 2014.

179 **"I saw kids who were sweet acid-heads"**: Marshall Berman, "Introduction," in Berman and Brian Berger, eds. *New York Calling* (London: Reaktion Books, 2007), p. 14.

179 **Downstairs, the Dom had become**: John Leo, "Swinging in the East Village Has Its Ups and Downs," *New York Times*, July 15, 1967.

179 **West Point cadet and reporter**: Lucian Truscott IV, "A Stockingful of Love, But No Re-Admission," *Village Voice* 14, no. 12 (January 2, 1969), http://blogs .villagevoice.com/runninscared/2010/06/lucian_truscott.php.

181 **Each night after they closed the bar**: Interview of Joyce Hartwell by the author, October 7, 2013, and several more times through 2013 and 2014.

181 **The Cow Palace**: Jeffrey Langer, "Fine Shows at Palace, Hippodrome," *Columbia Daily Spectator* 99, no. 30 (October 18, 1974); "The Dom Closes; To Be Cow Palace; A $3 Mixed Drink," *New York Times*, July 28, 1974.

181 **Johnny Ramone was in the audience**: Johnny Ramone, *Commando* (New York: Abrams, 2012), p. 25.

181 **"someone died at a Vanilla Fudge concert"**: Mark Stein, lead singer of Vanilla Fudge, told me in an email that he had no knowledge of the incident, but Joshua White recalled it in an interview. And Bill Graham's personal assistant Bonnie Garner tells the story in John Glatt, *Live at the Fillmore East and West* (Guilford, CT: Globe Pequot Press, 2014), p. 279.

182 **"from a hippie haven to Desolation Row"**: Lucian Truscott IV, "St. Marks Place, 1971: One-Way Street," *Village Voice*, August 26, 1971.

182 **was tired of being told to take the high road**: Douglas Martin, "James Forman Dies at 76; Was Pioneer in Civil Rights," *New York Times*, January 12, 2005.

182 **"If we can't sit at the table of democracy"**: Clayborne Carson, *In Struggle: SNCC and the Black Awakening of the 1960s* (Cambridge, MA: Harvard University Press, 1995), p. 160. Alternate language appears here: *Bridge to Freedom* (1965), transcript: http://www.pbs.org/wgbh/amex/eyesontheprize/about/ pt_106.html.

183 **"Black people must have absolute"**: LeRoi Jones, "The Legacy of Malcolm X, and the Coming of the Black Nation (1965)" in *Home: Social Essays* (New York: AkashiClassics Renegade Reprint Series, 2009; 1st ed. 1966), p. 279.

183 **"$500,000,000"**: Xerox copy of Forman's "Black Manifesto" found in the St. Mark's Church-in-the-Bowery archive. Also found in Marcus D. Pohlmann, ed., *African American Political Thought* (New York: Routledge, 2003), p. 269.

183 **On the morning of Sunday, October 5, 1969**: This account is based on the author's 2012–2014 interviews with Michael Allen, David Garcia, Stephen Facey, Tom Pike, and Nell and Bert Gibson, as well as records in the St. Mark's Church archives, including the group's list of demands, materi-

als about James Forman, and Michael Allen's correspondence to the vestry. The story is also told in Michael Allen's book *This Time, This Place*.

183 **For weeks, Allen had suspected**: Allen, *This Time, This Place*, p. 149.

183 **the Black Nationalist flag**: Ibid., p. 150.

184 **They expected Allen to reject their demands**: Interview of Nell Gibson by the author, June 16, 2013, and follow-up emails, especially December 26, 2014.

184 **"That was a hard moment"**: Allen, *This Time, This Place*, pp. 150–51.

184 **"Sunday was wonderful!"**: Interview of Tom Pike by the author, December 3, 2013.

185 **"We made public confessions"**: Interview of Nell Gibson by the author, June 16, 2013, and follow-up emails, especially December 26, 2014.

185 **"Little black baby"**: Ibid., pp. 168–70.

186 **"Mike was a wonderful, radical guy"**: Interview of Tom Pike by the author, December 3, 2013.

186 **"You know, Michael could have been bishop"**: Interview of David Garcia by the author, August 28, 2013.

187 **During his post–St. Mark's time as rector**: Michael D. Sorkin, "Rev. J. C. Michael Allen dies; activist priest who once had no religion," *St. Louis Post-Dispatch*, September 8, 2013.

187 **On a rainy day in October 1974**: When my parents told the artist Joan Mitchell that they were engaged during a dinner party at no. 53, Mitchell shouted, "Don't do it!" In the midst of her harangue about the evils of matrimony, the buzzer rang. My father answered it. It was the French-Canadian artist Jean-Paul Riopelle looking for Mitchell. They were having a tempestuous affair. "Don't let him in!" yelled Mitchell, who then took over at the intercom, yelling at Riopelle. At some point she buzzed him in and screamed at him down the stairwell until he finally went away, at which point she returned to the dinner table and continued trying to convince my parents not to get married. Her campaign was unsuccessful.

189 **"We woke up in a time"**: Interview of Peter Schjeldahl by the author, August 9, 2012.

Chapter 18

193 **Today Artie was wearing**: Interview of Carole Rosenthal by the author, September 19, 2013.

194 **"There has never been a band"**: He says he's not sure exactly where this piece ran—maybe *Newsday*?—but it appears on his website: http://www.robertchristgau.com/xg/nyet/nydolls-ms.php.

194 **where legend has it**: Interview of Adam Horovitz and Mike Diamond by the author, February 5, 2013.

194 **"when stupid on purpose became the new smart"**: Jeffrey Lewis, "A Complete History of Punk on the Lower East Side, 1950–1979," various performances of which are on YouTube. The lyrics from an August 26, 2004, performance are on the Jeffrey Lewis Message Board at http://jeffreylewisboard .free.fr/phpBB2/viewtopic.php?t=636.

194 **"hated by the rest of the country"**: John Rockwell, "The Pop Life: Growth, Change and David Johansen," *New York Times*, August 17, 1979.

195 **"probably the unluckiest band"**: Will Hermes, "Return of the Dolls, What's Left of Them," *New York Times*, July 23, 2006. Also, Morrissey's *Autobiography* (New York: Putnam, 2013). Poetically, The New York Dolls's 2006 album is called *One Day It Will Please Us to Remember Even This*.

195 **"People talk about CBGB"**: Interview of Jeff Roth by the author, May 20, 2013.

196 **"It was just an old, dumpy little bar"**: Ramone, *Commando*, pp. 31–32.

196 **"It was like a practice in front of ten people"**: Tony Fletcher, *All Hopped Up and Ready to Go: Music from the Streets of New York, 1927–77* (New York: W.W. Norton & Company, 2009), p. 334.

197 **"Kill yourself. Jump off a fuckin' cliff"**: The full archive of *Punk* can be found at punkmagazine.com. See http://www.punkmagazine.com/vault/ back_issues/01/editorial01.html.

197 **Collaborative Projects, Inc.**: The Colab movies are trippy! Here's a sampling: http://www.youtube.com/watch?v=0Qty7FOOnOs.

197 **"If you stayed long enough"**: Interview of Luc Sante by the author, May 2, 2013.

198 **One room of Moore's apartment**: Interview of Wells Moore by the author, September 10, 2013.

199 **"Never be poor"**: Interview of Tish and Snooky Bellomo by the author, March 13, 2013.

202 **Richard Hell and Tom Verlaine**: Richard Hell, *I Dreamed I Was a Very Clean Tramp* (New York: HarperCollins, 2013), p. 101.

203 **Singer Lydia Lunch caught her first glimpse**: Interview of Lydia Lunch by the author, May 14, 2013.

204 **"She was the welcoming committee"**: Interview of Jim Marshall by the author, May 15, 2013.

204 **"Lydia told me there were certain conditions"**: Interview of Jim Sclavunos by the author, May 16, 2013.

204 **"I told her I was interested"**: Interview of Nick Zedd by the author, May 15, 2013.

204 **"A good show for Teenage Jesus"**: Interview of David Godlis by the author, March 21, 2013.

204 **"Sex Pistols has Chuck Berry in it"**: Interview of J. G. Thirlwell by the author, April 12, 2013.

Chapter 19

206 **"The danger kept people away"**: Interview of Richard Manitoba by the author, March 21, 2013.

206 **"It was a slum"**: Hell, *I Dreamed I Was a Very Clean Tramp*, p. 137.

206 **"In 1975, I lived on St. Marks"**: Interview of Terry McCoy and Bob Contant by the author, February 12, 2013.

206 **His perfect day was rising at noon**: Interview of Joel Millman by the author, August 22, 2014.

207 **"The punks were out on the street"**: Interview of Libby and Al Forsyth by the author, February 5, 2013.

207 **"kids sitting in a circle holding daffodils"**: Interview of Angela Jaeger by the author, June 26, 2013.

207 **where the Hare Krishna mantra was first chanted in the West**: See http://www.nycgovparks.org/parks/tompkins-square-park.

207 **On December 23, 1974**: "Police Kill Gunman Holding 2 as Hostages in the East Village," *New York Times*, December 24, 1974.

208 **He was killed in a shootout**: One of the two policemen sent into the fray was Officer Donald Muldoon, who had been at the Ninth Precinct on Fifth Street since the 1960s. Muldoon's friend Officer George Ackerman describes Officer Muldoon as central casting for a refined, gentlemanly cop. "He did the Sunday *Times* puzzle in half an hour, loved wine, and wrote literary police reports that people would enjoy reading today," says Ackerman. "If my parents could pick any cop to come to the door, it would be Donny."

208 **Around this time, the writer Luc Sante**: Sante, 2003 afterword, *Low Life*, p. 365.

208 **"I knew my building might fall down"**: Interview of Luc Sante by the author, May 2, 2013.

208 **During this period, New York City lost**: Joel Millman, *The Other Americans: How Immigrants Renew Our Country, Our Economy, and Our Values* (New York: Viking Penguin, 1997), p. 80.

208 **"'White flight' wouldn't have been so bad"**: Millman, *The Other Americans*, Chapter 2, p. 67.

209 **"260,000 Italians"**: Interview by the author of Joel Millman, August 22, 2014, and his book *The Other Americans*, Chapter 2 (the number 260,000 appears on p. 66).

209 **A serious heroin addict at the time**: Interview of Jimmy Webb by the author, January 29, 2013.

210 **They often turned vestibules and doorways into toilets**: Interview of Anthony Scifo by the author, October 17, 2014.

210 **"It was a crash pad for all the junkies and alcoholics"**: Interview of Arthur Nersesian by the author, November 8, 2013.

212 **Forsyth decided to befriend him**: Interview of Libby and Al Forsyth by the author, February 5, 2013.

213 *Hispanic Study Report*: Jagna Wojcicka Sharff, "Life on Dolittle Street: How Poor People Purchase Immortality," Hispanic Study Project, Dept. of Anthropology, September 24, 1980, in *Hispanic Study Report*. A copy of this report is in Joyce Hartwell's personal collection.

214 **"that look that was just becoming"**: Rossner, *Looking for Mr. Goodbar*, p. 127.

214 **"a totally flipped-out hippie"**: Yuri Kapralov, *Once There Was a Village* (New York: St. Martin's Press, 1974), p. 73.

214 **Kapralov's seventies East Village**: Ibid., p. 117.

214 **"Poverty-stricken Puerto Ricans"**: Michael Brownstein, *Self-Reliance* (New York: Coffee House Press, 1994), p. 4.

214 **"Let's Do It" T-shirts**: Ibid., p. 195.

215 **"pooper scooper" law**: Department of Sanitation Press Release, October 27, 2011.

215 **"It wasn't just the criminality"**: James Wolcott, *Lucking Out: My Life Getting Down and Semi-dirty in '70s New York* (New York: Anchor Books, 2011), p. 49.

215 **"the Sunset Strip of bohemian striving and slumming"**: Ibid., pp. 226–30.

215 **"Rain-wet asphalt heat"**: Anne Waldman, ed., *Another World: A Second Anthology of Works from the St. Mark's Poetry Project* (Indianapolis: Bobbs-Merrill, 1971), p. 230. Poem written August 2, 1969.

215 **"Shots rang out"**: White, *City Boy*, p. 211.

215 **W. H. Auden left New York**: "Auden Starts New Job," *Daytona Beach Morning Journal* (AP), October 18, 1972.

216 **In July 1978, near the end of a renovation**: Robert McG. Thomas, Jr., "Blaze Damages Bowery Church Erected in 1799," *New York Times*, July 28, 1978.

217 **the Binibon**: Jack Henry Abbott with Naomi Zack, *My Return* (Buffalo, NY: Prometheus Books, 1987), p. 131.

218 **"I was packing my kids in the car"**: Interview of Paul Delaney by the author, September 12, 2013.

218 **"awesome, brilliant, perversely ingenuous"**: Terrence Des Pres, "A Child of the State," *New York Times*, July 19, 1981.

Chapter 20

219 **The St. Mark's Baths**: To the extent that the Baths show up at all in the press in the middle of the twentieth century, it is as a dangerous flophouse. The *New York Times* reported there on a 1934 veteran suicide, 1947 arrest of two suspected burglars, and 1955 murder of a trucker named James Trombetta while he sat there drinking coffee at 3:30 a.m.

219   **Owner Bruce Mailman spared no expense:** White, *City Boy*, pp. 228–29. The Baths was advertised in, for example, the July 1978 issue of *Blueboy*. "AIDS in New York: The First Five Years," New York Historical Society exhibit, 2013.

219   **Men could rent a locker:** Jane Gross, "Bathhouses Reflect AIDS Concerns," *New York Times*, October 14, 1985.

220   **"not too old to be repulsive":** Brandon Stosuy, *Up Is Up but So Is Down: New York's Literary Downtown Scene, 1974–1992* (New York: New York University Press, 2006), p. 181.

220   **"duck-footing in there":** Interview of Terry McCoy and Bob Contant by the author, February 12, 2013. Rudolph Nureyev was known to frequent gay bathhouses. See Toni Bentley, "The Brando of Ballet," Review of Julie Kavanagh's *Nureyev: The Life*, *New York Times Book Review*, December 2, 2007. Also see this *Muppet Show* clip of Miss Piggy sexually harassing Nureyev in a bathhouse: https://www.youtube.com/watch?v=-EJ1SBAO1HU.

220   **"You could pretend you were in jail":** The men quoted in this paragraph about their Baths experiences preferred to remain anonymous.

220   **"I managed to come at the stroke of midnight":** David B. Feinberg, *Eighty-Sixed* (New York: Viking, 1989), p. 6.

221   **According to gay nightlife impresario Scott Ewalt:** Interview of Scott Ewalt by the author, July 15, 2012.

221   **"Walking down St. Mark's Place at midnight":** Rosalyn Regelson, "'Not a Boy, Not a Girl, Just Me,'" *New York Times*, November 2, 1969.

221   **"hip people problems":** Interview of Perry Brass by the author, March 12, 2014.

222   **"St. Mark's Place now belongs":** Andrew Holleran, ed., *Dancer from the Dance* (New York: Bantam, 1979; 1st ed. 1978), p. 117.

222   **"just as the Polish barbers":** Ibid., p. 108.

222   **"*Gatsby* for the cusp-of-AIDS era":** Email from Carl Swanson to the author, January 31, 2013.

222   **"to fit into each day its maximum number of mistakes":** Peter Schjeldahl, "Those '80s," *Let's See* (New York: Thames & Hudson, 2008), p. 181.

222   **The art scene became a playground:** Richard Metzger, "East Village Preservation Society: Club 57," Dazeddigital.com, 2012.

223   **"They were taking matters into their own hands":** Interview of James Fuentes by the author, November 10, 2013.

223   **"It was an art world pre-commerce":** A 2013 Loren Munk painting called *The Decline and Fall of the Art World, Part I: The One-Percenters* at the Freight + Volume gallery shows a map of the East Village art world from the eighties. It's an intricate web of artists, zines, and small spaces with some internationally famous names like Basquiat visible in the tangle. The list of spaces includes: International with Monument, Nature Morte, Jake Worney Modern Art,

FUN Gallery, Pat Hearn, American Fine Arts/Vox Populi, PPOW, and Cash Newhouse Art.

223 **Mostly he was known:** Keith Haring, "Wednesday, February 22," *Keith Haring Journals*, New York: Penguin Classics Deluxe Edition, 2010, p. 132.

224 **Haring admired William S. Burroughs:** Morgan, *The Beat Generation in New York*, p. 97.

224 **clonking a texting NYU student:** Daniel Maurer, "When Art Attacks! Keith Haring's Self-Portrait Kicked Someone in the Head," Bedford + Bowery, January 16, 2015.

224 **"We felt the East Village":** Alexandra Kolossa, *Haring* (Los Angeles, CA: Taschen, 2009), p. 15.

224 **The mistress of ceremonies:** Interview of Ann Magnuson by the author, January 9, 2014.

225 **"the Tin Man, the Scarecrow, the Cowardly Lion":** The poet Sparrow has been my pen pal since 1991, when I was a freshman at Stuyvesant High School. He sent me a great email of stories about his time on St. Marks Place on November 22, 2013.

225 **Artist Kenny Scharf has said:** John Gruen, *Keith Haring: The Authorized Biography* (New York: Simon and Schuster, 1992), p. 46. Confirmed with Kenny Scharf via Facebook message reply to the author, March 5, 2015.

225 **naked performers once chased the audience:** Alan Moore, "ABC No Rio as an Anarchist Space," article awaiting publication.

226 **could hear Nomi's voice carry:** *The Nomi Song* (2004). Confirmed with Kenny Scharf via Facebook message reply to the author, March 5, 2015.

226 **"a little guy with a mystery":** Interview of Mark Howell by the author, August 15, 2012.

227 **"gay cancer":** Cynthia Carr, *Fire in the Belly: The Life and Times of David Wojnarowicz* (New York: Bloomsbury, 2012), p. 202.

227 **"You're all going to be dead in six months":** documentary *United in Anger: A History of Act Up* (2012).

228 **"You must have seen a lot of changes":** Carr, *Fire in the Belly*, p. 320.

228 **"I meet my guest":** Jay Blotcher, "Towel Boy at the St. Mark's Baths," Spring 1983, available online at http://www.jayblotcher.com/archives/200403/towel_boy_at_the_st_marks_baths_spring_1983_diary_entries_15.html.

228 **Bruce Mailman struggled to be:** Jane Gross, "Bathhouses Reflect AIDS Concerns," *New York Times*, October 14, 1985.

228 **"If you don't have it now":** Carr, *Fire in the Belly*, p. 279.

228 **"We didn't know who Klaus Nomi was":** Interview of Barbara Sibley by the author, January 27, 2014.

230 **"Madonna is the worst thing":** Interview of Scott Ewalt by the author, July 15, 2012.

230 **the New St. Mark's Baths was shut down for good:** See http://biotech.law.lsu.edu/cases/STDs/St_marks_I.htm.

231 **At his Astor Place Theatre memorial service:** Mireya Navarro, "Ritualizing Grief, Love and Politics: AIDS Memorial Services Evolve into a Distinctive Gay Rite," *New York Times*, November 30, 1994. See also "Bruce Mailman, 55, Owner of Businesses In the East Village," *New York Times*, June 12, 1994.

Chapter 21

232 **"I hated that place":** Interview of Arnie Weinberg by the author, November 4, 2013.

233 **Brokaw "jumped right in":** Interview of Tom Birchard by the author, October 30, 2014. Fun fact: Birchard's wife, Sally Haddock, runs the St. Mark's Veterinary Hospital down the block from the restaurant.

233 **"It was very embarrassing":** Interview of Myrna Hall by the author, November 2, 2014.

234 **Brokaw liked good food:** Interview of Libby and Al Forsyth by the author, February 5, 2013.

234 **"He was a great believer in the Horatio Alger story":** Interview of Lorcan Otway by the author, July 12, 2012.

Chapter 22

236 **Photographer Roberta Bayley:** Interview with Roberta Bayley by the author, November 1, 2013.

237 **Smiling, sweaty Billy Joel:** Billy Joel, "A Matter of Trust" (1986). See http://www.youtube.com/watch?v=6yYchgX1fMw.

237 **Joyce Hartwell had rented space:** Interview of Joyce Hartwell by the author, October 7, 2013, and several more times through 2013 and 2014. She also made available a trove of archival material.

238 **"I think she did a lot of good":** Interview of Charles Fitzgerald by the author, January 8, 2013.

239 **"Drugs were everywhere":** Interview of Sherry Sotomayor by the author, November 6, 2013.

241 **"A mother wouldn't think":** Interview of Joyce Hartwell by the author, October 7, 2013, and several more times through 2013 and 2014.

242 **"It was crazy!":** Interview of Richard Manitoba by the author, March 21, 2013.

242 **"Look, *Merk*":** Marky Ramone, *Punk Rock Blitzkrieg: My Life as a Ramone* (New York: Touchstone, 2014), p. 340. The band was called the Uncles, and their last show was at the Electric Circus, "an old town hall and ballroom carved out of three very old four-story brick row homes." Marky says it was hard for the teen band to compete with the "jugglers, fire-eaters, and tra-

peze artists," p. 25. He also loved hanging out at the Fillmore. A friend who worked there let him play there sometimes during off-hours and "feel the power of being onstage at a major venue," pp. 32–33.

242 **"When you live in a war zone"**: Interview of Priscilla and Jessica Forsyth and Ronald Hunter by the author, November 9, 2013.

243 **"I made $250 in two hours"**: Interview of Ann and Rachel Tyson by the author, January 10, 2013.

243 **"It was Upper East Side trash"**: Interview of Edmund Berrigan by the author, May 11, 2012. Interview of Anselm Berrigan by the author, July 12, 2012.

243 **An *Eyewitness News* report estimated**: VHS tape of this news report about pedophilia on St. Marks Place from circa 1989 provided by Joyce Hartwell.

244 **"a dirty sleaze"**: Interview with a police officer from the Ninth Precinct by the author, 2014.

244 **a sleek black town car**: Interview of Ben Laurence by the author, a former classmate at P.S. 41 and Stuyvesant High School, August 8, 2013.

245 **Spacely said he wasn't a snitch**: Interview of Peter Nolan Smith by the author, November 19, 2013.

246 **"I'd do drawings of him"**: Interview of Art Guerra by the author, September 8, 2014.

246 **Spacely roams the neighborhood**: *Story of a Junkie*, 1987. See http://www .youtube.com/watch?v=2IuJglN6siA.

246 **"It was rough"**: Interview of Colin Quinn by the author, May 7, 2014.

247 **It also shows him talking on his deathbed**: At around the one-hour mark of *Born to Lose: The Last Rock and Roll Movie*. See http://www.youtube.com/ watch?v=CLXYC6Gy4Lg.

247 **baby-faced beat cop**: Interview of George Ackerman by the author, October 28, 2014. Officer George is one of the nicest men in East Village history. He was close with Abe Lebewohl of the Second Avenue Deli. He took me and a bunch of other neighborhood kids to the New York City Ballet's *Nutcracker* in the eighties. Lately, he has worked as a security guard at Lincoln Center.

247 **bombing at One Police Plaza**: "Three NYPD Detectives Honored on 25th Anniversary of FALN Bombings," NY1 News, January 31, 2007.

248 **Kentucky Fried Chicken box**: Philip Messing, "Officials Shame NYC By Backing Terrorist in Parade," *New York Post*, June 7, 2014.

248 **One senseless tragedy occurred**: Leonard Buder, "Aiding a Neighbor, Boy is Killed in Fall Down Air Shaft," *New York Times*, September 5, 1985.

248 **Enz's owner, Mariann Marlowe**: Interview of Mariann Marlowe by the author, May 1, 2013.

249 **complaining of a horrible smell**: "Dismembered Body Found," *New York Times*, May 25, 1987.

249 **"When they came, they found"**: Interview of Steve Firestone by the author, March 27, 2013.

249 **"Christ or the antichrist"**: Mara Bovsun, "Psycho Made Human Soup, Dumped Bones in a Bucket after Slay of Swiss Beauty in 1989," *New York Daily News*, August 21, 2011.

249 **"David Rakowitz would sit in the park"**: Interview of Curtis Sliwa by the author, August 19, 2013.

250 **A squatter claimed to have found**: Mara Bovsun, "Psycho Made Human Soup, Dumped Bones in a Bucket after Slay of Swiss Beauty in 1989," *New York Daily News*, August 21, 2011.

Chapter 23

253 **"When the Gap opened there"**: Interview of Matthew Kasten by the author, September 5, 2014.

253 **"You've heard the name of the problem before"**: Jonny Xerox, "The Danger Is Here! What Are You Going to Do About It?" *East Villager* (September 15–30, 1984). Copy in the personal collection of Eileen Johnson.

256 **"We only did a few shows a year"**: Interview of Nicky Dirt by the author, November 7, 2013. All the Dirt quotes that follow are from this same interview.

256 **"To me, it was Archie Bunker with guitars"**: Email from Henry Rollins to the author, October 6, 2014. To the question of whether St. Marks Place was indeed more a place where fans hung out than where a lot of original hardcore music came from, Rollins said, "I don't know if it was a place where songs were written, but you would always see people hanging around. I was always under the impression that those who really made the music were not there, and it was more the fans and people hanging out, but it's really not my neck of the woods to say. As far as what is called 'hardcore,' like Agnostic Front and all that, I have not one of those records."

256 **"I used to beat up the artsy-fartsy faggots"**: Harley Flanagan interview on the site Dead Ramones, run by Sjarm Dertien, December 15, 2006. Kelefa Sanneh quoted from this interview in "United Blood: How Hardcore Conquered New York," *The New Yorker*, March 9, 2015, http://sjarm13.blogspot.com/2006/12/harley-flanagan.html.

257 **"St. Marks was hella wild"**: Interview of Danny Martin by the author, November 3, 2013.

257 **"Pussy Patrol"**: Interview of Guy Richards Smit by the author, September 15, 2013.

258 **"The neighbors hated it"**: Interview of Eileen Johnson by the author, November 8, 2012.

258 **One devotee, Jai Nitai Holzman**: Interview of Jai Nitai Holzman by the author, November 17, 2013.

258 **"They beat people up"**: Interview of Luc Sante by the author, May 2, 2013.

258 **"There was no anti-bullying campaign bullshit"**: Interview of Danny Martin by the author, November 3, 2013.

258 **where she did the Twist**: Interview of Louise Teiga by the author, December 8, 2013.

259 **wearing an elaborate outfit made of white plastic bags**: Nelson Sullivan, "The Now Explosion: Times Square to Tompkins Square, July 17, 1986," See https://www.youtube.com/watch?v=dlssfzFyWdI.

260 **"I always got ripped off"**: Interview of Curtis Sliwa by the author, August 19, 2013.

263 **"the good lampposts"**: Interview of Bill DiPaola by the author, October 2, 2013.

263 **East Village squatters at one point controlled**: Lincoln Anderson, "Jerry the Peddler Makes Pitch for Permit, but Parks Isn't Buying," *Villager* 77, no 8 (July 25–31, 2007).

264 **"The cost of heroin meant"**: Interview of Jerry Saltz by the author, August 7, 2013.

266 **"Someone dies in an apartment"**: Gary Indiana, *Horse Crazy* (London: Paladin, 1989), p. 91.

267 **"Gentrification is class war"**: Colin Moynihan, "20 Years after Unrest, Class Tensions have Faded and Punk Will Be Played," *New York Times*, August 2, 2008.

267 **Many officers from outside the district**: Robert D. McFadden, "Park Curfew Protest Erupts into a Battle and 38 Are Injured," *New York Times*, August 8, 1988.

267 **"I looked out the window"**: Interview of Jason Zinoman by the author, May 1, 2014.

267 **"The guy was swinging at people"**: Interview of Arnie Weinberg by the author, November 4, 2013.

268 **"I was feeling sick"**: Interview of Louise Teiga by the author, December 8, 2013.

268 **"I saw the tactical patrol force"**: Interview of Curtis Sliwa by the author, August 19, 2013.

268 **"We'll burn your fucking tanks!"**: Richard Sandler documentary *Brave New York* (2004), see http://www.fandor.com/films/brave_new_york.

268 **"something of a war zone"**: McFadden, "Park Curfew Protest Erupts into a Battle and 38 Are Injured."

268 **"The police panicked"**: Ibid.

268 **Businesses along Avenue A locked their doors**: Ibid.

268 **At least fifty people, including thirteen officers**: David E. Pitt, "Few Officers Face Charges in Park Melee," *New York Times*, March 22, 1989.

268 **Commissioner Benjamin Ward later admitted**: "Yes, a Police Riot," *New York Times* op-ed, August 26, 1988.

268 **There were 115 civilian complaints:** Pitt, "Few Officers Face Charges in Park Melee."

269 **"One of the most critical shots":** Interview of Clayton Patterson by the author, December 21, 2012.

270 **"Fly high" and "Hit hard":** Moynihan, "20 Years after Unrest, Class Tensions have Faded and Punk Will Be Played."

270 **ABC Community Center:** There's a protests timeline and ephemera here: http://gvh.aphdigital.org/exhibits/show/eastvillageprotest.

270 **On at least one occasion:** This was the case at an anarchist event I attended in the neighborhood circa 1991.

270 **"Blacks and Latinos couldn't understand":** Interview of Paul Krassner by the author, November 8, 2013.

270 **300 police officers evicted:** Marci Reaven and Jeanne Houck, "A History of Tompkins Square Park," *From Urban Village to East Village* (Oxford: Blackwell, 1994), p. 81.

271 **"bleeding like a sieve":** Interview of Curtis Sliwa by the author, August 19, 2013.

271 **To others, it was a symbol of the takeover:** The *Times* chalked the tension up to rage over gentrification, as "rising rents have displaced the historic culture of artists, musicians, social rebels and poor people." See McFadden, "Park Curfew Protest Erupts into a Battle and 38 Are Injured." Such descriptions of the gentrifying East Village in this 1988 article are eerily similar to those employed in the same paper in the 2010s to describe a supposedly new state of affairs in the East Village. For example, of Eighth Street: "One of downtown's last reliably funky and ramshackle shopping streets has been utterly neutered, scrubbed, and wine-barred" (Hugo Lindgren, "A Reason to Root for Dubai on the Hudson," *New York Times Magazine*, November 22, 2013).

271 **"You know when drug addicts are taking something over":** Interview of Jimmy Webb by the author, January 29, 2013.

Chapter 24

276 **"detachable penis":** Interview of John S. Hall by the author, August 20, 2013.

278 **@ Café at no. 12:** Jennifer Wolff, "At Two Cyber Cafes, They Eat and Drink, Hunt and Peck," *New York Times*, April 30, 1995.

278 **"We would roll joints":** Interview of Dan Oko by the author, January 14, 2013.

278 **"a street where you can see a young man":** N. R. Kleinfeld, "On the Street of Dreams," *New York Times*, November 22, 1992.

279 **"*Psst!* I got Sid's door!":** Interview of Adam Horovitz and Mike Diamond by

the author, February 5, 2013, and follow-up emails with Horovitz, December 28, 2014.

280 **"They didn't appreciate my Mohawk"**: Interview of Chloe Sweeney McGlade by the author, July 2, 2013.

281 **"[St. Marks] felt like the center of everything"**: Interview of Barry Joseph by the author, July 2, 2013.

282 **Yongman Kim**: Tom Roston, "Passing of a Video Store and a Downtown Aesthetic," *New York Times*, July 24, 2014.

282 **video rental promised to be a lucrative business**: Matt Phillips and Roberto A. Ferdman, "A Brief, Illustrated History of Blockbuster," Quartz.com, November 7, 2013.

282 **"The collection was very small and scattershot"**: Interview of Matt Marello by the author, January 14, 2014.

283 **"Where it said, 'Name two porn stars'"**: Interview of Guy Richards Smit by the author, September 15, 2013.

284 **"a USO show"**: Interview of Matthew Kasten by the author, September 5, 2014.

285 **"Before the Pyramid"**: Interview of Johnny Dynell by the author, October 8, 2014.

285 **"Pyramid was more kooky"**: Interview of Steven "Perfidia" Kirkham by the author, September 4, 2014.

Chapter 25

288 **"He was the Bruce Lee of skateboarding"**: Billy Rohan tells stories in one online version of Zoo York's Harold Hunter mix tape. See http://www.jenkemmag.com/home/2014/01/27/vhs-days-ep-4-harold-hunter-in-mixtape.

288 **"I had just come home from summer camp"**: Interview of Priscilla and Jessica Forsyth and Ronald Hunter by the author, November 9, 2013.

290 **"They promised to keep me safe"**: Interview of Miranda Lichtenstein by the author, May 18, 2013.

291 **"I wasn't allowed to go to Tompkins Square Park"**: Interview of Highlyann Krasnow by the author, January 22, 2014.

291 **"My whole family was crackheads"**: Ronald Hunter in an interview of Priscilla and Jessica Forsyth and Ronald Hunter by the author, November 9, 2013.

292 **"We put people anywhere we could"**: Interview of Joyce Hartwell by the author, October 7, 2013, and several more times through 2013 and 2014.

292 **where Boris Zuborev produced ridiculously high platform shoes**: Meagan Brant, "Shoe Design Find in an Unlikely Spot on St. Mark's," *Villager* 76, no. 31 (December 27, 2006–January 2, 2007).

293 **In his hoodie and with his cocky smile:** Harold Hunter's Zoo York Mix-tape, 1997; see https://www.youtube.com/watch?v=dgsTU_QZ1_c.

293 *Kids* **features explicit sex scenes:** There's a long story about that summer of filming here: http://narrative.ly/keep-calm-and-carry-on/legends-never-die.

294 **"Think of this not as cinema verité":** Janet Maslin, "Growing Up Troubled, in Terrifying Ways," *New York Times*, July 21, 1995.

295 **In 2006, Harold Hunter died:** Corey Kilgannon, "Harold Hunter, 31, Skateboarder With Celebrity Appeal, Dies," *New York Times*, February 25, 2006.

295 **"That night was crazy":** Ronald Hunter in an interview of Priscilla and Jessica Forsyth and Ronald Hunter by the author, November 9, 2013.

296 **"GG Allin is an entertainer":** The blurb is in the opening credits for the movie *Hated*. Margaret Eby, "How John Wayne Gacy and GG Allin Launched *Hangover* Director Todd Phillips' Career," *BK Magazine*, June 27, 2014.

296 **"You're trying to kill rock 'n' roll!":** *Hated* (1993).

296 **"Where other people stop, I accelerate":** https://www.youtube.com/watch?v=s5wz8XTdU5E.

297 **heading for "drugland":** There are at least two versions of this online. See https://www.youtube.com/watch?v=btAoo9AI9RI and https://www.youtube.com/watch?v=HmDdTSzJJ94.

Chapter 26

299 **"conventional members of society":** Loretta Lees, Tom Slater, and Elvin Wyly, *Gentrification* (New York: Routledge, 2008), p. 224.

299 **"The era of fear has had a long enough reign":** Alison Mitchell, "The New Mayor: The Overview; Giuliani Urges Dream of a Better City and End to Fear," *New York Times*, January 3, 1994.

299 **the term "gentrification":** Lees, Slater, and Wyly, *Gentrification*, p. 3.

299 **"Broken Windows Theory":** James Q. Wilson and George L. Kelling, "Broken Windows: The Police and Neighborhood Safety," *Atlantic Monthly* (March 1982). Access a PDF here: http://www.manhattan-institute.org/pdf/_atlantic_monthly-broken_windows.pdf.

301 **"I loved that shit":** Interview of Arthur Nersesian by the author, November 8, 2013. Also see Arthur Nersesian, *East Village Tetralogy: Four Plays* (New York: Akashic Books, 2006).

301 **the same set of writings by Khrushchev:** Luc Sante, "Commerce," in Berman and Berger, eds., *New York Calling*, p. 111.

301 **which moved from street buys to delivery services:** National Institute of Justice Report, "We Deliver: The Gentrification of Drug Markets on Man-

hattan's Lower East Side," 2002. Access a PDF here: https://www.ncjrs.gov/pdffiles1/nij/grants/197716.pdf.

302 **"The book tables were the worst for us"**: Interview of Terry McCoy and Bob Contant by the author, February 12, 2013.

302 **"The depressing part of St. Marks Place"**: Interview of Jonathan Kirschenfeld by the author, November 4, 2013.

302 *I Was a Quality of Life Violation*: *I Was a Quality of Life Violation* (2004). See http://www.imdb.com/title/tt0759919.

303 **"No Dancing" in six-foot tall letters**: Johnny Dynell, "Paul McGregor's Magic Flute: Remembering an East Village Nightclub Legend," *Next*, June 27, 2013.

303 **"the hardest-working middle-aged man in show business"**: Interview of Murray Hill by the author, October 6, 2014. Also see Ada Calhoun, "Meet Downtown's New 'It' Boy," *New York Times*, January 9, 2005.

304 **"If somebody didn't know that history"**: Interview of Mike Jackson by the author, July 4, 2012.

304 **Immigration expert Joel Millman**: Interview of Joel Millman by the author, August 22, 2014.

305 **In 1995, a judge said Hartwell**: J. A. Lobbia, "Stepping Off: Fifteen Minutes of Fame Are Up for East Village Rehab," *Village Voice*, September 5, 2000.

305 **Hartwell was more than one million dollars in debt**: Andrew Jacobs, "Neighborhood Report; Troubled Haven, Now Bankrupt, Still Fighting to Survive," *New York Times*, February 4, 1996.

305 **"Dinkins's people considered our work phenomenal"**: Interview of Joyce Hartwell by the author, October 7, 2013, and several more times through 2013 and 2014.

306 **NatWest bank on Second Avenue**: Rachel L. Swarns, "Owner of Second Avenue Deli Is Shot and Killed in Robbery," *New York Times*, March 5, 1996.

306 **Coney Island High, too, closed**: Robin Rothman, "Last Times at Coney Island High," *Village Voice*, July 20, 1999.

307 **In 2002, there were 276**: Tricia Romano, "A Crash Course in Cabarets," *Village Voice*, November 26, 2002.

Epilogue: i. Little Tokyo

311 **"I fought to get this job on this street"**: Interview of Zac Bogus by the author, November 4, 2013.

312 **The TV shows *Girls* and *Broad City***: Daniel Maurer, "Lena Dunham and *Girls* are Currently Camping on St. Marks," Bedford + Bowery, July 23, 2014; Daniel Maurer, "*Broad City* Filmed: Here's Ilana Hitting Her Mark on St. Marks," Bedford + Bowery, August 19, 2014.

313   **"St. Marks Place has a lot of chill people"**: Interview of Anna by the author, June 26, 2014.

314   **"Batsu means punishment"**: Interview by the author of various patrons of Sing Sing, June 26, 2014.

Epilogue: ii. The Nostalgics

316   **Boxy blue 1980s cop cars**: I also wrote about attending this reenactment for *The New Yorker*'s website. Ada Calhoun, "Reënacting the Tompkins Square Park Riots," NewYorker.com, May 20, 2014.

317   **average rent increased by 42 percent**: "Avenue A Retail Analysis," Columbia University GSAPP, Spring 2014.

317   **listed for $3,450 a month**: Craigslist, January 21, 2014.

317   **"That was really a huge turning point"**: Interview of Andrew W.K. by the author, December 2, 2013.

317   **"I can't tell you my real name"**: Interview of "E. V. Grieve" by the author, February 7, 2013.

318   **"ghost of the old East Village"**: "The Approval Matrix (Brilliant-Lowbrow)," *New York*, December 23–30, 2013.

318   **In the fall of 2014**: Cooper Union FAQ, January 15, 2014, http://cooper .edu/admissions/facts/faq#q16.

319   **"but not a hedge fund manager, who wouldn't 'get us'"**: Said by Bob Holman from onstage at a Bowery Poetry Club benefit reading, April 15, 2012.

320   **"The wall of Five St. Marks Place"**: Colin Moynihan, "A Threat Shadows a Relic from a Grim Era," *New York Times*, February 27, 2000.

320   **"When they painted over the mural of Spacely"**: Interview of Jimmy Webb by the author, January 29, 2013.

320   **"If hyper-gentrification were a person"**: Jeremiah Moss, Vanishing New York, March 2014, http://vanishingnewyork.blogspot.com/2014/03/on -spike-lee-hyper-gentrification.html.

320   **"There are a dozen bars"**: Interview of Judy Josephs by the author, April 23, 2013.

321   **"I took an oath in 1966"**: Interview of Jimmy McMillan by the author, August 28, 2013.

322   **writer Marc Spitz describes his memories**: Marc Spitz, *Poseur: A Memoir of Downtown New York City in the '90s* (Boston: Da Capo, 2013), p. 67.

322   **"Who wouldn't want to kiss a girl"**: Ibid., p. 69.

322   **"If you ask old people like me"**: Ibid., p. 359.

322   **"We're lucky"**: New York historian Eric Ferrara said this to me when I took his excellent East Village tour, July 12, 2012.

323   **In a piece called "The East Village Is Replaced"**: Bill Weinberg, "The East Village Is Replaced by Its Own Simulacrum," *Villager*, July 10, 2014.

323   **"Who works here?"**: Interview of Chuck Bettis by the author, January 27, 2014.

323   **Mondo Kim's closed**: Karina Longworth, "The Strange Fate of Kim's Video," *Village Voice*, September 12, 2012.

323   **the Cave (no. 120), an artists' collective**: Bradley Hope, "The Cave Collapses," *New York*, April 24, 2006.

323   **"Warhol was an idiot"**: Interview of Jim Power by the author, April 23, 2013.

324   **"Home Sweet Home"**: Interview of Jaime Darrow by the author, October 11, 2013.

Epilogue: iii. The Church and the Religion

327   **"There's something magnetic and chaotic about it"**: Interview of Penny Arcade by the author, October 20, 2014.

327   **During the anti-government protests**: Polly Kreisman, "Local Woman Helps Fund Medical Supplies in Ukraine," NY1, February 21, 2014.

327   **a burlesque house called Ali Baba**: Interview of Barbara Sibley by the author, January 27, 2014.

328   **"This older guy came in to look at the tile"**: Interview of Pete Langway and Kevin Beard by the author, October 27, 2014.

328   **People continue to order egg creams**: In 1972, Gem Spa briefly closed, prompting the *Village Voice* to write an obit: "Bye, Bye Miss American Egg Cream." Also in 1972, around the corner from St. Marks at the deli on Third Avenue, Leonard Marsh, Hyman Golden, and Arnold Greenberg started making juices to sell to health-food stores. This became Snapple.

329   **"'What would Sara Curry do?'"**: Interview of Eileen Johnson by the author, November 8, 2012.

329   **"crusty punks"**: A 1996 *New York Times Magazine* article reports that the "travelers" are often preyed upon by pedophiles; one they call "Leg Rub Steve."

329   **"They're trustifarians"**: Interview of Ann and Rachel Tyson by the author, January 10, 2013.

329   **"They just take"**: Interview of Jimmy Webb by the author, January 29, 2013.

329   **"They're filth"**: Interview of Hysen Gjonaj by the author, November 4, 2013.

330   **"trash sledding"**: A video of LES Jewels trash sledding can be found here: http://gothamist.com/2013/09/15/notorious_east_village_fixture_les.php.

331   **"gutter pirate"**: Gerard Flynn and Lincoln Anderson, "L.E.S. Jewels, godfather of crusties, is dead at 43," *East Villager*, September 19, 2013.

331 " 'Pee Phone' ": Bob Arihood, Neither More nor Less, March 19, 2009, http://neithermorenorless.blogspot.com/2009_03_15_archive.html.

331 **"LES Jewels, the most transgressive man I know"**: Post by "Rob" on SavetheLowerEastSide.blogspot.com, September 16, 2013, http://savethelowereastside.blogspot.com/2013/09/jewels.html.

331 **"I got one of the biggest ones"**: Interview of crusty punks in front of 30 St. Marks Place by the author, November 4, 2013.

331 **"Now you walk down the street"**: Interview of Charles Fitzgerald by the author, January 8, 2013.

332 **"I walked down these streets forty-five years ago"**: Interview of Richard Manitoba by the author, March 21, 2013.

332 **and all said the same thing: "Now"**: Interviews by the author of Hysen Gjonaj, November 4, 2013; Julian Baczynsky, November 4, 2013; and Amelia Hernandez, July 2, 2013.

BIBLIOGRAPHY

Books and Articles

Abbott, Berenice. *New York in the Thirties*. New York: Dover, 1939.

Abbott, Jack Henry, with Naomi Zack. *My Return*. Buffalo, NY: Prometheus Books, 1987.

Alger, Horatio. *Ragged Dick and Mark, The Match Boy*. New York: Macmillan, 1962. Impressively undermining introduction ("No doubt that what he wrote was bilge . . .") by Rychard Fink. *Ragged Dick* was originally published in 1867.

"All-Craft All Gone." *Villager*. November 20, 2002.

Allen, Michael. *This Time, This Place*. Indianapolis/Kansas City/New York: Bobbs-Merrill Company, 1971.

Allmen, Rick. *Stanley: The Don Juan of Second Avenue*. New York: Harper and Row, 1974.

Anasi, Robert. *The Last Bohemia: Scenes from the Life of Williamsburg, Brooklyn*. New York: Farrar, Straus and Giroux, 2012.

Armstrong, Hamilton Fish. *Those Days*. New York: Harper & Row, 1963.

Arnett, Frank S. "The Evolution of Manhattan," pp. 397–403 in *Tales of Gaslight New York*. Edison, NJ: Castle Books, 1985.

Badger, Emily. "How Many Gentrification Critics Are Actually Gentrifiers Themselves?" *Atlantic*, Cities blog. August 8, 2013.

Baraka, Amiri. *The Autobiography of LeRoi Jones*. Chicago: Lawrence Hill Books, 1997 (1st edition: 1984).

Bell, Barbara. "You Don't Have to Be High." *New York Times*. December 28, 1969.

Bergmann, Eugene B. *Excelsior, You Fathead! The Art and Enigma of Jean Shepherd*. New York: Applause Theatre & Cinema Books, 2005.

Berinère, Vincent, and Mariel Primois, eds. *Punk Press: Rebel Rock in the Underground Press 1968–1980*. New York: Abrams, 2012.

Berman, Marshall, and Brian Berger, eds. *New York Calling*. London: Reaktion Books, 2007.

Bernstein, Iver. *The New York City Draft Riots*. New York: Oxford University Press, 1990.

Berrigan, Ted. *The Sonnets*. New York: Penguin Poets, 2000.

"Black Hand Panics Spread in Schools." *New York Times*. June 18, 1926.

Blake, Mark, ed. *Punk: The Whole Story*. New York: DK Publishing, 2006.

Blau, Eleanor. "63 and an Activist, She Hopes to be an Episcopal Priest." *New York Times*. February 11, 1974.

Bleyer, Jennifer. "Like a Tree With Many Rings, a Building With Many Lives." *New York Times*. April 24, 2005.

Blinderman, Barry, ed. *Keith Haring: Future Primeval*. Normal, Illinois: University Galleries, 2009.

Bourdon, David. *Warhol*. New York: Harry N. Abrams, Inc., 1989.

Brant, Meagan. "Shoe Design Find in an Unlikely Spot on St. Mark's." *Villager* 76, no. 31 (December 27, 2006–January 2, 2007).

Brodhead, John. *A History of the State of New York*. New York: Harper & Brothers, 1853.

Brownstein, Michael. *Self-Reliance*. New York: Coffee House Press, 1994.

Buder, Leonard. "Aiding a Neighbor, Boy Is Killed in Fall Down Air Shaft." *New York Times*. September 5, 1985.

Buhle, Paul, and David Berger. *Bohemians: A Graphic History*. London: Verso, 2014.

Burdell, Edwin S. "A Symbol in Brownstone: The Story of the Foundation Building of the Cooper Union." *Cooper Union Alumni News* 17, no. 2 (February 1953). Available at library.cooperunion.edu.

Burrows, Edwin G., and Mike Wallace. *Gotham: A History of New York City to 1898*. New York: Oxford University Press, 1999.

Caro, Robert A. *The Power Broker: Robert Moses and the Fall of New York*. New York: Vintage Books Edition, 1975 (1st edition: Alfred A. Knopf, 1974).

Carr, Cynthia. *Fire in the Belly: The Life and Times of David Wojnarowicz*. New York: Bloomsbury, 2012.

Carroll, Jim. *The Basketball Diaries*. New York: Penguin, 1978.

Carroll, Patrick J. "Operation Pressure Point: An Urban Drug Enforcement Strategy." *FBI Law Enforcement Bulletin* 58, no. 4 (April 1989).

Casson, Herbert N. "The Story of the General Slocum Disaster," pp. 37–60 in *Tales of Gaslight New York*. Edison, NJ: Castle Books, 1985. Originally published in *Munsey's Magazine* (December 1904).

Champion, Miles. "Insane Podium: The Poetry Project, 1966–." PoetryProject. org. Accessed June 17, 2012.

Chesler, Phyllis. "All-Craft Foundation: Assessment and Recommendations." Unpublished manuscript. Courtesy of Joyce Hartwell. (July 1993).

"Chief and Gangmen Held for Murder." *New York Times*. January 11, 1914.

Christgau, Robert. "Bohemias Lost and Found." *Barnes & Noble Review*. January 19, 2009.

———. "Pioneer Days." *Barnes & Noble Review*. November 21, 2011.

Clay, Steven, and Rodney Phillips. *A Secret Location on the Lower East Side: Adventures in Writing, 1960–1980*. New York: New York Public Library and Granary Books, 1998.

"Club 57 and the Sweet, Sweet Smell of St. Mark's Place." BoweryBoys.blogspot
.com. May 1, 2009.

Cocks, Jay. "East Village Stars and Stripes." *Time*. April 7, 1986.

Cooper, James Fenimore. *New York*. New York: William Farquhar Payson, 1930.

——. *Satanstoe, or The Littlepage Manuscripts. A Tale of the Colony*. Albany: State University of New York Press, 1990.

Cooper, Lee. "Changes are Noted in Lower East Side; Indoor Markets Eliminating Pushcarts." *New York Times*. February 21, 1939.

——. "Fewer Tenements on the Lower East Side Now Unprotected Against Hazard of Fire." *New York Times*. August 8, 1940.

"Court Sanctions Stuyvesant Town." *New York Times*. December 3, 1943.

Cowley, Malcolm. *Exile's Return: A Literary Odyssey of the 1920s*. London: Bodley Head, rev. ed. 1964 (1st edition: 1934).

Crapsey, Edward. *The Nether Side of New York: Or, The Vice, Crime and Poverty of the Great Metropolis*. New York: Sheldon & Company, 1872.

"Crowd at Wedding Stampeded by Fire." *New York Times*. June 16, 1935.

"Cultural Revolution." Editors Note, *n+1*. April 29, 2013.

Curtis, Olga. *East of Third: Memories of Old Manhattan*. Berkeley Heights, NJ: Oriole Press, 1955. Rare Books Room, NYPL.

Day, Dorothy. "On Pilgrimage: October/November 1973." *Catholic Worker*, October–November 1973. Via the *Catholic Worker Movement*. http://www.catholicworker.org/dorothyday/Reprint2.cfm?TextID=534.

Dayton, Dorothy. "St. Mark's Back Within the Fold." *New York City Sun*. February 2, 1932.

Denison, Lindsay. "The Black Hand," pp. 79–92 in *Tales of Gaslight New York*. Edison, NJ: Castle Books, 1985. Originally published in *Everybody's Magazine* (September 1908).

The Downtown Book: The New York Art Scene 1974–1984. Princeton, NJ, and Oxford: Princeton University Press, 2006.

"Dr. Pauli Murray, Episcopal Priest." *New York Times*. July 4, 1985.

Ego, Les. *Zentences: Meditation Manual for Mini-Minds and Mystics*. New York: "The Catholic Union Mission" (self-published), 1971. Rare Books Room, New York Public Library.

"Everyone's Doing It—The New Now Look of the Frizz," *People*, May 26, 1975, pp. 8–11.

Feinberg, David B. *Eighty-Sixed: A Novel*. New York: Viking Adult, 1989.

Feininger, Andreas. *New York in the Forties*. New York: Dover Publications, 1978.

Feuer, Alan. "Last Bohemian Turns Out the Lights." *New York Times*. April 4, 2014.

"Finds Lower East Side Suited Only to Rich." *New York Times*. March 18, 1932.

Fink, Joseph, and Lloyd G. Sealy. *The Community and the Police—Conflict or Cooperation?* New York: John Wiley & Sons, 1974.

Fletcher, Tony. *All Hopped Up and Ready to Go: Music from the Streets of New York, 1927–77*. New York: W. W. Norton & Company, 2009.

"Found with Dynamite, Held in Palmieri Case." *New York Times*. March 6, 1927.

Franke-Ruta, Garance. "Everlasting Realities of the Bohemian Lifestyle." *Atlantic*. August 2013.

Franklin, Harold. *Run a Twisted Street*. Philadelphia: J. P. Lippincott Company, 1970.

"Gamblers Resist Raid." *New York Times*. May 9, 1912.

Gay, Peter. *Modernism: The Lure of Heresy*. New York: W. W. Norton & Company, 2008.

Ginsberg, Allen. *Collected Poems: 1947–1997*. New York: Harper Perennial, 2006.

Golden, Stephen A. O. "Talk is Strange in the East Village." *New York Times*. April 16, 1967.

Goldstein, Richard [of the *New York Times*]. *Helluva Town: The Story of New York City During World War II*. New York: Free Press, 2010.

Goldstein, Richard [of the *Voice*]. *Reporting the Counterculture*. Boston: Unwin Hyman, 1989.

Goodman, Paul. *Growing Up Absurd*. New York: Random House, 1960.

Goodwin, Maud Wilder, Alice Carrington Royce, Ruth Putnam, and Eva Palmer Brownell, eds. *Historic New York: Being the Second Series of the Half Moon Papers*. New York: G. P. Putnam and Sons, 1899.

Graham, Bill, and Robert Greenfield. *Bill Graham Presents: My Life inside Rock and Out*. New York: Da Capo Press, 2004 (1st edition: Doubleday, 1990).

Gray, Christopher. "Be There or Be Square, 1830 to the Present." *New York Times*. January 6, 2011.

———. "Streetscapes: 19–25 St. Marks Place; The Eclectic Life of a Row of East Village Houses." *New York Times*. November 8, 1998.

Green, Penelope. "The Prince of St. Marks Place." *New York Times*. December 12, 2012.

Griffis, William Elliot. *The Story of New Netherland*. Boston: Houghton Mifflin Company, 1909. Withdrawn from the Cooper Union Library.

Gruen, John. *The New Bohemia*. New York: Grosset and Dunlap, 1966.

Guthrie, William. *Offices of Mystical Religion*. New York: Century Press, 1927.

Hahne, Ron. *Black Mask and Up against the Wall Motherfucker: The Incomplete Works of Ron Hahne, Ben Morea and the Black Mask Group*. London: Salamander Press, 1993.

Hamill, Pete. "The New York We've Lost." *New York*. December 21–28, 1987.

Harrington, Michael. "'A San Remo Type': The Vanishing Village." *Village Voice*. January 7, 1971.

Harris, Charles T. *Memories of Manhattan in the Sixties and Seventies*. New York: Derrydale Press, 1928.

Harvey, Matt. "The East Village Isn't What It Used to Be . . . And It Never Was." *New York Press*. December 10, 2008.

Haynes, Jesper. *St. Marks 1986–2006: Twenty Years of Love and Friendships*. Self-published photo book, ca. 2010.

Hell, Richard. *I Dreamed I Was a Very Clean Tramp*. New York: HarperCollins, 2013.

Henahan, Donal. "Too Soon to Demand a 'War and Peace.'" *New York Times*. September 15, 1968.

Henderson, Eleanor. *Ten Thousand Saints: A Novel*. New York: Ecco, 2011.

Herlihy, James Leo. *Season of the Witch*. New York: Simon and Schuster, 1971.

Hertel, Fredrika W. *A Guide to Historic St. Mark's Church in-the-Bouwerie*. New York: J. Jay Devitt Co. Litho, 1949. Collected in George A. Trefethen, *Strawberry Bank's Bank—and The Marquis de Lafayette 1824*. New York: Newcomen Society in North America, 1950.

Hispanic Study Report: Phase One. Funded by Columbia University, National Institutes of Mental Health, and New York State Drug Abuse Control Commission. Presented to Commissioner D. Klepak Narcotic and Drug Research, Inc. October 15, 1976. Courtesy of the private collection of Joyce Hartwell.

"Hold-Up Suspects Captured in Store." *New York Times*. January 29, 1946.

Hollander, Kurt. *Low Rent: A Decade of Prose and Photographs from* The Portable Lower East Side. New York: Grove Press, 1994.

Holleran, Andrew, ed. *Dancer from the Dance*. New York: Bantam, 1979 (1st edition: 1978).

Holloway, Margurite. *The Measure of Manhattan*. New York: W. W. Norton & Company, 2012.

Horowitz, I. "Which Definition of Beat?" *Village Voice*. February 19, 1958.

Indiana, Gary. *Horse Crazy*. London: Paladin, 1989.

Ingraham, Joseph C. "Our Changing City: Old Lower Manhattan Area." *New York Times*. June 24, 1955.

Irving, Washington. *Diedrich Knickerbocker's History of New-York*. New York: Heritage Press, 1940 (1st edition: 1809).

Jackson, Kenneth T., ed. *The Encyclopedia of New York City*. New Haven, CT: Yale University Press, 1995.

Jacobs, Jaap. *The Colony of New Netherland: A Dutch Settlement in Seventeenth-Century America*. Ithaca, NY: Cornell University Press, 2009.

Jacobs, Jane. *The Death and Life of Great American Cities*. New York: Vintage Books Edition, 1992 (1st edition: Random House, 1961).

Jahn, Mike. "'Velvet' Rock Group Opens Stand Here." *New York Times*. July 4, 1970.

Janowitz, Meta F., and Diane Dallal, eds. *Tales of Gotham, Historical Archaeology, Ethnohistory and Microhistory of New York City*. New York: Springer, 2013.

Janvier, Thomas A. *In Old New York*. New York: Harper & Brothers Publishers, 1922 (1st edition: 1894).

Johnson, Jill. *Marmalade Me*. New York: E. P. Dutton & Co., 1971.

Jones, Hettie. *How I Became Hettie Jones*. New York: Grove Press, 1990.

Jones, LeRoi (Amiri Baraka). *Home: Social Essays*. New York: AkashiClassics Renegade Reprint Series, 2009 (1st edition: William Morrow and Company, Inc., 1966).

Jones, Thai. *A Radical Line*. New York: Free Press, 2004.

Joseph, Barry. *Waving the Mouse.* Unpublished novel set on St. Marks Place, 1995.

Kalish, Jon. "'Fug You': The Wild Life of Ed Sanders." NPR. May 4, 2012.

Kapralov, Yuri. *Once There Was a Village.* New York: St. Martin's Press, 1974.

Kashner, Sam. *When I Was Cool: My Life at the Jack Kerouac School.* New York: Harper-Collins, 2003.

Katzman, Allen, ed. *Our Time: Interviews from the East Village Other.* New York: Dial Press, 1972.

Kayton, Bruce. *Radical Walking Tours of New York City.* 2nd edition. New York: Seven Stories Press, 2003.

Kemsley, William. "Psychedelic Shopping," pp. 10–14 in *Ford Times.* January 1969.

Kent, Leticia. "High on Life and Deader than Dead." *Village Voice.* October 12, 1967.

Kessler, Henry H., and Eugene Rachlis. *Peter Stuyvesant and His New York: A Biography of a Man and a City.* New York: Random House, 1959.

Kleinfeld, N. R. "On the Street of Dreams." *New York Times.* November 22, 1992.

Kludt, Amanda. "Turning Japanese: The Changing Face of St. Marks Place Looks Asian." *Villager* 74, no. 20 (February 9–15, 2005).

Kolossa, Alexandra. *Haring.* Los Angeles: Taschen, 2009.

Kraft, Herbert C. *The Lenape-Delaware Indian Heritage: 10,000 BC to AD 2000.* Stanhope, NJ: Lenape Lifeways Books, 2001.

Kristal, Hilly. *CBGB's: Thirty Years from the Home of Underground Rock.* New York: Harry N. Abrams, 2005.

Landler, Mark. "Media: Press; Joey Skaggs, who delights in practical jokes on the press, has got a million of them." *New York Times.* January 29, 1996.

Landmarks Preservation Commission. Hamilton-Holly House, 4 St. Mark's Place, Manhattan. Built 1831. October 19, 2004: Designation List 357 LP-2157.

Ledoux, Urbain. *Mr. Zero?* Published by the author for the Old Bucks and Lame Ducks Club, and the Tub, located at 33 St. Marks Place, New York City. Copyrighted for them by the author in 1931. Copy in collection of the New York Public Library.

Lee, Erica. "On the Stoop of Rock n' Roll History." *New York Times* Local East Village Blog. October 22, 2010.

Lees, Loretta, Tom Slater, and Elvin Wyly. *Gentrification.* New York: Routledge, 2008.

Lehman, David. *The Last Avant-Garde.* New York: Doubleday, 1998.

Leland, John. "East Village Shrine to Riots and Radicals." *New York Times.* December 8, 2012.

LeSueur, Joe. *Digressions on Some Poems by Frank O'Hara.* New York: Farrar, Straus and Giroux, 2003.

Levins, Peter. "Robbery of Stewart Grave—One of N.Y.'s Biggest Mysteries." *Sunday News.* December 31, 1939.

Lincoln, Abraham. "Cooper Union Address." February 27, 1860. Available online at constitution.org/csa/lincoln/cooper.htm.

Lipton, Lawrence. *The Holy Barbarians*. New York: Julian Messner, Inc., 1959.

Live Sex Acts. New York: Portable Lower East Side, 1991.

"Lower East Side to Get Apartments." *New York Times*. February 4, 1962.

Lukas, J. Anthony. "The Two Worlds of Linda Fitzpatrick." *New York Times*. October 16, 1967.

Mack, Edward C. *Peter Cooper, Citizen of New York*. New York: Duell, Sloan and Pearce, 1949. Copy available in the Cooper Union Library.

Mailer, Norman. *Advertisements for Myself*. New York: Signet, 1959.

Marriott, Red. "Ben Morea: An Interview by Ian McIntyre (2006)." Libcom.org. March 24, 2012.

Mathews, John. "Wealthy Women as Teachers of Cooking." *Leslie's Weekly*. June 11, 1903.

McAuliffe, Kevin Michael. *The Great American Newspaper: The Rise and Fall of the Village Voice*. New York: Charles Scribner's Sons, 1978.

McDarrah, Fred W. *Kerouac and Friends: A Beat Generation Album*. New York: William Morrow and Company, 1985.

McGlone, Molly. "Excavating Experimentalism: Investigating Musical Space, The Electric Circus, and Nineteen-Sixties New York." Ph.D. dissertation, University of Wisconsin-Madison, 2010.

McNeil, Legs, and Gillian McCain. *Please Kill Me: The Uncensored History of Punk*. New York: Grove, 1996.

"Memorial of St. Mark's Church in the Bowery," 1899. Copy in the collection of the New York Public Library.

Metzger, Richard. "East Village Preservation Society: Club 57." Dazeddigital .com. 2012.

Miles, Barry. *In the Seventies: Adventures in the Counterculture*. London: Serpent's Tail, 2011.

Miller, Marc. H. "The East Village New York City: A Walking Tour and Poster." Brooklyn: Ephemera Press, ca. 2008. From St. Mark's Bookshop.

Miller, Mark Crispin, ed. *While We Were Sleeping: NYU and the Destruction of New York*. New York: McNally Jackson Books, 2012.

Miller, Terry. *Greenwich Village and How It Got That Way*. New York: Crown, 1990.

Miller, Tom. "I Remember Jerry." *Tucson Weekly*. April 27–May 3, 1995.

Millman, Joel. *The Other Americans: How Immigrants Renew Our Country, Our Economy, and Our Values*. New York: Viking Penguin, 1997.

Mitchell, Katie. *Two Suspicious Girls*. New York: Grove Press, 1973.

Molin, Marit. "David Godlis Took Abbie Hoffman's Apartment Because It Was a Steal." *New York Times* East Village Local Blog. August 24, 2011.

Moore, Alan W. "ABC No Rio as an Anarchist Space." Article awaiting publication, courtesy of Alan Moore.

Moore, Pamela. *Diana*. New York: Dell, 1961.

Morgan, Bill. *The Beat Generation in New York*. San Francisco: City Lights Books, 1997.

———. *The Typewriter is Holy*. Berkeley, CA: Counterpoint, 2010.

———. *Beat Atlas: A State-by-State Guide to the Beat Generation in America*. San Francisco: City Lights Books, 2011.

Mourik, Orli Van. "From Punk to Pucci." *Villager* 76, no. 29 (December 13–19, 2006).

Moynihan, Colin. "On a Changing East Village Street, a Source of Continuity." *New York Times*. January 6, 2014.

Murray, Pauli. *The Autobiography of a Black Activist, Feminist, Lawyer, Priest, and Poet*. Knoxville: University of Tennessee Press, 1989. Originally published as *Song in a Weary Throat: An American Pilgrimage* by Harper & Row, 1987.

Nersesian, Arthur. *East Village Tetralogy: Four Plays*. New York: Akashic Books, 2006.

———. *Gladyss of the Hunt*. Portland, OR: Verse Chorus Press, 2014.

Neumann, Osha. *Up against the Wall Motherfucker: A Memoir of the '60s, with Notes for Next Time*. New York: Seven Stories Press, 2008.

Neves, Irene. "The Trend to 'African Fashions for Everyone.'" *Life*. September 16, 1966.

Newman, Michael. "W. H. Auden, The Art of Poetry No. 17." *Paris Review*. Autumn 1972.

"Nine Persons Routed from Tenement Homes When Wall Cracks, Threatening Collapse." *New York Times*. March 10, 1938.

Northrop, H. D. *New York's Awful Steamboat Horror, and Other Dreadful Tragedies*. New York: D. Z. Howell, 1904.

O'Brien, Glenn, ed. *The Cool School: Writing from America's Hip Underground*. New York: Library of America, 2013.

"Obscenity Case Files: *Zap Comix* #4." Comic Book Legal Defense Fund. September 24, 2013.

O'Donnell, Edward T. *Ship Ablaze: The Tragedy of the Steamboat* General Slocum. New York: Broadway Books, 2003.

O'Kane, Lawrence. "The Bowery Awakens to an Upbeat Trend." *New York Times*. October 16, 1966.

O'Neill, Joseph. *Netherland*. New York: Vintage, 2008.

"On St. Marks Place, Help for Addicts." *New York Times*. December 6, 1987.

Padgett, Ron. *Joe: A Memoir of Joe Brainard*. New York: Coffee House Press, 2008.

———. *Ted: A Personal Memoir of Ted Berrigan*. New York: Figures, 1993.

Paikert, Charles. "The Ukrainians: The Little Nation on Second Avenue." *Daily News Sunday Magazine*. May 21, 1978.

"Parkhurst Raid Succeeds." *New York Times*. March 9, 1900.

Parry, Albert. *Garrets and Pretenders: Bohemian Life from Poe to Kerouac*. Mineola: Dover Publications, 2012 (1st edition: 1960).

Patterson, Clayton, ed. *Captured: The History of Film and Video on the Lower East Side*. New York: Seven Stories Press, 2005.

———, ed. *Resistance: A Radical Social and Political History of the Lower East Side.* New York: Seven Stories Press, 2007.

Peck, Abe. "Abe Peck on Why EVO Mattered." *New York Times* Local East Village Blog. February 25, 2012.

"Peg-Leg Pete's Bouwerie Tours." Various editions (Groovie, Gilded Age, Jazz Age, etc.) St. Mark's Historic Landmark Fund. 2012–2013.

"Police Kill Gunman Holding 2 As Hostages in the East Village." *New York Times.* December 24, 1974.

Portrait, Evelyn. "The Other Village—East." No date or source. Limbo's archive.

Ramone, Johnny. *Commando.* New York: Abrams, 2012.

Ramone, Marky. *Punk Rock Blitzkrieg: My Life as a Ramone.* New York: Touchstone, 2014.

Ratliff, Ben. "Outsider Whose Dark, Lyrical Vision Helped Shape Rock 'n' Roll." *New York Times.* October 27, 2013.

"Receiver Debated for 'Mr. Zero's' $37." *New York Times.* June 10, 1931.

Regelson, Rosalyn. "'Not a Boy, Not a Girl, Just Me.'" *New York Times.* November 2, 1969.

Reinholz, Mary. "Radical Priest Resigns, Then Later Rethinks, But Is Rejected." *Villager* 78, no. 23 (November 6–11, 2008).

Riffee, Mark. "Tribes of New York." The Local East Village blog. March 30, 2011.

Rivers, Larry. *What Did I Do?* New York: Da Capo Press, 2001.

Robbins, Tom. "Tuli Kupferberg: Model Village Citizen, 1923–2010." *Village Voice.* July 13, 2010.

Rockwell, John. "Rock Meets Disco: Where To Try It." *New York Times.* April 27, 1979.

Romano, Tricia, "The Safety Dance: You Can't Dance If You Want To," and "A Crash Course in Cabarets." *Village Voice.* November 26, 2002.

Rombes, Nicholas. *A Cultural History of Punk: 1974–1982.* New York: Continuum, 2009.

Rossner, Judith. *Looking for Mr. Goodbar.* New York: Pocket Books, 1975.

Rubenstein, Joshua. *Leon Trotsky: A Revolutionary's Life.* New Haven, CT: Yale University Press, 2011.

Rylance, J. H. "A Statement to the Members of St. Mark's Parish," *New York: Evening Post* Job Print, 1890. In *New York City Churches.* Presented at the Memorial Service, Middle Dutch Church, Second Ave., November Second, A.D. 1900. New York Public Library Collection. Also appears as: "St. Mark's Church in the Bowery, N.Y., A Statement to the Members from J. H. Rylance, Rector," 1890. Copy in the collection of the New York Public Library.

"St. Marks Block Set to Change." *Villager.* December 4, 2002.

"St. Mark's Church in the Bowery, New York. The tercentenary of the city of New York and our neighborhood," 1953. Copy in the collection of the New York Public Library.

"St. Mark's Honors Peter Stuyvesant." *New York World Telegraph.* January 30, 1939.

"St. Mark's In-the-Bouwerie: A Vital Expression of Present-Day Religion in New

York City: A Statement of Plans and Policies by the Rector, Wardens and Vestry," 1942? Copy in the collection of the New York Public Library.

St. Marks Place Block Association Newsletters and Flyers. Courtesy of Phillip Giambri. 1974–75.

"St. Mark's Sees Huston in Role of Stuyvesant." 1939.

Sanders, Ed. *Fug You: An Informal History of the Peace Eye Bookstore, the Fuck You Press, the Fugs, and Counterculture in the Lower East Side*. New York: Da Capo, 2013.

Sanderson, Eric W. *Mannahatta: A Natural History of New York*. New York: Harry N. Abrams, 2009. See also http://welikia.org.

Sanneh, Kelefa. "United Blood: How Hardcore Conquered New York." *The New Yorker*. March 9, 2015.

Sante, Luc. *Low Life*. New York: Farrar, Straus and Giroux, 1991.

Schafroth, Beatrice. *Rent Free in the East-Village*. New York: self-published text and drawings, 1985.

Schjeldahl, Peter. *Hydrogen Jukebox: Selected Writing of Peter Schjeldahl 1978–1990 (Lannan Series)*. Berkeley: University of California Press, 1993.

Shackleton, Robert. *The Book of New York*. Philadelphia: Penn Publishing Company, 1920.

Sharff, Jagna Wojcicka. *King Kong on 4th Street: Families and the Violence of Poverty on the Lower East Side*. Boulder, CO: Westview Press, 1998.

Shoenfeld, Oscar, and Helene Maclean, eds. *City Life*. New York: Grossman Publishers, 1969.

Shorto, Russell. *The Island at the Center of the World: The Epic Story of Dutch Manhattan and the Forgotten Colony That Shaped America*. New York: Doubleday, 2004.

Siegel, Allison B. "St. Mark's Place: Hardly a Saint in Sight." BoweryBoogie.com. May 3, 2012.

Sietsema, Robert. *Secret New York: The Unique Guidebook to New York's Hidden Sites, Sounds, and Tastes*. Toronto: ECW Press, 1999.

Skaggs, Joey. "Metamorphosis: The Miracle Roach Hormone Cure." JoeySkaggs.com. May 22, 1981. Accessed February 7, 2013.

"Slowdown Seen in 'Village' Boom." *New York Times*. March 4, 1962.

Smith, Mortimer. *My School the City: A Memoir of New York in the Twenties*. Chicago: Regnery/Gateway, Inc., 1980.

Smith, Neil. *The New Urban Frontier: Gentrification and the Revanchist City*. London: Routledge, 1996.

Smith, Patti. *Just Kids*. New York: Ecco, 2010.

"Snowfall a Boon to the Jobless." *New York Times*. March 10, 1928.

Solomon, Carl. *Emergency Messages: An Autobiographical Miscellany*. New York: Paragon House, 1989.

Solomon, Serena. "7-Eleven is 'Pringle-izing' the East Village, Anti-Chain Advocates Fume." DNAinfo.com. January 17, 2013.

Spitz, Marc. *Poseur: A Memoir of Downtown New York City in the '90s*. Boston: Da Capo, 2013.

Stansell, Christine. *American Moderns.* New York: Metropolitan Books, 2000.

Stein, Mark, with Larry Schweikrat. *You Keep Me Hangin' On.* La Vergne, TN: Lightning Source, 2012.

Stettner, Irving. *Adventures of a 2nd Avenue Patroller.* Saitama, Japan: Stroker Press, 2000.

——, ed. *Stroker Anthology: 1974–1994.* New York: Stroker Press, 1994.

Stinson, John D. "Randy Wicker Papers, 1958–1993, Biographical Note." New York Public Library Manuscripts and Archives Division. April 1995.

Stonehill, Judith. *Greenwich Village: A Guide to America's Legendary Left Bank.* New York: Universe, 2002.

Stosuy, Brandon. *Up Is Up but So Is Down: New York's Literary Downtown Scene, 1974–1992.* New York: New York University Press, 2006.

Strausbaugh, John. *The Village: 400 Years of Beats, Bohemians, Radicals and Rogues: A History of Greenwich Village.* New York: Ecco, 2013.

Sukenick, Ronald. *Down and In: Life in the Underground.* New York: William Morrow, 1987.

Talen, Bill. *What Should I Do If Reverend Billy Is in My Store?* New York: New Press, 2003.

Talese, Gay. "It's a Circus with Clowns and Animals and Even Poetry on St. Mark's Place." *New York Times.* December 21, 1961.

Taylor, Angela. "Downtown Boutique for an Uptown Crowd." *New York Times.* January 5, 1968.

Terry, Don. "Three Blocks of Unusual, That Is St. Mark's Place." *News and Courier.* November 1, 1929.

Theado, Matt. *The Beats: A Literary Reference.* New York: Carroll and Graf, 2001.

Thirlwell, Adam. "J. B. Him: Joe Brainard's Universal Prose." *Harper's Magazine.* July 2012.

Thompson, Victoria. *Murder on Astor Place* (Gaslight Mystery). New York: Berkley, 1999.

——. *Murder on St. Mark's Place* (Gaslight Mystery). New York: Berkley, 2000.

Tippins, Sherill. *Inside the Dream Palace: The Life and Times of New York's Legendary Chelsea Hotel.* New York: Houghton Mifflin Harcourt, 2013.

Trager, James. *The New York Chronology.* New York: HarperResource, 2003.

Trager, Oliver. *Dig Infinity! The Life and Art of Lord Buckley.* New York: Welcome Rain Publishers, 2002.

Trotsky, Leon. *My Life.* New York: Universal Library Edition, 1973 (1st edition: 1930).

Truscott, Lucian IV. "St. Marks Place, 1971: One-Way Street." *Village Voice.* August 26, 1971.

——. "A Stockingful of Love, But No Re-Admission." *Village Voice* 14, no. 12 (January 2, 1969).

"12-Foot Wall Hides Once Dazzling Shop." *New York Times.* August 26, 1915.

Tytell, John. *Paradise Outlaws: Remembering the Beats.* New York: William Morrow and Company, 1999.

Ulaby, Neda. "Amiri Baraka's Legacy Both Offensive and Achingly Beautiful." NPR. January 9, 2014.

Van Meter, William. "The Shop That Punk Built." *New York Times*. May 8, 2013.

Vitullo-Martin, Julia. "Not as Easy as A, B, C: Fighting Crime in One of Manhattan's Rougher Neighborhoods." *Wall Street Journal*. November 10, 2010.

Wakefield, Dan. *New York in the '50s*. New York: Houghton Mifflin, 1992.

Warhol, Andy. *The Philosophy of Andy Warhol*. San Diego: Harvest, 1977.

Watson, Edward B. *New York Then and Now*. New York: Dover Publications, 1976.

Watson, Steven. *The Birth of the Beat Generation*. New York: Pantheon, 1995.

Wetzsteon, Ross. *Republic of Dreams Greenwich Village: The American Bohemia, 1910–1960*. New York: Simon & Schuster, 2002.

White, Edmund. *City Boy: My Life in New York During the 1960s and '70s*. New York: Bloomsbury, 2009.

Wilcock, John. "The Village Square." *Village Voice*. September 4, 1957.

Wilkinson, Alec. "Anything Pink Rocks." *The New Yorker*. March 26, 2007.

Williams, Martin. "A Night at the Five Spot." *Down Beat*. February 13, 1964.

Wilson, Elizabeth. *Bohemians*. New Brunswick, NJ: Rutgers University Press, 2000.

Wolcott, James. *Lucking Out: My Life Getting Down and Semi-dirty in '70s New York*. New York: Anchor Books, 2011.

Woychuk, Denis. *Attorney for the Damned: A Lawyer's Life with the Criminally Insane*. New York: Free Press, 1996.

WPA Guide to New York City: The Federal Writers' Project Guide to 1930s New York. New York: New Press, 1939. Lower East Side section begins on p. 108.

Yablonsky, Linda. *The Story of Junk*. New York: First Back Bay Paperback Edition, 1998 (1st edition: Farrar, Straus and Giroux, Inc., 1997).

Yee, Chiang. *The Silent Traveller in New York*. New York: The John Day Company, 1950?

Zachter, Mort. *Dough: A Memoir*. New York: Harper Luxe, 2007.

Zukin, Sharon. *Naked City: The Death and Life of Authentic Places*. New York: Oxford University Press, 2010.

East Village Magazines and Newspapers

The East Village has produced a pretty remarkable number of literary magazines over the years. My father, Peter Schjeldahl, started *Mother: A Journal of New Literature* in Northfield, Minnesota, in 1964. When he moved to New York, he continued publication. Poets featured in *Mother 8*, published in May 1967, include Ted Berrigan, Ron Padgett, Harry Mathews, James Schulyer, and Ed Sanders. Schjeldahl also served as features editor for *Avant Garde* magazine, which was published from 1968 to 1971. Among the several articles he wrote for *Avant Garde* under various pseudonyms was issue 7's "The Satyricon of Petronius: A New Take, a translation by

Edgar A. Bunning, America's foremost Latin scholar." Schjeldahl, who knew no Latin, "translated" it in that he propped up three old translations on his desk and made a new one that was as different from them as they were from one another.

Other East Village zines include *The East Village Other* (headquarters at 147 Avenue A), which made the *Village Voice* look conservative. It was published from 1965 to 1972. At one point, its circulation was 65,000. Here's a short list of East Village magazines, nearly all of which are defunct:

Adventures in Poetry

Avant Garde

Between C and D (Catherine Texier and Joel Rose)

Birth (Tuli Kupferberg)

Black Mask (Ben Morea)

C (Ted Berrigan)

Culture Hero: A Fanzine of Stars of the Super World (Les Levine)

Cuz (Richard Hell)

The East Village Eye (For a while at no. 120; 1979–1987; online 2013: http://www
.east-village-eye.com)

The East Village Other (1965–1972)

East Villager (1980s)

The Eleventh Street Ruse

The Floating Bear (LeRoi Jones and Diane Di Prima)

Fuck You: A Magazine of the Arts (And the best-name award goes to Ed Sanders.)

Gandhabba

Just Another Asshole (Barbara Ess and Glenn Branca)

Live Sex Acts

Milk (Gillian McCain)

Modern School Magazine

Mother (Peter Schjeldahl)

Poetry Project affiliated: *Poetry Project Newsletter, Telephone, Adventures in Poetry, Un Poco Loco, Mag City, The 4, 3, 2 Review, The Harris Review, Reindeer, The 12th Street Punk*

Project Papers (Ed Friedman)

Punk (1976–1979; 1981–2007)

Rag, Caveman, Unnatural Acts, Little Light, Tangerine

The Rat

The Realist

The Recluse (Poetry Project, 2005)

Redtape (Michael Carter)

The Shadow

Stroker (by Irving Stettner, with frequent contributions from Henry Miller)

The World (Poetry Project, 1967–1983; 1992–2002)

Yugen (Hettie Jones and LeRoi Jones)

East Village Websites

1940sNewYork.com

98Bowery.com

BoweryBoogie.com

EVGrieve.com

Evhp.blogspot.com

EVTransitions.com

Forgotten-NY.com

FultonHistory.com

GVHP Off the Grid

Homeless Archives: http://homelessarchives.blogspot.com/

Jeremiah's Vanishing New York: Vanishingnewyork.blogspot.com

Leshp.org

NeitherMoreNorLess.blogspot.com

Newyork.nearsay.com

New York Songlines

Oldstreets.com

Rumur.com/astor-place (Michael Galinsky photo gallery of Astor Place peddlers in 1990)

ScoutingNY.com

StreetsYouCrossed.blogspot.com

TheLoDownNY.com

Walking Tours, Lectures, and Plays; Museum and Gallery Shows

Activist New York. Museum of the City of New York. 2014.

"AIDS in New York: The First Five Years." New-York Historical Society. 2013.

Beat Memories. Grey Art Gallery of New York University. 2013.

Clayton Gallery and Outlaw Art Museum. 2013.

The Decline and Fall of the Art World, Part I: The One-Percenters. Freight + Volume, August 2013. Contains a Loren Munk painting of the East Village art world.

Eric Ferrara, Lower East Side History Project Walking Tour. 2012.

Karen Finley: Written in Sand. Baruch Performing Arts Center. October 2–23, 2014.

The Haunting of St. Marks Place. Under St. Marks Theater. November 18, 2012.

Barry Lewis, Greenwich Village lecture at the New-York Historical Society, 2012. "If you live long enough, you see all the ironies of history ironed out," he said.

Jane Marx. Village Alliance Walking Tour. 2012.

Fred W. McDarrah: Save the Village. Steven Kasher Gallery. 2014.

The Museum of Reclaimed Urban Space. 2013.

"No Credit, Cash Only: Cookie in Film and Video," Participant, Inc. Opened October 16, 2014.

"Opposition: *Black Mask*, Ben Morea, and U.A.W.M.F." Boo-Hooray. 2014.

Punk: Chaos to Couture. Metropolitan Museum of Art. 2013.

"Punk Magazine Mutant Monster Beach Party." Boo-Hooray. 2013.

The Ukrainian Museum. 2013.

Why We Fight: Remembering AIDS Activism. New York Public Library Stephen A. Schwarzman Building. 2014.

The Yippie Museum. 2012.

INDEX

Page numbers in *italics* refer to illustrations.
Page numbers 341–82 refer to endnotes.

INDEX

ikely to be lowered. The plight of the men and
an age as forty is hard, almost hopeless, when
o seek for reemployment.

he words of a materialist. They are the words of a
how to blend justice with compassion.
n his biography of Cardozo, published after the
in 1938, wondered about the influence of his
ing Cardozo's humanistic and philosophic ap-
with Holmes', Levy suggested that if that particu-
ecame popular, "Law practice will become less of
re of a learned profession."
e no better eulogy to Benjamin Cardozo and his

regarded as the "head of the bar" of New York City. He was a
founder of the City Bar Association and its president in 1888
and 1889. He served as president of the New York State Bar
Association in 1906 and 1908 and of the American Bar Association in 1898 and 1899. Choate was a lawyer who firmly believed
in the greatness and integrity of his profession. The following
passage shows the depth of his feelings:

I maintain that in no other occupation to which men can devote
their lives is there a nobler intellectual pursuit or a higher moral
standard than that which inspires and pervades the ranks of the
legal profession. To establish justice, to maintain the rights of
man, to defend the helpless and oppressed, to succor innocence,
and to punish guilt, to aid in the solution of those great questions legal and constitutional which are constantly being evolved
from the ever varying affairs and business of men are duties that
may well challenge the best powers of man's intellect and the
noblest qualities of the human heart.

When Choate died in May of 1917, Elihu Root said, "He has
given his life for his country." To that must be added, "and for
the ideals of his profession."

BENJAMIN CARDOZO was one of New York's finest lawyers and
one of the country's greatest Supreme Court Justices. Nominated by Herbert Hoover in 1932 to replace the retiring Oliver
Wendell Holmes, Cardozo soon earned the older justice's
admiration:

I am sure that I should really love Cardozo if I knew him better.
I not only owe to him some praise that I regard as one of the
chief rewards of my life, but I have noticed such a sensitive
delicacy in him that I tremble lest I should prove unworthy of
his regard. All who know him seem to give him a superlative
place. I have seen him but once, and then his face greatly impressed me. I believe he is a great and beautiful spirit.

Cardozo was born in New York City in 1870. His ancestors
were Sephardic Jews. His great-great-grandfather, Aaron Nu-
nez Cardozo, was a British merchant who emigrated to the colo-

Benjamin Cardozo

nies in the mid-1700's. His great-great-uncle, Rabbi Gershom
Mendes Seixas, played a minor role in George Washington's
inauguration. Cardozo's father, Albert, was a New York judge,
who was forced to resign during the Boss Tweed scandals of the
1870's.

Young Cardozo's career bore no resemblance to his father's.
He was a political science major at Columbia and graduated
from Columbia Law School. Cardozo was admitted to the New
York Bar in 1891. His years as a judge began in 1913, when he
was elected justice of the supreme court in New York City. One
month later, Governor William Sulzer appointed Cardozo to the
Court of Appeals. The justices of that court had unanimously
recommended him for the job. Cardozo was already well ac-
quainted with the court's work, having published a study, *The
Jurisdiction of the Court of Appeals of the State of New York,* in 1903.

Benjamin Cardozo was called a philosopher-judge, a man
whose written opinions took on a distinctive, thoughtful, literary
tone. This can be observed in his analysis of the purpose of the
Court of Appeals:

The court exists not for the individual litigant but for the indefi-
nite body of litigants, whose causes are potentially involved in

---

the specific case at is
only the algebraic s
the formula of justic

In 1927 Cardozo bec
held in such preciou
ment to the Perman
The Hague.

But a man of Card
things. In 1932 Herbe
States Supreme Court.
that year. On the Cou
ments and continued to
for humanity. Legal hist

. . .his is an all round
general knowledge, and
the best of those who hav
ence for the use of lawyers

Cardozo was a pleasant,
to people and their needs
decisions, especially in that
Revenue, et al., v. Davis, a cas
ity Act. Davis was a sharehol
of Boston and wanted to st
required social security paym
tutionality, Cardozo wrote the

But the ill is all one, or at le
men are thrown out of work b
do or because the disabilities
doing it. Rescue becomes nec
The hope behind this statute is
rigors of the poor house as wel
such a lot awaits them when jou
. . . More and more of our po
industrial instead of rural and a
pressive that among industrial
women are preferred over the o
the older are commonly the firs

---

their wages are
women at so lo
they are driven

These are not t
man who knew
Beryl Levy,
justice's death
work. Compa
proach to law
lar approach
a trade and m
There can
work.

Notable Early New York Cases

The Trial of
Jacob Leisler, 1691

WHEN KING JAMES II was deposed in the Glorious Revolution in England because he was a Catholic, and his Protestant daughter Mary and her husband, William of Orange, both ascended the throne, there were political repercussions in the New York colony. Understandably so. While James was king, Protestant colonists feared a Catholic takeover and a possible invasion from the Catholic French in Canada. Now they feared it even more, thinking the French would invade to avenge the downfall of James and the crowning of a Protestant in his place. Francis Nicholson, King James' Lieutenant-Governor, fled New York to escape the angry and frightened colonists. Jacob Leisler, a popular merchant of German descent, took over power in the name of the Glorious Revolution, declaring his loyalty to William and Mary. No one challenged him, none tried to take his place.

Leisler had come to New York when it was still under Dutch rule. He was first employed by the Dutch West India Company, but his good head for business and his marriage to a rich widow soon made him one of the most respected men in the community. But an aristocrat he was not, nor did he aspire to be, in spite of his fortune and the fact that he held the titles of justice of the peace and captain of the militia.

At the time Leisler proclaimed himself Lieutenant-Governor and swore allegiance to King William and Queen Mary, he was extremely popular with the colony's skilled workers and common people. Leisler used his executive power to institute a number of democratic reforms: he convened a provincial assembly, gave the people of New York City their first mayoral election, and filled important government posts with people of his own class. As captain of the militia, Leisler was also in control of the fort on Manhattan.

It is unnecessary to say that Leisler made many bitter enemies this way. The upper class, former government officials and many of the clergy feared and hated him. After Leisler had assumed the title of governor, some members of the landed gentry fled to Albany certain that their privileges would be forcibly taken from them. Their fears were seemed realized when Nicholas Bayard returned to New York City and was promptly arrested for his "libelous" remarks about Leisler. Most of Leisler's foes now chose to flee to one of the other colonies.

Blissfully unaware of what was happening in New York City, William and Mary had appointed Henry Sloughter as the new royal governor of New York, but Sloughter had been delayed first in England and then by problems with his ship in Bermuda, and did not reach New York until two years later. When news of Leisler's naming himself governor reached Sloughter, he sent word that Leisler must surrender the fort on Manhattan and step down. Leisler refused at first, assuming that the orders were a fabrication of his enemies, but he immediately surrendered when he realized that Sloughter was arriving and, indeed, was the new governor. Leisler, his son-in-law Milborne, and several of their close followers were immediately arrested.

The trial took place shortly after Sloughter's arrival. Easily swayed, Sloughter fell under the influence of Leisler's enemies, the anxious and angry New York aristocracy. Leisler was indicted for treason. He was charged with murder, also, because of the death of Josiah Browne, killed in a clash with some of his followers. The indictment read:

Jacob Leisler (*et al.*) ... the 17th Day of March ... at Fort William Henry ... Falsely Malitious traiterously and felloneously Designeing ... their Said Majestys from their Royall State title power and government to Deprive ... Did Levy War against our said Lord and Lady ... Did make an assault on the said Abraham Gouverneur with one hand Gunn ... on ... Josiah Browne did Wound the said Josiah Browne ... of which Mortall Wound the said Josiah Browne ... Did Dye.

Jacob Leisler didn't stand a chance. Bayard, Stephanus Van Cortlandt, and William Pinhorne, fiercely anti-Leisler, conducted the questioning of the prisoner. The prosecution was comprised of William Nicolls, George Forewell and James Emott, three of Leisler's deadliest enemies. Leisler refused to plead to either of the charges, arguing that he had professed loyalty to William and Mary and had received a commission from them to govern. Leisler was referring to the commission sent to Nicholson who fled the colony thinking the French were about to attack. Since Nicholson never received the commission to act as governor, Leisler assumed it applied to him when he took over the office. Leisler's stubbornness only made his enemies hungrier for blood and he and Milborne met speedy convictions by a special Court of Oyer and Terminer.

A drunken Governor Sloughter signed the death warrant for Jacob Leisler and ordered anyone arrested who was found circulating petitions in his behalf. Several leading historians contend that Leisler's enemies had wined Sloughter until he was barely capable of speech and then persuaded him to sign the death warrant. On May 16, 1691, Jacob Leisler met the hangman.

The day was a remarkable one in New York. No carpenter in the city would supply a ladder for the gallows. It was raining heavily and the black clouds overhead echoed the mood of the people. People wept openly at the public execution. When Leisler was cut down, his clothing was cut into pieces and distributed among the onlookers. To the end Leisler maintained that he had served the Crown alone and forgave his enemies as he stood on the gallows.

The trial was one of the most ignominious miscarriages of justice in New York's legal history—a fact soon recognized by friend and foe alike. The verdict was reversed a few years later —of little help to the virtually murdered Leisler.

John André, 1780

Gentlemen: Major André, Adjutant General to the British army, will be brought before you for your examination. He came within our lines in the night on an interview with Major

John André

General Arnold, and in an assumed character; and was taken
within our lines, in a disguised habit, with a pass under a feigned
name, and with the enclosed papers concealed upon him. After
a careful examination you will be pleased, as speedily as possible,
to report a precise state of his case, together with your opinion
of the light in which he ought to be considered, and the punishment that ought to be inflicted.

THE AUTHOR of these words was George Washington, Commander in Chief of the American army during the Revolutionary War. The gentlemen he addressed were members of a special military board of inquiry, a court summoned by Washington
to try John André, adjutant to General Sir Henry Clinton of the
British army. The members of the board were Major General
Green, who was president of the board; and Generals Stirling,
Saint Clair, Lafayette, Howe, Steuben, Parsons, Clinton, Knox,
Glover, Paterson, Hand, Huntington and Stark. On September
29, 1780, the military board convened in a Dutch church in
Tappan, New York.

In the celebrated Benedict Arnold treason episode of the
Revolutionary War, Major John André was General Sir Henry
Clinton's emissary to Benedict Arnold. He was caught behind

American lines with papers handed to him by Arnold which gave such explicit details about West Point that had André been able to take them back behind British lines as intended, there is no question that the fortress would have fallen. Major André was arrested and Benedict Arnold escaped to the *Vulture,* a British ship anchored in the Hudson, south of the fort.

André impressed the military tribunal with his courage and honesty. He openly confessed to his actions and never once tried to shift blame on another. He took full responsibility for his deed. General Clinton, who had great affection for his adjutant, tried to save André by arguing to Washington that the young soldier had been traveling under the "sanction of a flag" and was, therefore, not a spy but a prisoner of war. André denied this, admitting that he knew when he started the mission that it was espionage in actuality, with grave consequences if it met with failure. Later, it was suggested to General Clinton that Arnold be exchanged for André, but the British general was forced to refuse, since he gave his word to the American traitor that he would be granted asylum should he seek it. At the close of the hearing André put himself "at the mercy of the board."

The decision was unanimous, as expected. The board found "that Major André, Adjutant-General of the British army, ought to be considered as a spy from the enemy, and that agreeable to the law and usage of nations it is their opinion he ought to suffer death." André's reaction to the decision was:

I foresee my fate, and though I pretend not to play the hero, or to be indifferent about life, yet I am reconciled to whichever may happen, conscious that misfortune, not guilt, has brought it upon me.

On September 30 Washington issued an executive order that André be hanged on October 1 at 5 o'clock P.M.

A military journal of that era gives us an account of André's execution. The author, a doctor, wrote:

He betrayed no want of fortitude, but retained a complacent

smile on his countenance, and politely bowed to several gentlemen whom he knew, which was respectfully returned.

André's last words were, "I pray you to bear me witness that I met my fate like a brave man." Many of those watching were deeply moved by the youthful Briton's courage. His charming personality and his talents in the arts had won André many American friends who now mourned him as a romantically tragic young man.

Major André died a spy's death, by hanging, despite his appeal that he be shot, the honorable way of military execution. Long forgotten by most Americans, Major André, his adventures and trial are among the most dramatic events in this country's military and legal history.

The People v. Harry Croswell, 1804

It is only by the abuse of the forms of Justice that we can be enslaved.—Alexander Hamilton, in defense of Harry Croswell

IN 1802 Harry Croswell, the editor of *The Wasp* of Hudson, New York, was arrested for libeling President Thomas Jefferson in his newspaper. He had reprinted a previously published report which said that it was Jefferson who had paid James Callender to write the scandalous *The Prospect Before Us*. In that book Callender had called George Washington a "traitor, perjurer and a robber" and had labeled John Adams "a hoary headed incendiary."

Croswell was initially indicted at Claverack, Columbia County. In January of 1803, however, the case was transferred to the State Supreme Court, and tried before Chief Justice Morgan Lewis. Croswell was convicted, and appealed on two grounds through writ of error. The appeal was granted and trial was set before the full Supreme Court in February, 1804. The court included, besides the Chief Justice, Justices Brockholst Livingston, Smith Thompson, and James Kent.

Alexander Hamilton

Alexander Hamilton was enlisted in Croswell's defense. In his famous brief, Hamilton insisted that freedom of the press meant the freedom to print the truth even if it was unsavory; that there was no concrete, established libel law in New York; that juries must be considered as the means for trying libel cases; and that truth, if not abused, is a sound defense in libel cases. Ambrose Spencer, New York's Attorney General, said that truth was immaterial to the case. Hamilton, in turn, branded Spencer's position as resembling the "tyrannical and polluted" British Star Chamber Court. Hamilton then cited pre-Revolutionary precedents, showing where truth was regarded as a justifiable defense in libel cases, making special note of the Zenger Case. Hamilton went on to say:

The liberty of the press consists in the right to publish with impunity truth, with good motives, for justifiable ends, though reflecting on government, magistracy, or individuals.

Brilliant though Hamilton's defense was, Croswell's conviction was upheld by the State Supreme Court. In spite of that, Hamilton's position on libel was incorporated into law by the state legislature one year later. It was made part of the state constitution of 1821 and is considered to be the basis for all laws involving libel suits in America.

Gibbons v. Ogden, 1824

GIBBONS V. OGDEN, one of Chief Justice John Marshall's hallmark Supreme Court decisions, has been deemed the "emancipation proclamation of American commerce." The case had a liberating effect on trade throughout the nation. Previous to the decision, several states operated as independent commercial spheres within the United States. *Gibbons v. Ogden* struck down that insularism and opened the door to flourishing trade among the states.

The case traced its roots to New York's practice of granting steamboat trading monopolies on its waters, based on the state's self-assumed right to regulate trade on all waterways within its borders. The practice had been initiated by the New York legislature and reinforced by the state's courts in an 1812 decision. This monopoly excluded vessels from other states from carrying goods to New York ports and precipitated a trade war between New York and New Jersey.

Aaron Ogden and Thomas Gibbons were partners in a steamboat business. When they decided to end the partnership, it was Ogden who got the New York steamship monopoly. Gibbons contested Ogden's right to use New York waters while he could not. In 1824, the case went to the United States Supreme Court.

The Court at that time lacked much of the formality that we now associate with it. A journalist covering the *Gibbons v. Ogden* case commented on how the justices donned their robes "in the same manner as a farmer puts on his frock, or the sportsman his hunting shirt," in full view of the court. Attendants were employed to help the justices "as a servant assists a lady in resuming her hat and mantle in an antechamber."

The "God-like" Daniel Webster represented plaintiff Gibbons. Webster was renowned for gifted, flowing oratory that

*Aaron Ogden and Thomas Gibbons, whose law suit established that
the federal government controlled inter-state commerce.
Chief Justice Marshall presided.*

made him one of the most charismatic lawyers in American history. Webster far overshadowed Thomas Addis Emmet, counsel for Ogden and the state of New York. In arguing against state monopolies, Webster called upon the Court to think of the United States as one nation, not as a motley collection of separate states. He said:

We do not find, in the history of the formation and adoption of the constitution that any man speaks of a general concurrent power, in the regulation of foreign and domestic trade, as still residing in the states. The very object intended, more than any other, was to take away such power. If it had not so provided, the constitution would not have been worth accepting.

On the other side, Thomas Addis Emmet argued for Ogden and New York that:

Why should not the contract of a state, in regard to its domain and property, be as sacred as that of an individual? . . . Who is to judge of that but the state legislatures?

Emmet emphasized the "states' rights" side of the issue, pointing out that the Federal Government should have no concern in the control of commerce within individual states' borders.

But John Marshall and the Court disagreed. In deciding for Gibbons, the Court ruled that the Federal Government had indeed the authority to regulate interstate commerce, that the "commerce clause" of the Constitution gave the Court the right to limit powers of individual states in that area.

With the Hudson River and Long Island Sound now open to interstate commercial traffic, New York City rapidly became the trading hub of the nation. As the city grew, its court system became equally large and important. Through the city's role as a commercial center, its courts became innovators in commercial law, and many precedent-setting cases involving United States trade and commerce passed through New York's courts.

So *Gibbons v. Ogden* served several functions. It struck down New York's navigational monopolies. It enhanced the reputations of John Marshall and Daniel Webster. It established the Federal Government as having power over the states in issues of interstate commerce. And, in the long run, it contributed to making New York a commercial center and the United States a trading giant of the world.

The People v.
Alexander McLeod, 1841

IN DECEMBER, 1837, William Lyon Mackenzie led a rebellion against the royal government in Toronto. Handily defeated by government troops, Mackenzie's forces fled and took refuge on Navy Island in the Niagara River, which divides Canada from New York state. Despite a proclamation of neutrality by the governor, some New Yorkers brought arms and food to the rebels. A steamer, the *Caroline,* was used to transport the supplies. The British and Canadian governments took great exception to Americans helping Canadian insurrectionists and interfering in their affairs.

On the night of December 29, 1837, the Canadians retaliated. Led by Captain Andrew Drew of the Royal Navy, Canadian troops crossed the Niagara River to the New York side and seized the *Caroline* and burned it. During the melee an American, Amos Durfee, was killed. The incident precipitated talk of war and eventually resulted in the controversial case of Alexander McLeod.

McLeod, a deputy sheriff in Ontario, served as an undercover agent for the Canadian government. He had been quickly dispatched to Buffalo where he could conveniently report on the activities of the *Caroline*. His misfortune, however, was that he was boastful. Three years after the burning of the *Caroline*, McLeod once more crossed the Niagara River, this time to a party held at an American tavern. After several drinks, McLeod boasted of how he spied on the *Caroline* and helped burn her. Furthermore, he added, he himself had killed Durfee. His boastful talk led to his arrest and imprisonment at the Lockport jail.

The arrest caused a storm of protest. Henry Fox, the British minister to the United States, wrote to Secretary of State John Forsyth, demanding McLeod's release. Fox argued that one man could not be held responsible for an incident involving many people three years before. London newspapers clamored for war. At no time, since 1812, were relations between America and England more strained. There were even reports that the British Mediterranean fleet had been ordered to sail for Gibraltar and remain on alert, pending a declaration of war.

On May 6, 1841, McLeod appeared before the New York State Supreme Court, asking to have the charges against him dismissed. The significant question was whether McLeod, a Canadian citizen and British subject, could be tried in America for his alleged offenses. The court ruled against McLeod, saying that aliens in the United States are indeed responsible for their actions and bound by the laws of the land; that the courts have jurisdiction over cases even if those cases are in diplomtic flux, and that the arguments McLeod was using for dismissal of the case would not even merit bail in Britain. The court honored McLeod's request that the trial be moved from the Buffalo area, where tensions were high and prejudice against the Canadian made a fair trial impossible. The trial was moved to Utica where McLeod was indicted on seventeen counts of murder and arson.

Part of his indictment read:

Alexander McLeod ... not having the fear of God before his eye, but moved and seduced by the instigation of the devil ... with a certain gun of the value of five dollars, then and there loaded and charged with gunpowder and one leaden bullet (which the said Alexander McLeod, in his right hand, then and there had and held), to against and upon the said Amos Durfee, then and there feloniously and willfully, and of his malice aforethought and with a premeditated design to effect the death of the said Amos Durfee, did shoot and discharge, and the said Alexander McLeod with the leaden bullet aforesaid, out of the gun aforesaid, then and there by the force of the gunpowder and shot sent forth as aforesaid, the said Amos Durfee in and upon the back of the head of him ... did strike, penetrate and wound, giving to the said Amos Durfee ... one mortal wound ... the said Amos Durfee, then and there ... did languish, and languishing, did die.

Responding to rumors that American agitators were planning to seize and lynch McLeod, Governor William H. Seward ordered additional protection for the prisoner. One hundred Oneida County militiamen were activated; a company of United States troops was dispatched to the scene. Nothing happened. No trouble ensued.

The trial itself went smoothly. McLeod's counsel, Joshua A. Spencer, summoned witnesses who backed McLeod's alibi of being miles from the *Caroline* at the time of its destruction. The prosecution's evidence consisted primarily of hearsay from persons who, through cross-examination, were revealed to be in favor of lynching McLeod. In his charge to the jury Judge Philo Gridley directed, "If you believe that this man is guilty of murder, then, fearless of the consequences, whatever those consequences may be—though they shall wrap your country in a flame of war—whatever the result, look to the God of Justice and say whether the prisoner be guilty or not." It took a mere twenty-eight minutes for the jury to return with a Not Guilty verdict. McLeod was given safe-conduct to the Canadian border, where he was hailed as a hero.

The case of Alexander McLeod is unique in New York legal history. It attracted national and international attention and in-

William Seward, the noted lawyer and statesman and Governor of New York.

spired an act of Congress in August of 1842, which gave Federal Courts total jurisdiction over such cases. America was brought to the brink of war with England. And all this was sparked by a few drunken boasts of a Canadian deputy sheriff in a tavern on New York's Niagara frontier.

"Big Thunder" on Trial, 1845

I could not stand idle and see thousands deprived of their natural and, as I conceived, social and legal rights. —Dr. Smith Boughton, alias "Big Thunder"

VIOLENCE, terrorism, mass protests, heated legislative debate, tar and featherings and midnight "Indian" raids characterized the Anti-Rent Movement, a farmers' rebellion in the 1840's. A state of insurrection and martial law was proclaimed, when all legal means failed to halt the revolt. Next to the American Revolution, the Anti-Rent Movement was the most widespread and devastating uprising in New York's history.

The rebellion was a protest against the feudal landlords who owned most of the Hudson Valley region. This seventeenth century landlord-tenant system, begun by the Dutch through their patroons and the British through their land grants, lasted for two centuries. The largest manors were those of the Van Rensselaer and Livingston families, who had hundreds of tenant farmers on their lands. The incredibly oppressive conditions they lived under were the direct cause of the rebellion. The manors exacted a heavy toll on a farmer's income. The levies averaged fifteen bushels of wheat per hundred acres per year, a large burden for the nineteenth century tiller of the soil to carry.

Strangely, it was the death of Stephen Van Rensselaer, a popular landowner, that signalled the beginning of the rebellion. He had been a generous man, aware of the harsh life his farmers led, and he had, consequently, not collected rents. How relieved his tenants must have been! But on his death, his son set about the grim task of collecting all the back monies due him as lord of the manor. Trouble followed. Farmers simply refused to pay. Sheriffs were summoned to help but the farmers banded together and chased them away. Word spread through the Hudson Valley and soon tenant farmers everywhere were stubbornly refusing to give up their crops to their patroons or lords of the manor. Anarchy prevailed until troops were called up by the governor.

Dr. Smith Boughton was one of the leaders of the anti-renters. He was a country doctor but his social activities made him very different from the usual conservative men practicing rural medicine. Boughton had been a rebel all his life: when he was at college, he had led a successful protest against compulsory chapel attendance and after practicing medicine for a short time, Boughton had traveled to Canada in 1837 to take part in Mackenzie's revolt. He returned home discouraged and penniless, but still burning with revolutionary fever. In the Anti-Rent Movement, Boughton found a new and worthy cause. He devoted the next years of his life to the farmers' uprising and, under the name of "Big Thunder," became one of the anti-renters' most eloquent public speakers.

In early December of 1844 the sheriff of Columbia County had been called upon to collect rents. On the road to the tenant farms he was ambushed by anti-renters dressed as Indians, one

John Van Buren, son of the president, was involved in many landmark legal decisions, including one which ended the feudal landlord system in New York.

of their favorite disguises. The rebels seized the sheriff's papers and burned them. At about the same time, a man who refused to shout, "Down with the rent!" when he was ordered to was shot and killed by a group of rampaging farmers. Infuriated, government officials arrested Boughton and several other anti-rent leaders and charged them with counts of robbery, conspiracy, assault, rioting and manslaughter. A jury acquitted the doctor on one count of robbery. There were hysterical celebrations by the anti-renters. "Big Thunder" was not so fortunate with his second trial.

Boughton had engaged Ambrose L. Jordan as his counsel. Jordan was noted for his remark: "I always stop the truth from coming out if I think it unpleasant to my client's cause." John Van Buren, son of the President, was prosecutor for the state. The two men detested each other. Judge John W. Edmonds, a loyal Democrat, presided over the case, giving Van Buren a distinct edge.

The trial was highlighted by a brawl between prosecutor and defense attorney, forcing the court to adjourn while the two lawyers spent the night in jail. In England the fight was dubbed "the latest sign of advancing civilization in America."

The significant issue in the trial was proving that Boughton had been on the scene at all. The anti-renters had been costumed as Indians when they attacked. Van Buren produced a key prosecution witness: Abraham Carle, a turncoat anti-renter. Carle testified that he had seen Boughton put on Indian dress and had actually helped the doctor remove the costume. Van Buren rested his case on the weight of this evidence. Jordan attacked Carle's testimony on the grounds of insanity. He summoned Carle's wife and mother, and both testified that Carle was insane. Jordan also produced several witnesses who testified that his client had been elsewhere at the time of the crime. Judge Edmonds now came to Van Buren's aid with information given him by a man hired to spy at Anti-Rent Movement meetings. This testimony was damaging to most of Jordan's witnesses and made the case against Boughton overwhelming.

In sentencing Boughton, the judge said:

Your offense, though in the form it is presented to us as robbery, is in fact high treason, rebellion against your government, armed insurrection against the supremacy of the laws.

Edmonds then announced that he was sentencing "Big Thunder" to life imprisonment at hard labor. The courtroom was stunned. The severity of the sentence sobered many of the extremists in the movement.

Boughton did not serve long in prison, however. When John Young became the new governor, he pardoned Boughton and thirteen other anti-renters two years after they had entered Clinton Prison.

Near the time of his death, Boughton wrote:

The man who attempts to overthrow an existing wrong or revolutionize a principle of government that is tyrannical must not expect to reap any reward—only in conscience and the satisfaction of knowing that his individual efforts bring a benefit to thousands. In this I am fully rewarded.

Dr. Smith Boughton was a New Yorker with a cause. He was "fully rewarded" when the feudal land-tenure system of New York was abolished in the Constitution of 1846.

The Willliam Freeman
Insanity Case, 1846

They have made William Freeman what he is, a brute beast; they don't make anything else of our people but brute beasts; but when we violate their laws, then they want to punish us as if we were men. —John DePuy, an Auburn free black man

At this juncture, had William H. Seward been found anywhere at night alone, and unprotected by powerful law abiding forces of the region, his body would probably have been discovered in the morning hanging from the nearest tree. —Charles Francis Adams, United States Congressman.

WILLIAM FREEMAN was born in Auburn in 1824, of Afro-Indian heritage. His father had died of brain damage and his brother and sister had been officially declared insane. In 1840 Freeman was convicted of horse thievery and sentenced to five years at Auburn State Prison. He was flogged repeatedly during these years. When he was released, friends noticed great changes in Freeman's behavior. He walked about with a strange look in his eye, mumbling unintelligible phrases, and vowing revenge upon the people who imprisoned him. Somehow or other Freeman became obsessed with the idea that John Van Nest, a prosperous farmer, had been responsible for sending him to prison. On March 12, 1846, armed with two knives, Freeman attacked and killed four members of the Van Nest family. The black man was apprehended and jailed the next day. There was never any question that he had committed the murders.

In spite of threats on his life and public pressure that would have destroyed a lesser man, William H. Seward, former governor of New York State, chose to defend Freeman. Seward, an abolitionist, was sympathetic toward blacks, and firmly believed that if a person were legally declared insane, he could not be charged with murder.

The trial began on July 10. Judge Bowen Whiting, who tried the case, was not Olympian about the issues involved. He had far more sympathy for Freeman's plight than most Auburn citizens. Whiting wrote:

I am crushed between the millstones of judicial tyranny and popular anger. But there will be a consoling reflection by and by that I was not guilty of hanging the poor wretches whom the State Prison tormentors drive to madness.

The state's prosecutor was the ubiquitous John Van Buren, who hoped the trial would lessen Seward's popularity and increase his.

The question of whether Freeman was insane at the time he committed mass murder became the main issue of the trial. Van Buren produced a parade of witnesses. Physicians, as well as local people stated he could distinguish right from wrong and was, therefore, sane. Seward countered with witnesses who testified of the change in Freeman after his release from Auburn Prison. The Reverend John Austin, a Universalist minister, testified that he had, at Seward's urging, recently visited Freeman in jail and that the prisoner had no conception of the enormity of his offense and even made absurd statements about Van Nest, saying that he would eat Freeman's liver if Freeman ate his. Seward called several phrenologists who testified that, judging from the curvature of the defendant's skull, he definitely was not sane. Seward's star witness, however, was Dr. Amariah Brigham, head of the Utica Insane Asylum. Brigham was a world-renowned authority in his field and considered to be the greatest expert on mental illness in America. Brigham stated flatly that Freeman was insane. In the cross-examination that followed, Van Buren and Brigham sparred vigorously. An excerpt of the examination reads:

Van Buren: Do you think stealing hens any evidence of insanity?

Brigham: It may or may not be. If you, Mr. Van Buren, should rob a hen roost tonight I should think you were crazy.

In his summation Seward reviewed Freeman's life history, from childhood to the present. He argued that it was impossible to judge a "maniac as a malefactor." He also said:

We labor under the further embarrassment that the plea of insanity is universally suspected. It is the last subterfuge of the guilty, and so is too often abused. But however obnoxious to suspicion this defense is, there have been cases where it was true; and when true it is of all pleas the most perfect and complete defense that can be offered in any human tribunal. Our Saviour forgave his judges because "they knew not what they did." The insane man who has committed a crime knew not what he did. If this being, dyed with human blood, be insane, you and I and even the children of our affections, are not more guiltless than he.

The summation was a landmark in establishing a justifiable insanity plea in murder cases. The entire text was later printed under the title, *Argument in Defense of William Freeman,* and was extremely successful, selling out four editions in the first publication year.

But Seward's reasoning and eloquence were to no avail. On July 23 the jury returned a verdict of guilty and Judge Whiting ordered the death sentence. Seward won an appeal to the State Supreme Court, however, as the judge had made several procedural errors. A new trial was ordered, but it never took place. William Freeman died on August 21, 1847. For months he lay dying in his cell, not knowing why he was there and not recognizing the people who came to visit him.

Despite the fact that after the trial he was "exhausted in mind and body [and] covered with public reproach," Seward continued to prosper. In addition to his success as an author, his legal business grew. He remained the leader of the Whig Party and eventually became Abraham Lincoln's Secretary of State.

Seward's performance in the Freeman case remains a model for the legal profession. Opposed by family, by neighbors and friends, by New York's nineteenth century judiciary, he followed his conscience and, in that, he was the victor.

The United States v.
Susan B. Anthony, 1873

Without having a lawful right to vote in said election district the said Susan B. Anthony, being then and there a person of the female sex, as she, the said Susan B. Anthony, then and there well knew contrary of the statute of the United States of America in such cases made and provided, and against the peace of the United States of America ... did knowingly, wrongfully and unlawfully vote. —From the indictment of Susan B. Anthony, leader of the women's suffrage movement

INDICTED FOR VOTING in a Rochester election in 1872, Susan B. Anthony was tried and convicted. Her penalty was a $100 fine which she never paid. Indeed, she refused to pay one cent. Her trial attracted national attention and her conviction made her a martyr. Her fellow worker, Elizabeth Cady Stanton, said of Susan B. Anthony:

In ancient Greece she would have been a Stoic; in the era of the Reformation, a Calvinist; in King Charles' time a Puritan; but in the Nineteenth Century, by the very laws of her being, she is a reformer.

And a reformer's soul she had. The story of Susan B. Anthony's trial at Ontario County Courthouse for the now seemingly ludicrous crime of "voting" provides us with a dramatic episode in the history of law in New York.

On November 1, 1872, Susan B. Anthony led fifty women to the polls in Rochester, New York, to test the right of women to vote under the 14th Amendment. Of the fifty, only she and fifteen other women succeeded in voting—all in the eighth ward, all as Republicans. Men and women alike were outraged by the incident. One local newspaper called for enforcement of the penalty for election law violation: the maximum of a five hundred dollar fine or three years in prison. On November 28 all sixteen women were arrested. They were indicted, bail was set at one thousand dollars, and the trial scheduled for the summer of 1873.

Susan B. Anthony

Susan B. Anthony was a tireless public speaker for women's suffrage. Hoping to turn public opinion in her favor, she made a lecture tour of Monroe County prior to the trial. One speech she made was titled "The United States on Trial — Not Susan B. Anthony." On May 23, in an attempt to thwart Miss Anthony, the district attorney succeeded in having the trial shifted to the Ontario County Courthouse at Canandaigua. In no way deterred, Miss Anthony set about canvassing the people of that county. In less than thirty days, she made twenty-one speeches. She was a dauntless, tireless woman—with a cause.

The trial began on June 17. Each session was announced by the tolling of the courthouse bell. At the sound of the bell, people dropped what they were doing and raced to the courthouse, hoping to find a seat. Henry R. Selden, retired justice of the Court of Appeals, represented Miss Anthony. Richard Crowley, United States Attorney, was the prosecutor. Judge Ward Hunt, of the United States District Court, tried the case. Hunt was hostile to the suffragist movement and a friend of Roscoe Conkling, the leader of the New York Republican Party. Conkling thought the case embarrassing and wanted it ended quickly.

The trial could hardly be called fair. Hunt denied Selden the right to let Miss Anthony testify on her own behalf, saying that she was an incompetent witness. Selden was allowed to testify and he stated that he had advised the women to vote, believing that they did indeed possess that privilege. The prosecution's witnesses substantiated the fact that Miss Anthony and her fifteen associates had voted. In his summary, Selden pointed out:

Miss Anthony believed and was advised that she had a right to vote. She may also have been advised, as was clearly the fact, that the question as to her right could not be brought before the courts for trial without her voting or offering to vote, and if either was criminal the one was as much so as the other. Therefore she stands now arraigned as a criminal, for taking the only step by which it was possible to bring the great constitutional question as to her right before the tribunals of the country for adjudication.

Selden's logic was to no avail. Hunt had made up his mind even before the trial began. He instructed the jury: "...the result must be a verdict on your part of guilty, and therefore I direct you to find a verdict of guilty." After several heated objections from Selden, the jury returned with the prescribed verdict.

The press condemned Hunt for his action. The Canandaigua court was branded a "stubborn and prejudiced" tribunal. The *New York Sun* called for Hunt's impeachment, saying that he assumed unauthorized dictatorial powers. Even some publications violently opposed to women's suffrage attacked Hunt's abuse of his office.

After the end of the trial, the judge had allowed Susan Anthony a chance to speak. He asked, "Has the prisoner anything to say why sentence shall not be pronounced?" Susan Anthony had a great deal to say and would not let the judge silence her. She talked until she saw fit to stop by saying, "I ask not leniency at your hands, but rather the full rigor of the law."

Conkling and Judge Hunt had no intention of imprisoning Miss Anthony. Their hope was to have as little furor over the case as possible. To make certain that Miss Anthony would not go to jail, Hunt eliminated the customary "that she shall be imprisoned until the fine be paid" from his sentence. Perhaps he suspected that she had no intention of paying it in the first place.

Two Famous Twentieth Century New York Cases

THE CASE OF CHESTER GILLETTE, tried and convicted in 1906 for the murder of Grace Brown, is one of the most famous murder cases in American history. It attracted the attention of the nation's major newspapers and was the basis for Theodore Dreiser's famous novel, *An American Tragedy*.

Gillette first met Grace Brown while the two were employed in a shirt factory, owned by his uncle, at Cortland. A love affair ensued, with Grace's affections becoming more intense and Gillette's less as the months went by. Grace felt what was described at the time, as a "pure, unselfish love" for Gillette. But as Gillette slowly became a popular young bachelor with the "society" of Cortland, he found Grace's attentions embarrassing and possibly even harmful to his newly found status. Grace sent Gillette a number of love letters which he did not answer. She finally wrote to tell him disastrous news: she was pregnant.

Gillette offered to take her on a honeymoon before the marriage. Grace readily accepted, although she was frightened about what her parents would think once they found out. Off she went, nevertheless, secure in the knowledge that soon she would be Mrs. Chester Gillette. The couple traveled to the Glenmore Hotel on Big Moose Lake in the Adirondacks. There Gillette checked in as Carl Graham from Albany, but registered Grace in her own name. Shortly after they were settled, Gillette rented a boat from Robert Morrison, the owner of the hotel, and rowed toward the southern part of the lake. They did not return that evening. The next day Morrison went out looking for the young people and found the boat overturned, with Gillette's straw hat floating on the water. Grace's body was recovered, but there was no sign of Gillette's.

However, Gillette was soon discovered alive and well at the Arrowhead Hotel on Fourth Lake. Why he did not go home but chose to stay in the vicinity will never be known. He expressed surprise at the news of Grace's death, but could produce no reasonable account of where he had been for the past two days.

He eventually confessed to having been with Grace during that time but denied having anything to do with her death. He was arrested for murder because of the contradictory, confused nature of his alibis.

Gillette's trial began at the Herkimer County Courthouse on November 12, 1906. Gillette was defended by Senator A.M. Mills and Charles D. Thomas. George W. Ward, the district attorney, prosecuted and Supreme Court Justice Irving R. Devendorf presided. The prosecution succeeded in weaving a strong web of circumstantial evidence around Gillette. The defense could do little to weaken it. Throughout the trial Gillette remained cool and collected, seldom showing any sign of emotion, in spite of the jammed courtroom and the growing conviction of everyone that he would be found guilty.

On December 4, 1906, Justice Devendorf read his charge to the jury. It took the twelve jurors just five hours to reach a verdict—guilty of first degree murder. On December 10, Devendorf passed the death sentence on Gillette and two days later the prisoner was transferred to Auburn State Prison.

All appeals failed. Gillette's mother, Louise, went on a speaking tour of the area, hoping to secure petitions for clemency for her son. At Utica's Majestic Theater, for example, she spoke to a crowd of twelve hundred, using the title "Chester Gillette, Guilty or Not-Guilty, A Mother's Plea for Her Son" for her speech. But even the heartbroken pleas of Mrs. Gillette could not save her son from execution. He died, silent and composed to the end.

CZOLGOSZ ASSASSINATES MCKINLEY, 1901 Buffalo in 1901 was a festive city, gaily decorated for the Pan-American Exposition. A local newspaper painted the scene:

Gradually, the Pan-American Exposition approached its climax in beauty and grandeur. Never before had the world seen a spot more beautiful than the cluster of highly colored buildings with their beautiful lighting arrangement. Europe sent hundreds of thousands to view it. Every home, hotel and place of accommodation was filled with enthusiastic and merry sightseers.

Leon Czolgosz

September 5 was designated "President's Day" since William McKinley would be visiting the fair. At the imposing Temple of Music the President, flanked by guards, greeted a seemingly endless line of wellwishers. On that line was Leon Czolgosz, a wire-worker from Cleveland, Ohio, who, when he stepped up to the President, shot him twice at close range. As guards and Secret Service agents beat Czolgosz to the ground, McKinley was heard to say, "May God forgive him." The wounded Chief Executive whispered that Czolgosz must not be harmed.

The assassin had actually planned to shoot McKinley the day before, during his visit to Niagara Falls, but he could not get close enough to the President. When Czolgosz arrived in Buffalo, he had a near-perfect plan. Carefully disguising his loaded pistol under a fake bandage on his right hand, he stood on line with the hundreds of excited people who were going to shake the hand of the President of the United States. Czolgosz presented a harmless view, even a pitiful one, as he stepped up and seemed to be awkwardly presenting his left hand to McKinley. When the shots rang out, the President's guards were totally surprised and unprepared.

Czolgosz was an anarchist. He freely admitted killing McKinley in cold blood. He considered him to be a "tyrant" and a puppet in the hands of big business. After all, hadn't he declared war against Spain to annex Cuba, the Philippines and Hawaii for the robber barons? Hadn't he insisted that the United States back gold (the root of all evil) as its monetary standard?

Czolgosz exhibited no regrets for his act and said, "I killed the President because he was the enemy of the good people; of the good working people." It never occurred to him that he would not die for what he did, but perhaps his scorn and hatred of the government was somewhat shaken when he learned that the Erie County Bar Association persuaded Robert C. Titus and Loron L. Lewis, both former Justices of the Supreme Court, to defend him and that the attorneys were paid with public funds.

Czolgosz's trial was brief, lasting only two days. He readily confessed to the crime and offered no resistance, except the refusal to answer some of District Attorney Thomas Penney's questions. The jury took just thirty minutes to return with a guilty verdict.

On his way to execution at Auburn Prison, Leon Czolgosz said, "I am not sorry for the crime, that's all there is about it." For Czolgosz, yes. But hardly for the American people, about whom he professed to care so deeply.

Legislative Pioneeering in New York

AMONG STATE LEGISLATURES, the New York Legislature stands out as one of the most forward-looking bodies of its kind in the nation. What follows is a survey of some of New York's legislative achievements which will give some idea of the many areas in which the New York Legislature has excelled.

Business Law

IN THE 1800's the Legislature took several major steps to control banking. The first significant law was passed in 1827 and set a 6% limit on interest. It also stopped bank officials from borrowing on more than one-third of their actual capital, and prohibited the payment of dividends from anything but bank profits. This law was followed two years later by legislation creating a bank safety fund, whereby 3% of a bank's capital was set aside as a fund to protect noteholders. The law also established a commission to supervise the safety fund system.

The Panic of 1837 left many of New York's banks in total disarray. The next year, the Legislature passed a law stating that with sufficient funds private individuals would be permitted to set up a bank. This measure greatly stimulated the economy. Also, noteholders received additional protection through this law, as the state ordered banks to deposit securities with the comptroller's office before issuing notes. In 1851 the state centralized its control of banking operations through creation of the State Banking Department.

Nineteenth century corporation legislation was many-faceted. New York's first general law dealing solely with business corporations was passed in 1811. The law, "relative to incorporation for manufacturing purposes," provided that five or more people could incorporate for manufacturing if they filed an acceptable certificate of information. The incorporation was good for twenty years. Later, the Constitution of 1821 limited corporation formation, requiring a two-thirds legislative vote "creating, continuing, altering, or renewing any body politic or corporate." The Constitution of 1846 put further controls on corporations, saying that all laws concerning them were subject to alteration or repeal and that only corporations involved with municipalities could be formed by special legislation. Other corporations were to be formed under general law. These laws prompted a marked incorporation increase.

The corporation law of 1848 included a provision that "nothing but money shall be considered as payment of any part of the capital stock." The law was amended in 1853, giving corporations leeway to issue stock to pay for "mines, manufactories, and other property necessary for . . . business." This New York law served as a model for corporation legislation in many other states.

The Legislature limited big corporations through capitalization control. Up to 1881 there was a two million dollar limit on capitalization and by 1891 that limit had been increased to five million. This limit on big corporations (and trusts) forced some New York firms to incorporate in other states. New Jersey, with its liberal incorporation statutes, became known as a "mother of trusts."

Early legislative attempts at controlling insurance companies proved largely ineffective. In 1905, however, the Armstrong Committee of the Legislature, led by Committee Counsel Charles Evans Hughes, made history in the investigation of insurance and gas corporations.

Hughes is certainly one of the more notable figures in the history of the New York Bar. He was born in 1861 in Glens Falls, and graduated from Brown University. He took his law degree from Columbia University in 1884. Hughes held a law professorship at Cornell from 1891 to 1916, when he left the bench to run against Woodrow Wilson for President. He was head of the New York State Bar Association in 1917, Secretary of State in the early 1920's, and was President of the American Bar Association in 1924. Hughes also served on the Hague Tribunal, was President of the New York City Bar Association, and became a Judge of the World Court in 1928. In 1930, he was confirmed as Hoover's nominee for Chief Justice of the United States.

Hughes' scrutiny of insurance executives during the Armstrong investigation revealed illicit campaign contributions, illegal account adjustments, payoffs to the press and to law makers, and improper loan practices. Hughes' work brought on prosecutions, resignations and even the decamping of several of the state's top insurance men. The investigations caused the resignation of the State Superintendent of Insurance. The Armstrong Committee also investigated gas corporation fraud and exposed inequities in that business. As a result of Hughes' brilliant work, the Legislature passed laws in 1906 placing stiffer regulations on insurance and gas corporations.

Canals

THE NEW YORK Legislature set a significant precedent by authorizing government funds for the construction of the Erie Canal. In 1817, the first section of the canal was begun at Rome. Eight years later, the 363-mile-long canal was completed, linking Albany, on the Hudson River, with Buffalo, on Lake Erie. To commemorate the occasion Governor DeWitt Clinton poured a vessel of Lake Erie water into New York harbor.

The canal's initial cost was approximately seven million dollars and its revenues soon paid for its construction. The canal promoted growth in scores of upstate communities and contributed to making New York City the nation's most important port. It has been said that the canal's opening "may be regarded as the single most decisive event in the history of American transportation."

But the canal and its prosperity brought on corruption, especially within state government. An infamous group, known as the "Canal Ring," manipulated appropriations for canal repairs.

In the early 1870's Samuel Tilden was appointed special prosecutor to investigate the management of the canal and in 1875,
issued a report to the Legislature which resulted in the governor
appointing a special investigating committee. In February of
1876, this committee published a voluminous report which confirmed Tilden's allegations. Indictments followed. Many of
those charged were Democrats, as was Tilden himself, but party
politics never played a part in the great attorney's battles against
corruption.

Civil Service

"TO THE VICTOR BELONG the spoils" was the phrase that characterized political patronage during much of the 19th century.
With the signing of the Civil Service Act on May 16, 1883, the
spoils system in New York politics went into a sharp decline.
Governor Grover Cleveland signed the law which Assemblyman
Theodore Roosevelt strongly supported. One observer commented, "It was most fitting, therefore, that the chief sinner
among the States should lead the van of reform, for the political
reform that is possible in New York is practicable everywhere in
the country."

Exams "for testing the fitness of applicants for the public
service" were set up by the new law. Certain public offices had to
be filled by those receiving highest test scores. Successful job
applicants were placed on probationary appointment and pro-
motions were based on competition and merit. A Civil Service
Commission was formed with "advisory and regulatory powers
for the administration of Civil Service."

Codification of Law:
The Field Code

NEW YORK'S David Dudley Field is probably the single most
important person in this country's codification of law. Field was

David Dudley Field, creator of the Code of Criminal Procedure.

a unique attorney, called by one contemporary, "a warrior type of lawyer, almost a figure out of the old Greek epics." Admitted to the New York Bar in 1828, he began his codification work eleven years later and labored in that task until his death. Field was motivated first by a lawyer's natural desire to simplify the great shapeless mass of American law into a form that could be readily understood and interpreted, and second by his own ego. As one observer commented, "Field has a dominant desire for self-expression in a world in which he felt himself to be a natural chieftain."

Field's codification ideas were enthusiastically received by the men forming New York's Constitution of 1846. The new constitution created a committee of three to study court procedure in the state. Field was appointed to that committee in 1847 and soon became the guiding force behind it. Through the authority of this body, Field developed his most successful code, the Code of Civil Procedure, passed by the Legislature and approved by the governor in 1848.

The Code of Civil Procedure simplified court procedure by reducing the number of Common Law pleas and proceedings.

Lawrence Friedman, in *A History of American Law,* cited the sixty-second part of the code, which he deemed its "heart: "

The distinction between actions at law and suits in equity, and the forms of all such actions and suits heretofore existing, are abolished; and, there shall be in this state, hereafter, but one form of action, for the enforcement or protection of private rights and the redress or prevention of private wrongs, which shall be denominated a civil action.

This part of the code, in effect, broke down the intricate, technical method of Common Law pleading, thus simplifying New York court procedure.

The Field Code has had immense impact, influencing legal procedure in all but a few states. At first, the code received its widest approval in western states. By 1860 Iowa, Minnesota, Indiana, Ohio, Nebraska, Wisconsin and Kansas had adopted it. In the next four decades the Dakotas, Idaho, Arizona, Montana, the Carolinas, Utah, Colorado, Oklahoma and New Mexico followed suit. In England, the code influenced the English Judicature Acts, significant measures of law reform. In New York the code was amended in 1849, 1851, and 1870. By 1880 it had grown from about four hundred sections to over three thousand and, alas, lost much of its original simplicity.

Field's International Law Code and his Penal Code met with some success, but his Civil Law Code, while being accepted in California, Idaho, and Montana, was repeatedly rejected in New York. On several occasions the code was passed by both houses of the Legislature, only to be vetoed by the governor.

In 1888, six years prior to his death, David Dudley Field was honored with the Presidency of the American Bar Association. This was certainly a small tribute to the chief proponent of American law codification. Field's doggedly stubborn genius left its mark, however. Of this genius it was said:

The world did not love David Dudley Field. He was too strong, too sure, too free of these soft human frailties that after all are the soil for men's affections.

Conservation

THE ROOTS of our state's present concern for its rich environment lie in the nineteenth century. During this time the Legislature enacted some very forward-looking ecology laws.

The story begins in 1872, with the lawmakers' creation of the first state park commission and continues on through 1883, when the Legislature stopped sale of Adirondack forest lands, repossessed through back taxes. In 1885 the Legislature passed its first Environmental Preservation Law, benefiting Niagara Falls. That same year the Legislature created the Adirondack Forest Preserve.

A law of 1892 established the Adirondack Park as a region "forever reserved, maintained and cared for as ground open to the free use of all the people for their health or pleasure, and as forest lands necessary to the preservation of the headwaters of the chief rivers of the state, and a future timber supply." This law was further strengthened by the Constitution of 1894 which halted lumbering in the Park and in the Forest Preserve. There are very few states that can boast of a state park system like New York's.

Constitutions of 19th Century New York

THE FIRST New York Constitution was adopted in 1777, by a convention led by John Jay, the constitution's main author, and Robert Livingston. In 1821, 1846, and 1894, constitutional conventions prepared new documents which were ratified by the voters. The 1867 constitution was rejected by the voters, except for its provision about the judiciary, which was returned to the electorate and eventually accepted.

The Constitution of 1821 contained several notable provisions. The constitution added "freedom of speech and the press, the right of *habeas corpus,* and protection against the seizure of private property for public use without just compensation" to New York's bill of rights. The constitution provided for an extension of male suffrage, reducing the gubernatorial term to two years, a guarantee of one Assembly representative for each of the state's counties, and a revised amendment procedure whereby amendments approved by both houses of two consecutive legislatures could be submitted for voter ratification.

The convention's 126 delegates consisted of sixty-eight farmers, thirty-seven attorneys, nine merchants, seven mechanics and five physicians.

The Constitution of 1846, influenced by the Anti-Rent Movement, did much to eradicate New York's feudal landlord-tenant patterns. Judicially, the state was separated into eight districts, a Court of Appeals was set up, and provision was made for electing judges, for the first time in New York history. In response to public demand, the constitution prevented the Legislature from deficit-spending without voter approval. Guarantees of protection against unreasonable bail, detention of witnesses, and cruel or unusual punishments were added to the state's bill of rights.

The Constitutional Convention of 1894, led by the distinguished lawyers Joseph Choate and Elihu Root, incorporated civil service, education, and forest preservation into its constitution. This constitution set up a definite process for convention delegate selection. Three delegates from each senatorial district and fifteen at-large delegates were to be elected for each succeeding convention. As with its counterparts in 1821 and 1846, the Constitution of 1894 easily received voter approval.

Education

SINCE THE late 1700's the New York Legislature has played an active role in the state's educational system. In 1784 the Legislature founded the University of the State of New York, headed by a Board of Regents, and delegated power to the Regents to set up secondary schools and colleges. Two years later, in the spirit of the nation's Northwest Ordinance, the Legislature directed the state surveyor general to reserve one lot in each developing township for "gospel and schools." A quarter of a million dollars in school aid, spread over five years, was appropriated by the Legislature in 1795, to help primary schools. To receive state aid, counties were required to show good faith by raising one-half of their designated grant. Even though this aid was in token amounts, it constituted one of America's first state programs of school assistance.

In the war year of 1812 the Legislature, led by Jedediah Peck of Otsego County, organized a system of common school districts for each county. School aid was apportioned according to township population. 1814 saw the lawmakers place greater responsibility on local officials, requiring that communities match their state school funding. In 1827, New York became one of the first states to set aside funds for teacher education. The first state normal school was started in Albany in 1844.

In response to reformer agitation the Legislature, in 1874, passed the Compulsory Education Law. While mild by today's standards, this law was a landmark in its time. Under its provisions children from the ages of eight to fourteen were compelled to attend school for at least fourteen weeks per year.

One of the most historic legislative acts was the passage in 1913 of the Regents' Scholarship Law. This law provided financial aid for deserving college students who enrolled in higher educational institutions within the state. Since then, thousands of New York students have received financial aid for their undergraduate and graduate studies.

Labor Legislation

As NEW YORK became more industrialized, it was necessary to legislate some sort of regulation of working conditions. While New York's most significant labor legislation came in the 20th century, we can find evidence of legislative concern for workers in the late 1800's. New York led the nation in promoting a program of comprehensive labor legislation.

Concern over workers' hours crystallized in the latter part of the 19th century. In 1870, a state law placed restrictions on hours of state employees. In 1883, the lawmakers created the Bureau of Labor Statistics which prepared annual reports for the legislature. A child labor law of 1886 banned children under thirteen from factory employment. In that same year, the State Inspection Bureau was formed, with authority to enforce the child labor law and the Compulsory Education Law of 1874. Two years later the Legislature set a twelve-hour maximum working day for street trainmen (employed on elevated railways, commuter lines, or subways) and later strengthened that law by placing a limit on working hours for all railroad employees.

By far the most significant legislation came in the first two decades of the 20th century. A child labor law of 1903 required children to have bona fide working papers, prohibited boys under ten and girls under sixteen from newspaper hawking, and placed the burden of responsibility on employers for children working in violation of the law. Sad to say, the law was poorly enforced.

Voters delegated more labor-controlling power to the Legislature in 1905 by approving a constitutional amendment giving the lawmakers authority to control hours, wages and working conditions for those employed under state-funded contracts. In 1910 the Legislature made its first stab at workmen's compensation. This law failed at its court test, the famous *Ives v. South Buffalo Railway Company* case.

The disastrous Triangle Shirt Company fire in 1911, involving the deaths of scores of women and young girls, spurred the Legislature to create a State Factory Investigating Commission, chaired by Robert F. Wagner and Alfred E. Smith. This commission's work inspired the most significant labor legislation created, to that date, in American history. The commission fathered laws controlling factory sanitation, industrial fire prevention, child labor regulations and, in 1913, a Workmen's Compensation Act that withstood judicial challenge.

The 1913 law mandated employer-purchased compensation insurance for workers in dangerous jobs and, if the employer had four or more laborers in such occupations, he had to buy insurance for all his employees. The law established a Workmen's Compensation Board to settle claims and a Workmen's Compensation Advisory Committee consisting of two employer representatives, two for workers, one for insurance carriers, one for self-insured employers, one for the State Medical Association and one for the New York State Bar Association.

Over thirty labor-related laws were enacted as a result of the Wagner-Smith Commission's work. The commission was lauded by the New York Federation of Labor:

Your legislative commission desires to call the attention of the delegates to the ... unprecedented number of labor laws placed on the statute books of this State. No Legislature in the history of the State Federation surpassed the session of 1913 in the passage of so many or so important remedial measures for wage-earners of our New York State, and we doubt if any state in the Union can now compare with our Empire State in its present code of labor laws.

Social Legislation

THE FIRST major legislative attempts at public welfare came in the relief field. In 1788 a New York law provided that "every city and town shall support and maintain their poor." While facilities created under this law were generally substandard, the law does mark an early effort at public welfare. In 1824, Secretary of State John Yates issued a report on the poor to the Legislature. This was the first major study on the subject. The report brought on passage of a law which established poorhouses in sixteen counties. At these institutions, the poor had to work for their lodging and, as before, the facilities were generally ill-kept.

In the areas of mental health and juvenile justice the Legislature made significant progress in the 19th century. In 1791, the lawmakers appropriated the first public funds to help the emotionally disturbed and in 1821, the first State Mental Hospital was organized in Utica. For its time, the Utica Asylum was a fine institution, headed by the famed Dr. Amariah Brigham. In 1864, urged on by Dorothea Dix, the Legislature investigated the state's asylums. As a result, power was given to the Legislature in 1865 to create state hospitals for the "chronic insane and the insane poor." Mistreatment of the insane in poorhouses was remedied in 1890 by a State Care Act prohibiting such action.

As early as 1825 New York operated "houses of refuge" for juvenile offenders. The greatest 19th century attempt at juvenile rehabilitation, however, came with the 1870 establishment of the Elmira Reformatory. This prison housed young criminals between the ages of sixteen and twenty who had no previous prison records. The Reformatory was established with the principles of vocational rehabilitation and moral instruction in mind. Prisoners were to attend classes and those with superior grades were made eligible for parole. Unfortunately, rehabilitation was later replaced by tight security at Elmira and the institution's original ideals were forgotten. The prison was a model, however, for similar institutions in other states. Juvenile justice progressed further in an 1884 law which gave judges the option of jail or a foster home for offenders under sixteen.

The Legislature made great social progress in the field of public housing. The first tenement house law, a largely ineffectual one, was passed in 1867. Two events spurred the Legislature to major housing reform. Jacob Riis, in 1890, published *How the Other Half Lives,* a damning book about the squalor of New York's tenements. In 1900, Laurence Veiller, a reformer in Riis' mold, arranged a public exhibition that vividly documented the deplorable conditions in New York slums. Riis himself became friends with Theodore Roosevelt, whose concern for reform found few equals.

Out of this case came the Tenement House Act of 1901. This legislation outlawed narrow dumbwaiter shafts, mandated installation of private water facilities in each newly constructed apartment, ordered stringent fire safety laws and instructed landlords to install fire escapes and waterproof basement floors in existing tenements. To supervise the law's application, a State Tenement Commission was formed, with Veiller as its secretary. New housing laws are being created to this very day but all are based on the pioneering work of Riis and Veiller.

A GUIDE TO

Historic Legal Sites
of New York

The Metropolitan Area
Judicial Districts 1, 2, 10 & 11

NEW YORK is one of the world's great trade centers, the head-quarters for scores of international and American businesses. New York leads the United States in the arts, with its great universities, with its citizens representing every nation on earth. New York has set the pace and standards for the legal profession, as well. The first session of the United States Supreme Court took place in New York. Many historic cases involving our commercial law were decided in New York. The first law professorship in the country was established at Columbia University. The state's first judicial system was organized by the Dutch in New Amsterdam. The city courts have rung with legal arguments from the state's most famed attorneys—Hamilton, Burr, Evarts, Tilden, Van Buren. In America, there is nothing like New York.

Following New York, Long Island has the oldest judicial system in the state. In the early Dutch settlements Dutch-Roman Law was enforced by the West India Company. During the period of control by the Netherlands, New England Yankees established colonies on Long Island and were independent enough to refuse to abide by Dutch Law. It was not until the British assumed power that Long Island became part of the New York judicial system.

We open our guide to legal sites with those in New York City and Long Island since it was in those two locations that the state's judicial system began.

MANHATTAN, NEW YORK COUNTY

Legal sites on Manhattan Island are listed geographically, beginning with the Battery, at the island's southern tip, and proceeding northward.

SITE OF THE STADT HUYS *(State House), 71 Pearl Street.*
The Stadt Huys was the city's first city hall and also functioned as a jail and court house. In 1641, the Dutch governor erected the Stadt Herbergh, a tavern in which he received visitors. This building became the Stadt Huys and in its front yard were the stocks and pillory. The site of this early center of government is at the intersection of Pearl Street and Coenties Slip.

SITE OF THE EXCHANGE, *Lower Broad Street, near Water Street*
On February 1, 1790, the first session of the United States Supreme Court was held in a building on this site, shamefully unmarked. Chief Justice John Jay presided over the session, which was attended by many eager onlookers. The New York Legislature, in its early days, also met here. The building, located approximately one block south of historic Fraunces Tavern, was demolished in 1799.

FRAUNCES TAVERN, *54 Pearl Street.*
This tavern was originally begun in 1719 by a wealthy Huguenot, Etienne Delancey. It was sold in 1762 to Samuel Fraunces, of West Indian heritage. For ten days in 1783, it was George Washington's residence. On December 4 of that year Washington made his farewell speech to his officers at Fraunces Tavern. The building was restored in 1907 and paintings of the colonial and revolutionary eras complement the decor.

UNITED STATES CUSTOM HOUSE, *south side of Bowling Green*
This building, carefully recreating French Renaissance architecture, was built between 1902 and 1907. The site it occupies is an extraordinary one, historically speaking. First came Fort Amsterdam, built by the Dutch in 1625. After the British seized New York, the fort became the focal point of the rebellion of Jacob Leisler against what he believed to be a Catholic plot against the King. In 1790, after the fort was razed, Government

House was erected on the spot. New Yorkers were certain their city would be named the capital of the young country and that the new building would serve as either the capitol or the president's home. These hopes soon died. The home was used as an official residence by Governors George Clinton and John Jay, however. It burned to the ground in 1815.

FEDERAL HALL NATIONAL MONUMENT, *Wall Street.*
Built in 1812 for customs purposes, the present building served for years as the United States Sub-Treasury Building. The original building was New York's first City Hall, erected in 1699. In 1735, the Zenger Case was tried in the building and in 1765, the Stamp Act Congress met there, as did the Continental Congress in 1785. The building was remodeled in 1788, under the direction of Pierre L'Enfant. It was renamed Federal Hall and on April 30, 1789, George Washington took the oath of office on the steps leading to the entrance. The building is of classical revival architecture, adorned with Doric columns. A statue of Washington stands in front of the building.

ALEXANDER HAMILTON GRAVE, *Trinity Church Cemetery, Wall Street.*
Alexander Hamilton is buried here. He was the first United States Secretary of the Treasury, leader of the Federalist Party, defender of Harry Croswell, and eminent member of the New York Bar. Trinity Church, an island of rest amid the heart of the city's financial district, is one of the noted architect Richard Upjohn's most famous creations.

NEW YORK COUNTY LAWYERS' ASSOCIATION, *14 Vesey Street.*
The Association's building, constructed in 1930, is the headquarters and meeting place for a number of Manhattan's lawyers. The building, slightly set back from the street, is highlighted by six Corinthian pilasters. The interior is Georgian architecture, with British decor.

THOMAS ADDIS EMMET GRAVE, *St. Mark's-Church-in-the-Bowery, 10th Street and 2nd Avenue.*
Emmet, a noted Irish patriot and a director of the United Irish-

Thomas Addis Emmet

men, was forced to leave Britain in 1802. In 1804 he came to New York and was licensed to practice law by a special act of the Legislature, strongly influenced by Emmet's friend, George Clinton. He soon became a prominent lawyer, particularly because of his defense of Aaron Ogden in *Gibbons v. Ogden,* a defense so eloquent that he earned the respect of Daniel Webster. A monument to Emmet stands in St. Paul's Chapel at Broadway, between Fulton and Vesey Streets.

DONGAN MEMORIAL, *St. Peter's Church, 22 Barclay Street.*
In 1911 the Knights of Columbus placed a tablet on the eastern pillar of this church, commemorating the rule of Thomas Dongan, Governor of New York from 1683 to 1688. The present church was built in 1840; however, the cornerstone of the original church was laid in 1785, making St. Peter's the oldest Catholic church in the city.

NEW YORK CITY HALL, *City Hall Park.*
This building, constructed of Massachusetts marble in Italian Renaissance style, was opened formally in 1811. Illuminated at

The Old County Courthouse

night, it is truly imposing. Throughout its rooms and halls are many portraits of New York historical figures. There is a plaque on the grounds of City Hall Park commemorating the reading of the Declaration of Independence to Washington and his army, on July 9, 1776, on that site.

SITE OF RICHMOND HILL, *corner of Charlton and Varick Streets.* Sadly, nothing marks the site of this once elegant country estate. The manor house was built in 1767 and surrounded by twenty-six acres of Manhattan farmland. John and Abigail Adams once owned the estate and Washington used it as his headquarters in 1776. In 1797 Aaron Burr purchased Richmond Hill but vacated the premises after his duel with Hamilton.

OLD COUNTY COURTHOUSE, *"Boss Tweed's Courthouse," 52 Chambers Street.* This courthouse was approved by the State Legislature in 1858 and was expected to cost little over $150,000. Construction of the building was stopped in 1871. Anti-Tweed officials accused the Tweed machine of bilking the city of $13,416,932. The Tweed politicians admitted to *only* a cost of $8,223,979.89! "Inflated" is a singularly mild adjective to use when describing the

Tweed machine's manipulation of building costs. The boss's men spent $7,500 alone for thermometers and almost $180,000 for three tables and forty chairs. These figures did not take into account Tweed's plans for a courthouse dome, a plan scratched when the scandal broke.

Tweed's courthouse remains today, despite many threats of demolition. It is a monument to the boss's Gilded Age and to his extravagance. There are few buildings left in the city that bring alive that colorful era so well.

NEW YORK COUNTY COURTHOUSE, *Foley Square.*
This building, replacing the Tweed courthouse, was completed in 1912, from a plan by architect Guy Lowell. Highlighted by its pentagonal shape, its beautifully carved pediment and Corinthian columns, the courthouse presents an impressive image. It can now handle only part of the judicial burden of Manhattan.

UNITED STATES DISTRICT COURT, *Southern District of New York, Foley Square.*
Supreme Court Justice Felix Frankfurter once said of this court, "It has a great tradition of eminent judges of the highest standard of judicial administration." Among the great judges of the court were Samuel Betts, the first American judge to become prominent in admiralty law, and Augustus and Learned Hand, two of the most noted men in the nation's judiciary. The Southern District Court was first convened on November 3, 1789, in the Exchange building, several months before the first session of the United States Supreme Court. The present court building, completed in 1936, is a towering structure, with a colonnaded base which complements that of its neighbor, the New York County Courthouse.

The court's dockets reflect this country's history, as chronological as if it were written in text form. The court has dealt with cases involving the Sedition Act of 1789, high seas piracy, draft resistance during the Civil War, prohibition, government scandal, censorship (notably the *Ulysses* and *Lady Chatterley's Lover* cases in the 1930's), espionage, and the first trial under the Smith "anti-communist" act. By virtue of its location in New

York City, much of the business law of this country has been created and defined in this court. Also because of its location, the court is the busiest in the Federal System.

SITES OF WASHINGTON, HANCOCK & TWEED HOMES, *Cherry Street, near Brooklyn Bridge.*
A plaque on the bridge's eastern pier, in Franklin Square, marks the site of 3 Cherry Street, where Washington lived at the time of his inauguration. John Hancock lived at 5 Cherry Street and Boss Tweed was born at Number 24. These homes, long since razed, are now marked only by the imagination.

NEW YORK LAW SCHOOL, *57 Worth Street.*
This Law School was founded in 1890 by a group of law professors from Columbia. Led by Theodore Dwight, Dean of the Columbia Law School, these legal scholars disagreed with the teachings and philosophy of the older school and decided that their best means of expression was through founding a law school of their own. Chief Justice Hughes and Woodrow Wilson have lectured at the school; Robert F. Wagner, Sr., and Associate Justice of the Supreme Court John Marshall Harlan are among its prominent graduates.

BURR HOUSES, *127–131 MacDougal Street.*
These three row-houses, of modest Federal architecture, were built for Aaron Burr, who never lived in any of them. Time and the fact that the buildings became commercial establishments have greatly altered their character.

NEW YORK UNIVERSITY LAW SCHOOL, *Washington Square.*
This leading private university was chartered in 1831 and began its teaching program the following year. The School of Law opened its doors in 1835 and is located on Washington Square, in the heart of New York's Greenwich Village. The present building was built in 1951.

THEODORE ROOSEVELT ASSOCIATION, *28 E. 20th Street.*
Theodore Roosevent was born here in 1858 and lived in the house until 1872. It is now a museum run by the Theodore

Roosevelt Association. Tours give the visitor a sampling of New York life just before the turn of the century.

APPELLATE DIVISION OF THE SUPREME COURT OF NEW YORK, *Madison Avenue and 25th Street.*
This is one of the most ornate courthouses in the United States. Designed by James Brown Lord and completed in 1900, it boasts a sculptured pediment, ornate Corinthian columns, and statues of Wisdom and Force by Frederick Ruckstuhl, Peace by Karl Bitter and Justice by Daniel Chester French. The courtroom was designed by Maitland Armstrong and is graced by Siena marble floors, dark oak furniture, a stained glass dome, and stained glass windows in which are inscribed the names of famous American judges. Murals depicting stages of justice in world history ("Mosaic," "Roman," etc.) lend their majesty to the Main Hall.

CHESTER ARTHUR HOME, *123 Lexington Avenue.*
This 1855 house was once the home of Chester A. Arthur, United States President and a member of the New York Bar. After Garfield's assassination, Arthur was administered the oath of office here on September 19, 1881.

THE ASSOCIATION OF THE BAR OF THE CITY OF NEW YORK, *42 W. 44th Street.*
This classically styled limestone building was finished in 1895 from the plans of Cyrus L.W. Eidlitz. It houses the administration of the City Bar Association, parent organization of the New York State Bar Association.

FORDHAM UNIVERSITY LAW SCHOOL, *140 W. 62nd Street.*
On September 28, 1905, Fordham University, a Roman Catholic university administered by the Jesuits, opened its doors to the first nine candidates to its School of Law. In September of 1961 the Law School moved from the university's Bronx campus to this new campus at Lincoln Center.

FRANKLIN DELANO ROOSEVELT HOME, *49 E. 65th Street.*
Franklin Roosevelt lived in this elegant town house. President,

legislator, and member of the New York Bar, Roosevelt spent many months here recuperating from polio. Mrs. James Roosevelt, the President's mother, lived at 47 E. 65th Street.

COLUMBIA LAW SCHOOL, *Columbia University, 116th Street and Amsterdam Avenue.*

First named King's College, Columbia University was established by Royal Charter in 1754. Many of the state's famous attorneys, including Franklin Roosevelt and Benjamin Cardozo, attended Columbia Law School. The first professorship of law at this distingushed Ivy League university was held by James Kent, the country's first major legal writer. Kent Hall, named after the Chancellor and built in 1910, houses most of the law school.

HAMILTON GRANGE, *287 Convent Avenue.*

This Federal-style country house was built in 1801 and occupied by Alexander Hamilton until his death. The house was moved to its present site from its original location, west of Convent Avenue. John McComb, Jr., one of the architects of the City Hall, designed the Grange. The building is presently closed to the public.

BRONX COUNTY

BRONX COUNTY COURTHOUSE, *851 Grand Concourse, Bronx.*
This courthouse, hearing cases of general jurisdiction, is also known as The Bronx City Building. It was built during the Great Depression. Ornate sculptures dress up its massive facade.

BROOKLYN COUNTY (KINGS COUNTY)

BROOKLYN BAR ASSOCIATION, *123 Remsen Street.*
The Brooklyn Bar Association occupies a four-story townhouse in the historic Brooklyn Heights neighborhood. The Association is an old one, tracing its founding back to 1872. The townhouse itself was built in 1854 and bought by the Association in 1918.

Richmondton, on Staten Island, is a restored colonial village complete with its original courthouse.

RICHMOND COUNTY

RICHMOND COUNTY COURTHOUSE, *Richmondtown, Staten Island.*
The first county seat, Stony Brook, was named in 1683 and its courthouse consisted of two rooms, one as jail. Improvements were made over the years but none was satisfactory and in 1729, the county seat was moved to Cocclestown, now Richmondtown. There have been three county courthouses built at Richmondtown: the first was burned to the ground during the Revolution; the second, a two-story, shingled building, was used until 1839 when the present one replaced it. The handsome Greek Revival building, with four Doric columns, still stands. The county offices were moved to St. George in 1898 and the courthouse could well have been razed had it not been for the efforts of the Richmond Historical District Association, which has restored the town, and now the fine old courthouse, repaired and repainted, is the center of the historical district, a mecca for tourists.

114

QUEENS COUNTY

QUEENS COUNTY BAR ASSOCIATION, *90–35 148th Street, Jamaica.*
Founded in 1876, the same year as the State Association, the
Queens County Bar Association occupies a building completed
in 1959. In 1960 the contemporary structure was cited by the
Queens Borough Chamber of Commerce for its "excellence in
Design and Civic Value."

QUEENS COUNTY COURTHOUSE, *Long Island City.*
The original county courthouse was built in 1666 in Jamaica,
then the equivalent of the shire seat. The building became so
dilapidated that funds were authorized to replace it. However,
the courthouse appears to have been still in use when British
soldiers tore it down for lumber. After the Revolution, sessions
were held in a church until the county seat was moved to North
Hempstead. The county courthouse there was built in 1787. But
the county seat was yet again moved, this time to Long Island
City, where the present county courthouse was built in 1876.
The building is still in use. It is three stories high, brick with
granite trim and cost $276,000, a staggering sum for that day.
Incidentally, it was here that the famous Ruth Snyder case was
tried and officials still have the sewing machine she used while
awaiting trial.

NASSAU COUNTY

NASSAU COUNTY COURTHOUSE, *Mineola.*
This county, once a part of Queens County, was named for
William of Nassau, Prince of Orange, who married Princess
Mary of Britain. They ruled jointly as King William and Queen
Mary. Nassau County was one of the first New York shires to
establish a charter form of government, with a county executive
at the helm. The present courthouse is a massive, four-story
building with the County seal engraved over the courthouse
door.

HOFSTRA UNIVERSITY LAW SCHOOL, *Hofstra University, Hempstead.*

This relatively new law school was established in 1969 with Malachy Mahon as its dean. The present enrollment in the contemporary school is nearly 700.

NASSAU COUNTY BAR ASSOCIATION, *15th and West Streets, Mineola.*
The Bar Association of Nassau County dates back to 1899. The Association's building, finished in 1932, is a unique structure, styled after the Middle Temple of the famed Inns of Court Law School, London. The building has received numerous architectural awards.

SUFFOLK COUNTY

SUFFOLK COUNTY COURTHOUSE, *Riverhead.*
The first British settlements in New York were in Suffolk County. As early as 1725 a courthouse-jail building was constructed in Riverhead to serve the region. A brick courthouse was erected in 1854.

Today's Suffolk County Courthouse is a part of a county building complex. Finished in 1929, the buildings were designed to house the county's executive, legislative and judicial departments. The central structure is a neo-Georgian building, accentuated by six dominating Corinthian columns topped by a pediment.

THEODORE ROOSEVELT HOME, *Sagamore Hill, Cove Neck.*
The home of Theodore Roosevelt, a member of the New York Bar, an assemblyman, a governor and 26th President of the United States. The indomitable Rough Rider is buried nearby at Youngs Memorial Cemetery. The grave borders a bird sanctuary and park, both named for the former president.

The Lower Hudson Valley,

Judicial District 9

This region might very well be called the birthplace of New York government. At Poughkeepsie, Dutchess County, New Yorkers ratified the Federal Constitution, while the first state constitutional convention was convened at Fishkill. The New York congress adopted the Declaration of Independence at a courthouse in White Plains. Westchester County was the home of John Jay, leader and, to a great extent, author of the first New York constitution. James Kent, whose work on the state bench had such an extensive impact on our modern judiciary, was a native of Putnam County. There are several fine nineteenth century courthouses, reminders of the area's rich history.

The Ninth Judicial District centers around the Hudson River. In colonial times and well into the 19th century, the river served as a commercial artery, connecting the region with upstate's farms and New York City's commerce. In early years the river was a watery highway, allowing the Ninth's justices to travel their circuits up and down by boat and, on occasion, to make an Albany journey.

DUTCHESS COUNTY

DUTCHESS COUNTY COURTHOUSE, *Poughkeepsie.*
Many distinguished New York attorneys have practiced in this county: the Livingstons, Jay, Van Buren and Smith Thompson, an Associate Justice of the United States Supreme Court.

Dutchess County was created a shire under the Dongan Act of 1683. Poughkeepsie, the county seat, was made state capital in 1777. Probably the most famous event in this city's history was New York's ratification of the Federal Constitution at the third Dutchess County Courthouse, July 26, 1788. As indicated by the 30-27 vote for ratification, the Federal Constitution met considerable opposition. George Clinton, first governor of New York and chairman of the convention on ratification, vocally opposed the document. The forces of approval, led by Jay, Robert Livingston and Hamilton, prevailed. Hamilton's gifted oratory and Jay's prestige particularly influenced the convention.

The present courthouse is the county's fifth, the first having been erected by the British colonial government in 1717. Constructed in 1902, the courthouse is a three-story red brick building with grey sandstone trim. On the Market Street side of the courthouse there is a bronze tablet, commemorating the 1788 proceedings. The tablet reads:

THE PEOPLE
OF THE
STATE OF NEW YORK
By Their Convention
Assembled in a Former
Court House
Which Stood
On This Ground
RATIFIED
The Constitution
Of The
United States of America
July 26, A.D. 1788

SITE OF OBADIAH BOWNE HOUSE, *Fishkill.*
This historic home was built in 1818 on the site of the razed building where the first state constitutional convention met. There, Samuel Louden printed the first copies of New York's Constitution and the first issues of *Journal of the Legislature.* The building was torn down after the Revolution and the Obadiah Bowne house built in its place. The Bowne House was demolished recently and replaced by the Hillcroft Apartments near the Penn-Central crossing.

FRANKLIN D. ROOSEVELT BIRTHPLACE, *Hyde Park.*
James Roosevelt, FDR's father, purchased the land for this estate in 1866. Franklin was born here in 1882 and lived here off and on throughout his life. The house and adjoining grounds and buildings constitute one of the Hudson Valley's famed 19th century manors. Hyde Park is a National Historic Site

ORANGE COUNTY

ORANGE COUNTY COURTHOUSE, *Goshen.*
This county once took in part of Rockland County, where court

The Orange County Courthouse at Goshen is a fine example of Greek-Revival architecture, popular during the early part of the 19th century.

first convened in Tappantown in 1712. Goshen, present county seat, witnessed its first court session in 1727. Courthouses were built there in 1737 and 1773. In 1842 the new courthouse was constructed. It is of Greek Revival style, rectangular in shape, and topped with a pediment. Six Doric columns front the brick courthouse. "Six over six" paned windows add their simple elegance to the structure. The courthouse's interior is highlighted by fireplaces, Egyptian trim, and a double circular stairway that leads upstairs to the courtroom.

LAWYERS' ROW, *Main Street, Goshen.*
Originally built as shops and private residences, these twenty-one brick townhouses, dating from around 1850, are now primarily occupied by attorneys. Many of the buildings have been restored, giving new life to their primarily Federal and Victorian architecture. The Orange County Historian's office is presently working on placing this historic neighborhood on the National Register.

ORANGE INN, *Main Street, Goshen.*
This tavern, the oldest continuously operating inn of Orange

County, occupies the site of Goshen's 1737 courthouse. Parts of that courthouse's foundation are rumored to have been incorporated into the tavern's base, but positive documentation is lacking.

ORANGE COUNTY COURTHOUSE, *Newburgh.*
This judicial hall was erected in 1842 and is the twin to the Greek Revival Goshen Courthouse. In fact, the same architect designed both buildings. In recent years the Newburgh Courthouse has been allowed to deteriorate. Its neighborhood was one of the city's blighted areas and, sadly, the courthouse suffered from the downgrading. Now, the courthouse has been partially restored and the building, at Liberty and Grand Streets, houses the Supreme Court Library and the County Probation Department.

PUTNAM COUNTY

PUTNAM COUNTY COURTHOUSE, *Carmel.*
This courthouse, one of the state's oldest, was erected in 1812 and is the only courthouse to serve Putnam County. In 1840 the courthouse was graced with a classical portico and a belfry, greatly enhancing the building's charm.

It is interesting to note the price tag on the 1812 structure. Base building costs totaled $3,882.86—roughly what it would cost to paint the building today. The courthouse was originally equipped with chairs for the exorbitant sum of $16!

SITE OF JAMES KENT BIRTHPLACE, *Old Route 22, Brewster.*
James Kent was born near Station 200 on Old Route 22 on July 31, 1763. The house was razed around 1850 and stones from its foundation were used in construction of the Old Southeast Presbyterian Church manse, a white-frame building that stands on the site today. A state historic marker which commemorated Kent's birthplace was stolen in 1959. Local historical groups will re-mark the site.

OLD SOUTHEAST PRESBYTERIAN CHURCH, *Route 22, Brewster.*

*The Putnam County Courthouse at Carmel is one of the oldest in
the state as well as one of the most architecturally graceful.*

James Kent's grandfather, Elisha, was founder of this church.
The present church, built in 1794, replaced the one at which
Kent preached.

ROCKLAND COUNTY

ROCKLAND COUNTY COURTHOUSE, *New City.*
Tappan, one of this county's earliest communities, boasted a
courthouse as early as 1669. The trial and hanging of Major
John André, convicted as a spy in the infamous Arnold affair of
the Revolution, took place in Tappan. Rockland County, created
from the southern part of Orange County, has always had its
county seat in New City. The present courthouse, constructed in
1928, is a large stone structure. Inside is a mural-map, painted
by artist James Monroe Hewlett, depicting the county history.

WESTCHESTER COUNTY

OLD WESTCHESTER COUNTY COURTHOUSE, *Bedford.*
This county has long enjoyed representative government. Un-

der Stuyvesant, the area was given Schepens' Court privileges. In 1665 two Westchester men attended Governor Nicoll's convention concerning the Duke's Laws and in 1683 Westchester sent four representatives to the Dongan Assembly.

This county courthouse, built in the period between 1786 and 1790, has a unique gambrel roof, making it the sole New York courthouse of that 18th century style to endure to the present day. In early American history such attorneys as Aaron Burr and Robert Troup practiced law in the Bedford Courthouse. John Jay's son, William, served on the bench here for several years. The courthouse was used by Westchester County until 1870 when it was relinquished to Bedford township control. The Bedford Historical Society has preserved this courthouse as a landmark.

WESTCHESTER COUNTY COURTHOUSE, *White Plains.*
In 176 White Plains, along with Bedford, was made a "shire seat" for Westchester County. As early as 1759 the British had constructed a courthouse in White Plains. It was at this courthouse that the fourth Provincial Congress adopted the Declaration of Independence. It was read to the public from the courthouse steps two days afterward.

The present courthouse, a massive structure with a Greek Revival front, was built to accommodate the growing needs of suburban Westchester County.

SITE OF DECLARATION OF INDEPENDENCE ADOPTION, *Mitchell Place and South Broadway, White Plains.*
A United States Air Force armory now stands on the site of the old courthouse where the Provincial Congress adopted the Declaration of Independence.

GRAVE OF JOHN JAY, *Palmer Estate, Rye.*
John Jay is buried here on a private estate. A truly distinguished member of the New York Bar, Jay was the first Chief Justice of the United States Supreme Court and was largely responsible for the drafting of New York's first constitution. The estate was formerly owned by Jay's brother, Peter.

JOHN JAY HOMESTEAD, *Katonah.*
In addition to the accolades cited above, Jay was President of the Continental Congress and author of several of *The Federalist Papers,* minister to Spain and American negotiator for the Treaty of Paris and the Jay Treaty.

The Jay Homestead, one of the Hudson Valley's fine estates, is built on land purchased in 1703 from the Indian Chief Katonah by Jay's grandfather, Jacobus Van Cortlandt. In 1787 Jay built a house on the site and it was enlarged in 1799 to elegant proportions. Jay retired to the mansion in his old age.

Today's Jay Homestead, a New York State Historic Site, is administered by the Taconic State Park and Recreation Commission. The restored home, containing relics of the family from Jay's era through the 1940's, is open to the public.

The Capital and the Catskills
Judicial District 3

The contrasting elements of New York's legal history are no better typified than in the third judicial district. The highest judicial body of New York, the State Court of Appeals, sits in Albany while in the remoter mountain townships of Greene County, local justices of the peace convene their evening traffic courts. Not only did James Kent practice in this district but the colorful court cases involving the Indian-clad anti-renters of the 1840's took place here, as well. In the town of Hudson in Columbia Country, Harry Croswell printed a controversial edition of his newspaper, *The Wasp,* an event that proved to be the catalyst for revision of New York's libel laws. And in the Village of Berlin in Rensselaer County, Henry Green poisoned his bride Mary Wyatt, resulting in the trial that inspired the folk ballad.

ALBANY COUNTY

NEW YORK STATE BAR ASSOCIATION HEADQUARTERS, *Albany.*
Known as the New York State Bar Center, this building is a

Association of the Bar of the State of New York.

unique legal site. The structure is a synthesis of three Albany townhouses plus a modern addition. The architectural firm of James Stewart Polshek and Associates worked with the Association on the building's design. In 1968 it won the Progressive Architecture Design Award. Ada Louise Huxtable of *The New York Times* praised the structure as "a sophisticated triumph in that most delicate, complex and poorly understood art of the environment: urban design."

The New York State Bar Center contains facilities for conferences, offices for the Association, a "Great Hall" lounge, and the Hinman Law Library. A series of colorful banners, designed by artist Norman Laliberte, brings additional life to the center. One series of banners depicts the evolution of the Great Seal of New York, from New Netherland of 1614 to the present day. Another series gives the artist's impression of the evolution of law in recorded history, beginning with ancient Egypt and ending with English Common Law. Laliberte has tied the series together with the quote, "The due administration of justice is the firmest pillar of good government." The words were those of George Washington, nominating Edmund Randolph of Virginia to the position of first Attorney General of the nation.

124

Court of Appeals building in Albany

NEW YORK STATE COURT OF APPEALS BUILDING, *Albany.*
The Court of Appeals is New York's highest court. Erected between 1835-1842, the building is of white marble, taken from the Sing Sing quarries of the Hudson Valley. Henry Rector, the building's architect, gave the court a Greek Revival flavor, popular in 19th century New York. Six Ionic columns add nobility to the building. A central rotunda, of classical decor, is lit from a domed skylight.

The Appellate Courtroom, planned by H. H. Richardson in 1881, is noteworthy for its Byzantine-styled fireplace, accentuated by Mexican onyx, and for the many fine portraits of judges that adorn its walls.

The Court of Appeals Building is located off Academy Park in downtown Albany, next to the Albany County Courthouse and directly across the street from the New York State Bar Center.

ALBANY COUNTY COURTHOUSE, *Albany.*
The city of Albany is one of the nation's oldest cities and was the site for the abortive national union congress of 1754. Albany has always been the county seat and has been the state capital since 1797. Many prominent New York attorneys, including Aaron Burr and Martin Van Buren, practiced law in Albany.

Today's Albany County Courthouse was built in 1914. It is a

neo-classic, granite-limestone structure, with majestic Ionic columns fronting the street, above the ground floor. A vast open space, illuminated by sky light, adds pleasant airiness to the interior.

NEW YORK STATE CAPITOL, *Albany.*

This landmark took over thirty years to complete. The capitol building is an eruption of architectural ornateness. Its red tile roof, ornamental carvings, balustrades, east-side exterior staircase, marble interior columns, arched windows, and dignified interior staircases all contribute to its architectural diversity. In the capitol one can view Gothic, Romanesque, Greek Revival and French-style architecture, making the building unique among government centers. Guided tours of the capitol, including the Legislature's chambers, are conducted frequently. The building is a "must" stop for those interested in New York State government and history.

SITE OF THE STADT HUYS, *the Plaza, at the foot of State Street.*

The Stadt Huys, a Dutch courthouse, was the site of the first Colonial Congress in 1754. The building served as a city hall and as the state capitol. Vacated by the government in 1808, it was a private residence until it was destroyed by fire in 1836. A plaque, situated in the park in Plaza circle, commemorates the building's site.

ALBANY LAW SCHOOL, *Albany.*

This law school, founded in 1851, was an offshoot of the University of Albany. Among its renowned alumni was President William McKinley, class of 1867. The law school merged with Union College, Schenectady, to form Union University in 1873. The present building, dating back to 1928, is an academic, Tudor-Gothic structure.

BERNE LUTHERAN CHURCH, *Berne.*

In 1845 this plain, brick, early American church was the site of the first New York anti-rent convention. Approximately two hundred delegates, representing tenants of New York's vast estates, met here to discuss their common grievances. The follow-

The New York State Capitol

ing year the state adopted laws that resolved much of the anti-rent issue.

Berne was the birthplace of Joseph P. Bradley, an Associate Justice of the United States Supreme Court. Bradley, as a boy, peddled charcoal in the streets of Albany to help support his family. He left New York at an early age and moved to New Jersey where he attended Rutgers. He is most famous for his deciding vote in the Electoral College which gave the presidency to Rutherford B. Hayes, rather than to Samuel Tilden who had won more popular votes. The Bradley home is located on Route 2, south of East Berne. It is a wood-frame home, dating to the early 1800's.

CHESTER A. ARTHUR GRAVE, *Albany Rural Cemetery, Watervliet.*
Chester A. Arthur is buried in this cemetery. He was a member of the New York Bar, graduate of Union College, and became twenty-first President of the United States when Garfield was assassinated. He was a strong supporter of Civil Service reform and a foe of political favors.

127

Chester A. Arthur

COLUMBIA COUNTY COURTHOUSE, *Hudson.*

The courthouse at Claverack, Columbia County's first seat, was the scene of Harry Croswell's indictment. In 1805 the county seat was moved to Hudson, then an important east coast whaling town despite the fact that its fleet had to journey over one hundred miles to reach the ocean. The first formal Hudson courthouse was constructed in 1835. Samuel Tilden and Martin Van Buren, among others, pleaded cases in this court's chamber. Today's courthouse, a domed classical building, was erected in 1907.

OLD COLUMBIA COUNTY COURTHOUSE, *Claverack.*

This 18th century structure stands at the intersection of Route 238 and Old Lane Road. A plaque on the building commemorates, erroneously, Alexander Hamilton's involvement in the Harry Croswell trial in 1803 at Claverack. Hamilton did not formally involve himself in the case until the 1804 session of the Supreme Court at Albany. The courthouse, built in 1788, is still standing and is now a private residence.

*Martin Van Buren, eight President of the United States was born
and raised in New York. His son was the famed lawyer, John Van Buren.*

GRAVE OF MARTIN VAN BUREN, *Kinderhook.*

Martin Van Buren, eighth President of the United States, Governor of New York, United States Senator, and a member of the New York Bar, is buried in the Kinderhook Village Cemetery. One observer portrayed the noted attorney as:

> . . . a bright blond (with) a snuf colored broadcloth coat with velvet collar; cravat orange with modest lace tips; vest of pearl hue; trousers of white duck; silk hose corresponding with vest; shoes morocco, gloves yellow kid and long furred Beaver hat with broad brim of Quaker color.

As far as dress was concerned, Van Buren was certainly a colorful lawyer.

LINDENWALD, *near Kinderhook.*

This was the home of Martin Van Buren. Judge William Peter Van Ness, Van Buren's legal mentor, built the house in 1797. Van Buren lived here from 1840 until his death in 1862. Soon after moving in, he commissioned architect Richard Upjohn, designer of New York's Trinity Church, to expand and renew the home.

Greene County Courthouse

CLERMONT, THE LIVINGSTON FAMILY ESTATE, *Red Hook, off Route 9, Columbia County.*
Clermont, home of the Livingstons, ranks as one of the fine patrician dwellings of the Hudson Valley. The original mansion was built in 1730 by Robert of Clermont, father of Robert R. Livingston, Chancellor of New York. The home burned in 1777 and was rebuilt by 1780. Several 19th century additions and some 20th century alterations have slightly modified the appearance of this fine Georgian home. The house, maintained by the Taconic State Park and Recreation Commission, is open from Memorial Day through October. The estate grounds are always open to the public.

GREENE COUNTY

GREENE COUNTY COURTHOUSE, *Catskill.*
Designed by architect William G. Beardsley and erected in 1909, the Greene County Courthouse is a revered landmark of Catskill. The county's judicial sessions were held in a school until 1812 when a wooden courthouse was built, which later burned. The present courthouse is highlighted by a pediment featuring

sculptures of judicial figures of the world. Among those featured are Pompilius, author of the first Roman laws; Justinian I; Papinian, considered by many to be the greatest Roman jurist; Solomon; Moses; and Justice, itself.

Greene County has a long legal history, from Harry Croswell who was involved with the *Catskill Packet,* an early village paper, to "Legs" Diamond, famed 30's racketeer, who was tried in the Catskill courthouse.

OLD GREENE COUNTY COURTHOUSE, *the Masonic Temple, Franklin and Bridge Streets, Catskill.*
The building, originally a courthouse, was erected in 1819 and sessions were held there until 1910. Its bell, now gone, was used to summon people to Sunday services. Besides the Masonic Temple, the building also is the office of the county treasurer.

ABRAHAM VAN VECHTEN HOUSE, *Snake Road, Catskill.*
Abraham Van Vechten lived in this home which was built in 1690. Called "Father of the Bar in New York State," Van Vechten (1752-1837) was an Albany attorney, noted for legal expertise. Among his friends were Hamilton, Jay, Burr, Livingston and Kent. Webster, Clay, Calhoun, Marshall and Seward visited Van Vechten here in his later years to seek advice and pay their respects. In one room James Kent is rumored to have written part of his *Commentaries on American Law.*

At the age of thirty-three, Van Vechten was sworn in as an attorney. His name was the first to appear on New York's list of lawyers and counselors.

SITE OF LYMAN TREMAIN BIRTHPLACE, *Oak Hill.*
Tremain, a member of the Greene County and State Bars, worked with Samuel Tilden in the prosecution of the Tweed Ring. He was born in a house east of the Lutheran Church on County Route 81. Nothing commemorates the site.

RENSSELAER COUNTY

RENSSELAER COUNTY COURTHOUSE, *Troy.*
The first courthouse for Rensselaer County, erected in 1828,

was an epitome of Greek Revival architecture. The courthouse, now gone, was a replica in part of the Temple of Theseus in Athens. Sing Sing marble was the courthouse stone. Today's courthouse, built in 1898, has a Greek Revival front but, beyond that point, bears little resemblance to its classical gem of a predecessor.

MARTIN I. TOWNSEND HOME, *165 2nd Street, Troy.*
Townsend (1810-1903) was often called the "Grand Old Man of the Troy Bar." In addition to his local accomplishments, he helped organize the Free Soil Party in 1848, was a delegate to the Constitutional Convention of 1867 and, as chairman of the New York delegation, had the honor of nominating Grant at the Republican Convention in 1872. Townsend was also one of the first New York attorneys to use insanity as a defense plea in a murder trial. Townsend lived in this home during the mid-nineteenth century.

SAMUEL TILDEN GRAVE, *New Lebanon Cemetery, New Lebanon.*
Samuel Jones Tilden was one of the most prominent lawyers in New York history. Tilden was a member of the Legislature, a governor, an unsuccessful candidate for president in 1876, a leader in the fight against political corruption, and a prime mover in the organization of the New York City and New York State Bar Associations.

SCHOHARIE COUNTY

SCHOHARIE COUNTY COURTHOUSE, *Schoharie.*
The present courthouse, built in 1870 in Victorian style of blue limestone, is the last in a series of the county's judicial buildings. The county's first court met in a wagon house; a later court used the upstairs of a Schoharie village store. County courthouses built in 1800 and 1845 were destroyed by fires; the village became a blazing inferno when the 1845 structure was burned. Today's courthouse once was also the county sheriff's office, the surrogate's office and the office of county clerk, but recent expansion of county facilities resulted in these offices being moved

and the building being used solely as a courthouse.

Several years ago, many county leaders were behind a movement to demolish the old courthouse and replace it with a modern building. Fortunately, the New York State Bar Association's Committee for the Preservation of Historic Courthouses was able to help convince the county board of supervisors to preserve the structure.

SULLIVAN COUNTY

SULLIVAN COUNTY COURTHOUSE, *Monticello.*
The county's first courthouse, built in 1811, ended the practice of holding court in private homes. Today's courthouse, dating back to 1910, is a Greek Revival, domed structure with an elaborately carved pediment. Four Ionic columns grace the building's front.

The situation in this county, before a courthouse was realized, was similar to that in many of our state's counties. Not only were private homes utilized, but taverns also served as courts. Generally speaking, the buildings with the largest rooms were chosen as makeshift courthouses. In early Monticello history, the tavern owned by Curtis Lindley served as a courtroom, making one wonder about the sober objectivity of the justice administered there.

ULSTER COUNTY

ULSTER COUNTY COURTHOUSE, *Kingston.*
The present courthouse, built in 1818, occupies one of the most historic sites in New York. The "Convention of the Representatives of the State of New York" wrote the state's first constitution and adopted that document on April 20, 1777 in a courthouse built on this site. The constitution was publicly read by the convention's secretary, standing on a barrel in front of the old courthouse, two days later. George Clinton, first Governor of New York, took his oath of office in that same Kingston courthouse on July 30, 1777. Ulster County's sheriff heralded the event with a public announcement from the courthouse steps.

Also, at Kingston, New York's first civil court session was held.

The present county courthouse is a two-story, colonial building, highlighted by an octagonal tower and neatly paned windows.

NEW YORK STATE SENATE HOUSE, *Kingston.*
In this one-story, rock-cut limestone structure the New York State Legislature met for its first session from September 10 to October 7, 1777. On September 9 of the same year John Jay inaugurated the first state court in the Senate House. The "house" was built by Wessel Ten Broeck in 1676. It contained only one room, the other rooms added in the 18th century. Fortunately it suffered little damage when the British troops burned Kingston in October of 1777. New York State acquired the Senate House in 1887 as a landmark. Adjoining the former legislature is a museum of colonial and Hudson Valley history.

SITE OF ANDREW OLIVER HOUSE, *Route 209, Marbletown.*
Next to the Marbletown Cemetery is a two-story, Federal stone house that stands on the site of the Andrew Oliver Home. The New York Legislature met for about one month in the Oliver home after the British burned Kingston.

VAN DEUSEN HOUSE, *Main Street, Hurley.*
This Dutch architectural gem, now privately owned, was built in 1723 and served as New York's capitol from November 18 to December 17, 1777.

Mountains of the Adirondacks

Judicial District 4

The Adirondacks provide a grand backdrop for the legal history of the area. Here, in the Fourth Judicial District, John Brown's body lay in state in the Essex County Courthouse. Here, at Elizabethtown, is the restored 19th century law office of Judge Augustus Hand. Here, in Warren County at Lake George Village, a fine 19th century courthouse was saved from demolition through community and Bar Association efforts. And here, at

Clinton County Courthouse

Johnstown, stands the state's only courthouse still in use that dates back to the American Revolution.

CLINTON COUNTY

THE OLD CLINTON COUNTY COURTHOUSE, *Plattsburgh.*
This unusual Victorian courthouse was built in 1890 and functioned as the county courthouse until 1976. It represents a stage in American architecture when experimentation in design was popular. The courthouse is one of several in Clinton County history. Court records in Plattsburgh date back to 1788 when a wood building functioned as a courthouse. During the War of 1812 the British attacked Plattsburgh and American cannon, while firing at the foe, bombarded and destroyed the courthouse.

SITE OF REUBEN WALWORTH HOUSE, *40 Court Street, Plattsburgh.*
Reuben Walworth, a Plattsburgh native, lived in a house once standing on this site. Walworth was the last Chancellor of New York, the first president of Albany Law School, and was called by one observer "the greatest artisan of our equity laws." The

first house on this site was destroyed by fire in 1812 and rebuilt in 1813. The house was razed in 1976 to make room for a parking lot, accommodating the Clinton County Government Center.

ESSEX COUNTY

ESSEX COUNTY COURTHOUSE, *Elizabethtown.*
John Brown's body lay in state in this courthouse after he was hanged for the Harper's Ferry insurrection. Brown is buried in North Elba, where he farmed from 1849 to 1854. The county courthouse, first located in Essex, replaced court sessions that had been held in a blockhouse. The present courthouse took twenty years to build and was completed in 1843. It is a plain-windowed building, of simple Greek Revival style.

THE HAND HOUSE & LAW OFFICE, *Elizabethtown.*
These buildings, maintained in period style, represent three generations of the Hand family. Judge Augustus C. Hand built the law office in 1839 and the house in 1849. Augustus' legal career encompassed positions as surrogate, Congressman, State Senator, and Judge of the Court of Appeals. From 1839 until 1917 the Hands used the office for law practice. Augustus' brother, Samuel, was one of the founders of the New York State Bar Association. Samuel's son, Learned Hand, was Judge of the United States Court of Appeals, New York City, and distinguished himself as one of the most respected judges ever to occupy that bench.

The law office today has on exhibit numerous appurtenances of the 19th century lawyer and a law library, once considered to be one of the state's finest.

FULTON COUNTY

FULTON COUNTY COURTHOUSE, *Johnstown.*

I am now carrying on a handsome building for a Court House, towards which I shall contribute £ 500. —Sir William Johnson,

136

May 21, 1772

And built it was. Today it remains the only colonial courthouse still in use in New York. The courthouse is indeed a gem, its courtroom a church-like judicial hall. It has seen America develop from thirteen colonies to independence and deserves the title, "New York's Bicentennial Courthouse." James Kent, among others, tried cases at the Fulton County Court's bar. One of Kent's cases tried at Fulton involved Aaron Burr as defense counsel.

The courthouse first served colonial Tryon County, renamed Montgomery County in 1784. When Fulton County was created by legislative act in 1838 the courthouse became its official hall of justice.

This courthouse is beautifully maintained. On July 24, 1972, it was honored by being placed on the National Register of Historic Places.

FRANKLIN COUNTY

FRANKLIN COUNTY COURTHOUSE, *Malone.*
This north country community, headquarters for the ill-fated 1866 Fenian attempt to seize Canada, has always been county seat. One of its first courthouses was a combination of court, jail *and* church. Today's courthouse was constructed in 1930.

WILLIAM A. WHEELER HOME, *Elm Street, Malone.*
Wheeler, probably the most distinguished member of the bar in Franklin County history, was district attorney in 1847 and Vice-President under Rutherford B. Hayes, 1877-1881. His home has undergone extensive change and presently is the Malone Elks Club.

HAMILTON COUNTY

HAMILTON COUNTY COURTHOUSE, *Lake Pleasant.*
This county, New York's least populous, is the only New York shire entirely within the bounds of the Adirondack Forest Preserve. In 1840, Lake Pleasant was made county seat and court sessions were held in a small wooden house. The present court-

house, fronted with classical columns, was completed in 1929.

MONTGOMERY COUNTY

FIRST MONTGOMERY COUNTY COURTHOUSE, *Fonda.*
Court sessions were held in this county landmark in July of 1837, the year the building was completed. In 1892, court functions were transferred to another location, but the county maintained the old building and used it for county offices. It remains in use today. However, renovations in 1966 greatly altered its exterior.

A glistening silver dome and Ionic columns dramatically accentuate the building and dominate the town of Fonda.

James Fenimore Cooper, extremely sensitive to criticism, sued a number of critics for libel. Several of his cases were tried in this courthouse. In 1841, an observer at one of the trials described Cooper as:

... presenting a grand appearance as he stood before the court, six feet high and finely proportioned, with a massive head and cultivated face, and his address to the jury showed that he had fine power of oratory.

ST. LAWRENCE COUNTY

ST. LAWRENCE COUNTY COURTHOUSE, *Canton.*
The boundaries of St. Lawrence County, the largest county in New York, were established in 1802. A makeshift court functioned in Oswegatchie Fort, near Ogdensburg. The first courthouse was built in 1803, with the help of masons brought in from Troy.

In 1828 Canton, a more centrally located community, was designated county seat. Today's courthouse was built in 1895. The building is constructed of Canton stone (a variety of marble) with Potsdam sandstone trim. It is an imposing Romanesque structure, complete with ornamental doorways and bell tower. A fire destroyed much of the courthouse in 1925, but the county chose to rebuild it in the 1895 style.

HOUSE OF SILAS WRIGHT, *3¹/₂ East Main Street, Canton.*
This home now houses the St. Lawrence County Historical Association. Wright's law office, within the building, is being restored. Wright was a county surrogate, a state senator, a Congressman, elected United States Senator in 1833, and Governor of New York during the anti-rent crisis.

HOUSE OF PRESTON KING, *602 State Street, Ogdensburg.*
King, a firebrand of the bar, ran an Ogdensburg paper, was a state assemblyman, a Congressman, and a United States Senator. An active supporter of Mackenzie's rebellion in Canada, King also became known for his abolitionist views and earned the dubious title, "Father of the Civil War." His home, now a private residence, is well-preserved.

SARATOGA COUNTY

SARATOGA COUNTY COURTHOUSE, *Ballston Spa.*
A modern county office complex in the Spa serves as courthouse. Built in 1973, the complex replaced an 1889 structure. The county's second courthouse, finished in 1817, was the scene of yet another James Fenimore Cooper libel suit against Horace Greeley.

One colorful saga concerning certain peculiarities of Saratoga County's 19th century courthouse reads:

For several years there has been a chronic charge that the constables sworn to attend juries in their deliberations were 'leaky vessels'; because the secret of how the jury stood on different ballots, if they remained out an unusual length of time, was sure to be known to the public. But the charge was illfounded. The courthouse itself is the telltale. Last spring, when the jury in the Dr. T. E. Allen matter went to their room, the author was engaged in the law library room adjoining. Soon voices were heard through the stovepipe hole in the partition wall, and the result of that trial was known to those in the library twenty two hours before it was officially announced.

SITE OF THE AMERICAN BAR ASSOCIATION FOUNDING, *City Hall, Broadway, Saratoga Springs.*
The American Bar Association was founded at Saratoga's City Hall in 1878.

WALWORTH ROOMS, *the Casino Museum, Broad Street, Saratoga.*
Reuben Walworth was last Chancellor of New York. His furniture, possessions and private papers are now part of this museum. Walworth lived in Saratoga during his tenure as Chancellor and was visited there by such noted lawyers as Webster, Seward, and Fillmore.

BATCHELLOR HOUSE, *20 Circular Street, Saratoga.*
George S. Batchellor rose to prominence as Ambassador to Portugal, as American delegate to the International Court at Cairo from 1897 to 1908, and as Assistant Secretary of the Treasury under Benjamin Harrison. His home, of oriental design, is now a private residence.

SCHENECTADY COUNTY

SCHENECTADY COUNTY COURTHOUSE, *Schenectady.*
This city was settled in 1661 and is one of New York's oldest communities. After the Revolution, the county courts convened in city hall and in Union College's first building, West College. Today's edifice, completed in 1911, is a striking four-story building. Eight magnificent Corinthian columns add dignity to the building's façade.

WARREN COUNTY

OLD WARREN COUNTY COURTHOUSE, *Lake George Village.*
This building, dating back to 1845, now houses the Lake George Institute of History, Art and Science. The courthouse, a stately red-brick towered building, was erected in two installments. In 1845 the main stone-brick courtroom was constructed; in 1879 the impressive tower section was added.

After the building of the Warren County Municipal Center in

1963, it was feared that the old courthouse might be razed or fall into disrepair. The Lake George Historical Association recruited support from the Committee for Historic Courthouses of the New York State Bar Association, from the New York State Historical Association, and from Stewart Udall, then Secretary of the Interior. Eventually the Lake George Historical Association established funding for building restoration.

HOME OF CHARLES EVANS HUGHES, *4 Center Street, Glens Falls.*
This house was the birthplace of Charles Evans Hughes. It is marked by a tablet placed there by the D.A.R. in the summer of 1976. Hughes, a giant of the New York Bar, achieved greatness in many fields of law, ending his phenomenal career as Chief Justice of the United States Supreme Court.

WASHINGTON COUNTY

WASHINGTON COUNTY COURTHOUSES, *Hudson Falls and Salem.*
Washington is one of the state's half-shired counties. The Hudson Falls (once called Sandy Hill) Courthouse was constructed in 1873. It is a white, cut-stone building, complete with mansard roof and has been, since its erection, a vital part of the community. Before the courthouse was built, court met "all over the place." At a session of 1796, at "Sandy Hill," an innkeeper, on whose premises court was being held, "invaded the courtroom and ordered the judges out, telling them that he needed the room for dinner."

The Salem Courthouse, built in 1871, serves the county to this day. It is smaller than its Hudson Falls counterpart and handles less of the county business. The courthouse is an unassuming building, blending in well with the fine residences on Salem's Main Street.

SITE OF HOUSE OF JUDGE WILLIAM E. DUER, *Town Road, east of Fort Miller.*
Duer, a prominent member of the early county bar, was county judge and gained fame as Assistant Secretary of the Treasury under Alexander Hamilton. Duer was a Revolutionary war hero

and also a land speculator, which finally caused his financial downfall. A plaque commemorates the site of his home.

From the Mohawk to Ontario, Central New York, Judicial District 5

Each of New York's judicial districts has its distinctive legal history. The Fifth District witnessed the historic trial of Alexander McLeod, which nearly caused a war between America and Great Britain. At the Herkimer County Courthouse Chester Gillette was convicted of murdering Grace Brown, the case that inspired Theodore Dreiser to write *An American Tragedy.* The Fifth District is the proud home of two of Horatio Nelson White's architectural masterpieces: Jefferson and Oswego Counties boast courthouses designed by this 19th century architect.

HERKIMER COUNTY

HERKIMER COUNTY COURTHOUSE, *Herkimer.*
This courthouse, built in 1873, remains a landmark in Herkimer's historic district. The courthouse was the scene of the famous Gillette murder trial (1906) and also witnessed the highly publicized Roxana Druse murder trial of the late 19th century, which resulted in Mrs. Druse's execution. Carved door panels grace the entrance of this towered building designed by Horatio Nelson White.

JEFFERSON COUNTY

JEFFERSON COUNTY COURTHOUSE, *Watertown.*
Horatio Nelson White also designed this courthouse. Its Norman tower and Romanesque windows are typical of White's style. The courthouse was built in 1862 and was one of the last designed by the architect.

Jefferson County is as sparsely populated today as it has been throughout its history. In the past, when there were lulls in court

Herkimer County Courthouse

sessions, judges and lawyers used to stage mock trials to occupy their time.

SITE OF ROBERT LANSING HOUSE, *Clinton Street, Watertown.*
Lansing, a prominent member of the Jefferson County bar, was Secretary of State under Woodrow Wilson. The site of his home, on Clinton Street, is now occupied by a Medical Arts Center. Lansing also maintained a cottage on Lake Ontario and was an active yachtsman, often sailing with members of the Dulles family who had a cottage on the Canadian side of the lake.

LEWIS COUNTY

LEWIS COUNTY COURTHOUSE, *Lowville.*
The first courthouse here was built in Martinsburg, under the direction of General Walter Martin, an early county leader. Prior to that, courts were held in individual homes and in the Lowville Academy. In 1864, in response to public agitation, the county seat was shifted to Lowville.

The Lowville Courthouse, constructed in 1855 and used as a

143

town hall until 1864, was of Greek Revival style, adorned with an impressive Ionic portico. The courthouse was rebuilt in 1919, maintaining its colonnaded front, while modernizing much of the interior.

OLD LEWIS COUNTY COURTHOUSE, *Martinsburg.*
This old courthouse, which stands on Martinsburg's main street (Route 26), was built in 1812. When the county seat was shifted to Lowville in 1864, the courthouse was bought and is now in private hands.

ONEIDA COUNTY

ONEIDA COUNTY COURTHOUSES, *Rome and Utica.*
The Rome Courthouse was built in 1851, replacing an 1848 structure destroyed by fire, and is in use to this day. It is a fine Greek Revival building, recently renovated under the historic redevelopment program in Rome. Early court sessions in Rome were held in Fort Stanwix, now a National Historic Monument.

Early Utica courts were convened in the Utica Free Academy and in the middle of the 19th century the city finally built a courthouse. The present building, once called Oneida County's "million dollar courthouse," is a massive structure with Greek Revival features. A county office building now adjoins the courthouse property.

OLD ONEIDA COUNTY COURTHOUSE, *Whitesboro.*
This courthouse, built in 1807, was made the Whitesboro town hall around 1860 and remains so to this day. Located on the village green, the courthouse was constructed on land donated by Judge Hugh White, the community's founder. After the county abandoned the building, title shifted back to the White family, who transferred the property to the town.

ROSCOE CONKLING HOUSE, *3 Rutger Park, Utica.*
Conkling, mayor of Utica in 1858, was a Congressman, Senator and leader of the state Republican Party. He purchased this 1830 home in 1867. The home is in Utica's Rutger Park, a group

of stately 19th century urban dwellings. Among the guests received by Conkling at his home was Ulysses S. Grant. The house, with some classical features, was designed by Philip Hooker.

TOWER HOMESTEAD & LAW OFFICE, *Main Street, Waterville.*
This palatial home was built by Reuben Tower in 1815. Reuben's son, Charlemagne, remodeled the home and practiced law in the small, brick office which still stands on the home's front lawn. Tower was a 19th century industrialist, making his fortune in Pennsylvania coal and Minnesota iron.

ONONDAGA COUNTY

OLD ONONDAGA COUNTY COURTHOUSE, *Syracuse.*
This courthouse, built in 1857, is being reconstructed on a new site. The building, made of Onondaga limestone from plans drawn by Horatio Nelson White, replaced an earlier structure that burned in 1856.

ONONDAGA COUNTY COURTHOUSE, *Syracuse.*
Erected in 1907, the present columned structure brightens the Syracuse nights with its floodlights. The courthouse interior includes marble pillars, ornate ceilings and murals depicting scenes from Central New York history (such as "The Discovery of Salt by Père LeMoyne"). The courthouse, Onondaga County's fourth, replaced the White courthouse mentioned above. The first county courthouse was completed at Onondaga Hill in 1810; earlier courts convened at Levanna and Ovid, both now located outside the county. The county seat was permanently moved to Syracuse in 1829.

SITE OF FIRST ONONDAGA COUNTY COURTHOUSE, *Onondaga Hill Town Hall, Route 5, west of Syracuse.*
The Town Hall building, once a schoolhouse, occupies the site where, in 1810, Onondaga County's first courthouse was completed. The courthouse, authorized by the legislature in 1801, was abandoned when the county seat was shifted to Syracuse in 1829.

SYRACUSE UNIVERSITY LAW SCHOOL, *E. I. White Hall, Syracuse University.*
This leading upstate university was chartered in 1870 under an original sponsorship of the Methodist Church. The now non-denominational university's College of Law was established in 1895. The present law building, a contemporary structure, borders Archbold Stadium.

POMPEY VILLAGE, *Route 20.*
Between 1795 and 1830, this small community, located east of the junction of Interstate 81 and U.S. 20, was the birthplace of thirteen members of the state legislature, one United States Senator, two New York governors, the mayors of five cities, and three State Supreme Court justices.

OSWEGO COUNTY

OSWEGO COUNTY COURTHOUSE, *Pulaski.*
Situated on the Pulaski village green, the Oswego County Courthouse is a charming, Greek Revival structure, completed in 1822. The building blends well with the small upstate town atmosphere that surrounds the Pulaski green. The courthouse's entablature and beautifully created portico add to its grace.

OSWEGO COUNTY COURTHOUSE, *Oswego.*
This courthouse, finished in 1860, was modeled after a Horatio Nelson White design. The courthouse is a dominating building, situated on a hill overlooking Oswego and Lake Ontario. As Oswego is the county's most populous settlement, most of the county's legal business is transacted here.

New York's Southern Tier
Judicial District 6

The rolling hills and rich valleys of the Allegheny Plateau dominate this district, the heart of New York's dairy country. Binghamton, the Broome County seat, is the major city of this largely rural region. Historic courthouses grace the region. At Wamps-ville, Madison County, the silver-domed courthouse glistens over distant corn fields. At Norwich the temple-like Chenango County Courthouse stands as proud guardian of the city green. And at Cooperstown, the ecclesiastical Otsego County Court-house adds historic flavor to this center of New York history. A notable site of the district is the Nelson Law Office at the Farm-ers' Museum, Cooperstown. Here one can view a restored 19th century attorney's domain, a re-creation of the profession's past. The office brings to life one chapter in the state's legal history.

BROOME COUNTY

BROOME COUNTY COURTHOUSE, *Binghamton.*
This county's first court session took place under the shade of an elm tree. The present courthouse, a domed Greek Revival build-ing, was built in 1898, on land deeded to public use by William Bingham, the city's founder.

SITE OF DANIEL DICKINSON HOUSE, *Front Street, between Clinton and Dickinson Streets.*
Daniel Dickinson's home, "The Orchard," was located on the west side of Front Street. Dickinson came to Binghamton in 1828 and established a law practice. He became mayor of Bing-hamton, a state senator, a delegate to the Democratic Presiden-tial Convention that nominated Van Buren, a lieutenant-gover-nor, a United States Senator, attorney-general of the state, and United States District Attorney for the Southern District of New York. Dickinson was a friend to Lincoln and his work earned the praise of Daniel Webster. His home burned to the ground in the 1870's and the surrounding land was made into a park. An apartment house now occupies the site.

GILES HOTCHKISS HOUSE, *Chestnut Street, Windsor.*
This house, the only stone one on the street, was built in 1823. Hotchkiss, a leading member of the Broome County Bar and a Congressman in 1863, was born here. The attorney was a trusted advisor to Lincoln. His home, now a private residence, is

Chemung County Courthouse

partly occupied by the "Old Stone House Museum," open by appointment.

CORTLAND COUNTY

CORTLAND COUNTY COURTHOUSE, *Cortland*.
In 1810 Cortland was named county seat, replacing the village of Homer, where the first judicial sessions had been held in a school. The present courthouse, an imposing capitol-like structure, was completed in 1922. It is on the National Register of Historic Places.

CHEMUNG COUNTY

CHEMUNG COUNTY COURTHOUSE, *Elmira*.
This courthouse, built in 1862, was designed by Horatio Nelson White and was entered on the National Register of Historic Places in August of 1971. Like White's other courthouses, this one exhibits his penchant for the Anglo-Norman style.

DAVID B. HILL HOUSE, *503 Lake Street, Elmira.*
This home, which has undergone extensive change, was Hill's local residence when he was Governor of New York. Hill was a prominent Elmira attorney who became a state assemblyman, then lieutenant-governor. In 1884, he automatically assumed the governorship when Grover Cleveland was elected President. After two terms as the state's chief executive, Hill was elected United States Senator, serving until 1897.

CHENANGO COUNTY

CHENANGO COUNTY COURTHOUSE, *Norwich.*
When Norwich became Chenango County seat in 1809, the town built a wooden courthouse. In 1836 the present court structure was completed. It is a fine Greek Revival building, supported by Doric Columns and situated in a central public square. Chenango County offices are housed in a modern structure to the rear of the courthouse.

DELAWARE COUNTY

DELAWARE COUNTY COURTHOUSE, *Delhi.*
In the 1840's, this county was the scene of much of New York's anti-rent agitation. Delhi, the county seat, built its first courthouse in 1798. In 1820 fire destroyed the court and another was erected. Today's courthouse was completed in 1871. The building is a beautiful red-brick structure, designed by Isaac E. Perry, architect of the State Capitol. The main court ceiling is highlighted by vaulted wooden beams.

ISAAC H. MAYNARD HOSE COMPANY, *Main Street, Stanford.*
Maynard, by far the most renowned member of the Delaware County Bar, studied law in Delhi after graduation from Amherst College. His career is highlighted by his appointment, in 1887, as Assistant Secretary of the United States Treasury and his appointment, in 1892, to the State Court of Appeals. As far as can be determined, this is the only fire department in the state named for a prominent attorney.

MADISON COUNTY

MADISON COUNTY COURTHOUSE, *Wampsville.*
Early county courts met in Sullivan, Hamilton, Morrisville and
Cazenovia. As the county's northern sector grew in population,
the communities of Oneida and Canastota demanded a courthouse. A compromise was reached, placing the county government at Wampsville which is midway between the rivals. The
present courthouse, a silver-domed structure, is visible for miles
across the upper Madison County countryside.

The indictments against upstate New York's infamous horse
thieves, the "Loomis Gang," were once kept in the Morrisville
courthouse. Determined to rid themselves of this legal evidence,
the Loomis boys broke into the Morrisville fire department, cut
the fire hose, and then proceeded to burn the county courthouse. Later, when they learned that the indictments had actually been transferred to the county clerk's office, they burned
that building also.

OTSEGO COUNTY

OTSEGO COUNTY COURTHOUSE, *Cooperstown.*
Archimedes Russell designed this church-like courthouse. An
imposing Gothic window juts out over the courthouse's arched
entranceway. Detailed brickwork can be seen throughout the
building.

Cooperstown has always been the Otsego County seat. The
county's first judge was William Cooper, father of James Fenimore Cooper, the novelist.

SAMUEL NELSON LAW OFFICE, *Farmers' Museum, Cooperstown.*
There is a re-creation of a 19th century village at the New York
State Historical Association's Farmers' Museum. Law and law-
yers were an integral part of village life in those days. One such
lawyer was Samuel Nelson who purchased the home of James
Fenimore Cooper in 1829 and built a law office on the property.
In the Farmers' Museum village that office has been restored
through the efforts of the Historical Association and the State

150

Samuel Nelson

Bar Association.

Today's Nelson Law Office is a small, dignified white-clapboard structure with two rooms: one a waiting room and clerk's office, the other, Nelson's personal office. The office is furnished in typical 19th century fashion but is not an exact replica of Nelson's.

Nelson was Chief Justice of the New York Supreme Court and in 1845 was appointed Associate Justice of the United States Supreme Court, serving in that capacity for twenty-seven years.

FENIMORE HOUSE, *Cooperstown.*
This building, headquarters for the New York State Historical Association, is built on the site of Judge William Cooper's home. Cooper was the first Judge of the Court of Common Pleas for Otsego County. The Association maintains a museum in the house and an art gallery. The gallery includes Tompkins H. Matteson's painting, "Justice's Court," which depicts frontier justice.

SCHUYLER COUNTY

SCHUYLER COUNTY COURTHOUSE, *Watkins Glen.*
Like many other New York counties, two towns fought to be

named county seat. Courthouses were constructed in Havanna, now Montour Falls, and Watkins, now Watkins Glen. Courts alternated between the two towns until, in 1866, Watkins Glen became the county seat.

The Watkins Glen Courthouse, a church-like structure, is undergoing renovation in a project sponsored by the Schuyler County Legislature.

OLD SCHUYLER COUNTY COURTHOUSE, *Montour Falls.*
Montour Falls acquired this courthouse after Watkins Glen became county seat. Although the building was erected around 1830, it is still intact and used for village offices, a police station and as a court for the local justice of the peace.

TIOGA COUNTY

TIOGA COUNTY COURTHOUSE, *Owego.*
This county once included parts of Broome, Chenango and Chemung counties. Its present boundaries were settled in 1836 and Owego was designated county seat. Today's courthouse, a regal structure, was built on the Owego public square in 1873. The courthouse is on the National Register of Historic Places.

The Owego Courthouse was dedicated with much ceremony. Speeches abounded. Reminiscences of the old 1823 courthouse and of the early Owego bench and bar filled the air. One attorney, Charles A. Munger, wrote a poem for the occasion. Part of his verse reads:

The old Court-house with all its fond
memories of yore,
With its low, dingy walls, narrow Bar,
creaking floor,
Its doves in the belfry, its rats in the
vault
Must sink 'neath the surgings of ruins'
assault.

TOMPKINS COUNTY

OLD TOMPKINS COUNTY COURTHOUSE, *Ithaca.*
Located on Ithaca's historic DeWitt Park, the old Tompkins County Courthouse was built in 1855, in a distinctive Gothic style. The courthouse is on the National Register of Historic Places and, in 1971, was made a state historic landmark by the New York State Historic Trust. Renovations, costing about $650,000, restored the building to its original design.

The Historic American Building Survey of the Department of the Interior has deemed the old courthouse "a historic structure of importance to New York State . . . a rare survival of its architectural type, particularly the magnificent original courtroom."

CORNELL UNIVERSITY LAW SCHOOL, *Myron Taylor Hall, Cornell University, Ithaca.*
Cornell's Law School was established on September 23, 1887. Myron Taylor Hall, which presently houses the law school, was completed in 1932, a gift of Myron C. Taylor, Roosevelt's ambassador to the Vatican and once a chairman of the board of U.S. Steel. The law school is an English Collegiate Gothic structure, highlighted by its fine carvings. Before becoming Chief Justice of the Supreme Court, Charles Evans Hughes taught law at Cornell from 1891 to 1893.

THE BOARDMAN HOUSE, *East Buffalo Street, Ithaca.*
Judge Douglass Boardman, a prominent member of the local bar, was the first Dean of Cornell Law School. The house, completed in 1867, is a modest Italianate building. Upon Boardman's death in 1892 the Ithaca Conservatory of Music, now Ithaca College, purchased the home. The house has deteriorated with time and there is currently a movement to restore it.

The Finger Lakes Region
Judicial District 7

Throughout New York history the Seventh Judicial District has been a breeding ground for causes. In Rochester, Monroe County, Frederick Douglass published his abolitionist *North Star* newspaper. At Palmyra, Wayne County, Joseph Smith received the vision that led to the Mormon Church's formation. Legal causes, too, have reverberated through the Seventh District. At the Ontario County Courthouse, Susan B. Anthony and her attorney Henry Selden brought the women's suffrage movement to the public's attention in a dramatic trial. At Auburn, Cayuga County, William H. Seward faced momentous opposition in his courageous defense of William Freeman, a black man accused of murdering several members of a prominent white family. Both Anthony and Seward lost their cases, but they set significant precedents that led toward the final vindication of their beliefs.

CAYUGA COUNTY

CAYUGA COUNTY COURTHOUSE, *Auburn.*
In frontier days the first courthouse in this Finger Lakes city was built of poles and roofed with brush. Today's courthouse is a splendid Greek Revival building, built in 1836 and reconstructed in the 1920's. Six Doric columns adorn the courthouse front.

SEWARD MANSION, *Auburn.*
Elijah Miller, William Henry Seward's father-in-law, built this home in 1816. The house, of post-Colonial architecture, is one of the most elegant in Auburn. Cast-iron griffins guard the front lawn. A statue of Seward stands beside the mansion.

Seward was one of New York's leading 19th century politicians. He began his political career at the age of 29 with his election to the state senate. In 1838 he became governor, in 1849 he entered the United States Senate, and then served as Secretary of State under Abraham Lincoln. He was noted for his abolitionist views, his purchase of Alaska, then termed "Seward's Folly," and his plea of insanity in defense of William Freeman in Auburn in 1846. The Seward Home is a completely preserved mansion and is open to the public.

LIVINGSTON COUNTY

LIVINGSTON COUNTY COURTHOUSE, *Geneseo.*
This county, in the heart of "Genesee Country," has had two architecturally fine courthouses. The first, built in 1823, was a neat, church-like structure, with the Ionic columns of Greek Revival architecture. This courthouse was replaced in 1898 by the present edifice, designed by Claude Fayette Bragdon, a Rochester architect. The courthouse boasts an elegant red brick exterior, accentuated by four white Doric columns and a small bell tower.

Geneseo and its courthouse served as a 19th century literary backdrop for Arthur Train's "Mr. Tutt" and his legal adventures. Train, a lawyer himself, spent much time in Geneseo and prosecuted cases in the Livingston County Courthouse. In his story, "Hermit of Turkey Hollow," Train accurately captured the Geneseo village atmosphere. Train wrote, "the smutty, little wooden railroad station, the memorial library of funeral granite, the horse trough in the middle of Main Street, the beautiful old court house."

MONROE COUNTY

OLD MONROE COUNTY COURTHOUSE, *Rochester.*
This courthouse, completed in 1896, is of Italian Renaissance architecture and is on the National Register of Historic Places. The main entrance, bordered by four Doric columns, leads to an interior courtyard. The courthouse is now used for general county offices. The new courthouse is in Civic Center Plaza.

There is an interesting feature in the old courthouse west wall. Stones from Ebenezer "Indian" Allen's grist mill are embedded in the wall. Allen, first settler in the area, ground grain for Indians and the few whites of that region around 1789. He left Rochester, accompanied by his white and Indian wives, in 1792. History does not record what happened to him.

SUSAN B. ANTHONY HOUSE, *17 Madison Street, Rochester.*

Old Monroe County Courthouse

This home is marked with a State Historic Marker and is on the National Register of Historic Places. Here the spirited Miss Anthony was arrested in a prelude to her famed trial for voting in 1873.

BARNARD FAMILY MEMORIAL, *West Bloomfield Road, Mendon Township.*

The Monroe County Historian's office, in 1976, set up a bicentennial marker commemorating three members of this lawyer-family. The marker reads:

BARNARD'S CORNERS

Major Timothy Barnard, an early 1809 settler was a Drum Major, Commissary Officer, and Paymaster and Express Messenger for General George Washington and General Jeremiah Wadsworth. He delivered to the northern governors the official dispatches announcing the surrender of Cornwallis in 1781. Timothy's son, Hon. Daniel D. Barnard, was this county's first Congressman and an ambassador to Prussia. Timothy's great-great grandson, Hon. Kenneth Keating, was U.S. Senator and ambassador to Israel and India.—Erected by the County of Monroe, 1976

HENRY R. SELDEN HOUSE, *8402 Ridge Road, Clarkson.*
A State Historic Marker identifies this house as Henry Selden's home. Not only was he Lieutenant Governor of New York and mentor for many early Monroe County attorneys, but he was Susan B. Anthony's lawyer and defended her during her trial for illegally voting in 1873.

JOHN MASTICK PLAQUE, HALL OF JUSTICE, *Old Monroe County Courthouse.*
JOHN MASTICK GRAVE, *Mt. Hope Cemetery, Rochester.*
These sites commemorate John Mastick, "pioneer lawyer of Rochester," who came to that city to practice law in 1812. The plaque reads:

In Memory of
One of the Brave Settlers Who Planted A City
1780—John Mastick, Esq.—1827
The Pioneer Lawyer of Rochester
He was the first to practice law in the wilderness village where men and women faced strange dangers and heavy toil. They found the forest primeval. They left a city of homes. A few dared and suffered. Many enjoy the good. Ye shall know them by their fruits.
—Erected by the Rochester Bar Association and the Rochester Historical Society, 1922.

ONTARIO COUNTY

ONTARIO COUNTY COURTHOUSE, *Canandaigua.*
As one approaches this Finger Lakes community from the east, the massive golden dome of the Ontario County Courthouse dominates the skyline. This courthouse, built in 1858, was the scene of the 1873 Susan B. Anthony voting trial. In the first county courthouse, constructed in 1794, Jemimah Wilkinson was tried for blasphemy. In western New York's first murder trial, at Canandaigua, famed Seneca orator Red Jacket represented the defendant. The second county courthouse, dating back to 1824, is still being used now as a town hall.

HUBBELL HOUSE, *164 Main Street, Canandaigua.*
Walter Hubbell, a Canandaigua attorney, built this 19th century home. Stephen A. Douglas, from the Canandaigua Academy, studied law at Hubbell's office. The law office which was an annex of the house has been moved behind the Granger Homestead.

THE GRANGER HOMESTEAD, *495 North Main Street, Canandaigua.*
Gideon Granger, a member of the local bar and Postmaster General under Jefferson and Madison, built this home. It is now a museum, run by the Granger Homestead Association. The Hubbell law office, to the rear of the Homestead, is presently being restored with period furnishings.

JOHN C. SPENCER HOME, *910 North Main Street, Canandaigua.*
Spencer, an Ontario County lawyer, was Secretary of State of New York in 1839, and Secretary of War and the Treasury in the administration of President Tyler. The latter nominated Spencer for the United States Supreme Court, but political maneuvering brought about his rejection. The Spencer House is now the Elm and Manor Nursing Home.

SENECA COUNTY

SENECA COUNTY COURTHOUSE, *Ovid.*
Three county buildings, nicknamed the "Three Bears," serve Seneca County from their hill in Ovid Village. The largest, "Papa Bear," was completed in 1845 and is still used as a courthouse. The courtroom in this building is meticulously preserved. The middle building, called "Mama Bear," once housed the Ovid office of Seneca County Clerk. "Baby Bear," the smallest building, is, along with "Mama," now vacant.

Ovid, together with Waterloo, is a Seneca County seat. Waterloo had sole possession of that honor until 1822 when Ovid regained its county courthouse functions in the southern part of the county.

SENECA COUNTY COURTHOUSE, *Waterloo.*
Waterloo was made county seat in 1817. In 1822, when the

Steuben County Courthouse

county was half-shired, Ovid was given court jurisdiction over the southern half of the county.

The Waterloo Courthouse was built in 1818 and is a three-story, column-adorned building, complete with a small, domed bell tower.

STEUBEN COUNTY

STEUBEN COUNTY COURTHOUSE, *Bath.*
The present courthouse, built in 1861, replaced an earlier structure that had been leveled by fire. The courthouse, with two white Greek columns, has been classified as being "midway between Greek Revival and the Victorian courthouse architecture."

Several years ago, the Steuben County Board of Supervisors considered razing the Bath courthouse and replacing it with modern facilities. The building was saved partly through the efforts of the State Bar Association's Committee for the Preservation of Historic Courthouses.

STEUBEN COUNTY COURTHOUSES, *Corning and Hornell.*

Steuben County is unique in the fact that it contains three county seats. In addition to the facilities at Bath, the county maintains courthouses at Corning and Hornell. The Corning Courthouse is of Greek Temple architecture while the Hornell building incorporates Greek Revival and Federal styles.

WAYNE COUNTY

WAYNE COUNTY COURTHOUSE, *Lyons.*
The building committee for the Orleans County Courthouse, in Adbion, journeyed to Lyons before making final plans for their courthouse. The Orleans and Wayne County courthouses bear such similarity that some have speculated that the same architect designed each. Both are fine examples of Greek Revival architecture.

The Wayne County Courthouse, dating back to 1854, replaced an earlier structure that had been gutted by fire. It was built of Lockport limestone, graced by an Ionic portico, and accentuated by a fine, proportioned dome. To this day the courthouse's esthetic qualities have been preserved.

YATES COUNTY

YATES COUNTY COURTHOUSE, *Penn Yan.*
This courthouse, a modest Greek Revival building, was built in 1835. It replaced the first courthouse, a New England-style building, that housed the county jail on the first floor and court-rooms on the second. Abraham Wagener, a leading Penn Yan citizen, donated land for this courthouse and in the process won the distinction of having his village named county seat.

Penn Yan village acquired its name in a peculiar manner. Its early settlers were primarily Pennsylvanians and Yankees. The two groups are represented in the abbreviated "Penn Yan" place name.

Western New York
Judicial District 8

When thinking of New York's judicial districts in terms of their historic sites, impressions immediately come to mind. New York City and Boss Tweed's courthouse are remembered, as are the Fourth District and its 18th century Fulton County Courthouse, the Seventh and its three-shired Steuben County, the Third and the Court of Appeals Building, the ultimate state judicial authority. Each district has its prominent symbols of legal heritage.

So it is with the Eighth Judicial District, the area encompassing New York's western extremity. For this author the Eighth immediately brings to mind two sites: the Erie County Courthouse at Buffalo, and the Orleans County Courthouse at Albion. Both structures exhibit notable architectural qualities. Both adapt beautifully to their environment. Each courthouse stands out as a fitting symbol of justice in New York.

ALLEGANY COUNTY

ALLEGANY COUNTY COURTHOUSE, *Belmont.*
The present courthouse actually consists of five official buildings which were consolidated into one in 1938. Carolina marble and fine cherry paneling decorate the structure. A Greek Revival façade adds stateliness.

Oddly enough, the courthouse's greatest claim to fame lies in the field of medicine. In the 1930's the American blood bank system was begun here.

In 1975-76 a modern wing was added to the courthouse, costing over four million dollars and greatly expanding county facilities. The wing stands in architectural contrast to the older courthouse section.

OLD ALLEGANY COUNTY COURTHOUSE, *Angelica.*
Built in 1819, this courthouse was the first officiad home for the county judiciary. It is a neat brick structure, with a window-paned bell tower. The courthouse is known as the birthplace of

161

the Republican Party in New York. It was here, in 1854, that that party's first state candidates were nominated.

CATTARAUGUS COUNTY

CATTARAUGUS COUNTY COURTHOUSE, *Little Valley.*
From 1867 until it was razed in 1967, a courthouse designed by Horatio Nelson White served the county. This building was typical of White's architectural style and was the last courthouse designed by the famous architect.

Today's county courthouse is a more modern structure built in 1967 in Little Valley. County offices are also maintained in Olean, the county's largest city.

OLD CATTARAUGUS COUNTY COURTHOUSE, *Ellicottville.*
This courthouse served the county from approximately 1830 to 1867. It is located on the village square and now houses village and town offices. A fire in the 1960s resulted in severe damage to the interior. However, every effort was made to rebuild the inside to the measurements and decor of the old.

CHAUTAUQUA COUNTY

CHAUTAUQUA COUNTY COURTHOUSE, *Mayville.*
This upstate village, county seat for Chautauqua County, is in the heart of New York's wine region. The first courthouse was a crude building, constructed of green wood. The last public execution in New York took place in the second court building. Today's courthouse was finished in 1909. It is fronted with an Ionic portico and topped with a bell tower.

RIPLEY VILLAGE
This village, located near the Pennsylvania border on U.S. 20, was once the "marriage capital of New York." Ripley boasted of a fast, convenient, "from clerk to justice" marriage service. Until the passage of the Todd Marriage Law, which mandated a three-day period between marriage license purchase and the marriage itself, Ripley was a veritable wedding factory.

ERIE COUNTY

ERIE COUNTY COURTHOUSE, *Buffalo.*

Known as the Erie County Hall, this magnificent structure was completed in 1876. It is a massive grey building, ornate and imposing. In 1884, the then new county building met this description:

It has three stories above the basement; the first being finished on the outside in rough granite; the two higher ones in dressed granite. The parapet of the cornice is seventy-four feet high, while the highest parts of the slate roofs are one hundred and five feet high. The whole is surmounted by a large, square, central tower, containing in its lower part an immense clock, with four dials, each nine feet in diameter, while at the extreme top is an observatory two hundred feet above the earth. On turrets, situated at the four corners of the tower, stand statues sixteen feet high, representing . . . Justice . . . Mechanic Arts . . . Agriculture . . . Commerce

---

In early Erie County legal history the "Three Thayers Execution" stands out. The three brothers were convicted of murdering John Love and publicly hanged. This spectacle drew a crowd of over twenty thousand people to Buffalo. Red Jacket, the famed Seneca Indian orator, left town before the executions, saying, "Fools enough there now—battle is the place to see men die."

FILLMORE HOUSE SITE, *Buffalo.*

A plaque, placed by the Buffalo Historical Society in the wall of that city's Hotel Statler, marks the site of the Millard Fillmore home. Fillmore, a member of the bar and the nation's thirteenth president, lived there, in Tudor-Gothic splendor, from 1858 until his death in 1874.

ALLEN HOUSE SITE, *Buffalo.*

Grover Cleveland, first Democratic president after the Civil War, lived in Buffalo and was elected Erie County Sheriff in 1870. A member of the New York Bar, Cleveland lived with his uncle in the Allen family homestead on Niagara Street. The

Millard Fillmore

home and most of the neighborhood have since been razed and are now part of the industrial section of the city.

WILCOX MANSION, *641 Delaware Avenue, Buffalo.*
From 1884 to the 1930's, this was Ainsley Wilcox's home. He was an important Buffalo lawyer who worked for Civil Service reform. It was here, on September 14, 1901, that Vice-President Theodore Roosevelt was sworn in as President on the death of McKinley. The house is now a National Historic Site.

SUNY AT BUFFALO LAW SCHOOL, *John Lord O'Brien Hall,* SUNYAB *North Campus, Buffalo.*
This law school was founded in 1887 as part of Niagara University. In 1962 the Buffalo Law School joined the State University system.

GENESEE COUNTY

GENESEE COUNTY COURTHOUSE, *Batavia.*
The county's first courthouse was built in 1802 on land donated

by the Holland Land Company, an early 19th century land developer. This building was replaced in 1843 by the present belltowered Greek Revival building, constructed of local Lockport limestone. The courthouse departs from the traditional rectangular Greek Revival form with its square shape.

Genesee County installed gas light in its Batavia courthouse in November of 1855. The county prosecuted the Batavia Gas Light Company in 1856, in one of the state's earliest environmental cases, charging it with responsibility for:

a certain offensive and unwholesome substance or tar generated and issue(d) . . . (that) runs away from the gas works, through a ditch and across a public street, all the time giving off . . . noisome, offensive and unwholesome smells and stenches.

NIAGARA COUNTY

NIAGARA COUNTY COURTHOUSE, *Lockport.*
In 1822 Lockport became the Niagara County seat. Its status as a key Erie Canal lockage point brought the village a "boom town atmosphere." A courthouse was built in 1823. This structure later proved inadequate for the expanding county government and a new courthouse was erected in 1886.

The main part of the 1886 building still stands today. Originally adorned with an ornate tower and topped with a goddess's statue, the courthouse was constructed of Lockport limestone. This stone was used in many of the elegant homes and public buildings of the region. The tower was dismantled and replaced by a dome and the courthouse front was given a Greek Revival façade. A modern office building was added to the courthouse's west side in 1955.

HOUSE OF WASHINGTON HUNT, *363 Market Street, Lockport.*
Hunt, a prominent county attorney, was elected Governor of New York in 1850. His home, now privately owned is being renovated and is on the National Register of Historic Places. His law office has been moved to the grounds of the Niagara County Historical Society, 215 Niagara Street, Lockport.

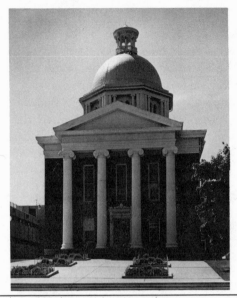

Orleans County Courthouse

SITE OF BELVA LOCKWOOD HOME, *Griswold Street, Royalton Township.*

A plaque marks the site where Belva Lockwood once lived. Lockwood was one of this nation's first woman attorneys. She was graduated from Washington University Law School in 1873 and admitted to the bar that same year. In 1879, Belva Lockwood was admitted to the bar at the United States Court of Claims and in 1884 and 1888 she ran for president as a candidate of the Equal Rights Party, becoming the first woman to formally run for that office. She made the ballot in several states and received several thousand votes. She died in 1917, a woman who was far ahead of her time.

ORLEANS COUNTY

ORLEANS COUNTY COURTHOUSE, *Albion.*
The first trial in the history of this county took place in 1825 in the house of Selah Bronson, a Gaines village blacksmith. The present courthouse was built in Albion in 1858, a beautiful

Greek Revival temple, red-bricked and silver-domed. It is well-preserved to this day.

Albion's acquisition of county seat status was not without dispute. Gaines also wanted the prestige. One historian recorded Albion residents' successful strategy:

Albion boosters were determined to have the county seat. So they dammed a swimming hole, built a mill and entertained the commissioners who were to make the selection. Filled with hard cider the solons were taken out to see the great wheel turning as a sign of local industrial progress; then just as the little lake ran dry, they were hustled away!

WYOMING COUNTY

WYOMING COUNTY COURTHOUSE, *Warsaw.*

Wyoming County has had but one courthouse. In 1842 the county completed, with state aid, a courthouse, county clerk's office, and jail. In 1936, a Greek Revival front was added and the courthouse dome removed.

The Warsaw courthouse has been, in recent years, the scene of the grand jury hearings on the Attica prison riots. Attica village and its penitentiary are located on the northern fringe of the county.

BIBLIOGRAPHY

BOOKS

——, *New York—A Guide to the Empire State,* compiled by the workers of the Writers' Program of the Work Projects Administration, Oxford University Press, New York, 1940.

——, *Transcriptions of Early Town Records of New York—Minutes of the Town Courts of Newtown, 1656–1690,* The Historical Records Survey, New York, 1940.

ANTHONY, Katherine, *Susan B. Anthony,* Doubleday & Company, Inc., Garden City, New York, 1954.

BAKER, Leonard, *John Marshall—A Life in Law,* The Macmillan Company, New York, 1974.

BLOOMFIELD, Maxwell, *American Lawyers in a Changing Society, 1776–1876,* Harvard University Press, Cambridge, 1976.

BURNHAM, Alan (ed.), *New York Landmarks,* Wesleyan University Press, Middletown, Connecticut, 1957.

CHESTER, Alden, *Courts and Lawyers of New York,* The American Historical Society, New York, 1925, v. I, II, III.

CHRISTMAN, Henry, *Tin Horns and Calico,* Henry Holt and Company, New York, 1945.

CONRAD, Earl, *Mr. Seward for the Defense,* Rinehart and Company, Inc., New York, 1956.

DORR, Rheta Childe, *Susan B. Anthony,* Frederick A. Stokes Company, New York, 1920.

DREISER, Theodore, *An American Tragedy,* Horace Liveright, New York, 1931.

EDWARDS, Charles, *Pleasantries About Courts and Lawyers of the State of New York,* Richardson and Company, New York, 1867.

ELLIS, David M. *et al., A History of New York State,* Cornell University Press, Ithaca, 1967.

ELLIS, David M., *Landlords and Farmers in the Hudson-Mohawk Region, 1790-1850,* Cornell University Press, Ithaca, 1946.

FLAHERTY, David H., *Essays in the History of Early American Law,* University of North Carolina Press, Chapel Hill, 1969.

FLICK, Alexander (ed.), *History of the State of New York,* Columbia University Press, New York, 1933, v. III.

FRIEDMAN, Lawrence, *A History of American Law,* Simon and Schuster, New York, 1973.

GRAVES, W. Brooke, (ed.), *The Government and Administration of New York,* Thomas Y. Crowell Company, New York, 1954.

HELLMAN, George S., *Benjamin N. Cardozo,* Whittlesey House—McGraw Hill, New York, 1940.

HILL, Henry Wayland (ed.), *Municipality of Buffalo, New York—A History,* Lewis Historical Publishing Company Inc., New York, 1923.

HORTON, John Theodore, *James Kent—A Study in Conservatism,* D. Appleton-Century Company, New York, 1939.

HURST, James Willard, *The Growth of American Law,* Little, Brown and Company, Boston, 1950.

169

JONES, Pomroy, *Annals and Recollections of Oneida County,* Pomroy Jones, Rome, 1851.

KAMMEN, Michael, *Colonial New York—A History,* Charles Scribner's Sons, New York 1975.

KELLY, Virginia, *et al., Wood and Stone—Landmarks of the Upper Mohawk Region,* Central New York Community Arts Council, 1972.

LEVY, Beryl Harold, *Cardozo and the Frontiers of Legal Thinking,* Oxford University Press, New York, 1938.

LEWIS, William Draper, *Great American Lawyers,* The John C. Winston Company, Philadelphia, 1907.

LINCOLN, Charles Z., *The Constitutional History of New York,* The Lawyers Cooperative Publishing Company, Rochester, 1906, v. I, II, III.

MANDELBAUM, Seymour J., *Boss Tweed's New York,* John Wiley & Sons, Inc., New York, 1965.

McADAM, David, *et al., History of the Bench and Bar of New York,* New York History Company, New York, 1897, v. I.

MITCHELL, Broadus, *Alexander Hamilton,* The Macmillan Company, New York, 1962.

NELSON, William E., *Americanization of the Common Law,* Harvard University Press, Cambridge, 1975.

REICH, Jerome R., *Leisler's Rebellion,* University of Chicago Press, Chicago, 1953.

RIDER, Fremont, *Rider's New York City,* The Macmillan Company, New York, 1924.

ROGERS, James Grafton, *American Bar Leaders,* American Bar Association, Chicago, 1932.

ROSSITER, Clinton, *Alexander Hamilton and the Constitution,* Harcourt, Brace and World, Inc., New York, 1964.

SARGENT, Winthrop, *The Life and Career of Major John André,* William Abbott, New York, 1902.

SCHWARTZ, Bernard, *The Law in America,* McGraw-Hill, New York, 1974.

SULLIVAN, Dr. James (ed.), *History of New York State,* Lewis Historical Publishing Company, New York 1927.

TILLOTSON, Harry Stanton, *The Beloved Spy,* The Caxton Printers, Ltd., Caldwell, Idaho, 1942.

VAN DEUSEN, Glyndon G., *William Henry Seward,* Oxford University Press, New York, 1967.

WHITE, Norval, (ed.), *AIA Guide to New York City,* The Macmillan Company, New York, 1968.

PAMPHLETS AND PAPERS

————, "New York State Bar Center," published by the New York State Bar Association, Albany.

————, "Preface to Tomorrow," published by the County of Monroe, 1971.

————, "The Counties of New York," published by the New York Telephone Company, 1948.

BURAK, H. Paul, "History of the United States District Court for the Southern District of New York," published by the Federal Bar Association of New York, New Jersey and Connecticut, 1962.

DOUGHERTY, J. Hampden, "William M. Evarts," Law Department of the Brooklyn Institute, 1901.

INGRAHAM, Granville S., "History—Gillette Murder Trial and Grace Brown's Love Letters," Charles E. Garlock, Herkimer, New York, 1907.

JOHNSON, Herbert Alan, "Crimes, Columns and Courthouses," loaned to me by the New York State Historical Association, Cooperstown.

RATH, Frederick L. (ed.), "An informal Guide to the Museums of the New York State Historical Association," published by the Association, 1975.

ROOT, Elihu, "Memorial of Joseph Hodges Choate," the Association of the Bar of the City of New York, 1917.

WALSH, John J., "Joshua A. Spencer and the Caroline Affair," from the papers of the Oneida Historical Society, Utica.

DOCUMENTS
New York State Bar
Association

Bylaws of the New York State Bar Association, adopted at the Annual Meeting, April 19, 1975.

Constitution of the New York State Bar Association, adopted at the Annual Meeting, January 26, 1973.

BERRY, John E., History of the New York State Bar Association, published in manuscript form, by the Association, 1952.

MILLER, Nathan L., "Seventy-Five Years of Achievement—Our Association in Retrospect," *New York State Bar Bulletin*, December 1952.

SEYMOUR, Whitney North, Jr., "The Choicest Fruit that Grows Upon the Tree of English Liberty," *New York State Bar Journal*, February 1975.

PERIODICAL ARTICLE

BLAUSTEIN, Albert P., "New York Bar Associations Prior to 1870," American Journal of Legal History, v. 12, 1968.

Articles from *New York History*, published by the New York State Historical Association, Cooperstown.

BACKUS, Oswald P., "Early Bar of Oneida County," Proceedings of NYSHA, 1915. From this point onward the fact that these articles are included in the Association's proceedings is assumed. The articles were published in the years given.

BONHAM, Milledge L., "Alexander McLeod: Bone of Contention," April 1937.

DAWSON, Edgar, "The First New York State Constitution," 1919.

FLICK, Alexander C., "Samuel Jones Tilden," October 1937.

HERSHKOWITZ, Leo, "The Troublesome Turk: An Illustration of The Judicial Process in New Amsterdam," October 1965.

HORTON, John T., "The Western Eyres of Judge Kent," April 1937.

JACKSON, Harry F., "Sam Dakin, Local Justice," January 1955.

JONES, Louis C., "The Berlin Murder Case in Folklore and Ballad," October 1935.

KELSAY, Isabel Thompson, "The Trial of Big Thunder," July 1935.

Lyon, F. D., "New York State Constitutional Conventions," January 1939.

May, Arthur J., "Susan B. Anthony—Perspective on a Pioneer," April 1947.

Moore, Frank C., "Constitutional Conventions in New York State," January 1957.

Smith, Frederic A., "Where New York Ratified the Federal Constitution," April 1937.

Smith, James Morton, "The Sedition Law of 1798 and the Right of Petition—the Attempted Prosecution of Jedediah Peck," January 1954.

Spaulding, E. Wilder, "New York and the Federal Constitution," April 1939.

Wheeler, Charles B., "John Jay," July 1926.

Acknowledgments

The guide to historic sites could never have been prepared
without the assistance of the following people.
Among the group are county historians, lawyers, judges and laymen.
To them goes deserved appreciation and thanks.

The Albany Institute of History and Art

The Association of the Bar of the City of New York

Mrs. Betty Auten, Waterloo

Mrs. Howard Bailey, Schoharie County Historian, Stamford

James Bailey, Essex County Historian, Elizabethtown

Mrs. Mary Biondi, St. Lawrence County Historian, Canton

Sally Brilyan, Washington County Clerk's Office

Brooklyn Bar Association

Miss Colleen A. Brown, Colgate University, Hamilton

Tom Cawley, *The Binghamton Press*

Gary Chatterton, Unadilla Forks

Glenn Chesebrough, Sylvan Beach

Clinton County Historical Society, Plattsburgh

M. Clute, Richard Weiss, Chemung County Historical Society, Elmira

George Cowen, Brookfield

Howard Davidson, Delaware County Historian, Bovina Center

Charles Dunham, Jefferson County Historian, Chaumont

Mrs. Violet Dunn, Saratoga County Historian, Saratoga

Arthur Einhorn, Lewis County Historian, Lowville

Erie County Chamber of Commerce, Buffalo

Franklin County Museum, Malone

Cheryl Gold, Clermont

William C. Greene, Allegany County Historian, Belmont

Mrs. Shirley Heppel, Cortland

County Historian, Cortland

Hickey's Grocery Store, Claverack

Walter Irving, Binghamton City Historian, Binghamton

Historic Ithaca, Inc., Ithaca

Mrs. Grayson Hinman, Windsor

Mrs. Shirley Husted, Monroe County Historian, Hilton

John Jay House Staff, Katonah

Mr. and Mrs. Don Jerge, Gasport

Mrs. Virginia Kelly, Oneida County Historian, Holland Patent

Frank Lorenz, Hamilton College Library, Clinton

Clyde Maffin, Ontario County Historian, Canandaigua

Arden R. McAllister, Orleans County Historian, Albion

Mrs. McAndrew, Glens Falls Library, Glens Falls

E. T. Mengarelli, Librarian, Supreme Court, Syracuse

David Millar, Hamilton College, Clinton

Brian Mohin, Orange County Historian's Office, Goshen

Charles Mooney, Albany County Historian, Albany

Nassau County Bar Association, Mineola

New York Historical Society Library Staff, Manhattan

Onondaga County Historical Association, Syracuse

Dr. R. Morris Palmer, Fulton County Historian, Gloversville

Miss Anna Patchett, Livingston County Historian, Geneseo

Eugene R. Perry, Tioga County Historian, Owego

Mrs. Wilhelmina Powers, Dutch-

ess County Historian, Poughkeepsie

Douglas Preston, Director, Oneida Historical Society, Utica

Public Relations Office, New York State Bar Association

Public Relations Office, New York State Historical Association, Cooperstown

Queens County Bar Association, Jamaica

I. Richard Reed, Niagara County Historian, Lockport

Miss Connie Rogers, Brookfield

Victor R. Rolando, Rensselaer County Historian, Nassau

H. Sass, Librarian, Erie County Historical Society, Buffalo

Frederic W. Shaw, Putnam County Historian, Putnam Valley

Anthony Slosek, Oswego County Historian, Oswego

Mrs. Mabel Parker Smith, Greene County Historian, Catskill

Mrs. Mildred Southhard, Washington County Historian, Fort Edward

Milo Stewart, Director of Education, New York State Historical Association

Frank L. Swann, Yates County Historian, Penn Yan

Robert Sweeney, Binghamton

Mrs. Pamela Vogel, Warren County Historian, Lake George

Judge John J. Walsh, Utica

John G. Wilson, Wyoming County Historian, Wyoming

Mrs. Doris Wickes, Hamilton County Historian, Speculator

Mrs. Shirley Woodward, Broome County Historian, Endicott

NOTABLE NEW YORK CASES

From John D. Lawson's *American State Trials*

IN THESE SEVENTEEN volumes Lawson presents a wide survey of unusual legal cases in American history. The New York trials depict a wide range of the judicial spectrum, varying from ones involving "blasphemy" to the Susan B. Anthony trial of 1873. For each case Lawson provides an annotation and a transcript covering significant portions of the trial.

What follows is a listing of Lawson's New York cases plus a brief summary for several of the more fascinating ones. It is hoped that this appendix will prompt the reader to explore further, into the exciting, readable world of Lawson's *American State Trials* (Scholarly Resources, Inc., Wilmington, Delaware, 1972).

VOLUME ONE

1. The Trial of Levi Weeks, for the Murder of Gulielma Sands, New York City, 1800.
Miss Sands' body was discovered on January 2, 1800. Weeks, her lover, was indicted for murder. The circumstantial evidence against Weeks did not hold up and he was acquitted. The case was prominent in the public eye, not only for its gruesome details, but for Weeks' defense counsels, Aaron Burr, Alexander Hamilton, and H. Brockholst Livingston (later an Associate Justice of the United States Supreme Court).

2. The Trial of Francis Mezzara, for Procurement, New York City, 1818.

3. The Trial of John Ury, for Inciting Negroes to Crime and for being a Romish Priest, New York City, 1741.
In 1741 a great fear of a slave uprising permeated New York. This mass hysteria, abetted by some suspicious fires, brought on the lynching of several blacks. John Ury, an "English, non-juring clergyman," who came to New York to teach, was arrested and charged with inciting riot and being a "Priest of Rome." Ury, a scapegoat in the matter, maintained innocence. Faced with a powerful prosecution, popular bias, and no defense counsel, Ury was convicted and hanged. This case marks a tragic point in New York legal history.

4. The Trial of Francis Wittenburgh, for Procurement, New York City, 1818.

5. The Trial of John C. Colt, for the Murder of Samuel Adams, New York City, 1842.

6. The Trial of Commander Alexander S. MacKenzie, for Murder, before a Naval Court of Inquiry, Brooklyn, New York, 1842.
Alexander S. MacKenzie, Commander of the American Warship *Somers,* was faced with possible

mutiny led by Midshipman Philip Spencer, son of Secretary of War John C. Spencer. The plot was discovered and Spencer placed in the brig. When trouble continued, urged on by Spencer's agitations from the brig, MacKenzie executed the midshipman and two of his co-conspirators. Prior to execution Spencer confessed to his deeds. Upon reaching New York MacKenzie asked for an inquiry into his personal conduct, received one, and was vindicated by the Navy.

7. The Trial of Mordecai M. Noah, for Breaking Open and Publishing a Letter, New York City, 1818.

8. The Trial of Alden Spooner, for Libel, New York City, 1818.

9. The Trial of Mordecai M. Noah and Alden Spooner, for Contempt, New York City, 1818.
Each of the above three cases resulted from fierce competition between the two men, who were rival journalists in an era marked by journalism that would make the muckraking of the late 1800's seem mild.

10. The Trial of Christian Smith for the Murder of Bornt Lake, New York City, 1817.
Smith admittedly killed Lake but a strangely "sympathetic" jury acquitted him. Judge William W. Van Ness, disgusted with the verdict, admonished the jury with the words, "I hope they will be able, upon future consideration, to reconcile their verdict to their consciences."

11. The Action of John M. Trumbull against Thomas Gibbons, for Libel, New York City, 1818.

12. The Trial of Paterick Blake, for the Murder of his wife, New York City, 1816.

VOLUME TWO

1. The Trial of Robert Stakes, for Cruelty to Animals, New York City, 1822.
Taken to court for beating his horses, Stakes was convicted. In his ruling, the judge said that "to treat a dumb beast with cruelty was a misdemeanor at common law."

2. The Trial of John Degey, for Disturbing Divine Worship, New York City, 1823.
Disturbed by a minister's sermon at the Ebenezer Baptist Church, Degey rose in protest, haranguing and interrogating the startled cleric. For his offense, Degey was convicted and fined.

3. The Trial of Teunis Van Pelt, for Bigamy, New York City, 1816.

4. The Trial of John Johnson, for the Murder of James Murray, New York City, 1824.

5. The Action of George Spence and Wife against Barney Duffey, for False Imprisonment, New York City, 1816.

6. The Trial of John Morris, for Assault and Battery, New York City, 1816.
Morris, angered by the way his son was disciplined at a city private school, quarreled with the school's headmaster. The quarrel erupted into a fight, and Morris was indicted and convicted of assault and battery.

7. The Trial of Alfred S. Pell, for Assault and Battery, New York City, 1818.

8. The Trial of Diana Sellick, for the murder of Hetty Johnson, New York City, 1816.

9. The Trial of Charles Gill, for Opening Another Person's Letter, New York City, 1818.

10. The Action of Patrick Duffey against George E. Matthewson and Others, for Assault and Battery, New York City, 1816.

11. The trial of John Dayton and Thomas Dyer, for Larceny, New York City, 1817.
The cargo of a boat capsized in the Hudson and floated to the Jersey shore. Dayton and Dyer retrieved a large amount of the merchandise, took it to Long Island and sold it. Because they talked too freely, they brought about their own conviction.

VOLUME THREE

1. The Trial of Susan B. Anthony, for Voting at a Congressional Election, New York, 1873 (see section three).

2. The Trial of Beverly W. Jones, Edwin P. Marsh, William B. Hall, for Permitting Women to Vote, New York, 1873.
These men were in charge of the election center where Miss Anthony voted. For permitting her to do so, they were convicted and sentenced to pay $25 fines plus the costs of prosecution.

3. The Trial of Archibald McArdle, for Assault and Battery, New York City, 1872.

4. The Trial of Harris Seymour, Moses Roberts, Holloway Hayward, Henry Howard, and James Ganson, for the Abduction of William Morgan, New York, 1827.
This case provides excellent insight into the Masonic movement in the early 19th century.

5. The Trial of Berthina Tucker, for Grand Larceny, New York City, 1820.

6. The Trial of Jared W. Bell, for Blasphemy, New York City, 1821.
In heated conversation with a storekeeper about the Hartford Convention of 1814, Bell remarked that "God Almighty was a fool" and "Jesus Christ was a fool." His indictment referred to him as "being moved and seduced by the instigation of the Devil, contriving and intending to scandalize and vilify the Christian religion," one of the stranger statutes of early America.

7. The Action of James Maurice against Samuel Judd for a Penalty, New York City, 1818.

8. The Trial of Raymer C. Wertendyke and James Pike for False Imprisonment and of Robert Browne for Assault and Battery, New York City, 1822.

9. The Trial of Antonio Ancarola, for Kidnapping, New York City, 1879.

VOLUME FOUR

1. The Trial of Charles Sprague, for Robbery, Brooklyn, New York, 1849.

2. The Trial of Thomas Hoag, for Bigamy, New York City, 1804.

3. The Trial of James W. Lent, for Assault and Battery, New York City, 1819.

4. The Trial of James Williamson, for Assault and Battery, New York City, 1819.

5. The Trial of Thomas Ward,

for the Killing of Albert Robinson, New York City, 1823.

VOLUME FIVE

1. The Trial of Emma August Cunningham, for the Murder of Dr. Harvey Burdell, New York City, 1857.

2. The Trial of Lawrence Pienovi, for Assault and Battery, New York City, 1818.

3. The Trial of Charlotte Greenwault and Sarah Moody as Common Scolds, New York City, 1819. Both women were acquitted of any offense under this obsolete law. The testimony of witnesses provides insight into the "crime." One witness testified that Sarah Moody "without provocation, came into the yard of the witness and accused her in plain terms of infidelity to her deceased husband." Charlotte Greenwault allegedly "abused (people) by bestowing on (them) the vilest epithets."

4. The Trial of Abraham Bogart, for Misdemeanor in Office, New York City, 1856.

5. The Trial of Eli H. Hall, for Robbery, Geneseo, New York, 1865.

6. The Trial of Joseph Pulford, for Kidnapping, New York City, 1819.

VOLUME SIX

1. The Trial of John Wood, for Sending a Challenge to a Duel, New York City, 1818.
Wood's challenge to a foe read: "I have an excellent pair of pistols as ever was used— i Should be very happy with your company tomorrow afternoon or morning, which is most convenient for you, to go along with me and try them; everything will be Prepared and we will have a fine time of it." The "fine time" never occurred and Wood was convicted of his offense.

2. The Trial of William Farquhar and John H. Clark, for Assault and Battery, New York City, 1816.

3. The Trial of Major John André, for Being a Spy, Tappan, New York, 1780 (see section three).

4. The Trial of David D. How, for the Murder of Othello Church, Angelica, New York, 1824.

VOLUME SEVEN

1. The Trial of Israel Thayer, Jr., Isaac Thayer and Nelson Thayer, for the murder of John Love, Buffalo, New York, 1825.
The trial of the "Three Thayers," certainly one of the most spectacular in Erie County history, is cited in section five.

2. The Trial of Alexander McLeod, for the Burning of the Steamboat, Caroline and the Murder of Amos Durfee, Utica, New York, 1841 (see section three).

3. The Trial of John Stuyvesant, for False Pretenses, New York City, 1879.

4. The Trial of John Ball, for Setting Fire to His Own House, New York City, 1817.

5. The Trial of John Langley, for Larceny and Embezzlement, New York City, 1819.

6. The Trial of John Scott, Jewitt Prime, Samuel Wynant, Oliver

Bancroft, Jacob S. Miles and Patrick Hildreth, for Riot and Assault, New York City, 1817.

7. The Trial of William Landon, for Breach of the Prohibition Law of the State, Albany, New York, 1855.

VOLUME EIGHT

1. The Trial of Leonard Simons and Eber Wheaton, for Libel, New York City, 1823.

VOLUME NINE

No New York cases are included in this volume.

VOLUME TEN

1. The Trial of Jacob Leisler, for High Treason, New York City, 1691 (see section three).

2. The Trial of Nicholas Bayard, for High Treason, New York City, 1702.

3. The Trial of Alexander Whistelo, for Bastardy, New York City, 1808.
Whistelo, a black coachman, was accused by a white woman of ill repute, of fathering her child. The court acquitted Whistelo, taking into account the fact that the child was white and spending much time on the question of how light a child's skin is when presumably half-black and half-white.

VOLUME ELEVEN

1. The Trial of James Phillips, for Larceny, New York City, 1819.
John Branson, owner of a hat store, had several hats stolen from a display in front of his shop. De-termined to catch the culprit, Branson placed a hat outside his store, attached it to a cord, and waited for the robber to return. Phillips attempted to swipe the hat, but was caught. The court acquitted Phillips, however, as the hat had remained attached to the building and, therefore, no merchandise had left the premises.

2. The Trial of Henrietta Robinson, for the Murder of Timothy Lanagan, Troy, 1854.

3. The Trial of Isaac Roget, for Conspiracy to Defraud, New York City, 1817.

VOLUME TWELVE

1. The Trial of John Weeks, for Larceny, New York City, 1818.

2. The Trial of Richard P. Robinson, for the Murder of Helen Jewett, New York City, 1836.

3. The Trial of James Gallaher and James McElroy, for Passing Counterfeit Money, New York City, 1820.
Stuck with a counterfeit $100 bill from a New Orleans bank, McElroy tried to pass it on, using Gallaher in the process. Gallaher was acquitted as an innocent pawn in the affair, but McElroy was convicted. The judge ruled that "getting stuck" is not an excuse for passing counterfeit bills.

4. The Trial of Daniel Allen, for False Pretenses, New York City, 1818.

VOLUME THIRTEEN

1. The Trial of John Moore and others, for Assault and Battery, New York City, 1824.
This case involved an early clash

between Protestant and Catholic Irish-Americans.

2. The Trial of James Melvin and others, for Conspiracy to Raise Wages, New York City, 1810.

This early labor-management case involved a strike by the Journeymen Codwainers, a shoemakers' union, against a city shop. The strikers were arrested, fined one dollar plus court costs, and scolded by the mayor for their "conspiracy."

VOLUME FOURTEEN

1. The Trial of Leon Czolgosz, for the Murder of President McKinley, Buffalo, New York, 1901 (see section three).

2. The Trial of Ruggles Hubbard and James Bell, Sheriff and Jailor, for Preventing an Attorney from Entering Jail to See a Client, New York City, 1815.

Hubbard and Bell, allegedly fearing conspiracy, prevented attorney William W. McClelan from seeing Zenos M. Bradley, his client. The two were indicted, brought to trial and convicted, the court deciding on the basis of the constitutional guarantee of right to counsel.

3. The Trial of James Dalton, for False Pretense, New York City, 1823.

4. The Trial of Isaac Cotteral and Peter Crannel, for Arson, Troy, New York, 1820.

5. The Trial of Henry B. Hagerman, for Assault with Intent to Murder, New York City, 1818.

6. The Trial of Albert W. Hicks, for Piracy, New York City, 1860.

7. The Trial of John Y. Beall, for Violation of the Rules of War and Acting as a Spy$ New York City, 1865.

VOLUME FIFTEEN

No New York cases are included in this volume.

VOLUME SIXTEEN

1. The Trial of John Peter Zenger, for Libel, New York City, 1735 (see section two).

2. The Trial of Harry Croswell, for Libel, Hudson, New York, 1803 (see section three).

3. The Trial of William Freeman, for the Murder of John Van Nest, Auburn, New York, 1846 (see section three).

VOLUME SEVENTEEN

1. The Trial of Martha Bradstreet, for Libel, New York City, 1817.

2. The Trial of Lieutenant James Renshaw, for Oppressive and Unbecoming Conduct, New York City, 1808.

3. The Trial of Lieutenant James Renshaw, for Sending a Challenge to a Duel, New York City, 1809.

4. The Trial of Henry Green, for the Murder of His Wife, Troy, New York, 1845.

UNITED STATES
SUPREME COURT JUSTICES
FROM NEW YORK

Justice	Home	Appointing President	Years in Office
John Jay	Katonah	Washington	1789-1795[2]
H. Brockholst Livingston	New York City	Jefferson	1806-1823
Smith Thompson	Stanford, Dutchess Co.[1]	Monroe	1823-1843
Samuel Nelson	Hebron, Washington Co.[1]	Tyler	1845-1872
Joseph Bradley	Berne, Albany Co.[1]	Grant	1870-1892
Ward Hunt	Utica	Grant	1872-1882
Samuel Blatchford	New York City	Arthur	1882-1893
Rufus Peckham	Albany	Cleveland	1895-1909
Charles Evans Hughes	Glens Falls[1]	Taft/Hoover	1910-1916 1930-1941[2]
Harlan F. Stone	New York City[3]	Coolidge/ Roosevelt	1925-1941 1941-1946[2]
Benjamin Cardozo	New York City	Hoover	1932-1938
Robert H. Jackson	Jamestown	Roosevelt	1941-1954
John Marshall Harlan, Jr.	New York City[4]	Eisenhower	1955-1971
Thurgood Marshall	New York City[5]	Johnson	1967-

[1] Place of birth as well
[2] Chief Justice appointment
[3] Born in New Hampshire, Stone moved to New York City to practice law and eventually became dean of Columbia Law School
[4] Harlan was born in Chicago, but practiced law in New York
[5] Marshall was born in Baltimore, but lived in New York and based much of his famed NAACP law practice from that city

PRESIDENTS
OF THE NEW YORK STATE
BAR ASSOCIATION

President	Year(s) in Office	Home	Judicial District
John K. Porter	1876, 1877	New York City	1
Samuel Hand	1878, 1879	Albany	3
Sherman S. Rogers	1800, 1881	Buffalo	8
William C. Ruger	1882, 1883	Syracuse	5
Elliott F. Shepard	1884	New York City	1
David B. Hill	1885, 1886	Elmira	6
Martin W. Cooke	1887, 1888	Rochester	7
William H. Arnoux	1889	New York City	1
Matthew Hale	1890	Albany	3
George M. Diven	1891	Elmira	6
J. Newton Fiero	1892, 1893	Albany	3
Tracy C. Becker	1894	Buffalo	8
William H. Robertson	1895	Katonah	9
Edward G. Whitaker	1896, 1897	New York City	1
Simon W. Rosendale	1898	Albany	3
Walter S. Logan	1899	New York City	1
Francis M. Finch	1900	Ithaca	6
William B. Hornblower	1901	New York City	1
John G. Milburn	1902, 1903	New York City	1
Richard L. Hand	1904, 1905	Elizabethtown	4
Joseph H. Choate	1906, 1907	New York City	1
Francis Lynde Stetson	1908	New York City	1
Adelbert Moot	1909	Buffalo	8
Elihu Root	1910, 1911	New York City	1
William Nottingham	1912	Syracuse	5

President	Year(s) in Office	Home	Judicial District
Alton B. Parker	1913, 1914	New York City	1
Alphonso Clearwater	1915	Kingston	3
Morgan J. O'Brien	1916	New York City	1
Charles Evans Hughes	1917, 1918	New York City	1
Henry W. Taft	1919	New York City	1
Nathan L. Miller	1920	Syracuse	5
William D. Gutherie	1921, 1922	New York City	1
William N. Dykman	1923	Brooklyn	2
Walter P. Cooke	1924, 1925	Buffalo	8
Arthur E. Sutherland	1926	Rochester	7
William C. Breed	1927, 1928	New York City	1
Frank H. Hiscock	1929—1931	Syracuse	5
Samuel Seabury	1932, 1933	New York City	1
Daniel J. Kenefick	1934	Buffalo	8
John Godfrey Saxe	1935, 1936	New York City	1
George H. Bond	1937	Syracuse	5
Joseph Rosch	1938	Albany	3
Fred L. Gross	1939	Brooklyn	2
Warnick J. Kernan	1940	Utica	5
John G. Jackson	1941, 1942	New York City	1
James McC. Mitchell	1943	Buffalo	8
Jackson A. Dykman	1944	Brooklyn	2
Lewis C. Ryan	1945, 1946	Syracuse	5
Robert E. Lee	1947	New York City	1
Mason H. Bigelow	1948	New York City	1
Neil G. Harrison	1949	Binghamton	6
Otis T. Bradley	1950	New York City	1
M. William Bray	1950*	Utica	5
Arthur VD. Chamberlain	1951	Rochester	7